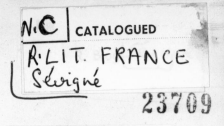

Marie de Rabutin Chantal
Marquise de Sévigné
1626–1696
From a pastel by Robert Nanteuil (*Musée Carnavalet*)
(*Photo : J. E. Bulloz, Paris*)

Letters from
MADAME LA MARQUISE DE SÉVIGNÉ

selected, translated, and introduced
by
VIOLET HAMMERSLEY

with a preface by
W. SOMERSET MAUGHAM, C.H.

London
SECKER & WARBURG
1955

Printed in England
by
Butler and Tanner Ltd
Frome and London
and
first published 1955
by
Martin Secker & Warburg Ltd
7 John Street, London
W.C.1

CONTENTS

		page
Preface by W. Somerset Maugham, C.H.		13
Translator's Introduction		20

THE LETTERS

1648

15 March	To the Comte Bussy de Rabutin	38

1668

4 December	To the Comte Bussy de Rabutin	40

1670

15 August	To the Comte de Grignan	42
19 November	To the same	43
15 December	To the Marquis de Coulanges	45
19 December	To the same	47

1671

9 February	To Madame la Comtesse de Grignan	48
24 March	To the same	50
4 April	To the same	52
8 April	To the same	53
17 April	To the same	54
22 April	To the same	55
26 April	To the same	57
18 May	To the same	60
23 May	To the same	61

		page
31 May	To the same	62
21 June	To the same	64
15 July	To the same	67
26 July	To the same	68
5 August	To the same	69
23 August	To the same	71
2 December	To the same	72
6 December	To the same	74
18 December	To the same	75
30 December	To the same	76

1672

5 January	To Madame de Grignan	77
22 January	To the same	78
29 January	To the same	80
3 February	To the same	81
5 February	To the same	83
26 February	To the same	84
16 March	To the same	85
30 March	To the same	87
1 April	To the same	88
6 April	To the same	89
8 April	To the same	91
27 April	To the same	92
29 April	To the same	94
6 May	To the same	96
13 May	To the same	98
16 May	To the same	99
30 May	To the same	100
17 June	To the same	101
19 June	To the Comte de Bussy	102
20 June	To Madame de Grignan	103
3 July	To the same	104
8 July	To the same	106
27 July	To the same	107

1673

5 October	To Madame de Grignan	109
10 October	To the same	110
16 October	To the same	112
2 November	To the same	112
8 December	To the same	114
28 December	To the same	116
29 December	To the same	117

		page
	1674	
5 February	To Madame de Grignan	118
	1675	
5 June	To Madame de Grignan	120
19 June	To the same	121
26 June	To the same	122
19 July	To the same	123
24 July	To the same	124
31 July	To the same and the Comte de Grignan	126
2 August	To Madame de Grignan	129
6 August	To the Comte de Bussy	131
7 August	To Madame de Grignan	132
6 September	To the same	133
11 September	To the same	134
17 September	To the same	135
20 September	To the same	136
29 September	To the same	137
27 October	To the same	139
13 November	To the same	140
24 November	To the same	142
4 December	To the same	143
	1676	
19 January	To Madame de Grignan	145
21 January	M. de Sévigné to Madame de Grignan	146
27 January	M. de Sévigné to the same	147
3 February	M. de Sévigné to the same	148
26 February	To the same	149
4 March	Note to the Comte de Grignan	150
24 March	To Madame de Grignan	150
10 April	To the same	151
17 April	To the same	152
29 April	To the same	152
6 May	To the same	154
10 May	To the same	156
15 May	To the same	157
17 May	To the same	158
19 May	To the same	159
28 May	To the same	161
1 June	To the same	162
4 June	To the same	164
8 June	To the same	165

		page
15 June	To the same	166
1 July	To the same	167
17 July	To the same	168
22 July	To the same	170
29 July	To the same	171
26 August	To the same	173
2 September	To the same	174
11 September	To the same	176
16 September	To the same	176
21 September	To the same	178
25 September	To the same	178
30 September	To the same	179
2 October	To the same	180
7 October	To the same	181
14 October	To the same	182
16 October	To the same	182
23 October	To the same	184
6 November	To the same	184
25 November	To the same	186
13 December	To the same	186

1677

11 June	To Madame de Grignan	188
30 June	To the same	189
21 July	To the same	191
23 July	To the same	191
11 August	To the same	192
18 August	To the same	193
21 August	To the same	194
6 September	To the same	195
24 September	To the same	196
1 October	To the same	197
7 October	To the same	198
15 October	To the same	199
20 October	To the same	201
27 October	To the same	202
3 November	To the Comte de Bussy	203
8 December	To the same	204

1678

18 March	To the Comte de Bussy	205
27 May	To the Comte de Grignan	206
18 December	To the Comte de Bussy	207

		page

1679

27 May	To Madame de Grignan	209
18 September	To the same	210
11 October	To the same	211
13 October	To the same	212
20 October	To the same	213
All Saints	To the same	214
2 November	To the same	215
22 November	To the same	216
24 November	To the same	218
1 December	To the same	219
6 December	To the same	220
27 December	To the same	222
29 December	To the same	223

1680

5 January	To Madame de Grignan	225
17 January	To the same	226
24 January	To the same	228
26 January	To the same	230
7 February	To the same	232
9 February	To the same	233
14 February	To the same	234
16 February	To the same	235
23 February	To the same	236
28 February	To the same	238
13 March	To the same	239
17 March	To the same	240
29 March	To the same	241
3 April	To the same	243
12 April	To the same	244
1 May	To the same	245
6 May	To the same	247
8 May	To the same	248
9 May	To the same	249
11 May	To the same	251
27 May	To the same	252
5 June	To the same	253
9 June	To the same	254
12 June	To the same	255
15 June	To the same	256
21 June	To the same	257
14 July	To the same	258
6 August	To the same	260

		page
21 August	To the same	262
28 August	To the same	263
11 September	To the same	265
29 September	To the same	266
9 October	To the same	267
23 October	To the same	268
6 November	To the same	268

1681

3 April	To the Comte de Bussy	271

1682

7 August	To the President de Moulceau	273
23 December	To the Comte de Bussy	273

1683

15 December	To the Comte de Bussy	276

1684

11 September	To Mademoiselle de Scudéry	277
13 September	To Madame de Grignan	278
27 September	To the same	278
1 October	To the same	279
5 November	To the same	281
26 November	To the same	282

1685

7 February	To Madame de Grignan	284
13 June	To the same	285
26 August	To the same	286

1686

13 December	To the President de Moulceau	288

1687

Epiphany	To the President de Moulceau	290
2 September	To the Comte de Bussy	291
22 September	To Madame de Grignan	291

page

1688

20 October	To Madame de Grignan	293
22 October	To the same	294
1 November	To the same	295
3 November	To the same	295
5 November	To the same	296
8 November	To the same	298
11 November	To the same	299
3 December	To the same	300
8 December	To the same	301
13 December	To the same	302
24 December	To the same	304
27 December	To the same	306
31 December	To the same	307

1689

3 January	To Madame de Grignan	309
Epiphany	To the Comte de Bussy	311
10 January	To Madame de Grignan	312
14 January	To the same	314
17 January	To the same	315
24 January	To the same	316
4 February	To the same	317
7 February	To the Comte de Grignan	318
23 February	To Madame de Grignan	318
2 March	To the President de Moulceau	319
11 March	To Madame de Grignan	320
25 March	To the same	321
13 April	To the same	322
19 April	To the same	323
24 April	To the same	324
27 April	To the same	325
5 May	To the same	326
18 May	To the same	326
25 May	To the same	327
15 June	To the same	328
22 June	To the same	329
26 June	To the same	330
17 July	To the same	331
24 July	To the same	332
30 July	To the same	334
6 August	To the same	335
12 August	To the same	336

		page
17 August	To the same	337
24 August	To the same	339
31 August	To the same	339
11 September	To the same	341
18 September	To the same	342
25 September	To the same	345
28 September	To the same	345
2 October	To the same	346
12 October	To the same	347
16 October	To the same	349
23 October	To the same	350
30 October	To the same	351
6 November	To the same	352
20 November	To the same	353
30 November	To the same	354
7 December	To the same	355
11 December	To the same	356
14 December	To the same	358
18 December	To the same	359

1690

22 January	To Madame de Grignan	360
1 February	To the same	361
18 March	To M. de Coulanges	363
26 April	To Madame de Grignan	364
12 July	To the Comte de Bussy	365
13 August	To the same	365
13 November	To the same	366
1 December	To the same	367

1691

26 July	To M. de Coulanges	369

1692

27 January	To the Comte de Bussy	371

1694

5 July	To M. de Coulanges	373
9 September	To the same	374

page

1695

3 February	To Madame de Coulanges	376
3 February	To M. de Coulanges	377
20 September	To M. de Sévigné	378
	A Selective Index of Persons	381
	Index of Places	388

LIST OF ILLUSTRATIONS

Madame de Sévigné by Nanteuil		*Frontispiece*
Madame de Grignan by Mignard	*facing page*	48
Statue of Madame de Sévigné at Saulieu	,, ,,	192
Châteaux des Rochers and de Grignan	,, ,,	266

PREFACE

By W. Somerset Maugham, C.H.

Well over a hundred years ago, Sainte-Beuve wrote that everything that could be said about Madame de Sévigné had already been said. Since then, however, a great deal more has been said. Such being the case, the reader of these lines must not expect me to tell him anything new. All I can hope to do is to remind him of certain facts that he may have forgotten. The events of Madame de Sévigné's life have been stated in sufficient detail by Mrs. Hammersley in the introduction to her translation of the letters which she has made for the delectation of the English reader, and for these I may refer him to that. I am inclined to think that French, for all its clarity, and apparent simplicity, is probably the most difficult of all languages to translate. To translate literally may land one in absurdities. One difficulty that confronts the translator is that the French word and the English one are often the same and yet are not used in quite the same sense ; another, is that a word may not have the same associations in English as in French and so, to translate it literally may sadly distort the author's meaning. It is to Mrs. Hammersley's credit that she has avoided these pitfalls, and her translation, though, so far as I have been able to judge, faithful, is easy, fluent and idiomatic.

Madame de Sévigné was a stylist of high quality. She was fortunate in the time of her birth. This took place at the very beginning of the second quarter of the seventeenth century. The best prose-writers of the preceding century, Montaigne, for instance, wrote with charm and naturalness ; but, as George Saintsbury justly remarked, their prose, " though exuberant and picturesque, was not planned or balanced, sentences were ill-formed and the periods haphazard. It was a conversational prose and had the diffusiveness of conversation." Jean Guez de Balzac, who lived through the first half of the seventeenth century, created the literary language of French prose, and (I am again quoting George Saintsbury) " taught French authors to write a prose which is written knowingly instead of a prose which is unwittingly talked ". Voiture, his contemporary, had a lighter touch than Balzac, and " helped to gain for French prose the tradition of vivacity and sparkle which it has always possessed as well as that of correctness and grace ".

Thus Madame de Sévigné had to her hand a perfected instrument which she had the tact, taste and talent to make admirable use of. Critics have noted that sometimes her grammar was faulty ; but style does not depend on syntax, it depends, I venture to suggest, on character ; and Madame de Sévigné had charm, unfailing humour, sympathy, affectionateness, common sense and keen observation. She wrote neither a treatise nor an history ; she wrote letters, and she knew very well that they must have a personal touch. Hers are as easy, and as apparently spontaneous, as those Jane Austen wrote to her sister Cassandra ; but she had the advantage of having subjects to write about of wider interest than had our own Miss Austen.

Newspapers then were few and dull. Letters provided people living away from Paris with the news of the day. Madame de Sévigné was in a good position to give it to her correspondents, since by her birth and connections she moved in high society. The subjects that excited the attention of the world she lived in were the sermons of eminent preachers, criminal trials, and the rise and fall of the King's favourites. When she went to Court she was graciously received. Once, Louis XIV danced a minuet with her, and afterwards she found herself standing beside her kinsman, Bussy de Rabutin. " One must acknowledge," she said to him, " that we have a great King." " Yes, without doubt," he answered. " What he has just done is truly heroic." But whether that witty, sarcastic man was laughing at her or at the monarch is not plain. On another occasion, Louis XIV, to the admiration of all present, talked to her for several minutes. But it was not often that Madame de Sévigné went to Court : she depended then for the latest news on an intimate friend. This was the Duc de La Rochefoucauld, the author of the imperishable maxims. He was a highly cultivated man, extremely intelligent, with a wide knowledge of the world. This knowledge had left him with few illusions. Sentimentalists have reproached him because, as a result of a lifetime's experience, he came to the conclusion that self-interest is the mainspring of men's behaviour. There is truth in that, but it is not the whole truth. The extraordinary, and heartening, thing about men is that though, in fact, self-interest *is* the mainspring of their conduct, they are capable on occasion of self-sacrifice, disinterestedness and magnanimity. The picture Madame de Sévigné draws of La Rochefoucauld is that of a good, high-minded and generous man ; and she never tires of remarking on his good nature, sweetness, amiability, and on his wish to please and to be of service.

During the seventeenth century in France persons of quality took a laudable interest in literature. They read Virgil with delight, and argued intelligently over the respective merits of Corneille and Racine. They discussed the niceties of style, and were ravished by a well-turned phrase. It was, in fact, a time of high civilisation. La Rochefoucauld was in the habit of passing some hours every day with Madame de La Fayette, author of the charming *Princesse de Clèves*, and in her house, in the Faubourg de Vaugirard, they would be joined by Madame de Sévigné and the witty Cardinal de Retz. In summer they sat in the garden, " the prettiest thing in the world ", with its flowers, its fountains and its arbour. What would one not give to have heard the conversation of those four cultured, brilliant and well-bred creatures ! Never can there have been talk of such savour before or since. Conversation in those happy days was cultivated as an art, and to talk well and entertainingly gave anyone, however modest his origins, an entry into that closed, aristocratic society. Voiture, the son of a vintner, was sought after for his caustic humour. The Duc d'Enghien said of him : " If Voiture were a gentleman (*de notre condition*) one couldn't put up with him." There was Madame Cornuel, daughter of the steward or agent of the Duc de Guise, who was famous for her wit and so was received in exclusive circles. At this great house or at that, Corneille could sometimes be induced to read an unpublished play, or La Fontaine his latest fables ; La Rochefoucauld's maxims would be admired or decried and a recent letter of Madame de Sévigné's be read aloud.

The malicious said that her letters were written for effect. What if they were ? If you have something to say, which you know will raise a laugh, or if you have a story to tell, which you think will interest, you put it as effectively as you can. I can see nothing blameworthy in that. Madame de Sévigné knew that her letters were passed from hand to hand, and there can be little doubt that she enjoyed writing them and enjoyed the pleasure they gave others. She could be serious enough when the occasion warranted, as, for example, when she gave an account of the death of Turenne ; but she had a wonderful sense of fun, and when she had something amusing to relate, she made, as the humorist does, the very most of it. She did not even disdain a pun. One I have noticed is brilliant, but since it is untranslatable I must give it in French ; she had a fine apartment that she wanted to let, but could not find anyone to take ; an apartment she said "*que tout le monde admire et que personne ne veut louer*". She claimed with justice that her letters were not studied. She might well have said what Jane Austen wrote to Cassandra : "I have now attained the true art of letter-writing, which we are always told is to express on paper exactly what one would say to the same person by word of mouth. I have been talking to you almost as fast as I could the whole of this letter." Madame de Sévigné's letters were written conversation, and the conversation of a woman who talked with wit, humour and spontaneity.

Most of them, as everyone knows, were written to her daughter, Madame de Grignan, whom Madame de Sévigné idolised in a manner that posterity has found exaggerated. Madame de Sévigné was a good-looking woman, with beautiful hair and a dazzling complexion. The censorious observed that her eyes were of different colours, her nose blunt and her jaw somewhat heavy ; but she redeemed these slight defects by the liveliness of her expression. Her daughter was a great beauty. It is a curious indication of the manners of the time that when Louis XIV was tiring of Madame de La Vallière, there was some talk of pressing the claims of Madame de Sévigné's daughter to the place which would shortly be vacant. What Madame de Sévigné thought of the project, we do not know, but Bussy de Rabutin, her cousin, looked upon it with favour. "I should be much pleased," he said, "if the King formed an attachment to Mlle de Sévigné, because the young woman is a great friend of mine and he couldn't have a better mistress." Nothing came of this and the young woman was married off to a member of one of the noblest families in France. Madame de Grignan had none of her mother's attractiveness. She was cold, avaricious, though wildly extravagant, proud and unbending. The two ladies were, in fact, so different that it is not surprising to learn that when, later, they were together in Paris, as they were on occasion for months together, they bickered a good deal. It was only when they were separated that they did not get on one another's nerves.

Madame de Sévigné had another child, a son, Charles by name, who seems to have inherited much of her charm, humour and good nature. It seems hard that she should have loved him so much less than she loved her daughter. He appears to have thought it very natural. When Madame de Sévigné divided her fortune between her two children, giving Madame de Grignan by far the larger share, he took it in good part. He was a great rake in his youth. Madame de Sévigné was the confidante of his amours, and she retailed them in her letters to her daughter with a surprising frankness. Charles de Sévigné was an unsatisfactory lover, and was soon discarded by the exacting objects of his passion. He complained to his mother that she was to blame for this, since he had inherited from her what is politely known as lack of temperament. Madame de Sévigné, left a widow at twenty-six, was abundantly courted, both, it appears, by men who wished to marry her and by men whose intentions were less serious. She remained a widow and chaste. In an age when marriages were made by arrangement, often when the parties concerned were children, conjugal fidelity was rare, and it was in the spirit of the time to ascribe it rather to natural frigidity than to virtue. Madame de Sévigné was a good Catholic, but she was not bigoted; and when her son eventually married, and became deeply religious (he ended his days in seminary), she found life with him not a little dull.

She was a great reader, especially during the long periods she spent at Les Rochers, the place in Brittany she had inherited from her worthless husband. She adored La Fontaine, and, indeed, quarrelled with Madame de Grignan because she did not share her admiration for the charming fabulist. She venerated Corneille, but did not much care for Racine. For all her sweetness and amiability, there was in Madame de Sévigné a certain toughness, and she found the tender author of *Bérénice* unduly sentimental. She read Montaigne with delight, Pascal, both his *Pensées* and the *Provinciales*, but her favourite author was Nicole, the Jansenist. His good sense and sound judgment appealed to her, and she delighted in his style.

During one of her sojourns at Les Rochers the peasants and the townspeople of Brittany, downtrodden and illegally taxed, revolted. They were punished by the Duc de Chaulnes, governor of the province, with barbarity. They were hanged, drawn and quartered by the hundred. Men, women and children were driven out of their houses into the street, and no one was allowed, under pain of death, to succour them. Madame de Sévigné wrote: "The mutineers of Rennes have run away long ago; so the good will suffer for the wicked; but I find it all for the best, so long as the four thousand soldiers who are at Rennes, under MM. de Forbin and de Vins, don't prevent me from walking about in my woods, which are very fine and marvellously beautiful." And again: "They've taken sixty bourgeois; they'll begin to hang them tomorrow. This province is a good example to the others; above all it will lead them to respect their governors, not to abuse them and not to throw stones in their garden." It has shocked Madame de Sévigné's readers to see with what complaisance she wrote of these wretched people's sufferings. It is indeed shocking. It cannot be excused, it can only be explained.

The seventeenth century in France was, as I have said, a time of high civilisation; but it was also a brutal time. Men were hard, cruel and unscrupulous. Fine gentlemen cheated freely at cards and boasted of it when they had cozened a fool out of his money. M. de Lenclos, a gentleman of Touraine and father of a famous daughter, ran the Baron de Chabans through the body with his sword as he was stepping out of his coach and could not defend himself. It is true that he had to flee from France, but I do not know that anyone thought the worse of him for the cowardly action. These cultured aristocrats, these elegant ladies—who were reduced to tears by Racine's pathos, who admired Poussin and Claude, who crowded to listen to the sermons of Bourdaloue and Massillon, who were so delicately sensitive to the sadness and beauty of the country—looked upon the peasants as hardly human. They used them as they would never have used their horses or their dogs. Madame de Sévigné shared the common opinions of her day. That the brutes should be hanged seemed to her only fitting, and when the Duc de Chaulnes was removed from the province to rule another that brought in a larger income, she wrote that she was heartbroken to lose her dear good Duke. I suppose the best one can say is that it is unfair to judge those of one generation by the standards of another. Perhaps it is well not to censure Madame de Sévigné too harshly for her indifference to the sufferings of these ill-used creatures when we remember how short a while ago we discovered that men, supposedly civilised, were capable of the cruelties we know of. It looks as though man, when his interest, his fear, his ambition, his pride, are concerned, remains very much what he always was.

The Comte de la Rivière, a relation of the lady's, and himself a voluminous letter-writer, said somewhere: " When you have read one of Madame de Sévigné' you feel a slight pang, because you have one less to read."

TRANSLATOR'S INTRODUCTION

Marie de Rabutin-Chantal, Marquise de Sévigné, was born in 1626 of an ancient Burgundian family. Her forebears were fierce barons, owning numberless coats-of-arms, feudal rights and moss-grown estates. The Baron, her grandfather, was killed out hunting, and her grandmother, the Bien-Heureuse Jeanne de Chantal, was left to bring up a son and three daughters of tender age. She did not, however, complete her task, and on hearing Saint François de Sales preach at Dijon, she then and there determined to give up the world and enter a convent. The call was unmistakable. She bade a heart-breaking farewell to her young son, who threw himself on the ground across the doorway, daring her to step over his body. So renowned were her good works, so great her sanctity, that in 1767 she was canonised by Pope Clement XIII. Marie's father, the young Baron, Celse Bénigne de Rabutin-Chantal, was brought up by his paternal grandfather. At an early age he married Mlle de Coulanges, a gentle heiress of a respectable "*famille de robe*". Madame de Sévigné was their only child. A madcap like his forebears, Celse Bénigne got himself involved in a duel, which was not well looked upon in Court circles, fled to the Ile de Ré, which at that time was invested by the English under Buckingham, and at Samblanceau he met his death at the head of his cavalry squadron, under de Toiras, on July 22nd, 1627. His broken-hearted widow left for Paris with the pious intention of burying her husband's heart in the Church of the Minims, Place Royale, thereafter going to live nearby with her parents, M. and Madame de Coulanges. But alas, she did not long survive her husband, and Marie was left in the guardianship of her maternal grandparents. When her grandfather, in his turn, was laid to rest at the Minims, her uncle, Abbé Christophe de Coulanges, was appointed her guardian, with the approval of Madame de Chantal, who wrote everlasting directions from her convent.

Marie was aged ten, and her uncle but twenty-nine, when she went to make her home with him at the Abbaye de Livry She and her "*Bienbon*", as she called him, remained faithful friends until his death, a close association of over forty years. She adored Livry, which is enclosed in the forest of Bondy, some twelve miles east of Paris. Round about the abbey were shaded gardens filled with honeysuckle. Some forty years later she wrote to her daughter: "I came here yesterday, and found the place in all the triumph of May—the spring has opened to the sound of the cuckoo, the thrush and the nightingale." It was at Livry, no doubt, that Mlle de Chantal acquired her passion for nature and the countryside, so unusual in a Frenchwoman.

The Abbé seems to have shown great common sense in the bringing up of the little girl, much on the same lines as if she had been a boy. He appointed as tutors the poets Ménage and Chapelain, who taught her literature, Italian and Spanish. She tells us she read Virgil in the original "in all the majesty of the text". Ménage was a great character, and possessor of a prodigious memory. He became somewhat embarrassingly attached to his pupil, but she laughed at him, teased him and kept him at arm's length with all the thoughtlessness of youth. When he told her she was making a martyr of him she replied: "I suppose I am your virgin." This upbringing, almost entirely surrounded by men, may have been responsible for certain masculine traits one observes in Madame de Sévigné's character. She was outspoken, frank, objective, and although full of feminine charm, and not averse from coquetry in her dealings with her admirers, she had less vanity than most women, did not crave for admiration, and judged herself severely. She loathed all forms of jealousy. There was in her a streak of good common sense, save in her relationship with her daughter, where all her defences fell clattering to the ground.

The *Bienbon*, though fundamentally good and upright, was not notably pious: indeed he often alluded to his shortcomings in this respect. Whether this may have influenced his niece, who can tell! It is clear that, in the matter of her own faith, she was faced with enormous obstacles, and only when fairly advanced in years did she arrive at a kind of stern philosophy, a belief in Providence, in Destiny. The word Providence is always on her lips. "*Cela est dans l'ordre, et dans l'ordre de Dieu*" is the refrain. Her son-in-law, M. de Grignan, writes of her last hours: "This person, so tender, so weak where those she loved were concerned, found courage and religion only when she felt that she had but herself to think of."

As Marie grew up there were many suitors for her hand, amongst whom, no doubt, was her favourite but tricky cousin Bussy de Rabutin, "*mon petit cadet*" as she called him, whom for some unknown reason she did not choose to accept: or was it he, frightened by certain direct qualities he could not live up to, who retreated? But he and she kept up a lively correspondence all their lives—a correspondence in which thrusts and ripostes were perpetually exchanged, ending, as with good duellists, in compliments and the warmest of handshakes. Bussy seems to have treated her very badly by publishing his outrageous *Histoire Amoureuse des Gaules*, in which he lampooned the ladies of the Court and his cousin; also by bringing her correspondence with Surintendent Fouquet to the King's notice, although he failed to implicate her, and later tried to make *amende honorable* for both lapses by publishing a most flattering portrait of her.

In accepting Henri, Marquis de Sévigné, a protégé of the Coadjutor Gondi [1] for his niece, the Abbé seems to have shown a singular lack of judgment and penetration. The Marquis was young, rich, handsome, of aristocratic birth, and Mlle de Chantal's inclinations may have played a major part in his decision. The young couple were married at two o'clock of the morning on August 4th, 1644, at the Church of St. Gervais and St. Protais in Paris before a large and fashionable assembly. Their marriage could never have been a happy one since, according to Bussy, the Marquis found his wife cold, and he was never faithful to her for a moment—"He loved many women," says Bussy, "but none so charming as his wife." He adored society, and frequented the brilliant gatherings at the Hôtel Rambouillet, where reigned its mistress, Catherine, Marquise de Rambouillet, "*l'incomparable*

[1] Cardinal de Retz.

Arthénice ". Here, of an evening, all the world would gather to hear Corneille read one of his plays—Bossuet was there, Racine (of whom Madame de Sévigné remarked : " *Il passera comme le café* "), Voiture, Ménage, and a bevy of beauties—Princesse de Condé, Duchesses de Longueville and de Chevreuse, Comtesse de La Fayette. As Lady Ritchie [1] writes : " A whole host of wits, writers, orators, are to be recognised : young Bossuet, l'Abbé Godeau—the whole book-shelf is there, bound in velvet and silk and gold-thread. . . ." Sévigné's wife looks at miniatures, whilst the young Marquis sits at the feet of Mlle Vigeau, making love to her.

The following autumn, 1646, a daughter was born to Madame de Sévigné—a daughter who was to fill her heart to the exclusion of all else, and to be the lodestar of her existence. " You are the grief and joy of all my days," she tells her. The child was christened Françoise Marguerite, and called by Rabutin " The prettiest girl in France ". In March 1648 a son was born, which completed the little family, but of conjugal bliss or family life there was to be little to boast of. The Marquis, having deposited his wife at Les Rochers, his Manorial Estate in Brittany, returned to Paris, threw himself into all manner of intrigues and dissipation, of which his affair with Ninon de Lenclos was perhaps the most innocuous. Ninon was also to be the mistress of his son, and most probably of his grandson, the young Marquis de Grignan. When she died at the age of eighty-five she was said to have lost few of her charms. On her tomb the following words were inscribed : " *Ci git le corps de Madame la Comtesse Ninon de l'Enclos qui mourut à l'âge de 85 ans. Elle fut renommée pour sa chasteté pendant les dernières années de sa vie.*" Sévigné made himself more conspicuous with Madame de Gondran, " La belle Lolo ", and was mortally wounded fighting a duel on her account in 1651, his adversary being the Chevalier d'Albret. It is not known how greatly Madame de Sévigné mourned her faithless husband, but she remained in retirement at Les Rochers for two years. His name was never subsequently heard to pass her lips, and on meeting d'Albret one day in a salon she swooned away.

Although she returned to Paris it was never again to plunge

[1] *Madame de Sévigné*, by Miss Thackeray (Mrs. Richmond Ritchie), Blackwood, 1881.

herself into the social vortex, and but seldom to attend Court functions, though she would always adore any Court gossip she could get hold of to recount to her daughter. Instead she made herself a côterie of intimate friends which was far more to her taste, foremost among these being Madame de La Fayette and the Duc de La Rochefoucauld. These two kept house together, and remained faithful through stress and storm and perennial ill-health on both sides, and of them Mlle de Scudéry wrote to Bussy: "*M. de La Rochefoucauld et Madame de La Fayette ont fait un roman* (*La Princesse de Clèves*) *des galanteries de la Cour de Henri Second: ils ne sont guère en âge de faire autre chose ensemble.*" Then there were her cousins M. and Madame de Coulanges, a charming if ill-assorted couple, Corbinelli, a faithful friend, and a host of others. Many of her friends had fallen, or were to fall, into disgrace. Bussy de Rabutin, who had incurred the King's anger on account of his book, was exiled; Fouquet, Minister of Finance to Louis XIV, was arraigned for misappropriation of funds and imprisoned for life; the Marquis de Pomponne was disgraced and exiled; and Cardinal de Retz, cousin of Sévigné—like him a great Frondeur [1]—was imprisoned but made his escape. Madame de Sévigné was an extremely loyal friend, and once her affections were engaged she stood up for those she cared for through thick and thin, despite her unalterable allegiance to the King. However blatantly he might conduct his love affairs, however ruthlessly he waged his perpetual wars, however summarily he disgraced his ministers and friends, *Le Roi Soleil* seems to have dazzled her completely. Once at Versailles he chose her out to dance with him and later she told Bussy: "I think the glory of his reign will eclipse that of all his predecessors." Amongst her friends we must not forget La Mousse and *le Bienbon*, her two beloved abbés, who were always at her side.

There were not wanting suitors for her hand, including possibly Bussy de Rabutin, but she had no inclination for remarriage, her first attempt having discouraged her; or maybe there was, as Bussy said, a certain coldness of temperament. (Her son reproached her for passing this on to her daughter when he himself could have done with a little more of it.) However it might

[1] *Fronde* = "sling". Civil war (1648–53) between Anne of Austria, married to Mazarin, and certain dissatisfied nobles who supported the Parlement.

be, she threw herself into the tasks of bringing up her children and retrieving her husband's scattered fortune with the Abbé's help. She showed a marked ability for managing her estates; and an ever growing love for garden and countryside. She might almost be called the pioneer of that splendid race of women gardeners of which Gertrude Jekyll, Miss Wilmot and Vita Sackville-West were and are such worthy descendants. That the first one should have been a Frenchwoman is notable indeed! She was game for anything, planting trees with her own hands and "watching them grow", or taking to the oars when a boat on the Loire, in which she was travelling, got stuck on the mud.

So her love for Les Rochers grew in her heart, and it is no exaggeration to say that it was closer to her than aught else save her daughter. Nothing that she has written of her green woods and their melancholy but might be said today—they are a true memorial. Edward FitzGerald's great-niece,[1] who visited Les Rochers, writes: "No engraving can do justice to the charm of Les Rochers, its soft grey stone set on the green carpet of its lawns, and against the shadowy emerald, yet sun-haunted background of its immense and silent woods."

When the time came for marrying off "*La plus jolie fille de France*", it is indeed ironical to think that her mother should have fixed on M. de Grignan, aged forty, who had recently been appointed Lieutenant Governor of Provence. This choice, as events turned out, was to mean a lifetime separation from the adored child. Madame de Sévigné writes of him to Bussy: "All his wives are dead, and by extraordinary good fortune his father and son as well, so that he is richer than ever before." No doubt she was persuaded that he would be recalled to Paris by the King, and given an appointment at Court, but this pious hope never materialised. Irony indeed that this worldly streak in Madame de Sévigné (who was not a Frenchwoman for nothing) should have been instrumental in ruining her happiness, since absence from the beloved daughter was not to be endured. It took her many years of pain and grief before she could begin to accept the sacrifice required of her. Had she but apprehended the darker side, which was to unroll itself, of Madame de Grignan's

[1] Mrs. Kerrich. She edited E.FG.'s posthumous *Dictionary of Madame de Sévigné*, 2 vols. Macmillan, 1914.

future, she might well indeed have yielded to despair. She has told us of her daughter's numerous miscarriages, of the tiny malformed infants, all skin and bone, who did not survive a twelve-month, of the poor little rickety boy, Adhémar, and his difficult growth, of beloved Pauline's blemishes, and of Madame de Grignan's lamentable health and disfigurement. Quite unknowingly she reveals the true diagnosis, the dread tru h: that M. de Grignan, having finished off two wives, undoubtedly infected Françoise with venereal disease, so prevalent at that period, and through her his children. Had Françoise, however, married nearer home, it is likely we should never have possessed the rich store of her mother's letters, these wonderful scintillating letters, magical and evocative, natural, almost colloquial, which were despatched every few days, by every Ordinary[1], to the daughter in her hated castle far away in Provence. In them she says everything that comes to her mind, pours out all the longing, recounts all the gossip, malicious or otherwise. She makes a gay frolic of little intimate things, food and drink, apothecaries and their ridiculous drugs, friends and their absurd weaknesses; she describes, without apparently a tremor, La Brinvilliers being burnt at the stake, and constantly and forever dwells on the melancholy and beauty of the woods where she walks by the light of the moon, "Endymion's beautiful mistress", thinking of her dear daughter. "*Je laisse trotter ma plume . . . c'est entre vos mains que mes lettres deviennent d'or.*" "My pen runs away with me." "The result," says Edward FitzGerald, "is all truth and daylight." These are the letters of a lover, waiting, hoping for an answer which, if delayed, throws him in a fever, and when it comes is a joy almost too great to be borne. When the wife of Talma the tragedian complained of his connubial shortcomings, she added: "*Avec lui tout f . . . le camp dans la tragédie.*" It might be said of Madame de Sévigné "*Avec elle tout f . . . le camp dans la correspondance.*" It was her Magician's Cave, where she could banish the nostalgia of those long solitary evenings spent in her distant home in Brittany, thinking, dreaming of the beloved one.

In considering her style we must remember, as Lyn Irvine [2] says, that a masque-like exaggeration of mood and experience was

[1] *See* f.n. p. 46. [2] *Ten Letter Writers.* Hogarth Press, 1932.

a persistent fashion in the seventeenth century. Those were days of unbridled emotions, strong drugs, extremes of all kinds, cynicism, cruelty, sensibility. When some illness overtook its unfortunate victim the doctors are described as breaking his jaws, hacking his head to pieces in the hope of resuscitating him. Crowds would assemble to watch criminals burn at the stake—Madame de Sévigné mixes with the crowd, despite " my extreme sensitiveness ", which she likes to dwell on. We observe on the one hand that accident or bereavement drove people to despair: they swooned, tears flowed, cries and screams were uttered; it appeared unlikely that the bereaved would survive. When Turenne was killed in battle, the groans and yells of his soldiers could be heard for miles. On the other hand laughter and mirth were more easily come by than in our sophisticated times. Madame de Sévigné tells of important visitors at Les Rochers rushing out to play games on the grass, laughing heartily, being overtaken by a shower of rain, and rushing in wet from head to foot, screaming with laughter, so that they overbalanced and fell to the ground.

The overmastering passion for this " dry stick of a daughter ", as Irvine calls her, or as Saint-Simon says, " *cet esprit aigre, altier, dominant* ", seems inexplicable. But it is possible that the shock of Madame de Sévigné's tragically short and disappointing marriage may have put her against men as lovers or husbands; and yet, being an artist to the very core, and possessing all the unsatisfied passions of an artist, she had to find an outlet, and in Françoise here it was, to her hand. It is most difficult to judge fairly of Madame de Grignan's response, since all her letters, and she wrote faithfully twice a week to her mother, were destroyed by her own daughter, Madame de Simiane, the beloved Pauline of the Letters—it is thought because they were considered unorthodox from a religious point of view. Madame de Sévigné's friends were aggravated by what they looked upon as extravagant maternal partiality, but one cannot escape the conclusion that Madame de Grignan had a great deal to put up with: pursued by over-anxiety in the matter of her health, by interference in her matrimonial concerns, by criticism of her domestic arrangements and of her extravagant ways, and relentlessly pursued by maternal love. Maternal love if you will, but with all the ingredients appertaining to a Grand Passion. To the Abbé d'Hacqueville she says in a moment of stress : " As I write my heart is so heavy methinks I shall die. I say this to you, who alone can enter into my feelings, knowing how sensitive, how thin-skinned I am. I tremble in every limb, I fear to lose my reason, I cannot sleep, and if for a moment I drop off into an uneasy slumber, I wake with a terrible start, and dare not close my eyes once more. . . . Wherefore does my daughter cease to write to me ? Is she sick ? Are her letters lost, stolen ? . . . Ah me ! How unfortunate am I to have no one with whom to share my pain, on whose bosom I can weep ! . . . I beseech of you to try and allay my fears by ascertaining for yourself the cause of this silence. . . . Dear friend—haste to answer, my state is pitiful. . . ." It is noteworthy that such cries, such anguish, are not heard when her son fails to write to her from the battlefield for weeks on end. On one occasion, when Madame de Sévigné visited the Château de Pomponne, she was severely lectured for six hours, we are told, by Pomponne's father, the pious old Arnauld d'Andilly, for idolising her daughter. And on one occasion she was refused Absolution by her Confessor on account of her maternal passion. We are left to wonder what were M. de Grignan's feelings on reading over his wife's shoulder the many passionate phrases addressed to her by her mother. Such a one as " Do you wonder if I cannot refrain from kissing your lovely face and bosom ? " was carefully suppressed by all save the latest of her editors.

The brother, Charles, seems to have been endowed with all the charm and humour Françoise lacked, and his relationship with his mother was delightful, on a less exalted plane. He was as pretty as Françoise, we are told, and Pomponne's brother, Abbé Arnauld, in his Memoirs of 1657, evokes the following picture of the Sévigné family : " I can see her now, as when she appeared to me for the first time, sitting back in her open carriage between her young son and daughter, all three so well endowed with brilliant looks and grace of bearing that they resembled none other than Latona surrounded by the youthful Apollo and Diana."

Charles adored his " Maman mignonne ", although she would scold him roundly for his most indiscreet, nay disastrous, love affairs with Ninon de Lenclos, Champsmeslé the actress, and harpies who fleeced and ruined him. In her eyes her "*fripon*" of a son was mad, feather-brained and stingy, but they laughed together, laughed hugely, read voraciously, and were perfect companions at Les Rochers, and when in 1676 a "torticolis" turned out to be rheumatic fever, he and his valet nursed her devotedly night and day, and he became her most capable amanuensis. When, after committing a hundred follies, Charles finally married a young woman of good Breton family and considerable fortune, his mother was gratified, and the young couple settled down at Les Rochers in a most exemplary manner—pious and domesticated. It could scarcely be expected that Madame de Sévigné would be satisfied with a daughter-in-law whom she found delicate and "*accablée de vapeurs*", as well as entirely negative. "*Elle n'est point ceci ni cela ; avec le temps je dirai, peut-être, qu'elle est cela.*" The best she is able to say is that she does not speak with a Breton accent. But affection grew for the poor wisp of a girl, and was returned in good measure.

So the years rolled by with endless interests in the country, occasional visits to Vichy for a cure, constant visits to Livry, visits to Paris where, in 1672, she settled in to the Hôtel de Carnavalet, Rue des Filles Bleues, Place Royale, a handsome, large, well-proportioned house, with ample room for all, for Bienbon "*une petite aile très jolie*", and spacious apartments for the whole Grignan family.[1] The upper floor was reserved for Madame de Sévigné and her daughter, the lower for M. de Grignan and his two elder daughters by a first marriage. "This is," she writes to her daughter, "a perfect arrangement." "*Enfin c'est une affaire admirable ... une belle cour, un beau jardin, un beau quartier, un bel air, et les bonnes petites Filles Bleues* (the Blue Nuns) *qui sont fort commodes ; et nous serons ensemble, et vous m'aimez.*" Later Madame de Sévigné appears to have become impoverished by over-generosity to her children and the default of tenants on her estate. She ceased to keep a carriage and joined her son and his wife at Les Rochers in order to economise.

But there were still the occasional and formidable peregrinations to Grignan—three weeks by road and river, full of peril and adventure. Again every few years her daughter visited her, visits never sufficiently protracted to satisfy the mother's hungry heart, although in 1680 she seems to have remained no less than eight years.

Towards the end of her life Madame de Sévigné lost many of

[1] The Carnavalet became a National Museum in 1866 (*see* f.n. p. 196).

her faithful friends—Madame de La Fayette, who had once told her: "*Croyez, ma chère, que vous êtes la personne du monde que j'ai le plus aimée.*" Bussy died in the same year, La Rochefoucauld soon after, Abbé de Coulanges in 1687. She must have suffered much through her great gift for friendship.

Of old age she wrote to President Moulceau: "*Si à vingt ans l'on nous fit voir dans un miroir le visage que nous aurons à soixante ans, nous tomberions à la renverse; mais c'est jour à jour que nous avançons; nous sommes aujourd'hui comme hier, et demain comme aujourd'hui, ainsi nous avançons sans le sentir, et c'est un des miracles de cette Providence que j'adore.*" Such a comprehension of life's span is rare indeed.

In her last years she was much occupied with the marriage of her grandchildren. Pauline de Grignan was snatched from the jaws of a convent to become Marquise de Simiane; the young Marquis chose a rich girl of plebeian origin. Her family was furious when his mother, excusing the misalliance, was heard to remark: "Even the best lands need manuring."

In 1690 Madame de Sévigné decided to start off once more for Grignan, and thereafter was to remain there until her death in 1696, save for one or two brief visits to Paris. To Bussy she writes: "When you see the date of this letter you will take me for a bird—I have passed courageously from Brittany to Provence."

One last tender service she was to render the beloved. When her daughter fell seriously ill she nursed her untiringly; but this illness was to kill, not the invalid who recovered, but her mother. As Madame de Grignan lay slowly convalescing Madame de Sévigné was struck down by an intermittent fever, and died on the 10th of April 1696.[1] Madame de Grignan survived her mother only nine years, dying at the age of fifty-seven, out of grief it was said at the early death of her son, who succumbed to smallpox, to which Madame de Sévigné's own son was also to fall a victim. It did not pass without comment that the beloved daughter was not present at her mother's deathbed.

The Château de Grignan, which was destroyed long ago, boasted immense, wind-swept terraces, a source of much disquiet for the poor mother on account of Madame de Grignan's supposed delicacy of the chest. To the Château they served as a vast esplanade, and as a roof-top to the chapel below. Festooned with

[1] Until recently thought to have been from smallpox.

balustrades they dominate vast horizons, all the way from the Comtat to Provence. It has been said that standing up there was like sailing a ship in the sky, and from the hold of the ship Madame de Sévigné set sail for Eternity. Clad in blue brocatel she was laid to rest in the family vault in the Collegiate Chapel at Grignan. In the Chapel, up above the high altar, can still be seen the monument erected by M. de Grignan in pious memory of his wife. She is seen, floating on a cloud, inclining her head ever so slightly, stretching out her hand ever so condescendingly to her mother, who is kneeling far below on a marble cushion at her feet. Death has thus set its seal on their relationship on earth—filial tolerance on the one hand, maternal adoration on the other, the cause of much comment at the time, and endless speculation thereafter.

In 1732 the following words were inscribed on Madame de Sévigné's tomb by the then owner of the Château de Grignan, Nicolas du Muy, Marshal of France:

Ci-git Marie de Rabutin Chantal,
Marquise de Sévigné,
Decédée le 18 Avril 1696.

His nephew, who inherited the property, embraced the cause of the French revolutionaries and in the *Gazette du Jour* it is told that the Société Populaire of Grignan, on the plea of performing a patriotic duty, overran the Church and Château, destroyed the contents, burning all the portraits save that of Madame de Sévigné and desecrating the tombs in the Chapel. One of Madame de Sévigné's descendants, the Comte de Castellane, who hastened with others to the scene, describes the sacrilege which took place in all its ferocious barbarity and horror. Fighting ensued, and the remains of the poor Marquise were torn asunder—a few remnants of brocatel, a few strands of hair, a rib, a tooth, falling into the hands of the vandals, who seem to have realised their value. After the holocaust a heap was made of skeletons, bones and skulls, which were thrown back into the open grave, and the marble tomb resealed.[1] Thus Madame de Sévigné's mortal remains were no longer to rest in solitary peace; no longer for her is the grave " a fine and private place ". Of the precious

[1] M. Gailly, who tells the story, says that Monmerqué and other editors suppressed these facts.

relics two fragments of brocatel alone are left—one at the Carnavalet, one at the Sorbonne Library. But the famous Letters are our heritage; and they are immortal.

The story of the successive editions of Madame de Sévigné's letters is intricate. It would seem that in 1714 the thought first struck her granddaughter Pauline, Marquise de Simiane, in collaboration with her cousin Abbé Celse de Bussy, son of the notorious Comte de Bussy, that the time was ripe for a selective edition of the many hundreds of letters addressed by Madame de Sévigné to her daughter Françoise, Comtesse de Grignan, Pauline's mother. These were known to be preserved, together with many corresponding letters and answers in the hand of Françoise, at the Château de Grignan in Provence, where Pauline's father was still living. Accordingly she spent two years at her ancestral home, during which time she transcribed and dispatched to her cousin in Paris, first a selection of 137 letters, with a *Préface* vouching for their authenticity, and then a further 50 letters, herself returning in 1716 to Paris where Abbé Celse had prepared an *Avant-propos* for their joint edition. No doubt they had been led to their task by his father's posthumous success, for after the publication of his *Mémoires* in 1696, four volumes of *Lettres de Bussy-Rabutin* had appeared in 1697, followed by three volumes of *Nouvelles Lettres* in 1709, the whole containing close on a hundred letters from the Marquise de Sévigné. The reputation of a correspondent who had delighted a distinguished circle of friends throughout her lifetime was thus widened and enhanced, and led to opinions being divided on the respective merits and epistolatory style of the two gifted correspondents. A matter of more speculative conjecture today is the real reason for Pauline's delay in publishing the first fruits of her labours, a delay which was to prove her undoing, as editor, in more ways than one. Whether or not her father's death, on the last day of 1714, so far from releasing her from family ties and obligations only strengthened her filial scrupulosity, or whether the two cousins of the younger generation agreed that the remarkable correspondence should be on a more grandiose scale, Pauline is known to have returned to Grignan in 1720 where, for the next six years, with the help of a secretary, she filled six quarto volumes with more than 2,500 pages, transcribing well over half the collection of letters available.

Once more the Abbé had to wait in vain for news from Grignan; but this time circumstances forced him to take matters into his own hands. In the autumn of 1723 he was nominated to the anti-Jansenist See of Luçon, a post not held for long, but one which was to estrange him from his cousin both physically and morally, as can be read in Pauline's own words, "*Je pleure ce pauvre abbé de Bussy, car je ne connais guère l'évêque de Luçon*"; in fact, by then more deeply concerned by religious scruples, she was to break off all relations with him after the series of disasters that followed close upon the first unauthorised edition of her grandmother's letters. Before leaving for his diocese, Celse de Bussy entrusted her transcriptions of the original 137 letters to the safe keeping of two literary friends, never intending that they should further the publication of so slight a volume. It seems most probable, however, that such a project was discussed by them with Voltaire, for it is to his hand that the experts attribute the editorship of what must be regarded as the *editio princeps*. Three copies only of this edition are known to exist, containing 37 letters written between 1671 and 1676, and printed in 1726 by Lefèvre of Troyes; the remainder are thought to have been destroyed. The same year saw the publication of two other mystifying editions, from Rouen and The Hague, both in two volumes and both including the original *Préface* and *Avant-propos*, the former without name of printer or place, while in the Dutch text the addition of one sentence, "*Voici ce que ma cousine m'écrivit en m'envoyant ce recueil*", established the *imprimatur* of Celse de Bussy. The Bishop, who evidently hastened to The Hague to establish his copyright after the clandestine publication by his two unscrupulous friends, neglected or had no mind to set his text in chronological order, though he did print his full quota of 177 against their truncated 138 letters. It is strange that Madame de Sévigné, usually so accurate in heading her letters with place, date, and time of day or night, almost always omitted the year, which must account for the wild confusion of arrangement in all but the Troyes edition, where the scholarly classification certainly points to Voltaire's editorship.

When faced with these pirated editions, Pauline exploded with rage, hoist with her own petard, but since they were printed and published in full accordance with the law, there was nothing she could do beyond firing off a few fulminating letters to the Chief of Police and to all the Dutch Gazettes. Expunge their memory she might, if only she could find a trustworthy editor to carry out her now stricter instructions when preparing her expurgated text for the press. She chose for her purpose a learned man of Aix, Chevalier Perrin, and entrusted to his enterprise, not the six quarto volumes of her transcriptions, but the whole vast store of original letters, fearing perhaps that he would take exception to her wilful excisions or, as M. Gailly suggests, that she herself might destroy the originals as soon as he had completed his task, since she is known to have made a holocaust of her mother's autographed letters shortly after she had sight of the first Perrin volumes. Be that as it may, it is by no means the end of Pauline's story. For years the Chevalier had worked, without a word from his patroness, cutting and editing along lines not laid down by her, and in 1734, from Simart in Paris, came the first four of his projected six-volume edition, with a Preface by himself. He concluded his task in 1737, having printed 402 letters in the first and 212 in the second publication. This proved to be Pauline's death-blow, for she died on the 3rd of July, 1737, having failed to elicit the return of her grandmother's letters from Perrin; but not before she had extracted a solemn promise from her son-in-law to burn the originals with his own hands. It was not until 1784 that her dread sentence was carried out under her son-in-law's dying eyes by his cousin's hand, and Pauline's direst wish was thus fulfilled. Perrin himself died in 1754, of indigestion, a few weeks before the publication of his eight-volume *édition générale* of 772 letters, which for so long held sway.

We must pass rapidly over the numberless editions which have appeared since 1754, and mention only the monumental work of Monmerqué who, after cutting out much of Perrin's work and going straight back to the first editions, produced the first work of modern scholarship in 1818–19. The year following he had the good fortune to be put in touch with a certain Marquis de Grosbois, who sent him a folio of 1,055 pages, lettered in gold, *Lettres de Madame de Sévigné*, the MSS. dating from the first half of the 18th century, but of unknown provenance. It proved a goldmine, and occupied Monmerqué for the last forty years of his life, but he did not live to see his completed work, in twelve magnificent volumes, inaugurate in 1862, under the auspices of M. Adolphe Regnier and with a lengthy biographical notice by M. Paul Mesnard, the famous collection known as *Les Grands Ecrivains de la France*. There the matter might have rested had it not been for the following extraordinary train of events.

At a public auction, which took place in January, 1872, at Semur-en-Auxois, the contents of a house belonging to the Massol family came under the hammer. One of the buyers, Madame Caquelin, antique dealer of Dijon, found herself, somewhat reluctantly and for a mere song, the possessor of six calf-bound volumes of manuscript. These, labelled *Lettres de Madame la Marquise de Sévigné*, were to be seen, day in day out, exposed to all weathers for thirteen months, on a bench outside her shop. Eventually, M. Charles Capmas, doctor-of-law at the University of Dijon, purchased the lot. He laboured to compose a labyrinthine introduction to what amounted to an arbitrary selection of textual variants, together with some few letters printed in full, and in 1876 issued his *Lettres inédites* as a two-volume supplement to Monmerqué, bequeathing the Dijon MSS. to the *Bibliothèque Nationale*. There the letters remained enshrouded till M. Gérard Gailly, the famous Flaubertiste, convinced that he held the key to their secret, came in the guise of Prince Charming to waken the sleeping Marquise. From a masterly introduction to the new edition of her letters,[1] we learn from M. Gailly that the Capmas treasure-trove is none other than the transcript made by Pauline de Simiane and her amanuenses, and that under his meticulous editorship the letters are to appear for the first time in their original form, complete and uncensored, straight from the lively pen, the eager brain, the loving heart of Madame de Sévigné. There was something Gallic, racy, one might almost say archaic in her mode of expression. She spoke of her style as rustic, and whenever we come across a passage with a whiff of the Hôtel de Rambouillet, or of Mlle de Scudéry, we may be sure it is a pastiche

[1] *Madame de Sévigné/Lettres/Tome* 1/1644–1675. *Edition nouvelle comportant de nombreux fragments inédits et restitutions de textes établie avec une introduction, des notes et un index par Gérard Gailly. Gallimard* (*Bib. de la Pléiade*), 1953.

of the affectations she so enjoyed laughing at. Yet it is interesting to note that many of her expressions are taken by Littré as terms of reference in his *Dictionnaire de la langue française*.

The aim of the translator has been to select, in chronological order, such passages from Monmerqué's text as will, within the scope of one volume, convey to the English reader a picture of Madame de Sévigné's life, friendships, philosophy, hopes, fears, joys and sorrows, as they were unfolded to her daughter. Grateful acknowledgement must be made to the expert guidance of M. Gailly, and to his publishers, Messrs. Gallimard, for their permission to draw on certain corrections to the text up to 1675, all of which are duly stated in the footnotes to this volume.

The story of the English versions is bizarre, to say the least. In editing Edward FitzGerald's *Dictionary of Madame de Sévigné* in 1914, his great-niece, Mrs. Kerrich, makes no mention of any English translation, but writes, " in order that the spelling of the *Letters* might present no stumbling-block to the general public, it has been altered in accordance with the accepted reforms introduced by Voltaire ", and mentions that the French texts of 1820 and 1826 were used, as well as the Capmas *Dijon Manuscript* of 1876.

Fifteen years later a spate of grandiose editions flooded the English market, three of which are worth recording. Copyrighted in 1927, printed in 1928 in the U.S.A. and distributed in this country by W. T. Morrell & Co., the limited Carnavalet Edition (7 vols.) was introduced by an American enthusiast, A. Edward Newton. No date is given for the translation, though high claims are made for it, and the text is said to be " newly re-edited, revised and corrected, including three hundred letters not previously translated into English ". The text will be found to be from the same source as that used in the two London editions of 1927. The first of these was issued by Spurr and Swift in a 10-volume edition limited to 1,000 copies under the title of *Letters from the Marchioness de Sévigné to her daughter the Countess de Grignan, with an introductory essay by Madame Duclaux* (*A. Mary F. Robinson*), who prints " The Editor's Advertisement " (unsigned and undated) and the " Preface to the Edition of 1734 " without further comment. She writes, on p. vi of her essay, the strangest account of her reasons for republishing the text of an outmoded and undated translation. " It is a rare piece of good fortune to have discovered this charming old translation of the Letters. From the point of view of the scholar, it is valueless: Monmerqué's edition, and especially Monmerqué revised by Mesnard, still keeps complete possession of the field. But, for an English reader, it is an immense advantage to hear the Marquise's voice speaking the elegant language of 18th-century Dublin. It is difficult to translate her prose exactly into English: as an Irishwoman she appeals to us at once. * * * That suspicion, that ghost, of a brogue dissipates any misunderstanding on our part."

The other edition was published by Routledge in two volumes, and reprinted the following year " with a few corrections ", under the title of *Letters of Madame de Sévigné to her Daughter and her Friends. Selected with an Introductory Essay, by Richard Aldington.* This contains a note on the text, " This is a selection of the nine volumes, printed for J. Walker, London, 1811 (now very scarce), which was itself translated from the enlarged Paris edition of 1806, in eight volumes," on which Mr. Aldington limits his comment to a single sentence, " A reprint of the bulk of Madame de Sévigné's letters in an early 19th-century translation needs no apology."

A comparison of these three texts proves them to be printed from an identical source, with one or two verbal changes, especially in the footnotes, where Mr. Aldington has Duchess for Dutchess, and Tuileries for the Irish (?) Thuileries of Madame Duclaux, and all keep the uncongenial anglicised form of " The Rocks " for " Les Rochers ". It is on this none-too-accurate text that English readers have had to subsist for close on 150 years.

Then, in 1946, came Mr. Arthur Stanley's *Madame de Sévigné: her letters and her world*, in which the author himself translated 246 letters out of a possible 1679, filling in their background discursively as he went along. Mr. Stanley's task was admirably fulfilled. The first third of the book deals at length with the early life of his subject, notably with the trial of Fouquet and the intrigues of the Fronde, and other later events not included in this book. The present selection of 272 letters may be regarded as complementary to his volume, since Madame de Sévigné is here allowed to tell her own story, aided by notes of historical value, and once again it can be claimed that the greater number appear in an English translation for the first time.

1648

To the Comte Bussy de Rabutin [1]

Les Rochers, 15 March [1648].

You are indeed a churlish fellow to have so neglected me for two whole months. Have you forgotten who I am and the exalted rank I hold in our family? Indeed, I shall not allow you to forget it, and if despite what I say, you should rouse my anger still further, I shall reduce you to a mere docket.[2] You well knew I was near the end of my pregnancy, yet I observe in you no more concern for my health than were I an unravished maiden. Very well then! However much you may stamp and rage, I shall now break the news to you that I am brought to bed of a boy,

[1] Roger de Rabutin, Comte de Bussy (1618–93), second cousin of Mme de S., for whom she coined the word *Rabutinage* to express the ties of their sincere friendship since childhood. Followed Condé in the Fronde, then enlisted in the King's Service (1653). *Mestre-de-camp-général de la cavalérie légère*, with Turenne in Flanders. Himself a suitor for his cousin's hand, he urged her to wed the Prince de Conti; when later she refused to advance him money, he revenged himself by writing a sarcastic caricature of her in his *Histoire amoureuse des Gaules* (1659). For this book he was ordered to the Bastille and then exiled to his estates in Burgundy. Member of the Academy (1665). During his 18 years' retirement he translated Ovid and Martial, wrote his memoirs, and composed a Genealogy of the Rabutin family dedicated to Mme de S., of whom he wrote: "*Vous êtes de ces femmes qui ne devraient jamais mourir, comme il en a qui ne devraient jamais naître*".

[2] In armorial bearings the term "*lambel*" or "*brisure*" was used to designate the junior branch of a family.

and that the very milk he suckles is envenomed by hatred for you. I also intend that the many other sons I bear shall be your enemies. You have not been as clever as I, you mere fashioner of daughters ! [1]

But a truce to this banter, dear cousin ; truth must come before politics. I intended throughout my letter to scold you for your laziness, but, in so doing, I have put too much strain upon my affections and I must, here and now, confess that I and M. de Sévigné dote on you, and oft-times find ourselves conversing of the pleasure your company affords us. . . .

[1] Bussy had three daughters only by his first marriage to Gabrielle de Toulongeon. In 1650 he married Louise de Rouville, and had two sons and two daughters, his second son being Celse-Roger (1669–1736) (*see* Introduction).

1668

To the Comte Bussy de Rabutin

Paris, 4 December 1668.

Have you not received my letter, in which I granted you a reprieve, and proclaimed my intention of not smiting you to the ground? I expected an answer to this noble gesture, instead of which you never gave it a thought but rose up and grasped your sword again, as indeed I bade you. I only hope you will never use it against me.

I have a great piece of news for your satisfaction. The prettiest girl in France [1] is being given in marriage, if not to the handsomest, certainly to one of the most deserving of men, to M. de Grignan,[2] whom you have known a long time. But his wives having died most accommodatingly, as well as his father and his son, he is left more wealthy than ever. To add to this, a noble birth, great possessions and amiable qualities, render him most acceptable in our eyes. There is to be none of the usual bargaining attached to these occasions, for our predecessors will have paved the way. He appears equally gratified with his new alliance, and

[1] Her daughter, Françoise Marguerite (1646–1705), born 10th October.

[2] François Adhémar de Monteil, Comte de G. (1629–1714); head of ancient Provencal House of Adhémar (*Monteil d' Adhémar = Montélimar*); since 1663 Lt.-General of Languedoc. Twice widowed, his first wife being Angélique d'Angennes, sister of Julie de Montausier, youngest daughter of the Marquise de Rambouillet (*ob.* 1664); his second, Marie-Angélique du Puy-du-Fou, by whom he had a son who died (*ob.* 1667).

as soon as news has reached us from his uncle, the Archbishop of Arles[1]—the Bishop of Uzès,[2] another uncle, being in Paris—the matter should be concluded, we hope by the end of the year.

I am punctilious, as you know, and have not failed to turn to you for advice and approbation.

The world appears satisfied, which is gratifying, since we are foolish enough to set store by its good opinion.

[1] François Adhémar de Monteil de G., Abp. from 1643 to 1689.

[2] Jacques, brother of above, Bp. from 1660 to 1674.

1670

To The Comte de Grignan

Paris, Friday 15 August [1670].

Should I continue to correspond with you, this is only on the understanding that my letters require no answer, and to prove the reliance I place in you, I proceed to offer my congratulations on the honours which have been conferred on you. These I feel are as much addressed to M. de Grignan as to M. le Commandant,[1] and there is, I think, a wholly personal element in their bestowal.

I observe such a lively interest exists between you and a certain lady that it would be absurd of me to pretend to give you any news of her. Not only can I tell you nothing you do not already know on the subject of her love for you, but her actions, her conduct, her solicitude and her languor, all proclaim it openly. I consider myself extremely perceptive in the affairs of the heart, and not without experience. What I see gives me much satisfaction, and I should not know how to improve upon it. Rejoice, be not ungrateful, and if there is a little corner in your heart still untenanted, it would make me most happy if you assigned it to me, for there is a very large one in mine for you. I scarcely need to tell you what loving care I bestow on your wife, how carefully I watch over her health, and trust the ship with its little cargo

[1] The Comte de G. had been nominated (29.11.69) to the military and administrative post of Lt.-General of Provence and had left Paris in April to support the 13-year-old Governor, the Duc de Vendôme.

will come safely to port.[1] Should you be an expert in love you will be able to judge of the extent of mine. Would to God your good wife were as fortunate as Deville,[2] who has been brought to bed of a boy, who looks to be three months old. My daughter says: "It is too bad that Deville should have stolen my son, for two boys are never born in the same house." I have given to her, that is my daughter, a book for you of extreme beauty, written by Pascal's friend,[3] who produces nought but what is perfect, pray read it with all your attention. Do not neglect either your voice or your figure; and since you are loved, pray continue to please.

To The Same

Paris, Wednesday 19 November [*1670*].

Madame de Puisieux [4] says that if you long for a son you must give yourself the trouble to produce one. I endorse this sentiment as perfectly reasonable. You have endowed us with a daughter; [5] we return you the gift. Never was a birth more propitious. I must tell you that last Saturday Françoise and I went to the Arsenal [6] for a walk when her pains started, so on our way home I wanted to collect Madame Robinet,[7] but she would not let me. She made an excellent evening repast.

The Coadjutor [8] and I wanted to prepare the room for her confinement, but she tried to persuade us it was a false alarm.

[1] Madame de G. was expecting a child.

[2] Wife of Comte de G.'s factotum. She occasionally supplied Mme de S. with a bulletin of her mistress's health.

[3] Pierre Nicole (1625–93), Jansenist, author of *Essais de Morale*.

[4] Charlotte d'Estampes de Valençay (1597–1677), widow of the Vicomte de P., Secretary of State to Henri IV and Louis XIII. Renowned for her wit.

[5] Mme de G. gave birth to a daughter, Marie-Blanche, on the 15th of November. In the previous year she had had a miscarriage at Livry.

[6] Public gardens much in vogue.

[7] Famous Parisian midwife.

[8] Jean-Baptiste, nicknamed "Seigneur Corbeau", and, at his own request, "Pierrot"; the Comte de G.'s brother, Coadjutor to his uncle, the Abp. of Arles, whose Dignity he succeeded to in 1689.

Finally, just as I insisted on getting la Robinette, the pains became so violent that it was clear her labour had started. No midwife—what to do! I was in despair. She appealed for help and cried out for a nurse; it was none too soon as Deville, whom we had urged to hasten here by coach, brought the child into the world fifteen minutes after her arrival. Almost at the same moment Pecquet [1] appeared, who assisted the delivery. All was happily over when la Robinette turned up, who was much taken aback, thinking she had all night before her. She had remained to oblige "Madame la Duchesse".[2] Hélène [3] was heard to say "It's a boy". I passed on the news to the Coadjutor, after which, examining more closely, we discovered it to be a girl.

Having placed all our hopes on devotions and votive offerings to Almighty God, we are somewhat downcast that "*La Signora met au monde une fille*".[4] I can assure you it has taken us down a peg or two, and nothing could make up for the disappointment save Françoise's perfect recovery; she has not had so much as a touch of milk-fever. Her daughter has been christened Marie-Blanche.[5] What else can I tell you? Your wife's good health may console you for the sad news that our beloved Duchesse de Saint-Simon [6] is dangerously ill of the smallpox, and not likely to recover.

Farewell, dear friend. Make what you can of these confused impressions—you know well what my feelings are towards you. Ill-natured folk pretend that Blanche d'Adhémar has not the makings of a great beauty, and the same persons add that she resembles you; in that case you may be sure my heart is hers.

[1] Jean P. (1622–74) famous anatomist, Fouquet's doctor and Mme de S.'s.

[2] Anne de Bavière, Duchesse d'Enghien, second daughter of Edward, Count Palatine and Anne de Gonzague.

[3] Hélène Delan, Mme de S.'s maid.

[4] Allusion to La Fontaine's Conte, *L'Ermite*, where the lady in question dreams her future son will be Pope.

[5] Marie-Blanche took the veil at the Convent of the Visitation at Aix, at the age of sixteen, and died there some 45 years later.

[6] Diane-Henriette de Budos, who died 13 days later; first wife of Claude, father of the memoirist.

To The Marquis de Coulanges [1]

Monday, 15 December [*1670*].

I am now going to tell you something so surprising, so astonishing, so marvellous, miraculous, triumphant, so unbelievable, so singular, extraordinary, unexpected; the biggest, the smallest, the most rare, the most commonplace, the most notorious and, until now, most secret, the most brilliant and yet obscure, and most to be envied; in short, something unique in the whole of history with one exception, which however may not be an exception,[2] something which we in Paris cannot believe (how much less in Lyons?). Something which calls for universal commiseration; something which will rejoice the hearts of Mesdames de Rohan and d'Hauterive,[3] finally something which will take place on Sunday, when those who are present will not know if they are standing on their head or their heels, something which will take place on Sunday and perhaps on Monday will not have been accomplished. My lips are sealed; I give you a guess—three guesses. You give it up? Well then, I capitulate!

M. de Lauzun [4] is being married at the Louvre on Sunday—Guess to whom? I give you four, I give you ten, I give you a hundred to one. Mme de Coulanges [5] says: "How mystifying! I know—Mme de la Vallière?" [6] Certainly not, Madame.—

[1] Philippe-Emmanuel, Marquis de C.—"le tout petit Coulanges", (1633–1716), son of the brother of Mme de S.'s mother and her lifelong friend, for she was 7 when he was born. Author of light verse, nicknamed "Le Chansonnier". Councillor, later *Maître des Requêtes*. A congenial *bon-viveur*.

[2] Possible reference to the marriage of Louis XII's widow to the Duke of Suffolk, three months after the King's death (*Monmerqué*).

[3] The Princess de Léon, sole heiress of the Duc de Rohan, and Mme d'H., daughter of the Duc de Villeroy; both had married beneath them.

[4] Antonine Nompar de Caumont, Marquis de Puyguilhem (1633–1723), who since 1668 had been Col.-General of the Dragoons. In 1685 he went to the Court of James II, bringing the Queen of England to France after the Revolution. In 1692 created Duc de Lauzun. Famous for his *Mémoires*.

[5] Marie-Angélique du Gué Bagnols, renowned for her witty and sarcastic epigrams. Niece of Chancellor Le Tellier's wife and so cousin of Louvois; friend of Mme de Maintenon.

[6] Louise, originally the companion of *Madame* (Henrietta of England), favourite of Louis XIV.

"Surely then, Mlle de Retz?"[1] No indeed, how provincial you are!—"How dense I am", say you—"Mlle Colbert?"[2] Still less.—"I know, Mlle de Créquy?"[3]—Colder and colder: I shall be obliged to tell you. On Sunday, at the Louvre, with the King's sanction, he will wed Mademoiselle, Mademoiselle de . . . Mademoiselle . . . try again! Mademoiselle, I swear it, on my honour! On my sacred word of honour! Mademoiselle, *the great Mademoiselle.*[4] *Mademoiselle*, daughter of the late *Monsieur*. Mademoiselle, grand-daughter of Henry IV, Mademoiselle d'Eu, Mademoiselle de Dombes, Mademoiselle de Montpensier, Mademoiselle d'Orléans, Mademoiselle, first cousin to the King, Mademoiselle destined for a throne. MADEMOISELLE, the only consort worthy of MONSIEUR.[5] Is not this a fine subject for conversation? Should you exclaim, be indignant, maintain that it is all an invention, a tissue of lies, that we are making fun of you, that you do not find the joke a good one; should you, in fact, turn round and rend us, we shall consider you are justified, for in your place we should do likewise.

Adieu: the other letters carried by this ordinary[6] will bear witness to the truth of our story.

[1] The Cardinal's niece, later Ctsse and Dsse de Sault.

[2] The Minister's second daughter, future Dsse de Beauvillier.

[3] The Duc de C.'s heiress, who was to marry the son of Mme de S.'s friend, Psse de Tarente.

[4] Anne-Marie de Bourbon (1627–93), only daughter of Gaston de Foix, Duc d'Orléans (1608–60), only brother of Louis XIII. She inherited the fortune of her mother, wife of Henri de Bourbon, Duc de Montpensier.

[5] Philippe d'Orléans, brother of Louis XIV.

[6] Mme de S., in a letter dated 18 May 1670, tells her daughter that through the good offices of the Coadjutor of Rheims, arrangements have been made with M. Dubois for the regular and speedy delivery of their letters. Since 1627 *Bureaux de dépêches* had been established in various towns throughout France, from which *courriers ordinaires* set out once or twice a week. Letters left Paris for Provence on Wednesday and Friday, and took five days; they took ten days from Provence to Brittany. Mme de S. also employed *extraordinaires* (*homme exprès à toute bride*), who did not always prove so reliable.

To The Same

Paris, Friday 19 December [*1670*].

To be knocked all of a heap—that is what happened to us last night at the Tuileries ; [1] but we must start by retracing our steps. You have shared in the joy and transports of ecstasy of the Princess and her happy lover. As I told you, it was on Monday that the news was made public. Tuesday was passed in talking it over, in astonishment, and in congratulations. On Wednesday MADEMOISELLE made a deed of gift to M. de Lauzun of the title, names, and endowments deemed necessary for the marriage contract which was drawn up the same day. In the meantime she gave him no less than four dukedoms : that of the county of Eu, the premier dukedom of France, carrying the highest rank, the dukedom of Montpensier—of Saint-Fargeau, of Châtellerault, estimated at a total of twenty-two millions ; when the marriage contract was signed he at once assumed the title of Duc de Montpensier.

Yesterday morning, being Thursday, MADEMOISELLE was in expectation of the King's promised signature, but at seven o'clock of the same evening His Majesty, having been persuaded by the Queen,[2] by Monsieur, and several dotards, that this marriage would injure his reputation, summoned MADEMOISELLE and M. de Lauzun to his presence, and declared before M. le Prince [3] that their marriage was banned. M. de Lauzun mustered all the loyalty and courage he possessed, not unmixed with despair at so cruel a humiliation, and behaved with great dignity. MADEMOISELLE, true to character, cried and screamed and lamented and was seized with violent pains. She took to her bed and lived all day on slops. What a beautiful dream ! Or subject for a novel or for the theatre, and still more for great gossip and argument in which, believe me, we indulge day and night and from dusk to dawn. Do you likewise, " *e fra tanto vi bacio le mani*."

[1] The Royal Palace, begun in 1564, and frequently altered ; later superseded by Versailles. Gardens designed by Le Nôtre.

[2] Even the Queen, Marie-Thérèse, daughter of Philip IV of Spain, who never interfered, spoke out strongly to the King, as did MONSIEUR. Monsieur le Prince said to the King that he would attend Cadet Lauzun's marriage and knock him down as he came out of Church.

[3] Le Prince de Condé, of royal blood.

1671

To Madame la Comtesse de Grignan [1]

Paris, Monday 9 February [*1671*].

You say my ring has reached you safely, likewise have your letters reached me, and as I read them I cannot restrain my tears; my heart would fain break in two. I had dreaded you would scold me, that I should learn you were ill, had met with an accident, and lo and behold! it is all the other way: you tell me you love me in so convincing a manner that my tears flow afresh. When I have the good fortune to learn all this, and that you are proceeding on your journey without misadventure, it leaves me in the pitiful state I have described. How good to know you are thinking of me, speaking of me, and that you can better express your feelings by the written than the spoken word. Whichever way you choose is equally precious to me, who truly am privileged to understand the meaning of love. You make me sensible of the great tenderness of my feelings towards you, and if, as you say, you think of me sometimes, believe me, my dearest dear, you are ever in my thoughts—are indeed what the devout call "a habit of thought" which, if we were dutiful, should belong exclusively to God. I am incapable of distraction and am constantly at your side; I can see your coach relentlessly moving onwards, nevermore in my direction; I am a wanderer on the

[1] After several postponements, she had left on 5 Feb. to rejoin her husband in Provence.

Françoise Marguerite de Sévigné
Comtesse de Grignan
1646–1705
by Pierre Mignard (*Musée Carnavalet*)
(*Photo: J. E. Bulloz, Paris*)

high road, and sometimes fear I may fall by the wayside; I am in despair at the ceaseless rain; the thought of the Rhône in flood terrifies me. A map lies open before me; I know by heart where you will lie tonight; it will be at Nevers, and Sunday at Lyons where this letter will await you. Hitherto I have had only two letters from you—a third will console me; I crave no other consolation. I find myself incapable of being in a crowd, or of sustaining a conversation—it will get better no doubt. The Duchesses de Verneuil and d'Arpajon [1] want to distract me; I beg to be excused. The kindness of people in these parts is scarcely credible! I spent all of Saturday with Madame de Villars.[2] She understands my feelings; we spoke of you and I wept. . . . I shall sup tête-a-tête in the Faubourg [3] tonight and this must be my share of the carnival. Every day I have a Mass said in your intention, this is no superstitious act of devotion. . . . If you really wish to please me, take good care of yourself, and write to me. I throw you kisses without end, and must ever weary you with enquiries after your good health, sleep soundly in your pretty bed, eat up your good broth, and muster all the courage I am so notably lacking in. . . .

I have had the following accounts of yesterday's festivities: [4] Two thousand lanterns illuminated the courtyards and entrances to the Hôtel de Guise. The Queen entered Mlle de Guise's resplendent apartments, where all the ladies in their jewels knelt before her, without distinction of rank, after which supper was served. Forty ladies sat at the table, the repast was sumptuous. The King arrived, cast an eye of utmost gravity on the proceedings, but did not take his place at table. The company then proceeded upstairs to the ballroom, where the King, holding the

[1] Charlotte Séguier, daughter of the Chancellor, widow of the Duc de Sully, now married to the Duc de Verneuil, natural son of Henri IV; and Catherine d'Harcourt-Beauvron, Dsse d'A, who was to befriend Mme de G.

[2] Marie de Bellefonds, wife of Pierre, Marquis de V., Ambassador to Spain, and later to Savoy. A great friend of the family.

[3] Faubourg St.-Germain, with Mme de La Fayette, Rue de Vaugirard, opposite the Petit Luxembourg (*see* f.n. p. 56).

[4] Given to celebrate the marriage on 7 Feb. of Marie-Angélique, sister of the Prince d'Harcourt, to Pereiro de Mello, Duc de Cadaval. She was a near cousin of the Grignans. The Hôtel de Guise was replaced by the Hôtel de Soubise in the eighteenth century: now Repository of the National Archives.

Queen's hand, took the floor and honoured the assembly by executing a few quick steps, after which he left to sup with lesser company at the Louvre. MADEMOISELLE refused to go to the Hôtel de Guise,[1] which is all I know on that matter . . .

God be with you, my own most precious one. You are the love of my heart, the joy and grief of all my days.

To The Same

Livry, Tuesday in Holy Week, 24 March [*1671*].

Three hours have passed since my arrival, and I am hastening to pour myself out to you. I left Paris accompanied by the Abbé,[2] Hélène, Hébert and Marphise,[3] with the sole object of leaving the world and its sound and fury behind me for two whole days, until Thursday evening. I am trying to delude myself with the idea that I am a solitary, as in the Trappist Monastery, and that I am devoting myself to prayer and recollection, that I intend to observe a strict fast for innumerable intentions, and to exert myself by walking instead of remaining closeted in my room ; and above all to suffer boredom for God's sake. Instead of all this, my dear, I shall be thinking of you, which I have not ceased doing since my arrival—indeed, to such an extent, that I was constrained to seat myself on the little mossy bank where you used to lie, at the further end of your favourite shady walk, and write to you. Every place reminds me of you, and a sword has entered my soul. You are everywhere present—in the house, the Church, in the garden, in the countryside, everything I see holds some memory of you which wrings my heart. I see you, feel you, my thoughts turn endlessly round in my head, leaving a vacuum which cannot be filled. It is useless to think, to tear myself to pieces—my loved one is gone, is two hundred leagues away. She has left me

[1] She had quarrelled with her sister, the Duchesse de Guise.

[2] " The Abbé " *par excellence*, " *le Bien Bon* " of these letters ; Christophe de Coulanges, Prior of Notre Dames des Anges at Livry, Mme de S.'s maternal uncle and guardian, who often jokingly referred to himself as her husband, since he looked after her affairs. Brother of the Marquise de la Trousse.

[3] Hélène was the maid, Hébert the footman, Marphise the Marquise's little dog.

desolate. Yes, I am left to mourn endlessly and am at the end of my strength. What weakness I betray! But after all, how can I fight against a weakness which is inherent in human nature? I do not know how you will judge of my letter, and you may misread what I intend to convey. If you do, so be it, and at any rate it will have served to relieve me of an intolerable weight which is all I can ask. You would not believe how this place has affected me, and I must ask you not to allude to it in your letters, but to honour my weakness and my tears, of which my love for you is the unwitting cause.

(Livry), Thursday in Holy Week.

Had I wept for my sins as much as I have wept for you since I came here, I should indeed be in a state of grace and well prepared for my Easter duties and to celebrate my jubilee. I spent my time here as I had intended, save that your image haunted me more than I had conceived possible. How strange that I should possess an imagination so vivid that I can call up the past as if it were there in very truth, and in so doing, destroy myself. I know not how to escape from you! Our Paris house fills me with boredom, and Livry appears still more tedious. As for you, I doubt not that you have to make an (effort) to remember me at all, for your surroundings do not bring me to life as mine do you. But I have found some solace in all that I have suffered here, from the complete silence and solitude, the melancholy of the Offices, the solemn chanting of *Tenebrae* (which I was hearing at Livry for the first time), the strict canonical fast, and the great beauty of these gardens, which would have charmed you as it has me. Alas! how I have longed for you, and I know that you, who are apt to shun solitude, would have welcomed it here. I am forced to return to Paris where I shall find your letters, and shall be present at the Mass of the Presanctified, when the Passion sermon will be preached by Père Bourdaloue [1] or Père

[1] Louis B., born at Bourges (1632–1704), "*Le roi des prédicateurs et le prédicateur des Rois*", a Jesuit renowned for the uncompromising severity and high moral tone of his sermons, usually preached at Notre-Dame: respected by all sects and parties.

Mascaron:[1] I have always greatly revered the fine sermons of the Passion. Adieu, my dear Countess—this will be my missive from Livry which I will finish in Paris. Would that I had had the strength not to write to you, but, instead, had offered all I have endured to God. Of how much more value this would have been than all the penances in the world, and yet I was so cowardly that I preferred to seek consolation by telling you of my distress!

To The Same

Paris, Saturday 4 April, [*1671*].

I was telling you the other day of the manner in which Madame de Nevers[2] dresses her hair, and how La Martin exaggerated the style of it. I have now seen a modified form which enchants me, and I must describe it to you in order to stop you covering your ears with innumerable little puffs which do not stay in curl, are unbecoming, and as out of date as the wiggeries of Catherine de Médicis. Yesterday I saw the Duchesse de Sully and the Comtesse de Guiche,[3] whose head-dresses are charming. I am converted. This style is made for you, you will look an angel, and it takes no time to do. My only preoccupation is lest this cascade of falling hair from an uncovered pate should provoke toothache. *Trochanire*,[4] who has just arrived from Saint-Germain,[5] wants you to picture the following: a blonde head with hair

[1] Jules M., born at Marseilles (1634–1703), Bp. of Tulle, 1671, and in 1679 of Agen. Oratorian of remarkable eloquence, then preaching at St. Gervais, Mme de S.'s parish. Said, at his death, to have left but 2,000 Calvinists in his diocese from the 30,000 at the time of his translation.

[2] Hortense Mancini, Duchesse de Mazarin (the Cardinal's niece), married to the son of Marshal de la Meilleraye, Duc de Nevers.

[3] Respectively the daughter of Abel Servien, Marquis de Sable, married to the Duc de Sully, and his sister, daughter of the Duchesse de Verneuil, married to the gallant Comte de Guiche, son of Maréchal de Gramont.

[4] Marie Godde de Varennes, Marquise de La Troche, wife of a Councillor in the Rennes Parliament. She added her own note to this letter.

[5] Château de Saint-Germain-en-Laye, a royal residence dating from the Renaissance.

parted in the middle to within an inch of the pad, the hair cut on each side of the head in stages and twisted into loose curls, which hang just below the ear. The effect is pretty and girlish, as of a big nosegay on either side of the face. The hair must not be cut too short as it requires a natural wave which the curls tend to reduce, so that the wearers are apt to become uncurled, much to their discomfiture. Ribbons are worn in the ordinary way and a large curl tied between the pad and the dressed hair is sometimes allowed to hang over the shoulder. Have we drawn a clear picture of this fashion? I might try it out on a doll for you, and after all I have said, I tremble lest you should recoil from the trouble involved, and just stick on a yellow wig like a "*Chère*".[1] What is certain is that Montgobert's style is quite outdated. If you can overcome your idle ways, and do not shrink from toothache, I shall hope to see you like the rest of the world. I know you will be perfectly suited by a style which would make an older and plainer woman appear ridiculous.

To The Same

Paris, [*Wednesday*] *8 April* [*1671*].

Your letters have begun to arrive on Sundays, an auspicious sign! Dear heart!—what charming letters you write. . . . You say you have gone into retreat and have a call to visit the convent of the Sisters of Mary.[2] Do not overdo yourself in devotions and meditations, which tend to melancholia. It is sometimes wiser to skim the surface than to probe the depths. . . .

Let us turn to your brother's affairs! Ninon [3] has dismissed him. Weary of unrequited love, she requested the return of her letters, which were duly despatched. This was a great relief to me. I used to whisper a little pious saying into his ear,

[1] *Les Précieuses*, still young at the period of the Hôtel de Rambouillet, when visibly ageing would call each other "*Chère*", by which name they were widely known.

[2] Les Sainte-Marie d'Aix-en-Provence.

[3] Ninon de Lenclos (1620–1705), mistress of his father in 1650, and later of his nephew, the young Marquis de Grignan.

and remind him of his good intentions in the past, and beseech of him not to stifle the voice of conscience . . . The young Merveille [1] has not broken with him, though no doubt she will. That is why my son crossed Paris to fetch me yesterday and tell me the adventure which befell him. Having found a favourable opening (dare I say it ?) he failed to. . . . Strange indeed ! And for the young woman a novel experience. The gallant left hastily and in disorder, thinking he was bewitched, and, best of all as you will agree, he was dying to tell me of his misadventure. How we laughed you can imagine ! And I told him I was enchanted to think he was being punished from whence he'd sinned. He turned on me and told me I was the cause of his discomfiture by transmitting my frigid nature to him instead of to his sister. In fact he said a lot of nonsensical things, and I no less. It was a scene out of Molière to the life. In vain to tell him that, all the world over, love is bound up with tragedy—nothing would console him. The little " Chimène " reaffirms he does not care for her and she is already consoling herself elsewhere. It is a rumpus which makes me laugh. Would I could turn him from his evil ways which are so displeasing to God !

To The Same

[*Paris,*] *Friday 17 April* [*1671*].

My son [2] still suffers from ills, which cause his precious ladies to doubt the strength of the passion he professes. He confessed to me yesterday, that his excesses during Holy Week were such, that he was taken with a loathing and disgust which made his stomach turn over ; in fact he dared not let his thoughts dwell on it lest he should vomit. There revolved ceaselessly in front of his eyes a basketful of kisses, and of what besides ? Breasts, thighs, hips, a basketful of every kind of thing, and in such abundance that, like a horse surfeited with oats, he was revolted

[1] Mlle Champmeslé, famous interpreter and mistress of Racine.
[2] Charles de Sévigné became deeply pious after his marriage.

and felt he could never again look on a woman. This is no new story, and I took advantage of it to preach him a short homily on his failings. We discoursed on the Christian virtues and he has fallen in with my mood, all the more that he has not fully recovered.

He showed me some of the letters he had extracted from this play-actress. I have read nothing to equal the frenzied passionate tone of them. He weeps, he dies a thousand deaths. He believes what he writes, and the next moment laughs at himself. Believe me, he really is not worth his weight in gold.

Farewell, my sweet child . . . I trust you still care for me . . . Your love is the very breath of my existence. It would be unworthy of mine, were I to keep on reminding you of it. Allow me to send warm kisses to the poor Count. I am inclined to the belief that we both love you to excess.

To The Same

Paris, [*Wednesday*] 22 *April* [*1671*].

Do you really and truly think I prefer Madame de Brissac [1] to you? Do you believe, knowing me as you do, that her ways please me more than yours? that her wit captivates me to the detriment of yours? and that, in my eyes, your beauty is eclipsed by hers or that anyone in the world can equal Madame de Grignan? Meditate on this at your leisure, and you will be persuaded that your convictions are the right ones.

To turn to your brother: he is everybody's darling and as weak as water. Three of his friends took him out to supper last night. These gentlemen are too wise to be caught themselves, your brother can do all the paying there is to be done. Miserable fellow that he is, he finds nothing better to do than to obey, and then blurt it all out to me, calling himself a fool. I tell him I am ashamed of him and needs must convict him of leading a life unworthy of a gentleman, and that one day his sins will find him

[1] Duchesse de B. (1646–84), sister of Saint-Simon, an inveterate flirt.

out. He has broken with the actress. After blowing hot and cold (his intentions were honest), no sooner was her back turned than he made fun of her. Ninon has left him; when she loved him he was dissatisfied, now that she loves him no longer he is in despair, to add to which, she hasn't a good word to say for him. She says of him: "His spirit is made of pap, his body of chewed string, and his heart is like a pumpkin fried in ice and snow" . . . He recounted his follies to M. de La Rochefoucauld,[1] who dotes on any form of originality, and agrees with what I say that my son errs less from the head than from the heart. His impulses, which are all aflame in a trice, are both honest and reprehensible; in fact he has the soul of a lunatic. We ended by laughing heartily, in which your brother joined, who is ever the best company in the world, and agrees with everything that is said. I am his confidante, and abase myself in order to make him speak, and to have the right to chide him. . . . He wants to come with me to Brittany for five or six weeks, if his military duties permit. What a sorry tale! But knowing how great is your interest, I hazard you will not be bored.

You speak with such loving kindness of our project to visit you in Provence. Believe me, I and M. l'Abbé fervently desire it, indeed, look forward to it with agreeable anticipation. It is merely a question of the most suitable moment for us all. We were telling our dear d'Hacqueville [2] the other day of our projected peregrination from Brittany to Provence, and he advised us against it for this year. . . . In the spring I could go to Burgundy, where a lot of business awaits me, thence to Provence, Chalon, the Saône, Lyons, the Rhône, and behold I am at Grignan!—a mere nothing—and as I should be bringing you back with me I should not be continually haunted by the terror of another parting, which seems to deprive me of my very life . . . Any delay in the overwhelming joy of seeing you cannot be otherwise than a matter of regret to me, but the happiness of anticipation brings with it a measure of inward peace . . .

[1] François de Marsillac, Duc de La R. (1613–80), famous moralist, author of *Les Maximes* (1665); devoted friend of Mme de La Fayette and frequenter of the "*Corps de Veuves*" of Saint-Germain.

[2] *L'Abbé*, or *Le grand d'H.*, King's Councillor, friend of de Retz, an ever-obliging friend, sometimes referred to as *Les d'Hacqueville.*

All you tell me of la Marans [1] is divine, especially the torments she will endure in Hell, where doubtless you will bear her company and forever continue to hate her? Think of it! You will be bound to each other for all eternity! Surely this is enough to make you wish to save her soul; I feel I am well advised in suggesting it to you. She came to see Madame de La Fayette the other day, where she found me and M. de La Rochefoucauld. She arrived bare-headed, straight from the hands of the barber, where she had been cut and chopped and turned into a regular barber's block, powdered and frizzed, still hot from the curling-tongs. She was taken aback, knowing she would be found fault with. Madame de La Fayette said: " Are you quite mad? Really, Madame, you have turned yourself into a figure of fun." M. de La Rochefoucauld: " My dear mother, by my faith, come nearer that I may verify whether you are like your sister [2] whom I have just been seeing." Her hair had also been chopped. " My dear mother, you are a perfect sight!" This with the biting sarcasm you can imagine—just what you would expect of him. I was laughing behind my sleeve. She was so disconcerted that she was unable to bear the ridicule, put on her hood, and sulked until fetched by Madame de Schomberg [3] in her carriage, the only one available. I hope this story will divert you.

To The Same

Paris, [*Sunday*] *26 April* [*1671*].

It is Sunday 26th April, and this letter will not leave till Wednesday; it is however not so much a letter but an account of what

[1] Françoise de Montalais, widow of the Comte de Marans, nicknamed *Merlusine* (the wicked fairy) after her attendance at Mme de G.'s miscarriage in 1669. She called La Rochefoucauld " My son ".

[2] Mlle de Montalais, lady-in-waiting to Henriette d'Angleterre, who was involved in the Spanish letter scandal.

[3] Marie de Hautefort, widow of Marshal Charles de S., son of Henri de S., Comte de Nanteuil.

happened to Vatel [1] at Chantilly,[2] given me by Moreuil [3] for you benefit. I wrote on Friday to tell you he, Vatel, had stabbe himself. This is the story in detail.

The King arrived on the evening of Thursday; the hunt, th lanterns, the moonlight, the throng, the supper-tables spread o a carpet of jonquils—all went famously. At some tables the joint were missing on account of additional diners who had not bee expected. Vatel, horror-struck, kept repeating: "My honour i lost, my honour is lost, this is a disgrace from which I canno recover." To Gourville: [4] "I'm losing my reason, I have no slept for twelve nights, help me to issue fresh orders." Gourvill tried to calm him. He was obsessed by the thought of the joints which had not failed be it said, at the King's table,[5] but only a the twenty-fifth table. Gourville informed Monsieur le Prince The latter went to Vatel's room and said: "Vatel, all is goin magnificently, the King's supper was sumptuous." Vate answered: "Monseigneur, your goodness overwhelms me, know the joint failed at two tables." "Nothing of the sort," Monsieur le Prince repeated, "do not distress yourself, all wa in order." When night fell there were fireworks, which wer obscured by cloud; they had cost sixteen thousand francs.[6] A four in the morning, Vatel, who was wandering about all ove the place, met a purveyor with two small consignments of sea fishes. He cried out: "Is this all?" The man, who did no know that Vatel had been sending emissaries to scour the fishing ports, answered: "Yes, sir." There being no sign of othe purveyors, Vatel's distress grew, and he thought no more fis

[1] In reality Watel, major-domo to the Grand Condé, after having serve Fouquet. A character made famous by this passage.

[2] A fortress in the Middle Ages; rebuilt by the Connétable Montmorenc in the sixteenth century, and further embellished under Louis XIV and XV

[3] First Gentleman of the Condé household (1625–1703): de La Roche foucauld's brother-in-law, after being his secretary. Wrote his *Mémoires* subject of a Sainte-Beuve *Lundi*.

[4] J. Hérauld de G.

[5] It is recorded in the *Gazette* that at Chantilly there were four principa tables: the first for the King and for Monsieur, the second for the Prince d Condé, the third for the Duc d'Enghien, the fourth for the Duc de Longuevill and fifty-six additional tables. [*Monmerqué*].

[6] Gourville said that the whole fête cost M. le Prince more than 180,00 livres.

would arrive. He went to Gourville, and told him he could not survive this further disgrace, that his honour and reputation were at stake. Gourville only laughed at him. Thereupon Vatel went straight to his room, leaned his sword against the door-post and ran it through his heart, only falling dead at the third thrust. Meanwhile the catches of fish began to arrive from every side.[1] They looked for Vatel to distribute the fish, and when they reached his room they battered the door in, and found him lying in a pool of blood. Monsieur le Prince was informed and was completely overcome; the Duke [2] burst into tears, for it was on Vatel that his journey to Burgundy depended. Monsieur le Prince informed the King with suitable gravity, everyone commended Vatel's integrity, commended and deplored his courage. The King complained that he had put off the Chantilly meeting for five years because of all the fuss and bother he knew it would entail; he then ordered the Prince to confine himself in future to two tables only, and leave all the rest, and swore he would not tolerate these excesses. But, alas! For poor Vatel it was too late.

Gourville, however, tried to make good the loss of Vatel, and the loss was made good; an excellent dinner was served, followed by a cold collation, supper, a stroll through the forest, games, a stag-hunt; jonquils perfumed the air and the scene was one of enchantment. Saturday the same programme, and that evening the King left for Liancourt where a *medianoche* [3] had been ordered. This is the tale Moreuil wishes you to be told. Of the sequel I know nothing, and wash my hands of the whole affair. Monsieur d'Hacqueville, who was present, will no doubt supply further details . . .

[1] The *Gazette* relates that on the 25th Their Majesties, having heard Mass at the Château, were served with a prodigious display of the finest and most appetising fishes.

[2] Condé's son, who was about to preside over the *Etats provinciaux* in his father's place.

[3] Spanish term signifying a meat meal taken immediately after midnight when a fast day is followed by a feast day.—(*Dictionnaire de l'Académie de 1694*).

To The Same

Monday morning, at the hour of departure, 18 May [*1671*].

At length, at last, dearest daughter, I am ready to step into my coach, and bid you farewell.[1] That is a word which, addressed to you, will ever hurt me to pronounce. I am off to Brittany, and wonder how, when already two hundred leagues away from each other, the distance can be further stretched? Well, I have found the way. You think your town of Aix not far enough removed, and I that Paris is too accessible; so you have gone to Marseilles to get further from me, and I am going one better by leaving for Vitré. But, little one, how I shall miss our intercourse, which gives me such consolation and entertainment! . . . And what shall I find to tell you from the deep solitude of my woods?

I am relieved at what you say about your health, but, for God's sake, be careful, do not dance, do not have a fall, rest as much as possible, and, above all, see that you are at Aix for your confinement, where you can be sure of obtaining medical assistance. You know what a hurry you are always in, so get settled there sooner than later. I scarcely know how I shall bear up when the time comes. . . .

I propose to take your brother away with me to wean him from his immoral ways. You can imagine how little his mistresses will mind, but I shall be glad to have him . . . Of course I believe what M. de Grignan affirms. Ah! My dear Count—I can well believe no-one in your place would have acted with more restraint than you have; you are convincing, and your tone invites one's indulgence, but do remember that the youth, beauty, happiness, the very life of the woman you love are prejudiced by the recurrence of the strain you impose upon her. Dear child—I return once more to you after parting with your husband. Rumours reach me here that you and he are gambling, and heavy losers. Heavens above! Why draw down on yourselves such misfortunes! And why this continual drain on your resources?

[1] Mme de S. was going to Les Rochers, her estate in Brittany, 3 miles south of Vitré.

I find a constant drip so irksome, but I must stop lest, like the constant drip, I too become irksome to you. Adieu, dear one, a hundred times adieu.

To The Same

Malicorne,[1] *Saturday 23 May.*

I have found a letter from you on my arrival here, thanks to an ingenious contrivance on my part. I wrote to you on Monday, the day I left Paris; since then I have continually gone further and further from you, with such sorrow and poignant memories in my heart that my distress has made me poor company indeed. I carry a likeness of you, in my pocket, which I constantly study. It is charming; your presence dwells within me and my heart is filled with a great tenderness for you. It constitutes the whole of my equipment, and with it I increase the distance between us by three hundred leagues! We have been greatly tried by the heat and one of my fine horses was left behind at the first stage at Palaiseaux, but the other six held good. We start at two in the morning to avoid the great heat, and today we stole a march on dewy dawn, hoping to surprise Sylvia and her wood nymphs, at Malicorne where I shall rest tomorrow. . . Seldom, if ever, have I found myself in more agreeable surroundings, nor tasted of better fare.

I needed all the water I could find to slake my thirst after six days of extreme heat which we have endured. Our Abbé is well, my son and la Mousse [2] are a great solace. We have been reading Corneille again and recalled all my favourite passages. We have also read a new work of Nicole, which bears the stamp of Pascal and *L'Education d'un Prince*, but of this last one could never weary.

We shall arive at Les Rochers on the 27th where I hope to find a letter from you, which alone can afford me any happiness. . . . Dearest daughter, for God's sake, if you truly love me, take every

[1] A fine château, 6 miles from Le Mans, belonging to the Marquis de Lavardin.

[2] L'Abbé Pierre de la M., Dr. in Theology, supposed natural son of M. Du Gué, the father of Mme de Coulanges.

care of yourself. How I long for your presence! How I deplore your activities! Will you never have a rest from this continual and wearisome state?[1] I must try to understand M. de Grignan, but, when all is said and done, he should take pity on the woman he loves. . . .

Remember that your letters will reach me every Friday, but remember also that I never see you, that you are a thousand leagues away, that you are with child, suffering—think . . . nay do not think, I will do all the thinking as I roam up and down these alleys, spacious and melancholy as the thoughts which fill my mind. However many times I tread them the absent one will not be there! Adieu, dearest child. You do not speak enough of yourself. Always note the date at the head of my letters. Your brother greets you. He is a great distraction for me and tries his best to please me. You can picture us talking and reading. La Mousse holds his own, and the Abbé I adore, if only because he adores you. He has made over all his fortune to me, but tell no-one, as the family would eat him up. . . . I send a kiss to that monster de Grignan, despite his delinquencies.

To The Same

Les Rochers, Sunday 31 May [*1671*].

We have reached our poor Rochers at long last, my dearest. How is it possible to gaze once again at these familiar walks, these emblems,[2] this little study, these books, this room, without such discouragement as is akin to despair? Some few memories are agreeable, but how many more are so poignantly sweet as to be well-nigh unbearable. Those which concern you are among the latter. Cannot you realise the effect of all this on a nature like mine?

If, my child, you keep well, I shall put off going to you till the coming year. Brittany and Provence are not compatible. It is a strange fact about long journeys that, if one's feelings on arrival were each time to be renewed, one would never again

[1] A third pregnancy. [2] Cut on the tree-trunks.

leave home, but Providence sees to it that we forget. Providence renders the same service to women in labour. God allows it lest the world should come to an end, and lest journeys to Provence should cease! Mine however will be a great joy to me, but what a sad thought that there should be no immediate prospect of your leaving home . . . Walking in the woods I sometimes indulge in day-dreams of such a sombre hue that I come home as if stricken with fever . . . A reception was prepared here for my son's return. Vaillant [1] had placed fifteen hundred men under arms for the occasion, well turned out, each with a new ribbon to his cravat. They proceeded in good order, to await us a mile or two away, when what do you think we discovered? Monsieur l'Abbé had announced our arrival for Tuesday. We calmly arrived Wednesday, little dreaming an army had been mobilised in our honour. We were greatly vexed, but what excuse could we offer?

Mademoiselle du Plessis [2] is as you left her. She has a new friend at Vitré, whom she makes much of, for the reason that she is endowed with no less than a great intellect, having read every novel and having received two letters from the Princesse de Tarente.[3] I have maliciously got Vaillant to say I was jealous of this new friendship, that I would endeavour to conceal it, but felt it deeply. Her response was worthy of Molière . . . My plantation of young trees is of surprising beauty. Pilois [4] brings them up with such admirable rectitude that they soon reach the sky . . . Do you remember my giving you a suitable motto? I have cut one out of the bark of a tree for your brother. "*Vago di fama*",[5] a good epigram, don't you think? Alas! dearest, what rustic epistles are these! Not so long ago I could write of Paris happenings as well as anyone. I confine myself now to giving you personal news, and I am persuaded you will prefer it. I am enchanted with my companions, the ever admirable

[1] Bailiff at Les Rochers.

[2] A much-despised neighbour at the Château d'Argentré.

[3] Daughter of Wilhelm V, Landgrave of Hesse-Cassell (1625–93); widow (1672), of the Duc de la Trémouille, Henry-Charles, Prince de T., Baron de Vitré. She was thus Mme de S.'s *suzeraine* in Brittany. Aunt of second Dsse d'Orléans.

[4] The gardener at Les Rochers.

[5] "Greedy of fame".

Abbé, La Mousse, and my son, who are inseparable from each other and from me. We are always losing or looking for each other, and when I am too busy they are put out and think me ridiculous for preferring my farmer's fables to those of La Fontaine. Love me always and for ever; my existence depends on it, my soul yearns for it; as I told you the other day you are all my joy and all my sorrow. What remains of my life is overshadowed by grief when I consider how much of it will be spent far from you.

To The Same

(In answer to letters of 30 May and 2 June)

Les Rochers, Sunday 21 June [*1671*].

At last, my dear, I breathe again. I heave a sigh like M. de la Souche,[1] a weight is lifted from my heart, which allowed me no rest or respite. God is a witness how greatly I suffered when two weeks passed without a letter from you! It is not an affectation, but a deadly reality when I say that my life, in very truth, depends on your letters. I must confess to you that I was at the end of my tether. I was so distraught with anxiety lest you should be ill that I would have welcomed a letter from you to any other correspondent. Better to be forgotten by you than endure such torments . . . I found no comfort save in confiding my troubles to d'Hacqueville, who is so level-headed, and yet can understand better than anyone the immensity of my passion for you, whether because he shares it, or because he loves me so much, or a combination of the two I know not; certain it is that he enters into all my feelings, and this binds me to him with the closest ties . . . But guess what happened to these cherished letters I was waiting for so impatiently! They had been sent to Rennes because your brother was there . . . You can guess what a racket I made at the post. . .

You tell me how well you are looking. Am I to believe that I should be able to identify you in a crowd? You say you are

[1] Molière, *L'Ecole des Femmes*, II. 6.

not pale, not emaciated, not at your last gasp like Princesse Olympie,[1] not sick unto death as I have been picturing you! How happy this makes me God alone knows! In His name then, enjoy yourself, look after yourself . . . let M. de Grignan help in the good work. As I told you, I am certain you are pregnant of a male child; this should encourage him and make him the more zealous. I am glad you can turn your mind to dress. Do you recollect how tired we grew of that old black mantle you wore? No doubt it was meritorious but scarcely attractive to the onlooker.

I fear you will find it difficult to lengthen your short skirts. This fashion has reached us here; the young ladies from Vitré, Mesdemoiselles de Croque-Oison and Kerborgne [2] wear them just above the ankle. I adore these names and call la Plessis Mlle Kerlouche.[3] As for you, the Queen of Provence, you will set the fashion there, which rejoices me . . .

I wanted to know what weather you were having in your Provence and how you were enduring the plague of bugs, but you have forestalled my curiosity. As for us it rains incessantly, and we find it useless to say: Rain, rain, go to Spain! as it indubitably comes back again! Our workmen are scattered. Pilois has gone home, and instead of addressing me at the foot of a tree, you must do so at my fireside or the Abbé's study, to whom I owe more than I can ever repay. We have much business on hand, and have not as yet made up our minds whether to face the *Etats*,[4] or to run away. The one certain thing, my best one, which you will readily believe, is that we do not forget our poor exile. Alas! she is too dear and precious for that. We talk of her frequently, but however much I may talk of her, I think of her the more, every day and all night, during my walks, and when I most appear to forget her; at every hour, and whatever subject crops up,

[1] Ariosto, *Orlando Furioso*, X. 24.

[2] Their real names were de Kerqueoison and de Keramborgne. Mme de S. often simplified rather than caricatured the Breton names, *i.e.* Mlle de Kerikivili for Quenec'hquivili.

[3] Because she squinted.

[4] The provincial *Etats* were assemblies attended by representatives of the clergy, the nobility and the commoners, which took place periodically by order of the King for the purpose of regulating the local administration of the province, raising funds, etc.

when discoursing on other matters, and finally, as I should think of Him were I but moved by the love of God to the exclusion of all else. All the more that ofttimes I do not mention your name, for one should guard against exaggeration and check it for the sake of good manners and diplomacy. I must remember my old teaching and avoid being ponderous. We read and are very studious here. La Mousse has begged that I should read Tasso with him. I am familiar with it, having been well-grounded,[1] and find it entertaining. His Latin and his good sense make him an apt pupil and my sound training makes me a good teacher. Your brother reads aloud to us various trifles and plays, which he recites like Molière ; also verses, tales, romances. He is most diverting, has a ready wit, and woe to us should we take anything he says seriously. He leaves us in a fortnight to do his military service, not I assure you without regret. . . . You who know Les Rochers can picture me here, but I am at a loss when I think of you. I conjure up a Provence, a house at Aix, finer maybe than yours ; I can also picture Grignan, but it is bare of trees, which I hate, and there are no grottoes in which to keep cool ; I cannot imagine where you walk, and am sure the wind on the terraces will sweep you off your feet. If only it could carry you here on a whirlwind, I would open my windows wide to receive you, God knows !

Your daughter is charming; as yet she has not ventured to copy her mother's nose, neither has she . . . I will say no more ! She has adopted another alternative and has a little square one. Are you not sorry ? This time you must pass it over. Stare at yourself in the glass and that will ensure a happy end to the good work you have begun. . . .

"*To my good and beautiful one in her Château d'Apollidon.*" [2]

[1] Chapelain and Ménage had been her tutors.

[2] Castle built by the magician Apollidon, *Amadis de Gaule*, II. 1.

To The Same

Les Rochers, 15 July [1671].

Were I to write and tell you of my day-dreams my letters would be the longest in the world, but that would be impracticable, and I must be satisfied with writing what can be written, and dreaming dreams for which I have both leisure and opportunity. La Mousse has slight toothache or a chill in his gums and the Abbé a slight pain in his knee, which leaves me free to roam at will in my domain. I like to walk about until eight o'clock every evening. My son is absent, hence a silence, a calm, a solitude reign here which belong to no other place. I will not tell you, my best one, of whom I am thinking, nor how tenderly. Who guesses right need not be told. If you were not pregnant and the hippogriff were still alive, what a gallant and unforgettable gesture it would be to ride over and visit me on his back, for he takes but two days to go round the world. You could come and dine and be with M. de Grignan again for supper, or sleep here, which I should like still better and be back in the family pew [1] for Mass. . . .

Mademoiselle du Plessis often graces us with her presence. Yesterday she was telling us how at her sister-in-law's wedding feast, twelve hundred roasted joints were consumed. This was such a tall order that we were turned to stone. Taking my courage in both hands I said: "Mademoiselle, reflect. Is it not twelve roasted joints you mean? Surely you are making an error!" "No, Madame, twelve hundred, or at least eleven hundred—I cannot affirm whether it is eleven or twelve for fear of committing myself, but I can assure you it is one or the other!" This she repeated at least twenty times, not conceding as much as a chicken. We suggested there must have been three hundred cooks present to offer such a bill of fare, and it must have required a great meadow spread with tents, and we think that if really there were only fifty persons to partake of the feast they must have started a month ahead. All this banter would have amused you.

[1] The family pew, which was in the gallery of the church, still exists at Grignan.

To The Same

Les Rochers, [*Sunday*] *26 July* [*1671*].

Please note that I write to you twice a week, dear daughter, this in passing and no reproach intended, for I dearly love my task. Today I begin my letter somewhat in advance; it will not go till tomorrow, and before I seal it I may wish to add a word.

Picture me yesterday, Friday, sitting reading quite alone in my room, with a book held tenderly in my hand. I saw my door opened by a tall, distinguished woman, in fits of laughter, and a man she was hiding behind her equally convulsed, and the man was followed by another woman who was splitting her sides, and I, not knowing why they were laughing, started to laugh myself. I must tell you that I was expecting Madame de Chaulnes,[1] who was coming to spend two days here, but I couldn't make her out at first. She it was who brought Pomenars [2] along, and it was his idea to give me a surprise. La Murinette Beauté [3] was of the party and Pomenars was so gay that he quickly banished dull care. They played a game of battledore and shuttlecock—then partook of a light collation. Afterwards we walked in the woods, talking of you. The Great Walk reminded us of your fall there, which made us blush . . . Then we spoke of Mlle du Plessis and her nonsense, and how one day, with her face close to yours, she said something so foolish that you gave her a smack, and I, hoping to smooth things over, said to her mother: "these young things got so excited that they took to fisticuffs, your daughter teased mine and mine hit her—such fun to watch!" With this device I managed to delight Mme du Plessis in your childish tiff, and to pass off the box on the ear. La Murinette approves of all you do and swears that, when next she comes too near Plessis,

[1] Elizabeth le Féron, widow of the Marquis de Saint-Mégrin, wife of Charles d'Albert d'Ailly, Duc de C., Baron de Pecquiguy, Governor of Brittany and later ambassador to Rome.

[2] Jacques Troussier, Vicomte de La Gabetière, Marquis de Pontménard, an eccentric known as Pomenars, lived at Château Couëbo near Ploermel.

[3] Nickname of Marie-Anne de Murinais (1649–1707), who married in 1674 Henri de Maillé, Marquis de Kerman. Cousin of Dsse de Chaulnes.

she will emulate you and give her one on the ugly side of her face . . .

As for you, my dear, how I pity you with your Aunt d'Harcourt.[1] What a menace ! what an incubus ! what a bore ! I should suffer more than anyone, and only from your hand would I swallow such a dose. I fear boredom more even than death and I long to have a good laugh with you and Vardes [2] and Sire Corbeau.[3] Ah ! get rid of that Trump of the Last Judgement. I have hated her for twenty years, and for twenty years have owed her a visit . . . My little grand-daughter is amiable and her nurse is perfection. . . . The little one requires dressing, so naturally I will give her her first dress, I being her godmother, and it will cost me less than 'tuppence', leave it to me and do not dream of thanking me.

I am wondering if these gnats you speak of are not really your over-heated blood, so treacherous and dangerous for you. I would advise you to take cooling potions and good soups ; do not be afraid of being well-nourished, for overheated blood leads at this time of year to agues which are highly deleterious. For dear sake, little one, remember my advice and take cooling drinks.

To The Same

Les Rochers, [*Wednesday*] *5 August* [*1671*].

I am relieved that you have heard all the news from Monsieur de Coulanges. You will also have learned of Monsieur de Guise's [4] death, which appals me by reason of the effect it will have on Mlle de Guise.[5] You know that nothing can disturb me less than Guise's death were it not for my all too vivid imagination and the dread I have of self-recrimination. Well, Mlle de Guise cannot reproach herself in any way over her nephew's

[1] Anne d'Ornano, Comtesse d'H., maternal aunt of M. de G.

[2] François-René du Bec-Crespin, Marquis de V. (1621–88). Governor of Aigues-Mortes. Long exiled for his part in the Spanish letter scandal.

[3] The Coadjutor of Arles (*see* f.n. p. 43).

[4] The Duc de Guise had recently died of smallpox.

[5] His aunt Marie de Lorraine, later Dsse de Joinville.

death. She was opposed to his being bled, and it was the amount of blood they drew which caused the seizure. What a charming little incident in truth! My view is that if one falls ill in Paris one falls dead. Mortality is too high in that city. How I beg of you, my dearest dear, to be cautious, and if any child at Grignan were suspected of smallpox, send it immediately to Montélimar. Your good health is my greatest preoccupation.

I must tell you, who are a Breton, something of our *Etats*. Rumour had it Monsieur de Chaulnes was arriving on Sunday evening. On Monday he sent me a letter by messenger, to which I replied by dining in his company. Two tables were spread in the same room, fourteen places were laid at each table, Monsieur presiding at one, Madame at the other: the repast was of excessive proportions—too many good things—the roast meats were carried out untouched, and as for the pyramids of fruit, they were tall enough for the doors to be heightened to admit them. Our forefathers never anticipated such contraptions: they made doors to accommodate themselves. Enter a pyramid, the kind of pyramid which obstructs the view of the other side of the table, not, be it said, that this is not sometimes an advantage. Enter the said pyramid with the addition of twenty porcelain dishes, duly dropped at the door, making such a commotion and clatter as to drown the violins, hautbois and trumpets. After dinner Messieurs de Locmaria [1] and de Coëtlogon [2] performed some extraordinary figure dances with two Breton ladies, minuets with an air unrivalled by the professionals: they danced gipsy and native steps with an assurance and a delicacy which charmed the spectators. I thought of you constantly and recalled the times I had seen you dancing, with such a sharp pang, that my pleasure was turned into pain. You would have liked prodigiously to watch Locmaria dancing: the violins and figures at court are not in it, it is really superb. He must know at least a hundred different steps and is incomparable in this kind of thing. After the ball the crowds who had come for the opening of the *Etats* surged in. I had never witnessed it before and thought it a grand sight. I believe ours excel any other. Our province boasts a larger contingent of the nobility, for none are absent at the Court or at the

[1] Louis-François du Parc, Marquis de L, later became a General.
[2] René-Hyacinthe, Marquis de C., Governor of Rennes.

war; only our little colour-bearer[1] is away and he may return himself one day . . . As for the Governor, for him it means a turn-over of forty thousand crowns, any amount of gratuities, presents, pensions, extensive repairs to roads and towns, fifteen or twenty gaming tables, endless diversions, games, a series of balls, play-acting, and, three times a week, a grand display. Behold, the *Etats*! I forgot to mention the consumption of wine, a detail others would not forget so easily. What fairy tales I'm telling you, but my pen runs away with me here where there is so little else to talk about.

To The Same

Les Rochers, Sunday 23 August [*1671*].

When you wrote to me, you were, I understand, with your President's wife, Madame de Charmes.[2] Her husband, methinks, was an intimate friend of Monsieur Fouquet? Anyhow, dear daughter, you are not alone, and how wise of Monsieur de Grignan to force you out of your retreat in order to entertain his guests, but he might have spared everyone his capacious beard; possibly it will not prejudice him with you, for when he wore his hair[3] "in a wild mop" you thought him a perfect Adonis. It is remarkable how indelible an impression is left on the mind by some happy, or unhappy memory of the past. That autumn, when all seemed propitious, ended in such disaster that even now to think of it brings me out in a sweat, but one must thank God for a happy end to the affair.[4] Your reflections on Monsieur de Guise's death made a deep impression on me as I read them wandering through the glades where I dream at my leisure and stroll sometimes till nightfall now that la Mousse has toothache. Do not imagine that being alone does me any harm, save for the

[1] Charles de Sévigné, who was *Guidon des Gendarmes-Dauphin*.

[2] M. de Charmes was President of the Aix Parliament, an intimate friend of Fouquet.

[3] *See* f.n. p. 97.

[4] Mme de G.'s miscarriage at Livry, on seeing her handsome brother-in-law, the Chevalier, mount a high-spirited stallion.

heartache from which I fain must suffer. I am not an object of pity. My disposition is gay, all is fish that comes to my net, and I greatly prefer being alone here than in the midst of a crowd at Vitré. I have been here for a whole week, undisturbed, which has cured my heavy cold. I have drunk gallons of water, have not spoken a word, have eaten nothing, and got well despite the long walks I have taken.

Madame de Chaulnes, Mademoiselle de Murinais, Madame Fourché [1] and a fine wench from Nantes came on Sunday. Madame de Chaulnes came in saying she must see me, that she was at the end of her tether and would swoon away, whereupon she flung herself on my bed, and in one second was sound asleep. We continued to talk until she woke up, having fallen in love with the pleasant informality of Les Rochers. We walked in the garden whilst the others played games. I made her tell me about Rome,[2] and how she and Monsieur de Chaulnes got married, for I love to indulge my curiosity. At that moment, and without warning, it started to pour and a deluge of rain threatened to drown us all. We ran, screaming, falling, stumbling, and on arrival at the house we lit great fires, divested ourselves of every stitch down to our chemises, I having to supply fresh garments, our shoes put to dry meanwhile, and all this amid gales of laughter. What a way to receive the wife of the Governor of Brittany in her own kingdom! The poor lady left, preferring I am sure the insults we heaped on her head to the onerous duties which awaited her at home. She has made me promise to write you this adventure and to come over to help her out for the next eight days. I felt I could not do otherwise than say yes. . . .

To The Same

Les Rochers, [*Wednesday 2*] *December* [*1671*].

Well, my sweet dear, now that my first transports of joy are over, I am already longing for Friday's letter to finish the good

[1] Wife of a Breton Deputy.

[2] The Duc de Chaulnes, now Governor of the province of Brittany, had previously held the appointment of Ambassador to Rome.

work and to give me entire satisfaction. So many things can go wrong with a woman after child-birth and Monsieur de Grignan says you will chatter to such an extent, that at least nine more days must elapse before I can be wholly free from anxiety and proceed on my journey. I shall await Friday's courier, and the following Friday's should reach me at Malicorne. I cannot express the relief I feel. I am so happy that I cease not giving thanks to God, for the anxiety over your confinement weighed on my heart night and day, as if you, with your own hand, had placed a heavy stone there. I have had a stream of congratulations, numberless letters from Brittany and Paris. The little fellow's health has been drunk far and wide. I provided the liquor and supped the company as I do on the eve of Twelfth Night . . .

M. de Montmoron [1] rushed round and among other things we talked of mottos, on which subject he is an expert. He says he has never set eyes on the one I suggested to Adhémar. He knows the rocket, which goes off with the words: "*da l'ardore l'ardire*", "My ardour—thence my hardihood"—but he prefers the other: "*Che peri, pur che m'inalzi*", "May I perish if so be I can rise." Whether this is mine or comes from some other source, he finds it very apt.

What say you about Monsieur de Lauzun's plight [2]? To think he should be a prisoner today when so much fuss was made about him only a year ago! *Vanity, vanity, all is vanity!*

It is said that the new Madame [3] sits loose to her exalted rank and thinks small beer of physicians and less still of remedies. When her private physician was presented to her she is alleged to have told him she would not require his services, that she has never been purged or bled, that when indisposed she is cured by a two league walk—"*Lasciamo la andar, che fara buon viaggio*": "Let her go, she will travel safely."

You see I am writing to you as if it were already three weeks

[1] Charles de Sévigné, Comte de M., Councillor to the Rennes Parliament, a cousin.

[2] Lauzun had been arrested on 25 Nov. and taken by d'Artagnan across the Alps to Pignerol, whither he had conducted Fouquet 7 years previously. Lauzun remained 10 years in exile.

[3] Elizabeth-Charlotte of Bavaria, aged 19. Mother of the future Regent Philippe d'Orléans.

since your labour. I begin to think it is time to remind Monsieur de Grignan of the promise he made me. Please reflect that this is the third occasion on which your child's birth has taken place in the month of November. Next time, unless you hold him in check, it will be in September. Ask this one favour in return for the lovely gift you have just made him. Another way of putting it—you have endured far more than if you had been severely beaten. Can one who loves you wish you thus to suffer, year in, year out? I have said enough, but I swear I will not return to Provence if you are pregnant and I hope he will heed my threat. For myself, I should be in despair, but I will abide by my wager, and this not for the first time. Farewell, divine lady—Kisses to the little one whom I love tenderly, but the extent of my love for his mother far outstrips that which I bestow on him. I long for news of you, of the gathering, and details of the christening. I must exercise patience, and that is a virtue for which I have little use . . .

To The Same

Les Rochers, Sunday 6 December [*1671*].

I needed your last letter to reassure me, as much as those of a week ago. I was so elated at the news of your safe delivery, that it could scarcely last and I began to dread any possible complication which might ensue. I wanted fresh letters, and here they are, containing the best of news. You have had pains in your stomach, and milk-fever, but all is happily over. The Coadjutor tells me your little son had retention of urine for three hours, and that you were distraught. What a storm in a tea-cup! Your maternal love blinds you to realities. Need one feel to that extent? He is blond which attracts you—you love blonds. Monsieur de Grignan is right to be jealous, he says you drop him for the first-comer, he means the last one! The Coadjutor writes me details worthy of Monsieur Chais and Madame Robinet.[1]

As for you, dear Count, I pity you. It is evident you are

[1] Celebrated Paris gynecologist and midwife of that period.

quite displaced, by this little wisp of a boy, he will restore the balance in your household which was sadly wanting. Adieu, my very dear Adhémar, and you, my much loved and charming young mother. As Barillon [1] once put it, "He who loves you more than I, does so to excess." At such a distance one can say and do little which is not out of place. One weeps when one should laugh, and laughs when one should weep . . . these are some of the drawbacks of separation.

To The Same

Paris, Friday 18 December [1671].

I have this moment arrived, dear one. I am at my aunt's,[2] surrounded by the family, hers and mine, all embracing and questioning me, but I must escape from them just to send you a line. Monsieur de Coulanges insists on my going home with him, because Madame de Bonneuil's son has smallpox in the house. She, most obligingly, tried to cover it up, but the plot was laid bare, and my little girl [3] was removed to Monsieur de Coulanges'; I am waiting to return with her as my aunt wishes to witness [our] meeting. It would really have been intolerable had I exposed the child to infection, and been banished from my friends for six weeks because Madame de Bonneuil's son had smallpox! . . .

Study your looks, get fatter, dear one, indulge yourself and remember your good resolutions, and if Monsieur de Grignan cares for you he will give you time in which to recover, if not there is nothing to hope for, and you will remain a skeleton like Madame de Saint-Hérem.[4] How well-inspired I am to put this idea into your head! Nothing could be a greater warning to you . . .

As for your little son, what you tell me about him is not

[1] Paul de B. d'Amoncourt, Ambassador to Whitehall.

[2] Henriette de Coulanges, Marquise de la Trousse, who was to linger on till 30 June, 1672.

[3] Marie-Blanche, her granddaughter.

[4] Anne Legras, Marquise de Saint-Hérem, wife of the Master of the Royal Wolfhounds—" hideous at 18 ", according to Saint-Simon, she lived to be 90.

calculated to alter my opinion of the bad effects of chocolate—I am convinced it corroded his inside. Thank heaven they applied wet packs, which doubtless saved his life.

To The Same

Paris, Wednesday 30 December [1671].

Surely the inclination to write to you a dozen times a day is an infallible sign that I do not altogether dislike you! . . . I have questioned Rippert [1] closely on your state of health: I am not pleased with you, and you deserve a scolding. You treated your confinement as if you were the wife of a Swiss Colonel. You do not take enough nourishing soups, you were already gossiping the third day after your confinement and up on the twelfth, and you are surprised at turning into a scarecrow! How I hoped you would have taken pride in getting stronger and fattening yourself up. Where on earth did you get this idea of copying Madame de Crussol? [2] . . . It annoys and upsets me very much to see your beauty impaired, you know well how I prize it. Ought you not, for my sake, to try and preserve it?

You speak the truth when you say that Provence is my spiritual home since it is yours. Paris chokes me, and I wish I were well on the way to Grignan. But, dear heart, what loneliness you are preparing for yourself by returning home to your château. You will be like Psyche on the mountain-top! [3] . . . Farewell, my angel. Monsieur de Coulanges loves you, I am pleased to be with him,[4] and to exorcise the smallpox. That big house with Madame de Bonneuil in your place scarcely tempts me? [5] . . . I hate your letters addressed to "*Madame la Marquise de Sévigné*". Why not call me *Pierrot*? It would give so tender an impulse to read what is inside.

[1] Gentleman of the household, who accompanied Mme de G. on her travels.

[2] Julie-Françoise, Ctsse de Sainte-Marie, Dsse d'Uzès, only daughter of Mme de Montausier (*see* f.n. p. 79).

[3] Allusion to La Fontaine's *Amours de Psyché*, Bk. II.

[4] Rue du Parc-Royal.

[5] Her own house in Rue de Thorigny.

1672

To Madame de Grignan

Paris, Tuesday 5 January.

Yesterday, 4 January, the King received the Dutch Ambassador [1] in audience. He insisted on Monsieur le Prince, M. de Turenne,[2] M. de Bouillon [3] and M. de Créquy [4] being present at the interview. The Ambassador presented his letter to the King, who did not read it, having a duplicate in his pocket. He spoke at length, trying to justify his conduct as set out in the letter, and assured His Majesty that the Ministers of the United Provinces had scrupulously examined themselves, but could find nothing either lacking in respect, or to which the King could take exception, despite which they understood that the great French armament programme was directed solely against their country. He affirmed they were ready to do whatever His Majesty decreed, and begged the King to remember the many favours accorded to them by

[1] Peter Grotius, son of the famous Jurist, Hugo G. (1583–1645). Louis XIV was resolved from the start to grant nothing, having every intention of prosecuting a war against Holland with the help of the King of England, under the terms of a treaty signed the preceding June between them. War was declared, in fact, on 6 April.

[2] Henri de la Tour d'Auvergne, Vicomte de T. (1611–75), Marshal of France, brilliant strategist, simple and modest.

[3] Godefroi-Maurice de la Tour, Duc de B., son of Turenne's elder brother, himself brother of the Cardinal and the Comte d'Auvergne.

[4] François de Créquy (1624–87), Marshal of France (1668), one of Louis XIV's Great Captains.

his predecessors to whom they owed their greatness in the past. The King replied with remarkable courtesy and ease, saying that he well knew how much his enemies had been worked upon, and he thought it only prudent to protect himself from being taken unawares. He added that he increased his army and navy in order to defend himself; a few orders remained to be given, and in the spring he would act as he thought best, in conformity with his honour and the good of his country; he thereupon made the Ambassador a sign with his head indicating that he did not wish for any reply. The letter contained a replica of all the Ambassador had said, save for an assurance of obedience to the King's wishes, provided the United Provinces should not be expected to break with her allies.

The same day M. de la Feuillade[1] presented himself at the head of the regiment of guards, and took the oath at the hands of a Marshal of France (as is the custom). The King, who was present, informed the regiment that he had appointed Monsieur de la Feuillade to be their *mestre de camp*, and then and there placed the pike in La Feuillade's hand. This was an unprecedented favour on His Majesty's part, as the ceremony is usually performed by some emissary on behalf of the King . . .

To The Same

Ten o'clock of the evening, Paris, Friday 22 January [*1672*].

At last, dearest, I tear myself away from my little granddaughter's bed-time ceremony in order to write to you. Should you be jealously inclined, I scarcely know how to spare your feelings. She is the most enchanting child I have ever known, lively, gay, and has the prettiest ways imaginable . . .

Nothing but talk of war which is now inevitable. We await the decision of the Queen of Spain,[2] but in any case, we intend

[1] François d'Aubusson, Duc de la F. (1625–91), Colonel of the Guards and future Marshal; a soldier of courage but no great ability.

[2] Anne-Marie of Austria, widow of Philip IV of Spain, mother of Charles II, Regent until her son attained his majority in 1676. [*Perrin*].

fighting. If she declares herself for us we shall fall on Holland, if it be the other way we shall seize Flanders, and when the squabble begins it will not be so easy to call a halt. Our troops are on the march in the direction of Cologne, M. de Luxembourg [1] opens hostilities. There is a movement of troops in Germany . . .

You often speak with admiration of my letters, but for fear of starting an interchange of compliments, I refrain from alluding to yours, yet one is sometimes constrained to speak openly. Your letters contain passages of incomparable beauty, your style is without flaw. D'Hacqueville and I read with delight certain brilliant turns of phrase, and your accounts touching the King and the indignation you feel with Lauzun and the Bishop [2] are set out in a masterly manner . . .

Dearest, hearken to a most touching incident concerning the benevolence shown by your gracious Sovereign which should redouble your zeal and loyalty to him. I heard on unimpeachable authority that M. de Montausier [3] begged the King for a favour for one of his friends, the grant of a small abbey, which was refused. He left the King in anger and was heard to say : "Only Ministers and Mistresses have any influence in this country." These not very well chosen words came to the King's ears, who sent for Monsieur de Montausier, chided him for losing his temper, reminding him of past favours, and the next day appointed Madame de Crussol [4] Lady-in-Waiting at the Palace. These are the gestures of a Titus . . .

[1] François-Henri de Montmorency-Bouteville, Duc de L. ; Marshal of France in 1675.

[2] Bp. of Marseilles, Toussaint de Forbin-Janson, referred to as *L'Evêque*, *Dom Courrier*, sometimes as *la Grêle*.

[3] Charles de Sainte-Maure, Marquis de Salles, later Duc de M. (1610) married Julie d'Angennes de Rambouillet. She became *Gouvernante des Enfans de France*, while he was entrusted with the education of the Dauphin.

[4] Julie-Françoise de Sainte-Maure, Ctsse de C., niece of M. de Grignan's first wife (*see* f.n. p. 40). Only daughter of Julie, she became the possessor of the famous " Guirlande de Julie " on her mother's death. Dsse d'Uzès in 1680.

To The Same

From the Convent of Sainte-Marie du Faubourg, Friday 29 January. Feast of Saint François de Sales,[1] *and anniversary of your wedding-day. I must be in my dotage making anniversaries out of everything and nothing* [*1672*].

Here I am, my dear one, in the place of all others where I have wept most bitterly at your departure when you have had to leave me; the very thought of these partings sends a shudder through me. For an hour or more I have been walking alone in the garden while our good Sisters are at Vespers, which, for me, are spoilt by indifferent singing, and I have had the good sense to absent myself. My dear, I am at the end of my endurance, the thought of you utterly destroys me. In this garden which is haunted by your presence, in which I have seen you a thousand times, I have felt I would die of grief. I dare not tell you the extremity I am in, for you are severe and have no pity for human frailty. There are days and hours when I am not mistress of myself, I am weak, I do not pretend otherwise. A man whom I had sent to enquire for the Chevalier de Grignan,[2] chooses this very moment to present himself and reports that the Chevalier is *in extremis*. This news is scarcely conducive to drying my tears. I believe the Chevalier is leaving you his fortune, and I entreat you not to follow the dictates of your heart in this matter and give it all away, your brothers-in-law are all more prosperous than you. I dread unspeakably the loss of the Chevalier. It seems hard that a wretched little jelly of a man like Monsieur de Rohan [3] should be snatched from the jaws of death, whereas a charming, well-born, good-looking man of unimpeachable character whose loss is universal, just dies on our hands! Had I been free to do so I would not have left him, for I do not fear infection, but I was not my own master. . . .

[1] (1567–1622). Bp. of Geneva from 1602: beatified 1661, canonised 1666.

[2] Charles Philippe, Chevalier de Malte, Mme de G.'s handsome brother-in-law. He died of smallpox 1 Feb., when the title passed to his brother Joseph.

[3] "Le Petit Duc de R", who survived till 1727.

Yesterday evening, Mme du Fresnoy [1] supped with us. She is a nymph, a goddess, but Mme Scarron,[2] Mme de La Fayette and I set out to compare her with Madame de Grignan and decided she was not her equal—not so much on account of her bearing and complexion and the way she holds herself, but her eyes are most peculiar! Her nose cannot compare with yours, your mouth is perfection whereas hers is unshapely, and she is so withdrawn, so reserved that one feels she would not pronounce a word which did not perfectly match her appearance. One cannot picture her joining whole-heartedly in any conversation. Where she is there l'Abbé Têtu [3] is to be found, he does not leave her by a hair's breadth. As for your wit, the ladies think it incomparable, and laud your conduct, wisdom and good sense. I have never heard such lavish praise. I had not the courage either to join in, or to perjure myself by protesting . . .

Farewell, my very dearest. In my present state I cannot write as I would. You could do without my lamentations, but you must blame yourself if they are forced upon you, and since you praise the length of my letters you surely dare not complain. I embrace you and must return to the garden, and hear the tail-end of Benediction and then visit the sick who are as unhappy as I. Here comes Sœur Madeleine-Agnès, who salutes you in Christ.

To The Same

Paris, Wednesday 3 February, 1672, at ten in the evening.

. . . I have been closeted for an hour with Monsieur de Pomponne.[4] It would take more reams of paper than I own to tell

[1] Daughter of an apothecary, married to Elie du F., Steward to Louvois, whose mistress she was for many years. He procured her the post of Woman of the Bedchamber to the Queen in 1673 (*Mémoires de la Fare*).

[2] Françoise d'Aubigné, widow of Paul Scarron, author of *Roman Comique*; future Dsse de Maintenon.

[3] Jacques T., Abbé de Belval (1626–1706), Member of the Academy (1665), assiduous friend of Mme de Coulanges, nicknamed *Têtu-tais-toi*.

[4] Simon Arnauld, Marquis de P. (1618–98), son of the Jansenist Arnauld d'Andilly and nephew of "le grand Arnauld", exiled to Verdun after the fall

you how joyful was our meeting, and how rapidly we reviewed together a thousand chapters of our life-history. I found him unchanged, he is still perfect and thinks I am worth more than, indubitably, is the case. His father desired him to oblige me in all matters, and many reasons impel him to do so. For one thing my responsibilities in regard to the government of Provence serve as an admirable pretext for our community of interests. This chapter alone was never closed. I spoke at length of the Bishop, for he can listen as well as discourse. He grasped the picture I drew of the prelate, and it was evident that he could not think it right for one of his holy calling to assume the prerogative of a Governor. He is so wise himself that, unlike many persons I know, he inspires one with wisdom. In short, dearest daughter, wishing for no more appreciation than you already shower on me, I left him, my heart full of happiness in the thought that our friendship might be of some service to you. We agreed to correspond. Being supremely eloquent he likes my natural, untutored style . . .

Last night the Princesse de Conti [1] had an attack of apoplexy. She is unconscious, speechless and without a pulse. They are torturing her to keep her alive. Her house is filled with a hundred demented folk crying and screaming. I do not know what the outcome will be . . .

The Chancellor [2] died a noble death. His great mind, prodigious memory and natural eloquence, as well as his piety, came to his assistance in his last hours. One could compare him to a torch which flares up before it is finally extinguished. Le Mascaron attended him and was dumbfounded by his answers and citations. Those round him wept to hear his paraphrasing of the *Miserere*. He recited passages from the Scriptures and the Fathers of the Church far better than could the bishops who surrounded him. Indeed, his death was one of the most moving sights possible. What is even more so is the fact that he died compara-

of Fouquet (1662), permitted to return to his estates near Meaux. Minister of Foreign Affairs 1671–9, after serving as Ambassador to Stockholm. One of Mme de S.'s most intimate friends.

[1] The Princesse de Conti, died the following day (*see* f.n. p. 83).

[2] Pierre Séguier (1588–1672), friend of Mme de S., of great learning. President of the Commission charged to judge Fouquet.

tively poor, no wealthier indeed than when he first came to Court . . . He left seventy thousand livres, and what is that for a man endowed with private means, Chancellor for forty years . . . It is not yet known who will hold the seals of office.

Farewell, my charming one. I love you far better than I love myself. Your daughter is amiable and diverts me, she improves daily in looks and methinks the little baggage plays no small part in keeping me alive.

To The Same

Paris, Friday 5 February. I was born a thousand years ago today [1] *[1672]*

How delighted I am, my dear one, that you enjoy my letters, but I don't think they are as agreeable as you make out, although it would be an exaggeration perhaps to describe them as frigid. As for the Princesse de Conti,[2] she died eight hours after I sealed my last packet, that is on Thursday at four in the morning, without regaining consciousness, or uttering a sensible word. She asked for her maid, Céphise, and called loudly upon God . . . She died uttering a great cry and in the midst of a convulsion so severe that she dug her nails into the flesh of a woman who was holding her. Impossible to describe the utter desolation which overcame those present. Monsieur le Duc, the Conti princes, and others wept without restraint. La Gesvres [3] decided to have the vapours, and la Brissac to utter screams and throw herself about, so that she had to be turned out of the room, no-one knowing any more what they were doing. The King, who

[1] Mme de S. was forty-six.

[2] Anne-Marie Martinozzi, niece of Mazarin, widow (1666) of Louis-Armand de Bourbon, Prince de Conti, brother of the Great Condé, who died young, She was the mother of the Conti Princes. Her epitaph ran thus: "She sold her jewels during the famine of 1662 to feed the poor of several provinces. Spending nothing on herself, she restored the sum of eight hundred thousand livres where it was due . . . and after sixteen years of persevering labour, at the age of thirty-five years, she passed like a flash into eternity."

[3] Marie-Françoise du Val, Dsse de G.

appeared to be deeply moved, pronounced a paneygyric, saying the Princess was more renowned for her virtues than for her wealth. She left twenty thousand crowns to be distributed to the poor, and a like sum to her servants. She wished to be buried in her parish in a pauper's grave. Yesterday I saw the body of this saintly princess laid out on her bed. She was sadly disfigured by the martyrdom to which she had been subjected in the effort to bring her back to life, her teeth were broken, her head severely burned; such is the state the unfortunate sick can be reduced to when they are spared a rapid death by apoplexy. To reflect on this death, so cruel to her family and friends, so happy for herself, I find most edifying.

To The Same

Paris, Friday evening, 26 February [*1672*].

. . . Paris is in a state of commotion. The messenger to Spain is returned. He reports that, not only is the Queen of Spain determined to abide by the Treaty of the Pyrenees in which she is pledged not to attack her ally, but that she will go to the support of the Dutch with all that she possesses. Thus the biggest war in history is ushered in, and for what? When we attack Flanders the Dutch will call on the Spaniards. God preserve us from the Swedes, the English and the Germans! I am greatly disturbed by this news. If only a good angel would descend from heaven and throw oil on the waters and make peace! . . .

Madame Scarron, who sups with us nightly and whose company is enchanting, plays with your little daughter. She thinks her pretty, anyhow far from plain. The child kept calling L'Abbé Têtu her *papa*. He gave us convincing reasons why this was not the case and we believed him. I kiss you my love. I told you so much in my last letter that I find myself at a loss today, but never, I can assure you, where my feelings towards you are concerned.

To The Same

Paris, Wednesday 16 March [1672].

You speak of my departure: ah, my beloved child, I live in this charming anticipation. Nothing keeps me back save the condition of my poor aunt, who is suffering from dropsy. It breaks my heart to see her thus and to listen to her wise and tender sayings. Her courage, patience, resignation are wholly admirable. Monsieur d'Hacqueville and I follow her gradual decline day by day. He knows so well the working of my heart, and how sad I am not to be free, here and now, to go to you. I fain must follow his advice and we shall see what happens between now and Easter. If her condition continues to deteriorate as fast as it has been doing, she will, by then, have died in my arms, but if she is easier and appears to linger, I shall start as soon as Monsieur de Coulanges returns. Our Abbé and I are in despair, we think of little else. You cannot desire to see me as ardently as I to embrace you. Pray curb your ambitions, for you can never emulate mine in this respect.

My son tells me they are wretched in Germany and have no idea what they are there for. The death of the Chevalier greatly upset him.

You ask me, my dear child, if I am still as enamoured of life. I must confess I find it full of poignant grief, but the thought of death is even more repugnant. To think the inevitable end leads through those dread portals induces such sadness in me that I would willingly turn back and retrace my steps. What a predicament I am faced with; embarked on the sea of life without any option of my own, I am equally constrained to leave it. How?—when?—through what door?—at what time?—in what manner?—Shall I suffer a thousand torments, driving me to despair?—Shall I have a seizure?—a fatal accident? How shall I face my God empty-handed?—Will fear, necessity, be my only passports?—and my only feeling be that of terror?—and what hope can there be for one who is neither worthy of Heaven nor of Hell?—How cruel a dilemma is this! What folly can be greater than to pledge one's salvation to hopeless indecision although it is natural enough, and as easy to understand as is the empty vacuity of our days. I destroy myself in these thoughts and considerations, and so great is my dread of death, that I hate life as its precursor, even more than I hate the thorns and prickles which bestrew our path. You will say I long for immortality. By no means; had I been consulted I should have elected to die in my wet nurse's arms, which would have spared me much trouble, and insured my reaching heaven without a pang; but a truce to all this!

I am vexed that someone should have deprived me of the pleasure of giving you *Bajazet*.[1] It is that beast of a Barbin,[2] who hates me because I cannot produce a few *Princesses de Montpensiers*.[3] Your criticisms are just and agree with mine. I would have liked to send you la Champmeslé to bring the play to life. Bajazet is an icicle . . . There are some agreeable moments, but no thrilling passages as in Corneille and, above all, let us beware of comparing Racine to Corneille. The former surpassed himself in *Alexandre* and *Andromaque*. *Bajazet* cannot touch them, so people think, and if I dare to venture a popular opinion, which is also mine, Racine writes plays for Champmeslé, and not for posterity. If ever he grows up, and ceases to fall in love, it will be a different story.[4] So hurrah for our old friend Corneille! Forgive him a few indifferent verses for the sublime heights to which he raises us: such master-strokes are inimitable . . .

I thought you would be satisfied that your daughter should be the image of the Coadjutor; apparently your son aspires also to resemble him, but meaning no offence to the Coadjutor whence, I ask, does the child derive his pretty mouth and his charms? We are to take it he is like his sister, which troubles me. I do love you for not again being with child. If you think your beauty is wasted, you must find solace in the assurance that you are not again about to die . . .

Farewell, my child; I shall never end. I defy you to say you understand how much I love you.

[1] Racine's tragedy received its 1st performance 4.1.72.
[2] A famous bookseller, on the Sainte-Chapelle steps at the Palais de Justice.
[3] Mme de La Fayette's novels had greatly enriched the *Libraire Barbin*.
[4] This came to pass with *Mithridate*, *Phèdre* and *Athalie*.

TO THE SAME

Paris, Wednesday 30 March [*1672*].

How kind of you, dearest, to say you like my letters and wish they were longer, and like them less when they are short. But in order to please you, Grignan, most unfortunate man, is obliging enough to pore over these volumes. I remember his observing how much he admired those persons who could endure wading through long epistles; he seems, however, to have changed, but I trust you to keep from him those he would find tedious . . .

Here are some reflexions which occur to me when I hear of your and M. de Grignan's losses at the card-table. Beware—it is far from agreeable to find oneself in the position of dupe, and be sure that a never changing run of good or ill luck is not in the order of things. Not long ago I was told of that fraud at the Hôtel de la Vieuville over a game of *fredon* (three of a kind), do you remember? Do not imagine everyone plays as you do. It is my deep interest in you which prompts me to say this, and I know you will take it as it is meant, as coming from someone who loves you.

You may also like to hear that Kéroual's [1] lucky star has followed her. The King of England is enamoured of her, and as she shews a slight inclination not to hate him the result is that she is eight months gone with child; strange indeed! La Castelmaine [2] is out of favour, and that is how things are done in that Kingdom over the sea. Since we are gossiping I will reveal to you, with M. de Grignan's permission, that the young son of F...... [3] and the Chevalier de Lorraine [4] (I dare not be more explicit) is being brought up, pell mell and all above board,

[1] Louise-Renée de Penancoët de K. had accompanied *Madame* (Minette) on her Treaty of Dover mission in 1670. Charles II created her Duchess of Portsmouth, 1672. Louis XIV revived for her the title of Dsse d'Aubigny when she returned to France, 1684.

[2] Her rival, Barbara Villiers, created Duchess of Cleveland in 1670.

[3] Mlle de Fiennes, lady-in-waiting to the Queen.

[4] Born a d'Harcourt, favourite of *Monsieur*, brother of the Comte de Marsan, implacable enemy of *Madame*. *See Monsieur* by Philippe Erlanger, 1953.

with Mme d'Armagnac's [1] children; and when the Chevalier returned great play was made of family likenesses which the Chevalier confirmed, and thereupon took such a liking to the boy that they no longer made any secret of his origin. Madame d'Armagnac will continue to lavish her kindness on him in the name of the Chevalier de Lorraine. How tedious for you if you have already heard this scandal. Adhémar is much better placed than I to recount all the tittle tattles, and I can safely leave it in his hands.

To The Same

[Paris,] Friday 1 April [1672].

Guitaud [2] tells me of your wish that I should come to Provence, and I am transported with joy; to hear it thus indirectly adds so greatly to my satisfaction. But nothing I hear can increase my own desire to come . . . alone my aunt is cause of the delay; indeed she is so ill that it is inconceivable she should last, but I will keep you informed of what is at the moment my greatest preoccupation . . .

The Chevalier de Lorraine called the other day on la Fiennes, who played up like anything and assumed the airs of a maiden all forlorn. The Chevalier, with his most engaging manner, which I admire so much, said: "Why do you repine, Mademoiselle? Nothing out of the ordinary has occurred. We loved, we love no longer, at our age constancy is scarcely to be expected; far better to forget all that has passed and resume our old habits and mode of address . . . Who made you a gift of that charming little dog?" His tirade, as you can well imagine, struck the knell of this grand passion.

What book are you reading? I am engrossed in Christopher

[1] Catherine de Neufville, Ctsse d'A, his sister-in-law, married to Louis de Lorraine, *Grand Ecuyer de France*, noted for his handsome features and sometimes called *Monsieur le Grand*, herself a member of the Queen's household.

[2] Guillaume de Pechpeyrou-Comminges, Comte de G., Marquis d'Epoisses, devoted friend and neighbour at Bourbilly.

Columbus' Discovery of the Indies,[1] but I am still more diverted by your daughter. I find her irresistible. She strokes your portrait in so engaging a manner that I fain must give her a hug. I admire the way in which, by arranging the curls on the top of your head, you anticipated the new vogue in hairdressing. You were ever a forerunner of fashion. Farewell, dearest child, I truly believe nothing can equal the depth of my passion for you.

To The Same

Paris, [*Wednesday*] *6 April* [*1672*].

. . . In view of my aunt's illness I am hard put to it to know what to do. The Abbé and I are literally boiling over with impatience, and should it seem likely she was to drag on indefinitely, we are resolved to start for Provence ; good nature has its limits. You may be assured that my wish to be off exceeds yours to see me start. You think I exaggerate, but that is impossible where my feelings on this matter are concerned. I do not forget to give my poor aunt your kind messages. She is convinced her death is not far off but, ever ready to oblige and in order not to distress my cousin, the poor creature makes a pretence of welcoming the remedies which no longer can assist her. But when subterfuge becomes useless she will, I am persuaded, look death in the face with fortitude and resignation . . .

As for M. de la Mousse, I have apprised him of your great desire to see him. He is deterred only by the thought of the perils of the journey. Pray write to him as you suggest, and for our part we shall be delighted for him to join our company and shall encourage him by telling him of the pleasure you will derive from his visit . . .

How alarmed I am at events in Provence ; and although the smallpox has so far spared your little one, what of the plague? I am greatly concerned. Even your sunshine will not prove a protection to the victims. I pray your good Governor to tighten up his restrictions and regulations . . .

[1] Probably in an Italian translation of the book written by his son.

On Saturday the Duke had a stag hunt in honour of "*Les Anges*",[1] followed by a supper at Saint-Maur, which was composed of the finest sea fishes. The company afterwards repaired to a small house adjacent to the Hôtel de Condé where, more scrupulous than we are in Brittany, and immediately on the stroke of midnight, a sumptuous *medianoche* was served consisting of delicious savoury meats; this unwarranted laxity did not meet with general approval, but provoked admiration of Madame de Grancey's charming manners. Also present were the Comtesse de Soissons,[2] Mesdames de Coëtquen [3] and de Bourdeaux,[4] several gentlemen besides the Chevalier de Lorraine; there were bagpipes and violins; but of the Duchess and of Lent not a murmur, the one was confined to her apartments, the other to the cloisters . . .

How I rejoice you are not with child! For God's sake, dear one, enjoy your good health while it lasts, take advantage of the respite and do not add to your many cares by harbouring regrets.

The old MADAME [5] is dead of apoplexy; MADEMOISELLE inherits the Palais du Luxembourg, to which we shall now have access. In order to make a nuisance of herself MADAME had all the trees razed on her side of the garden which thus became lop-sided and ridiculous. Providence has stepped in, and MADEMOISELLE will have them razed on the other side, and has put in Le Nôtre [6] to deal with it, as he has at the Tuileries. She was not brave enough to attend her stepmother's last hours, which was neither Christian, nor heroic . . .

M. de La Rochefoucauld is again crippled with the gout, and in such a high fever that you can never have seen him more afflicted. He begs you will take pity on him, and if you could see the state he is in I defy you not to relent.

[1] The remarkably beautiful Rouxel sisters, daughters of Marshal de Grancey by his second wife; Elizabeth, later lady of the bed-chamber to Marie-Louise, Queen of Spain, and Marie-Louise, Ctsse de Marei, mistress of the Duc d'Enghien. *Monsieur* was the lover of the elder, who never married.

[2] *See* f.n. p. 104.

[3] Marguerite de Rohan Chabot, Marquise de C., wife of the Governor of St. Malo, mistress of the Chevalier de Lorraine.

[4] Widow of Antoine de B., late Ambassador to Whitehall.

[5] Marguerite, daughter of the Duc de Lorraine, second wife of Gaston de France, Duc d'Orléans, uncle of the King.

[6] André Le Nôtre (1613–1700), designer of Louis XIV's parks and gardens, and Controller of the Buildings at Versailles.

My dear child, having long coveted a heart *adamantino* I wish to retract, for how can I desire to love you less than I do, whatever pain may accrue to me? Are you not of the same way of thinking? May our hearts remain unchanged, you cannot be deceived where mine is concerned . . .

To The Same

Paris, Friday 8 April [1672].

War is declared, and departure is in everyone's mouth. Canaples [1] craves the King's permission to serve under the King of England. Marshal du Plessis,[2] who is at the same time a bourgeois and a Canon of the Church, will hide his talents under a bushel and remain in Paris, where he will assess the course of the fighting. With such a great reputation nothing he does can come amiss. He told the King he envied his children who have the honour and good fortune of serving His Majesty, and that finding himself useless he courts an early death. Whereupon the King embraced him tenderly saying: " M. le Maréchal, the rest of us work in order to attain the reputation you have acquired; how good it is to rest on these achievements ". Indeed I esteem him wise not to jeopardise the fruits of his life's work.

The Maréchal de Bellefonds [3] is spending Holy Week at La Trappe, but before leaving spoke in no unmeasured terms to M. de Louvois [4] who, as general under the Prince, wishes to relieve him of some of his responsibilities. He then placed the whole matter before His Majesty, and won out of hand . . .

M. and Madame de Chaulnes are returning to Brittany. At such a time as this the best place for a Governor is in his own province.

[1] Alphonse de Créquy, Comte de C., brother of the Duke and the Marshal. " *Courtisan imbécile* ", according to Saint-Simon.

[2] César de Choiseul, Comte du Plessis-Praslin, had distinguished himself in many campaigns: commanded the King's army during the Fronde, and defeated Turenne at Rethel. His son was to meet his death before Arnhem.

[3] Bernardin Gigault, Marquis de B., Master of the King's Household.

[4] *See* f.n. p. 93.

We are in for a bloody war, and I confess I am consumed with anxiety. Your brother is very near my heart, we are good friends, he is dutiful and loving, and I, like a harsh stepmother, rule over him and his affairs. I should indeed be ungrateful if I found fault with either of you, for both I think are very pretty specimens of my handiwork. I must end my letter by telling you that when I was dressing this morning I was attended in my room by a Burgundian gentleman, one from Provence, and one from Brittany.

To The Same

Paris, [*Wednesday*] *27 April* [*1672*].

. . . The King leaves tomorrow. The computation is there will be an exodus of no less than one hundred thousand men from the capital. I have spent four whole days in bidding good-bye. I went yesterday to the Arsenal to bid farewell to the Grand-Master [1] who had sent for me; he was not there. [But] I found La Troche grieving for her departed son, and the Comtesse [2] for her husband: the latter was wearing a soft grey felt hat she kept bashing down on her head at the excess of her displeasure. No hat has ever received more cavalier treatment; a mobcap or hood would have been more suitable to the occasion. Off they both went this morning, wife to Lude, husband to the war, and what a war! The most cruel and devastating since Charles VIII marched through Italy: the King has been warned. The Yssel [3] is defended by twelve hundred pieces of cannon, sixty thousand foot soldiers, three townships and yet another wide river. The Comte de Guiche,[4] who knows that country, shewed us the map at Madame de Verneuil's the other day, an astonishing

[1] G.M. of the Ordnance, Henri de Daillon, Comte, later Duc du Lude, First Gentleman of the King's Household, Governor of Saint-Germain and Versailles; always idolised by Mme de S.

[2] Renée-Eléonore de Bouillé, his first wife, who hunted dressed as a man, and spent most of her time pursuing this pastime on their estates in Maine.

[3] Modern *Ijsel*, the Scheld.

[4] Armand de Gramont, son of Marshal Antoine de G., who had recently been exiled by the King for refusing to resign his colonelcy of the Gardes Françoises in favour of his younger brother, the Comte de Louvigny.

sight. Monsieur le Prince is absorbed in his plan of campaign. He was accosted a few days since by a crazy loon who boasted he could counterfeit money. "No, my friend" said the Prince, "I thank you. But if you can devise a way by which we can cross the Yssel without being attacked I shall be grateful, for I know of none." The Marshals d'Humière [1] and de Bellefonds are to serve as his Lieutenants-General . . .

The two armies will join up, the King will be in command of MONSIEUR; MONSIEUR, of M. le Prince; M. le Prince, of M. de Turenne; M. de Turenne, of the two Marshals, as well as of the army of Marshal de Créquy. The King told M. de Bellefonds that he must implicitly obey M. de Turenne. The Marshal replied without a moment's hesitation (therein lay his mistake) that were he to observe so blind an obedience he would show himself unworthy of the honour conferred on him by His Majesty. The King entreated him to reconsider his decision, thereby proving his goodwill, for otherwise it would entail his dismissal. Bellefonds repeated that he quite understood his future was at stake and that he was forfeiting His Majesty's favour, but rather than lose the King's esteem he must refuse to obey M. de Turenne, for to do so would be to demean the rank to which H.M. had raised him. The King said: "In that case, M. le Maréchal, we must part." The Marshal, making a profound obeisance, left the King's presence. M. de Louvois,[2] who detests him, left orders that he should forthwith repair to Tours, his name has been erased from the King's household, and being in debt for the sum of 50,000 crowns, which he has no means of discharging, he is a ruined man; but he is quite content and will enter the Trappist monastery. His carriages, which were a gift from the King, he has offered, unreservedly, to His Majesty . . . All who know him are inconsolable . . .

M. d'Aligre,[3] who is eighty, has received the seals of office, he has become a depository, a kind of pope.

[1] Louis de Crevant, Duc d'H., Marshal of France (1668), cousin of the Comte de Bussy, Governor of Lille.

[2] François-Michel Le Tellier, Marquis de Louvois (1639–91), Secretary of State for War (1666), Postmaster-General, taking Dubois, who took a special interest in Mme de S.'s correspondence, to the wars with him.

[3] Etienne d'A. (1592–1677) succeeded Séguier, and though in his dotage was Chancellor from 1674–7.

I have just made a round of visits, ending up with M. de La Rochefoucauld. He is heartbroken, having seen off all his sons to the war but, notwithstanding, he sent you messages and we conversed at length. All are mourning sons, brothers, husbands, lovers; one cannot be indifferent to this exodus of the whole country. Dangeau [1] and the Comte de Sault [2] have been to say their farewells and inform us the King, in order to avoid tears and lamentations, left incognito this morning instead of tomorrow as had been given out. He was twelfth to leave, the others running after, but instead of going to Villers-Cotterets he went to Nanteuil where "certain persons", who had also vanished, may be found.[3] Tomorrow he will leave for Soissons as arranged: and if you do not call this a chivalrous action pray name one! Sorrow is universal and defies description: the Queen is appointed regent, and the heads of sovereign states have come to pay their respects. Strange war indeed which starts so inauspiciously . . .

I approve of your visit to Monaco. It seemed, as you say, rather cruel to travel a hundred leagues only to find yourself back at Aix! But it fits in with my enforced delay. I adjure you write often! Without your letters I am lost. Enchanted to hear you are not pregnant; it makes me love M. de Grignan with all my heart. Tell me if it is due to restraint on his part, or to consideration for you, and if you are not delighted to get about, to visit the country, and to await me without that constant dread of falls and miscarriages? . . .

To The Same

Paris, Friday 29 April [*1672*].

Off you go, dear child, on your great adventure; best to do it while you are in the right mood . . . I would be happier if

[1] Philippe de Courcillon, Marquis de D. (1638–1720), Catholic convert, ready poet, successful courtier and card-player, author of *Journal de la Cour de Louis XIV*. Member of the Academy (1684–1720).

[2] François-Emmanuel, later Duc de S., great grandson of the Connétable de Lesdiguières, whose name the latter assumed; *ob.* 1681.

[3] Allusion to Mme de Montespan.

only you were not such a dare-devil, but you will want to perform prodigies and drive where no carriage has ever ventured before. I am worried, believe me dearest, do not try to go one better than Providence; pray ride on horseback or in a litter, think of the horror of broken heads and limbs, and write from Monaco without fail.

I find I get on famously with the Comte de Guiche. I have met him several times at M. de La Rochefoucauld's and at the Hôtel de Sully; he makes straight for me, and seems to think I possess a nice wit; we conversed at length, and he told me his sister,[1] was hopelessly crippled as a result of being bled. It excites both pity and fear. I have not seen him and his *Chimène*, (*Madame de Brissac*) together. They are so perfectly sophisticated that no-one puts a ribald interpretation on their passion, and it is thought that each one has his or her good reasons for observing the proprieties. . . .

My aunt is no longer *in extremis*, and we are resolved to start in May; I will write to you punctiliously. Meanwhile I am moving into my new little house which is charming [2]: you will like your apartments, that is if you still love me when a hundred leagues no longer divides us. I enjoy settling in with the charming prospect of having you here. Farewell, my sweet angel, I am yours without discriminations or limits of any kind.

Friday evening.

. . . Our Cardinal [3] took his departure yesterday. There is not one man of quality left in Paris, all are with the King or deputising for him, or in their own homes, and these are few and far between. I estimate that M. de Sully[4] possesses more courage than any man who crosses the Yssel: young, strong, rich, he has seen everyone leave with no more emotion than if they were picking up shells on

[1] Catherine-Charlotte de Gramont, Psse de Monaco, wife of Louis Grimaldi, Duc de Valentinois, P. de M., favourite of *Madame* (Minette).

[2] In the Rue Sainte-Anastase. Mme de S. was not to rent the Hôtel de Carnavalet till 1677.

[3] Paul de Gondy, Cardinal de Retz (1614–79) usually referred to thus.

[4] Maximilien de Béthune, Duc de S., son of Charlotte Séguier.

the beach and he were looking on. I will not say than if they were hunting, for in that he would surely have participated. Off to Sully for the summer, he is wiser than those who are ruled by *l'opinione regina del mondo* : he has chosen the part of a philosopher. Mourning is general and hearts are heavy for those friends and relatives exposed to great peril. Even the King did not remain unmoved when he left so precipitately ; we are assured that " certain persons " who received him at Nanteuil will not be returning as soon as anticipated to Saint-Germain, as in the course of the next three months they will, in some country retreat of their own choosing, be engaged in a " certain undertaking."[1]

To The Same

Paris, Friday 6 May [*1672*].

Dear daughter, I feel an urge to gossip to you which I cannot resist. Yesterday I attended a service at the Oratory for Chancellor Séguier ![2] The expenses were borne by painters, sculptors, orators, musicians, in a word by the fine arts. Le Brun[3] designed the mausoleum which reaches to the vault and sparkles with a thousand lights. It is adorned by symbols suitable to their subject, and which serve to extol his memory. Four skeletons standing below bear the insignia of his office, one his *mortier*,[4] another his ducal coronet, a third his orders and a fourth his mace as if at the moment of his death, they had deprived him of his worldly honours. The four Arts—Painting, Music, Eloquence, and Sculpture are depicted lamenting the loss of their patron ; in the foreground stand the four Virtues—Fortitude, Justice, Temperance and Religion. Four Angels or Genii stoop from above to receive and welcome his immortal soul. The mausoleum is

[1] Mme de Montespan was brought to bed on June 20th of the future Comte de Vexin.

[2] Chancellor of France. *See* Letter of 3 Feb.

[3] Charles Lebrun (1619–90). Chancellor, and Rector of the Academy. Colbert was his patron.

[4] Velvet cap worn by High Court Presidents. S. had been *Président à mortier du Parlement de Paris*.

further enriched by the figures of angels supporting the catafalque which is suspended from the dome. Nothing more splendid can be conceived than this masterpiece of Le Brun, and in addition the church is hung with paintings, emblems and mottos relating to the feats of arms or incidents in the life of the Chancellor. Madame de Verneuil [1] offered to pay a high price for the entire decoration, but it was resolved that a whole gallery [2] should be dedicated to this work as a mark of gratitude and esteem in perpetuity. The assembly, though large, was orderly: I was sitting in the proximity of M. de Tulle,[3] M. de Colbert, and M. de Monmouth, [4] who is as handsome as in the days of the Palais Royal, and who by the way is joining the King's army. A young Oratorian arrived to deliver the funeral oration. I told M. de Tulle to take his place, as his eloquence alone could be worthy of the occasion. Well, dear child, the young preacher started in a trembling voice, and the audience one felt to be as nervous as he. At first he spoke with a Marseillais accent (his name is Laisné),[5] but gaining assurance, he soon entered on a discourse so enlightened, so moderate, praising the deceased in such measured terms, avoiding pitfalls and ending in passages of such inspired eloquence that all, all I say, of those present were moved to the heart by this noble tribute. He is only twenty-eight and an intimate friend of M. de Tulle who is removing him to his diocese. We nicknamed him Chevalier de Mascaron, but I think he may even excel his elder. As for the singing it was inspired. Baptiste [6] had further perfected the King's music, and augmented the fine *Miserere*, and at the *Libera* the whole audience was dissolved in tears. These strains were straight from heaven . . .

I must be crazy to send you such a rigmarole, no doubt it indulges my garrulous disposition! . . . A kiss for Grignan on his right cheek, just under his tangled mop [7] . . .

[1] Charlotte Séguier, Dsse de V. by her 2nd marriage.

[2] In the Hôtel Séguier, Rue de Grenelle, not far from the Oratory.

[3] Mascaron.

[4] Natural son of Charles II, beheaded 1685.

[5] Vincent Léna, born at Lucca 1633, educated at Marseilles, distinguished for his eloquence, died at the age of 44 in 1677. [*Monmerqué*].

[6] Jean-Baptiste Lully (1633–87), thus always referred to by Mme de S.

[7] Allusion to some *bouts-rimés* of Mme de G. (*touffe ébouriffée*). *See* Letter p. 71.

To The Same

Paris, Friday 13 May [*1672*].

You are right, dear daughter, in saying that Livry's extraordinary beauty would help to distract me, were it not for the grief I feel at my aunt's lamentable condition, and for my urgent longing to go to you. I am also much disturbed at Mme de La Fayette's protracted state of languor. After spending a month in the country, resting, purging, and generally refreshing herself, she returned to Paris as blithe as a lark: no sooner did she get back, however, than she was stricken with an attack of tertian fever which gives her bad dreams and literally burns her up, and she is reduced to a skeleton. Nevertheless this lady's illness does not preoccupy me as does my aunt's; hers is a real embarrassment. But trust to us, leave it in our hands; it might entail an endless delay were we not to go to Provence this year. Despite your professed intention to return with me, let us start by coming to you, and if the Abbé can be of any assistance in straightening out your affairs, pray take advantage of his good intentions. Much can be accomplished in a short time, take pity on our growing impatience and help us to bear with it, and believe that not a moment will be lost, even at the sacrifice of some decorum. You see how I am torn in half by duty and desire . . . I can well understand your longing to see Livry once again . . . God willing, you shall do so in the Abbé's lifetime.

I was given an account the other day of the habits of your Provençal spring, and where and when your nightingales can be heard. But I confess I see nothing there but stones and barren rocks, olive and orange groves, the bitter flavour of which would deter any songster: it is for you to rehabilitate your country in my eyes . . .

M. de Turenne has gone to Charleroi at the head of twenty thousand men, no one knows his intentions. My son is still in Germany; in future the news will, I fear, be disquieting. It seems that Ruyter,[1] who is reputed the greatest living sea captain,

[1] Michael-Adriensz de R. (1607–76), Admiral to the Dutch Republic.

has defeated Comte d'Estrées [1] in a running fight in the English Channel. We know nothing, but hope the King, who has placed an embargo on any news leaking out, will not go so far as to conceal his victories . . .

To The Same

Paris, [*Monday*] *16 May* [*1672*].

Your letter is superb, dearest daughter, and reads like a novel whose heroine I am in love with. I take the deepest interest in every detail from your pen, and have great difficulty in believing that this journey through the most beautiful country in the world, this land of fragrance where you are received as a queen, that this wonderful new adventure which surely can never be tedious, is otherwise than pleasurable to you; and although you may occasionally wish for my company, I am assured and overjoyed to know it has afforded you such distraction . . .

My son writes dutifully, but the war causes me grave anxiety; his regiment is shortly joining the King's arms. We hear of the siege of Maestricht as less formidable than fording the Yssel. Letters from the front unnerve me, and how much worse it will be in a fortnight's time! I and M. de La Rochefoucauld console and lament with each other; he is the father of three or four sons in whom his heart is deeply engaged. Yesterday Madame de Marans visited Madame de La Fayette; so black was her mood that she might have come from making a pact with the devil, and shortly be expected to deliver the goods. I fear she has been left repining by some faithless warrior . . .[2] Madame de la Fayette asks to be kindly remembered to you, and wishes me to say she is in a poor way but this does not reconcile her with the thought of death; indeed she dreads it all the more. I must confess that I myself do not find life entirely agreeable,

[1] Jean d'E. (1624–1707), Vice-Admiral (1670), Marshal of France (1681). Governor of Brittany. *Vice-roi de l'Amérique* in 1686.

[2] M. le Duc, Condé's eldest son, by whom she had a child.

but no philosophy of yours can turn me wholly against it. I am sorry, dear little one, but whatever you may say, I cannot alter my somewhat frivolous outlook . . .

To The Same

Paris, Monday 30 May [1672].

. . . Livry just now is beautiful beyond description, the trees are a tender green, honeysuckle is rampant everywhere, and so far I have not sickened of the smell, but how unfavourably you must compare my poor little thickets with your groves of orange ! . . .

Here is a tragic little tale from Livry. Do you remember that pious and devoted postulant who never dared raise his eyes or turn his head as if—I remarked at the time—a glass of water were poised on top of it ? Well—piety has driven him mad ; one fine night he stabbed himself five or six times, was found on his knees in his cell, stark-naked and bleeding profusely. Goodness to God, my dear brother, what is all this ?—and who has attacked you ?—Father, he answered coldly, I am making penance. —So saying he swooned, was put to bed and his wounds dressed, when it was found his condition was of the utmost gravity. After three months of devoted care he recovered and was returned to his parents at Lyon. If this does not strike you as a remarkable face-about I shall be surprised and will give you yet another example, that of Madame Paul ! [1] Madame Paul falls hopelessly in love with a great lout of twenty-five, whom she had engaged to work in her garden. The woman becomes so distraught that she marries him ; he is brutal, mad, and will end by pounding her into a jelly, having already threatened her more than once. But she is prepared to accept anything at his hands. Never have I witnessed so engrossing a passion. All is on a grand scale in this affair, sketched in on a huge canvas with every colour of the rainbow. It diverts me to watch the whims and caprices of love, but I admit I am frightened by the violence of this man's assaults. What presumption to attack Madame Paul, the exponent

[1] Respected widow of the gardener at Livry.

of austere and homely virtue, as we had thought! How indeed is it possible to feel safe anywhere? Here are some pretty tales, dear one, in return for your pleasant discourses.—

Madame de La Fayette is still far from well, M. de La Rochefoucauld is crippled; we sometimes converse in so lugubrious a manner that there seems nothing left but to bury us as soon as possible. Madame de La Fayette's garden is a dream of beauty, all flowers and scents. We sit there many an evening, as the poor woman dare not drive. I often wish you were discreetly hidden behind the fence, and could hear us discourse of distant lands we have explored [1] . . .

To The Same

Paris, Friday 17 June. 11 o'clock of the evening [*1672*].

I have just heard a sad piece of news, dear child, but can give you no details as yet: all I know is that M. de Longueville [2] was killed at the crossing of the Yssel [3] which is a heavy blow. I was with Madame de La Fayette when the news was brought by M. de La Rochefoucauld, and we learnt at the same time that M. de Marsillac had been wounded and the Chevalier de Marsillac [4] killed in action; an avalanche of bad news, and only M. de La Rochefoucauld's iron self-control prevented him from breaking down completely; but he cried his heart out . . . I flew to M. de Pomponne in a state of panic, who was able to reassure me, reminding me that my son was in the King's army and nowhere near the fighting. It was M. le Prince's battle, and they say he is wounded, that he has crossed the river in a small boat,

[1] Allusion to *Terres inconnues* on the map *Tendre*, in Mlle de Scudéry's *Clélie*.

[2] Charles d'Orléans, Comte de Saint-Paul 1668, and in 1671, by a deed of his elder brother, Duc de L. Youngest son of the Dsse de L., he bore a striking resemblance to La Rochefoucauld, whose mistress she had been. A reckless character, he was only 23 at the time of his death.

[3] In reality, the Crossing of the Rhine. [*Monmerqué*].

[4] Respectively the eldest and the 4th son of the Duc de La Rochefoucauld, the former François VII, Prince de La R. (1637–1714), later Governor of Berry. (*See* f.n. p. 241); the latter, Jean-Baptiste, Chevalier de Malte.

that Nogent[1] is drowned, Guitry[2] killed, Messieurs de Roquelaure[3] and de La Feuillade wounded and the casualties are heavy. As soon as I know more I will inform you . . . anyway the Yssel is crossed, M. le Prince crossed the river on several occasions, giving orders in his divinely imperturbable way. We are told the enemy have retreated into their lair . . . Farewell dearest one, I think I am out of gear, and although my son is with the King's army there will be so many more alarms that I faint, I die in anticipation . . .

To The Comte de Bussy

Paris, 19 June, 1672.

The death of M. de Longueville, Guitry, Nogent, and many others; Monsieur le Prince, de Marsillac, and de Vivonne . . .[4] and a thousand more wounded draws a baleful and melancholy picture of the war. I do not understand how they can have swum the Rhine. The fantastic tale of men on horseback jumping into the river like hounds pursuing a stag, neither drowning themselves in the attempt nor being clubbed to death on reaching the opposite bank, passes all belief, and my brain reels . . .

Adieu, my dear cousin, I must away to dine. I find your son[5] handsome and charming. I am so gratified you value my letters. It is impossible to receive your homage without being greatly flattered.

[1] Armand de Bautru, Comte de N., *Maréchal de Camp*, married to Lauzun's sister, Diane-Charlotte de Caumont, who wore widow's weeds for the remaining 48 years of her life. [*Gailly*].

[2] Guy de Chaumont de G., Grand Master of the Robes.

[3] Gaston de R., (*duc à brevet* 1652) Governor of Guyenne 1676.

[4] Louis-Victor de Rochechouart, Duc de V. (1636–88), Marshal of France, Mme de Montespan's brother, later disgraced for his conduct in Sicily.

[5] Amé-Nicolas, his eldest son, a pupil at the Collège de Clermont (Lycée Louis-le-Grand). Taken prisoner at Philisbourg. Later Marquis de Bussy.

To Madame de Grignan

Paris, 20 June [1672].

. . . My son is in mortal peril. The war which waxes ever more violent, the couriers who bring us nothing but tidings of death and disaster, the dread of hearing bad news ; the desolation of those poor souls in the extremity of grief among whom my life is passed, added to which my aunt's precarious state of health and my longing to be with you, all combine to tear at my heart-strings, to destroy me, and to make me live a life so contrary to my temperament and natural inclinations that I know not how I endure. You cannot conceive what Paris is like, everyone in tears and yet fearing to give way . . . Madame de Longueville's [1] plight is heartrending, I have not seen her, but this is what I am told. Mademoiselle de Vertus,[2] having lately returned to Port-Royal [3], she and M. Arnauld [4] were fetched to break the terrible news. Her hurried return confirmed Madame de Longueville's worst fears. " Mademoiselle," she said, " tell me, how is my brother ? " (the Grand Condé.)—She dared not probe further. —" Madame, he has survived his wounds, there has been a battle." " And my son ? "—There was no answer.—" Ah ! Mademoiselle, my son, my dear son, tell me, is he killed ? "— " Madame, I can find no words in which to tell you." " Ah ! my son, my poor son, was his death instantaneous ? Did he not have a moment of grace ? O, merciful God, what a holocaust ! " Uttering a cry she sank down on her bed in the last stages of grief. She went into convulsions, then into a swoon ; deathly silence was followed by stifled moans, bitter tears and wild cries to heaven, indeed the whole gamut of extreme suffering. She

[1] Anne-Geneviève de Bourbon, Psse de L. (1619–79), sister of Condé and Conti had retired from the world on the death of her husband, Duc Henri II, in 1663. Her son was buried at the Orléans chapel of the Celestins in Paris, but his heart was taken to Port-Royal des Champs, where his mother erected a sumptuous monument to his memory.

[2] Catherine de Bretagne de V., sister of the Dsse de Montbazon. She died at Port-Royal, whither she was taken by the Dsse de L. and Mme de Sablé.

[3] Famous Cistercian abbey near Marly, headquarters of the Jansenists.

[4] Robert A. d'Andilly (1589–1674), one of the " *solitaires* " of Port-Royal.

sees only a chosen few, and out of obedience takes a little nourishment; she gets no rest and her already poor health has visibly deteriorated: I earnestly hope she may die, and how indeed is it possible she should survive such a loss! . . .

In the midst of our griefs what you tell me of Madame Colonne [1] and her sister [2] is too divine, and distracts me despite everything. What a picture you draw!! The Comtesse de Soissons and her sister Mme de Bouillon [3] are furious at the behaviour of these madcaps, and say they should be shut up, and they have set their faces against this escapade. It is thought the King however does not want to annoy the Connétable on account of his high standing in Rome. Meanwhile we shall await their arrival, disguised no doubt as *Mademoiselle de l'Etoile*—what a perfect simile! . . .[4]

Evening of the same day, 10 o'clock.

It is two hours since I sealed my packet, and as I return from town I find a letter which tells me a truce has been declared. It is evident that Holland is in a state of alarm and will submit: the King is in the seventh heaven; but what a sword in the heart of Madame de Longueville and other bereaved mothers! . . .

To The Same

Livry, Sunday evening (continuation of a letter dated 3 July, 1672).

. . . I am sorry one of my postal packets was mislaid; as it contained much news I fear this may have caused you to lose

[1] Marie Mancini, former mistress of Louis XIV who had married her to Lorenzo-Onufre (Prince) Colonna, Constable of the Kingdom of Naples.

[2] Hortense, Dsse de Mazarin, married to Marshal de la Meilleraye, who took her title. Disguised as men the sisters had run away from the Palazzo Colonna in Rome and gone in pursuit of the Chevalier de Lorraine and his brother, the Comte de Marsan. The King did not wish them to be arrested on their arrival at Aix.

[3] Olympe Mancini, usually known as "Madame la Comtesse", mother of Prince Eugene of Savoy, and Marie-Anne, Dsse de B., patroness of La Fontaine, wife of the Grand Chamberlain; sisters of the above.

[4] Character in Scarron's *Roman Comique* (1651).

the thread . . . You must, however, have received detailed accounts in which you will have learnt that the (Rhine) was badly defended. The miracle was to have swum it on horseback. M. le Prince and his Argonauts rowed in a boat; the first troops they encountered on landing begged for quarter when, as ill luck would have it, M. de Longueville, who was not aware of this, having remounted his horse which he had pulled across behind him, pushed on to the terrain where the enemy was intrenched, and in the ardour of battle killed the first man he closed with, himself falling, riddled with bullets. Longueville was closely followed by M. le Duc, after him his father M. le Prince, the rest on their heels; hence the dreadful massacre which could have been avoided had they been cognisant of the enemy's wish to surrender. But are not all things predestined?

The Comte de Guiche,[1] in fighting a successful action, covered himself with glory, his failure would have been accounted a crime. He made it his business to discover whether or no the river was fordable. He decided it was when, in fact, it was not, despite which whole squadrons got across in good order; true it is he took the first plunge. The thing had never previously been attempted: it succeeded. The count surrounded the enemy and compelled them to surrender. You can see that his good luck did not desert him and, as ever, went hand in hand with his honour. But of course you must know all, and more than all, I am telling you.

A certain Chevalier de Nantouillet was unseated by his horse and sank, rose, sank and rose once again, this time grabbing his horse's tail and swimming with him to the bank. Once landed he sprang into the saddle and in a moment found himself in the thick of the fighting; with a couple of bullets in his hat, he came back rejoicing. Such spirit is comparable to that of Orontes, Prince of the Massagetes.[2]

Yes—it is a fact that M. de Longueville made his confession before leaving for the war; as he was never one to boast, he did not even tell this to his mother. He made use of our friends (at Port-Royal) for his confession, absolution being deferred for

[1] *See* f.n. p. 92. He had been banished from 1662–71, following the scandal over MADAME (Minette); esteemed as brave as he was handsome.

[2] Allusion to Mlle de Scudéry's *Artamène, ou le Grand Cyrus*.

two months: there is no cause to doubt this, and it affords Madame de Longueville infinite consolation. This man was the soul of charity, distributing his gifts far and wide, but always in the strictest secrecy. Never was there one of more solid virtues. It might perhaps have been better had he possessed a few amiable vices, a little pride, a little vanity possibly; as it was he was near to perfection: "*pago lui, pago il mondo*" [1]; praise and adulation passed him by . . . His sad death was but a nine days wonder; that of MADAME's [2] created much more sensation . . .

Goodbye, farewell, divine one; I miss your letters so badly, you alone can console me for their absence.

TO THE SAME

Paris, Friday 8 July [*1672*].

At length, dear daughter, you are at Grignan, awaiting me stretched out on your bed: as for me I am in the throes of departure, and if I were to give way to day dreaming I should never start at all; but I am resolved to go, and if you receive one more letter from me that will be as much as you can expect. Pray be as idle as you know how till I come, in order to get over it before I arrive: how true it is that our temperaments are scarcely compatible, but, as you so truly say, our hearts, being quasi related, naturally turn to one another . . .

M. de Longueville has left behind him a trail of mourning females, who throw discredit on the profession. They all wanted to pour out their woes to M. de La Rochefoucauld, but fearing ridicule more than all else, he sent them to the right about . . .

[1] Guarini's *Il Pastor Fido*, II, 5. Richard Fanshawe, in *The Faithfull Shepheard* (1647) translates it, "*and if she's pleas'd, what others think| It matters not.*" (*Lui satisfait, le monde devait être satisfait.*)

[2] Minette's tragic death, following so soon after her triumphant success in obtaining her brother's signature to the Treaty of Dover, had plunged the Court in gloom.

Longueville's boy is that same little "apostle" you had heard tell of![1] It is one of the best stories of our time . . .

Despite what you are told, pray have some scorpion oil[2] prepared before we come, in order that we may face the remedy and the disease at one and the same time . . . You will soon have to stock up your dovecotes, your rabbit warrens and even your poultry yard to satisfy the requirements of your numerous guests. I am talking nonsense. We shall be furious if you increase them by so much as a pigeon, and to tempt M. l'Abbé with good cheer will be a certain way of ending his life: as it is you keep too ample a table. La Mousse has been somewhat troubled at the prospect of fleas, bugs, scorpions, bad roads and noises he might encounter, so he says. It has all grown into a kind of bugbear. When I laugh at him he only repeats: "What kind of figure shall I cut among so many persons of consequence, I who am nothing?" We call these sentiments self-glorifying humilities.

To The Same

Lyons, Wednesday 27 July [1672].

. . . I shall not start until Friday morning and shall sleep at Valence where I have some reliable boatmen on the look out for my arrival. I have asked, above all, not to be handed to yours who, methinks, are rogues and thieves. I have excellent introductions, and shall be passed on from hand to hand like a princess. I shall be at Robinet[3] at 1 o'clock of the afternoon, and if you are not there to fetch me I shall remain stationary until you appear. It is no use telling you how happy I am; the dear Abbé is well . . . La Mousse is alive. We long for you, and at the thought my heart leaps for joy.

[1] Himself a *bâtard adultérin* (*see* f.n. p. 101), he left this son by the Maréchale de la Ferté five hundred thousand francs. Some years later, when Louis XIV had his bastard offspring by La Montespan legitimised, he did not forget Longueville's boy. [*M.*] He was inadvertently killed at Philisbourg in 1688.

[2] Against gnats, bugs and fleas.

[3] On the Rhône: port of call for Grignan.

So far we have travelled safely and in comfort. Yesterday one of my horses was drowned at the horsepond and I am thus reduced to five which is none of my doing. We shall not do you credit I fear . . . I shall not have my coach at Robinet: count on our being five, the Abbé, La Mousse, two serving maids and myself . . . Madame de Coulanges keeps trying to persuade me to send you messages that I intend remaining with her all summer, I wish you could hear her! She will come and see us and rejoice our hearts I know. Farewell, dear daughter, your little one is safely in Paris, and far more surrounded than I am: I love the child, and it was a happy inspiration to leave her where she is. Here comes Madame de Rochebonne[1]—I feel I am embracing her brother (M. de Grignan) and there will be nothing left for him! What bliss to think I am getting ever nearer to my beloved and beautiful Countess!

[1] Thérèse-Adhémar de Monteil, Csse de R., M. de G.'s younger sister, who resembled him closely.

1673

To Madame de Grignan

Montélimar, Thursday 5 October [1673].

A terrible day,[1] my dearest, and I must admit I am worn out. The state I left you in has added to my distress. I can only think of your footsteps leading you in one direction, mine leading me in another, and were this so to continue, you and I would never meet again in this world. When I am with you, then only is my heart at peace, which is its natural state and one giving full satisfaction. The events of this morning were exquisitely painful. No doubt your philosophy will prompt you as to the cause of my acute suffering, from which, I can assure you, it will take me a long time to recover: your image is always before my eyes and present in my heart and in my thoughts. I cannot think of you without weeping, neither can I refrain from thinking of you, wherefore my state of mind is well nigh unendurable; perhaps the very extremity of my grief is a proof it cannot indefinitely be protracted. I find myself searching for you everywhere, and your absence leaves a void which nothing can fill. For fourteen months my eyes rested on you perpetually, whereas now I stare into space, and present sadness is accentuated by the joys which have fled. I must grow accustomed to this state, but never sufficiently so, I fear, not to pine for your presence and

[1] The day of Mme de S.'s departure from Grignan, after a visit extending over 14 months, to Paris and that of Mme de G. to Aix. Montélimar is only a few leagues from Grignan.

to embrace you once again. I feel I was sparing of my kisses when I bade you goodbye. Why did I not tell you again and again what your tenderness means to me? And how came it that I failed to commend you to M. de Grignan's good care? And why did I not sufficiently thank him for his kindness and attentions to me? . . . In a word, dearest one, I exist for you alone, would that God's grace might one day inspire me to love Him as I do you! . . . Never, I think, has journey equalled the melancholy of ours. We never open our mouths. Adieu, beloved. Alas, this return to mere letter writing! Pity me that I should have had to leave you.

To The Same

Lyons, Tuesday 10 October [*1673*].

. . . I want once again to remind you that, should you intend to avoid the dangers of winter travel,[1] you must be ready to alight from your coach, as I did, at any given moment; a litter would be admirable, or to ride on horseback as do Mesdames de Verneuil and d'Arpajon. M. de Verville's [2] coach broke down last year, and we were advised another route by following the bed of the Rhône. I got out, the horses swam and the coach was flooded, this occurred two leagues from Montélimar. At the season you propose to travel the river will be in flood and quite unnavigable, you will have to come overland, the risk is far too great, the dangers untold. My forethought and care for you leave me no option but to warn you, and though you may scoff M. de Grignan will uphold me, and in the end you will come round to my view. Peace is now a certainty, and doubtless we shall go to Paris, but should war with Spain be declared, with no foreseeable end, it will scarcely be encouraging, in as far as fresh appointments are concerned in the world of governors, and I should think it would

[1] Mme de G. was considering a visit to her mother the following winter.
[2] Charles de Grolée, Governor of Montélimar, whose son was to buy out Charles de S.'s *guidon* in 1676 [*Monmerqué*].

be a wise move if M. de Grignan attended the Court at Versailles sooner rather than later . . .

Tuesday evening.

I scarcely had the strength to open your letter, without weeping bitter tears. The thought of you at Aix, distraught, wearing yourself out body and soul, destroys me utterly. It seems as if you were escaping from me, eluding me, and I were losing you for ever. I so well understand your nostalgia, you were accustomed to my presence day in, day out . . . I had always hoped you would return with me, but you know how harshly you contradicted me, I was forced to acquiesce and appear to agree with you but, believe me, it is cruelly unnatural that I should return to Paris alone. If you find you can come this winter, I shall rejoice indeed and be comforted. In this case I shall, as you say, only have three months to endure, but meanwhile I go further and ever further from you, and the dread future is all unknown. I long for your letters; the pleasure is a mixed one, but my interest in your doings is so great that I cannot afford to be without them . . . Here is a sound piece of advice. Do not put your pot on to boil too early of a morning lest the ingredients should turn into a watery soup: the thought of an "oille" [1] pleases me as being more nourishing than a plain meat: like you, I only add one other ingredient to the bitter chicory leaves, which are good if they happen to suit you and, in spite of the fact that I am ugly and unknown in this part of the world, I have never been better in my life. . . .

[1] From *olla*, a kind of stew or soup of Spanish origin, containing various meats and herbs.

To The Same

Bourbilly,[1] *Monday 16 October* [*1673*].

Here I am at last, dear child, in my ancestral home where my forebears reigned triumphant according to the custom of those days. Here I am renewing acquaintance with my lovely green fields, my little river,[2] gorgeous woods and pretty mill just where and as I left them. Honest folk dwell here, better men than I, but, having just left Grignan and said goodbye to you, I am dying of melancholy. If I followed the dictates of my heart I should weep all day long, but I recollect your admonitions and turn away from such indulgence.

How well I remember you here! Bussy was with us, who always chased away dull care, and once you called me "step-mother" in a stern voice, do you remember? The trees in front of the house have been pruned to form a most agreeable pleached alley right up to the front door. Everywhere the crops are abundant, to bursting, and "of Charon not a murmur" [3] or in other words not a penny farthing. The rain is pouring down, I am not used to these perpetual storms, and they drive me mad . . . I cannot accustom myself to doing without you; and, if you love me, you must prove it in the coming year. Adieu, dearest, I have only just arrived and am a little weary. When my feet are less cold I will tell you more.

To The Same

Paris, *Thursday 2 November* [*1673*]

I must announce my arrival to my very dear one after four long weeks on the road, but none of it was as wearisome as my

[1] Ancestral château and estate of the Rabutin Chantals, between Epoisses and Semur in Burgundy, in which Mme de S. had a life interest. Long supposed to have been her birthplace, but her birth-certificate proves she was born "*à la Place Royale au Marais dans la circonscription de la Paroisse de Saint-Paul* (5.2.1626).

[2] The Serein, tributary of the Yonne.

[3] Allusion to Lucian's *Dialogue* between Charon and Mercury. In trans. by Wm. Tooke, *Charon, or The Surveyors General.*

first night, albeit in the best bed in the world. I never closed my eyes, counted the hours on my watch and rose at crack of dawn for " what to do in bed if not to sleep ? " [1]

I had my cooking pots already on the stove, an " oille " in the one, a soup in the other, steaming away. We arrived yesterday, being All Saints Day: good day, happily accomplished. We made a halt at M. de Coulanges' ; I dare not tell you of my weakness, of my folly on reaching Paris ; I felt the moment approaching when my face would play traitor, but I turned it off by saying the cold wind had reddened my nose : I found M. de Coulanges who warmly embraced me, the next moment M. de Rarai appeared . . . followed by Madame de La Fayette, M. de La Rochefoucauld, Madame Scarron, d'Hacqueville, the Abbé Têtu, and you can well imagine the clamour and all that was said and done and the rejoicings : " And what of Madame de Grignan ? Tell us about your journey ? " and questions and answers without rhyme or reason, head or tail. Supper and bed and the glorious and peaceful night I have described.

This morning, at the stroke of nine La Garde,[2] l'Abbé de Grignan,[3] Brancas [4] and d'Hacqueville, walked into my room in slippers for what is called an undress conference . . . I forgot to tell you I had your letters of 15, 18, 22 and 25 October. I perfectly understand your so lucid exposition, and I can never be sufficiently grateful for your tender affection of which I am convinced, nor for the confidence you place in me. Dear daughter in this you do me justice, for nothing is nearer my heart than your interests, whatsoever they may be. Your letters keep me alive, pending your arrival.

I am glad M. de Grignan's small worries have cleared up, for in Provence one must mind one's p's and one's q's . . . I hope his health is improved and the fever abated since, alas, it is

[1] Allusion to La Fontaine's *Fable*, " The Hare and the Frogs."

[2] Antoine Escalin des Aimars, Marquis de La G. : M. de G.'s 1st cousin of his mother's side.

[3] Louis-Joseph, brother of Mme de S.'s son-in-law, whom she refers to as " *le bel Abbé* " or " *le plus beau des prélats*."

[4] Charles de Villars, Cte de B. (1618–81), descended from the illustrious Neapolitan family of Brancaccio. He arranged Mme de G.'s marriage and was *Chevalier d'Honneur* to the Queen. The *Ménalque* of La Bruyère, " *d'une distraction légendaire* ".

beholden to him to have to draw the sword. I hate this paltry little war.[1] . . .

To The Same

Paris, Friday 8 December [1673].

Dearest child—I must start by telling you of the death of the Comte de Guiche.[2] The poor fellow, who was in M. de Turenne's army, died of languor and prostration, and the news only reached us on Tuesday morning. Père Bourdaloue broke it to the Maréchal de Gramont, who had long been apprehensive on account of his son's failing health. He lodges in a small apartment at the gates of the Capuchin Convent.[3] Ordering everyone to leave the room, he threw his arms round the good Father, saying he knew only too well what he had come to tell him, that it was his death warrant, which he accepted from God's hands, he was losing what was in very truth the centre and core of his being, the object of his tenderest love adding that he had never experienced the extremes of joy or of sorrow save through this dutiful and beloved son. So saying he flung himself on the bed, extenuated with grief, grief too deep for words. The priest wept in silence, but at length addressed him gently, in his own inimitable way, speaking to him of God and of God's goodness. They remained closeted together for six hours, after which and in order to complete the great sacrifice the Marshal was led to the Capuchin church where the good nuns were keeping vigil for his son. The Marshal was so weak that he fell to the ground and had to be lifted and half carried in; his face was unrecognisable. M. le Duc saw him in this pitiable state and wept when telling us about it at Madame de La Fayette's. Later the poor Marshal returned to his little closet like a man stricken, sentenced to die; the King has written to him. No one sees him.

[1] The once independent principality of Orange had revolted. M. de G. at the head of 600 men, reached the town on 21st Nov. and received its capitulation.

[2] *See* f.n. p. 92. Died at Kreuznach on 29th Nov., aged 36.

[3] Close to the Hôtel de Gramont, in what is now the Place Vendôme.

Mme de Monaco[1] is inconsolable, and is seen by none. Nor is La Louvigny,[2] but that because she feels no grief. Does this creature's good fortune not surprise you? All in a moment she has become Duchesse de Gramont! The Chancelière[3] is in the seventh heaven. The Comtesse de Guiche[4] observes the proprieties, and cries when she is told that on his deathbed her husband desired his regrets and excuses to be conveyed to her. She says: "He was an amiable man and a kind one, had he loved me at all I should have returned his love with passion. I am greatly moved by his death, for I had always hoped that one day his feelings towards me would change." That is the truth, the plain unvarnished truth . . . Poor d'Hacqueville took on himself the burden of going to Frazé, thirty leagues distant, to break the news to the Maréchale de Gramont,[5] carrying a letter in which the poor deceased expressed deep repentance, wished to make amends and a public confession of his sins . . . His last gesture is a fine one, and the curtain goes down on his rich and prosperous widow. The Chancelière has learnt such a lesson, from watching her granddaughter's unhappy marriage that she will not rest until she has made it up to her. If there were a King of Ethiopia handy she would gamble her last farthing to procure him for the young woman. We confess we are baffled and cannot think of a suitable husband for her. You will, I know, suggest M. de Marsillac, but neither side is willing, and the other dukes are all too young. Try and think of someone, for time presses. Goodness me, what a lot of details I am giving you, but sometimes you say you have a fancy for them.

[1] Catherine de Gramont, his sister. *See* f.n. p. 95.

[2] Marie-Charlotte de Castelnau, sister-in-law of the Comte de Guiche.

[3] Relict of the late Chancellor Séguier, grandmother of the Ctsse de Guiche: Madeleine Fabri, daughter of Treasurer for War. *See* p. 176.

[4] Marguerite de Béthune-Sully, daughter of Charlotte Séguier by her 1st marriage. She became Dsse du Lude in 1681.

[5] Françoise-Marguerite de Chivré, his mother, daughter of Hector, Seigneur du Plessis, de Frazé, et de Rabestan. She married the Marshal in 1634.

To The Same

Paris, Thursday 28 December [1673].

Today as ever is, I shall begin my letter, hoping to finish it tomorrow. First and foremost let us deal with the chapter concerning your project of coming to Paris. Janet [1] will have told you that La Garde was chiefly responsible for saying it was necessary you should obtain leave to come . . . but you will not have it that this is of such vital importance, and your arguments appear irrefutable. Well—I cannot put up any more fight and must bow to the inevitable; and when you add: that I, *who more than anyone should weigh the pros and cons of your actions in regard to the future, want to involve you in heavy expenses which may seriously embarrass you*:—what is there left for me to say? No, my dear child, as God is my witness, I not only do not wish to injure you, but should hate to be thought a foolish, frivolous, ill-advised mother who tries, for sentimental reasons, to turn you from the straight path which, in your wisdom, you have cut out for yourself. Nevertheless I thought you were coming, you had given me your word, and when I consider what you are spending at Aix in play-actors, revelries, and feasting for the carnival, I must asseverate that it would cost you less to come here where, as you well know, you need not contribute a farthing piece. M. de Pomponne and de La Garde point out many ways in which you and M. de Grignan's presence is essential for the prosecution of his affairs, and I add my injunctions to the effect that I am ready to receive you, and my hopes run high; happily you are not pregnant and require a change of scene. I have gone as far as to allow myself to hope M. de Grignan would spare you to me for the whole summer, and that yours would not be a mere two months escapade such as men indulge in. My friends all insist on my claims, but you do not see the force of my reasoning, wherefore I must yield to yours and try to submit. I will accept this heavy set-back as a well deserved chastisement sent by God to try me; a more painful one could scarcely have been devised, but I must once and for all make the sacrifice and learn to spend

[1] A gentleman of Provence, greatly attached to the de Grignans.

the rest of my existence separated from the one of all others I love best, whose disposition and tastes conform most nearly to mine, and who, I truly believe, cares for me now more than she has ever done. All this must be offered to God . . . and I will even extol the ways of Providence whereby the grand and the beautiful things in your life walk hand in hand with an abyss of utter wretchedness. Our enforced separation is the ruin of my days and half my nights. This is no exaggeration, but the simple, sincere expression of my thoughts . . . The subject is closed, I will say no more but will try and meditate on your strength of mind, and emulate your admirable wisdom, which I never cease to envy.

To The Same

Paris, Friday 29 December, 1673.

M. de Luxembourg's army is being heavily contained at Maestricht by M. de Monterei [1] and the prince of Orange. He cannot retreat and would be annihilated should no reinforcements reach him. M. le Prince starts in four days time with M. le Duc and M. de Turenne, the latter serving under the two princes, all working in perfect harmony. They command twenty thousand foot and ten thousand cavalry. All, save the volunteers, have marching orders including La Trousse and your brother, who returned yesterday. Scarcely are their boots pulled off than back they are in the mud. The assignation is for March 16th at Charleroi . . . This is great news and has spread like wildfire; no one knows where to turn for funds . . .

[1] Governor of the Spanish Netherlands.

1674

TO MADAME DE GRIGNAN

Paris, Monday 5 February [1674].

Dear daughter, today, many years ago, a creature was born into this world whose destiny it was to love you above all else beside. Do not, I pray, go searching high and low for an answer to this riddle : " *Cet homme-là, Sire, c'était moi-même* ".[1] It was three years yesterday since you left me to go and live in Provence where, alas ! you have been living ever since. Were I to attempt to make you understand all the bitterness and pain I suffered and still suffer from that untoward event my letter would never end . . .

The Archbishop of Rheims [2] was returning yesterday from Saint-Germain in hot haste like a tornado. Doubtless he thinks himself the first in the land, but then so does everyone else. They were driving through Nanterre,—*gallop-a-gallop-a-gallop*, when they encountered a man on horseback,—*have-a-care, have-a-care, have-a-care.* The rider tried to avoid a collision, not so the horse, and the coach and six drove straight into them, the rider went head over heels, the coach went over the rider and to such purpose that it overturned into the ditch. The rider, far from being crushed or maimed for life, then and there sprang into the saddle

[1] From an *Epistle* by Marot to François Ier, on being disrobed.

[2] Charles-Maurice Le Tellier, younger brother of M. Louvois, (1642–1710), cousin of the Coulanges. Former Coadjutor, he had succeeded to the Archbishopric in 1671.

and was off like a streak of lightning, and is still galloping, the while the Archbishop's footmen and coachman yell out: "stop him, stop the thief, beat him till he drops." In telling the story the Archbishop adds: "If I'd caught the rogue I'd have broken both his arms and cut off his ears." . . .

Farewell, my dear blessing; how my heart yearns for you! I am sending this to Lyons . . . Do not for one moment think that my joyous anticipation will grow less. I am wrapped up in the thought that I shall see you, welcome you, clasp you to my heart with a fervour and wealth of affection far surpassing what is common to mankind, or what we treasure most in this world.[1]

[1] A few days after this letter was written M. and Mme de G. arrived in Paris, he returning to Provence in May 1674, his wife remaining until May 1675.

1675

To Madame de Grignan

Paris, Wednesday 5 June [1675].

Yesterday the Duchesse de la Vallière took the veil.[1] Madame de Villars had promised we should go together, but owing to some misunderstanding, we feared we should not find seats. Despite the Queen's wish to limit the attendance, we only had to present ourselves at the door in order to be admitted. Madame de la Vallière, beautiful and courageous as ever, bore herself with notable charm and dignity: her beauty struck all the onlookers, you will be surprised to hear that M. de Condom's [2] address was much less inspired than was expected.

I received your letter from Mâcon.[3] I am still unable to read your letters without the fountains starting to play, my heart turning to wax, so that I am left without strength or resistance . . . Pray have no qualms about my health; never shall I forget that avalanche of philosophy you let loose on me on the eve of your departure. I try to turn your lessons to advantage, but I am frail

[1] *See* f.n. p. 45. She entered the Carmelites of the Rue Saint-Jacques under the name of Sister Louise de la Miséricorde. For three years she had put up with the insults of her rival and hard words from the King. She often said: "What I shall suffer at the Carmelites will often remind me of how much those people caused me to suffer."

[2] Jacques-Bénigne Bossuet (1627–1704), friend of the de S.s. Bp. of Condom, 1669; of Meaux, 1681.

[3] Mme de G. had recently started on her return journey to Provence.

by habit and despite your admonitions I ofttimes fail and give way. By the time this letter reaches you the Cardinal [1] will have departed . . . It will be a sad day for me, as I am greatly attached to him, his fine qualities, his conversation and the many kindnesses I have received at his hands. His was a mind and soul of such a high order it could scarcely be expected he would share the common lot of man: those whose rule in life is to pursue the great, the heroic course are apt to retire from the world in their good time, leaving their friends to mourn . . . I must finish my letter, dearest, in order not to overwhelm you. Alas! What a sad alternative is that of reading your letters to the joy of seeing and touching you! One thing I cannot reproach myself with is indifference to my loss.

To The Same

Paris, Wednesday 19 June [1675].

Believe me, my dearest child, the ordeal of parting with you at Fontainebleau was worse than any I have endured, but I found it cruelly painful to bid farewell to Cardinal de Retz at M. de Caumartin's [2] yesterday, four leagues from here. I repaired there on Monday and found him surrounded by his three faithful companions, whose sorrowful countenances moved me to tears, and I was well nigh overwhelmed by the kindness and tenderness His Eminence deigned to shew me, and by the dignity of his bearing . . . After partaking of dinner we walked in the most lovely woods in the world, where we conversed for many hours and on all manner of subjects . . . I wanted to return to Paris, but was persuaded to stay the night: I slept little and next morning, speechless and in tears, I embraced our Cardinal and hurriedly left . . .

M. le Duc is laying siege to Limbourg. M. le Prince is with

[1] de Retz.

[2] At Boissy-Saint-Leger, the country house of Louise Lefèvre de C., Councillor of State, friend and agent of de Retz, and his 2nd wife Catharine-Madeleine de Verthamon, sister of Mme de Guitaut.

the King whose concern you can easily imagine. I do not think my son is present at either siege, that of Limbourg or that of Huy. He sends you loving embraces. I expect letters from him, but with what impatience I await yours! Like you and more than you I find the time between one "ordinary" and the next altogether too protracted. How often do we deplore the flight of time when, as you say, it suddenly stops dead, and in the end we are dissatisfied either way. It seems I can never get used to not seeing you, not coming across you, not meeting you, not expecting you: I am weighed down by your absence, and know not how to turn my thoughts in any other direction. Our Cardinal's departure nearly put you in the shade but you and he are so inextricably mixed up in my mind that when I can force myself to think calmly it becomes apparent that you are responsible for the love I bear him. I do not seem to have taken full advantage of your philosophic instructions; but I am delighted to hear that you yourself are not above all human weakness . . .

To The Same

Paris, Wednesday 26 June [1675].

Answer to a letter of 19 June.

I have this moment received the sad news of our poor little Marquis's illness.[1] I am greatly alarmed, and cannot think it wise to bleed a child of his tender years with all the agitation it involves: in my young days such a thing was never done. Madame de Sanzei [2] opposed it in the case of her son, and gave him a worm powder instead which cured him. I am terrified for our little one lest by overdoing it he should go the way of the King's children and those of M. le Duc.[3] I shall have no rest until I hear he is improving. How greatly I pity you and M. de

[1] Mme de G.'s little son aged three.
[2] Anne, sister of Philippe de Coulanges.
[3] The Duc d'Enghien had just lost two children at a few days' interval. The Dauphin was now the only legitimate royal offspring alive. [*Perrin*].

Grignan! tell him what I feel for you both. Heaven knows I am most grievously distressed.

What you tell me regarding the Cardinal's future plans is true enough and I know, once his debts are discharged, how enamoured he is with the notion of making you the recipient of his generosity: I think you should be informed of so obliging an intention on his part, but as you will have at least two years to meditate on how best you may reject his favours, you need not, my dear one, take measures thus far ahead.[1] May God spare him to us for many a long day . . .

M. de Turenne is in a good strategic position, his army has not been in action as we believed; all are reported well both in Flanders and on the Rhine.

To The Same

Paris, Friday 19 July [1675].

Guess where I am writing from, my dearest: from M. de Pomponne's, as you will see from Madame de Vins's [2] little note herewith.

Accompanied by her, the Abbé Arnauld [3] and d'Hacqueville, I have been to see the great procession of Sainte Geneviève.[4] We were home by two o'clock, much sooner than many spectators who will not get back till nightfall. I assure you the procession was a grand sight. Monks and nuns, priests from every parish, the Canons of Notre-Dame, and finally the Archbishop, clad in his pontificals, proceeded on foot all the way to the (Cathedral). The Archbishop blessed the crowds as he passed, but as his right

[1] It would require another 2 years to pay off the Cardinal's debts.

[2] *née* Ladvocat, M. de Pomponne's sister-in-law, Marquise de V., known as the *petit ministre* from her great interest in Mme de G.

[3] Antoine A., Abbé de Chaumes, eldest son of Arnauld d'Andilly, author of *Mémoires*, in which he refers to "*l'illustre Marquise de S., dont le nom seul vaut un éloge à ceux qui savent estimer l'esprit, l'agrément et la vertu.*"

[4] On occasions of dire necessity, at the order of the King; in this case harvests had been destroyed by 2 months' incessant rain.

hand is useless, the Abbé of Sainte-Geneviève, with the mitre and crozier, like the Archbishop (barefoot) and preceded by a hundred and fifty barefooted monks, walked at his right also blessing the crowds. This he did fasting and with an air so humble and devout that it became apparent that he would presently, and in person, celebrate Mass at Notre-Dame. The legislators in their red robes and representatives of the other professions followed the Saint's shrine which is encrusted with gems and borne aloft by twenty men, barefoot, and clad in white. The Provost of the Guilds, together with four councillors, remained at Sainte-Geneviève [1] as hostages until the return of the precious reliquary. Doubtless you will wonder what purpose was served by its removal and display. It was done as an intercession that rain should cease and warm weather return, and as these hopes were fulfilled the very moment the plan was conceived, maybe we owe the King's return on Sunday to the same fruitful source. . .

I saw a letter of yours yesterday to the Abbé de Pontcarré ; [2] it is divine, not a word in it which could hurt a fly or offend the most vulnerable ; he has sent a copy to His Eminence, the original being guarded as closely as the reliquary.

Farewell, very dear and well beloved daughter, you are the soul of truth and I believe every word you say of the tenderness you bear me. You are the best judge as to whether or no I am grateful.

To The Same

Paris, Wednesday 24 July [*1675*].

It is very warm today, my dear love, so instead of tossing and turning in my bed, I am indulging my whim which is to rise at the unearthly hour of five in order to converse with you . . .

I am waiting until the weather gets cooler to purge myself, and for a little cease-fire in Brittany to start on my travels. Mesdames

[1] The old church in Rue Clovis, on site now occupied by the Panthéon.
[2] Pierre Camus de P., Grand Almoner, known as " le gros Abbé ".

de Lavardin [1] and de la Troche, M. d'Harouys [2] and I put our heads together to consult over the prospects of our journey, for we do not want to find ourselves caught up in the fury of battle which is raging in our poor province and which daily grows fiercer: these devils have been pillaging and setting fire right up as far as Fougères, too near Les Rochers to be pleasant. An exchequer has once more been sacked at Rennes, and Madame de Chaulnes has been threatened and is half dead with terror. I was advised yesterday she had been arrested, and even the more moderate among the hotheads have notified M. de Chaulnes, who is at Fort Louis, that if the reinforcements he has asked for set foot in Brittany, Madame de Chaulnes runs the risk of being torn to pieces. It is only too true that reinforcements are being sent, and rightly enough, as half measures are useless, but I do not think it wise to start whilst such disorder prevails. We must hope the harvest may scatter the crowds, for after all the wheat has to be garnered, meanwhile there they are, six or seven thousand of them, the cleverest of whom cannot boast a word of French . . . In any case we must wait and see the outcome of this tornado, and I am not sorry to put off my departure . . .

I must tell you, dear one, that the famous *cassolette* [3] has turned up, and it closely resembles a *jubilé*.[4] It weighs more and is less handsome than we thought; it is an antique which passes by the name of *cassolette*, of inferior design, quite suitable for Grignan, but not I think for Paris. The good Cardinal admired it as he professes to admire good music about which he knows nothing. You must thank him quite simply and let him think we are delighted with his gift . . . He is well, much better than in the winter; a diet of meats, simply dressed, has entirely restored him. . . .

Madame de Montlouet is suffering from smallpox to the sorrow

[1] Marguerite-Renée de Rostaing, Marquise de L., "*la Gazette ambulante*", one of Mme de S.'s most intimate friends. Widow of Henri de Beaumanoir Marquis de L.; her son Henri Charles was Lt.-General in Brittany, married to the sister of the Duc de Noailles.

[2] Guillaume d'H., Seigneur de la Silleraye, Treasurer of the Breton *Etats*, b.-in-law of "le petit Coulanges".

[3] An incense-burner which Cardinal de Retz had presented to the Sévigné family.

[4] A clock.

of her daughter, and the mother is in despair because her daughter will not leave the sick bed and take the air as she is ordered to do: these ladies are not celebrated for their wit, but of their good feeling there can be no doubt, it is as spontaneous and natural as ours. I find it difficult to respond adequately to what you tell me of your affection, and the place it occupies in your life, save by speaking of the joy it gives me and the gratitude I feel: whatever the motives are which lie behind these sentiments of yours they are most agreeable to hear. M. de Pomponne says: "It appears that Madame de Sévigné adores Madame de Grignan, do you know what motives lie behind this passion?" I will tell you if you like: just simply that she adores her, and he might add that, to her undying satisfaction, she is adored in return . . .

To The Same and The Comte de Grignan

Paris, Wednesday 31 July [*1675*].

Dear one, I acquainted you with my reasons for delaying our journey. M. de Forbin [1] is leaving at the head of six thousand men to punish our poor Brittany, in other words to ruin her: he is going by way of Nantes, so I and Madame de Lavardin will proceed by Le Mans. We are estimating how long it will take us. M. de Pomponne indicated to M. de Forbin that he owned land in Brittany, and told him the names of my son's properties. Sainte Geneviève's shrine has brought us lovely weather . . .

Here is a sad little story of something which took place three days ago. A poor lace-maker living in the Faubourg Saint-Marceau, was taxed ten crowns on his possessions which he found himself unable to pay. When further demands were made he asked for a respite which was not allowed. Thereupon his wretched bed and platter were seized. Seeing himself so ruth-

[1] Bailli de F., Capt.-Lt. 1st Co. King's Musketeers, under orders to suppress Breton insurrection, which had started early in the year owing to heavy new taxation, especially on tobacco. The Marquis de Vins was in command.

MONSEIGNEUR,

This award is due to favour rather than to merit.[1] Wherefore I will add nought.

LE COMTE DE GRAMONT.

Adieu Rochefort.

TO MADAME DE GRIGNAN

Paris, Friday 2 August [*1675*].

I am thinking, dear one, of your shock and grief when the news reaches you of M. de Turenne's death. The Cardinal de Bouillon [2] is inconsolable: he first heard of it from one of M. de Louvigny's [3] gentlemen, who wished to be the first to offer his condolences and stopped the Cardinal's coach on its return to Versailles from Pontoise. The Cardinal did not, it seems, take in what was said to him, and the young man thereupon hastily retreated: the Cardinal sent post haste to fetch him back, and when he learnt of the tragic death he swooned and was conveyed to Pontoise where he lay for two days and nights, spent in cries and lamentations and without nourishment of any kind passing his lips . . . On no account omit to write to him, I esteem that you express yourself well on any subject whatsoever; on this one the heart speaks for itself. We breathlessly await letters from the front . . . We are told that (on the occasion of Turenne's death) the soldiers' cries could be heard at a distance of two leagues, nothing would hold them back and they clamoured to be led into battle in order to avenge their leader, saviour, protector, defender, by whose side they had known no fear, and for the sake of whose honour no quarter could be given. A

[1] Quotation from *Le Cid*, I. III.

[2] Emmanuel de la Tour d'Auvergne (1644–1715), Grand Almoner; Turenne's nephew. Head of the Benedictine Abbaye de Saint-Martin at Pontoise.

[3] Antoine-Charles, Comte de L., second son of Marshal de Gramont, whom he succeeded in 1678: Cte de Guiche after death of his eldest brother.

gentleman, who was near M. de Turenne when he was killed and who was on his way to inform the King, told us this with tears in his eyes. It seems the ball struck M. de Turenne directly across the body. You might well imagine that he fell and died upon the instant, yet he had enough life left in his body to crawl a few yards and even to clench his hands in a final spasm; then his cloak was thrown over him where he lay . . .

I think I told you the Grand-Master is created Duke; he cannot complain, for he will ride in the front coach as Marshal of France, and the King has addressed him in terms far surpassing any honour yet conferred on him. His Majesty instructed him to hand over his title deeds and qualifications to Pomponne; he answered: "Sir, I will give him the patent conferred over my grandfather, all he needs do is to have it copied.[1] We must offer him our congratulations. M. de Grignan will have a great deal to do (upon all these promotions) and may well get himself into hot water, for they aspire to the title of *Monseigneur*,[2] and are not to be persuaded of the injustice of their claim."

It is alleged that when M. de Turenne bade farewell to Cardinal de Retz he addressed him in these terms: "Sir—I am no windbag, but you can take it from me, were it not that my country may, in the present crisis, require my services, like you I would gladly have resigned, and I can assure you, if I come out of this alive, I shall not die in the anteroom, waiting to dance attendance upon my master, but follow your example and hope to give myself a breathing space between life and death."

Farewell, dearest, so passionately do I love you that, methinks, the extreme limit has been reached, further one cannot go, and should anyone wish to solicit my affection he must need be satisfied with the little I have left, a few crumbs, such for instance as I scatter before your portrait.

[1] He was governor to Gaston d'Orléans, but never a Duke.

[2] Title reserved for Princes of Royal blood, Ministers, and certain high functionaries.

To The Comte de Bussy

Paris, 6 August, 1675.

I must stop writing to you of my daughter's departure, and endeavour to keep it to myself, but I can never get used to her absence. You ask me how and where I am, and what I do to distract myself. I am well, I am in Paris, and I amuse myself with trifles; but I am being laconic and must develop my theme. I am going to Brittany, where I have much business to transact, but the unrest which prevails there will make my task more difficult. M. de Forbin is proceeding there at the head of six thousand men. I await the result of this chastisement. If the rebels think better of it and come to heel, I shall spend part of the winter there myself.

I have suffered from the vapours, and my triumphant health, to which you are accustomed, has suffered some horrid set-backs which I find very mortifying.

For the rest you know how I live. I spend my time with five or six intimates whose company I value, and in the performance of a thousand dull duties, no small matter I assure you. But what vexes me is that, whereas our poor existence is made up of a number of days which we spend doing little or nothing, we grow old and die before we have had time to turn round. I resent this a great deal; life is far too short, and old age is ever on the heels of youth. I should like to make sure of living a hundred years, and all the rest to remain in the realm of uncertainty; do you not agree, dear cousin? . . .

I must say you are a first rate almanac; as a soldier you predicted everything that has happened in Germany, but not the death of Turenne, however, nor the cannon-ball fired at random which picked him out among all those who surrounded him. For myself, who believe in destiny, I see this cannon loaded from all eternity, and Turenne led to the appointed place, and if so be his conscience was clear what better end could any man wish for? What better end indeed than to die at the zenith of his fame? He lived to see the retreat of the enemy and the fruit of three months exploits. The brightest star grows dim after a space, and how much happier for the Comte d'Harcourt [1] had he died after the capture of the Isles Sainte-Marguerite; or Marshal du Plessis Praslin [2] after the battle of Rethel . . .

You must know how universally Turenne is mourned, and all about the eight new Marshals of France? We shall be terribly uneasy until we hear that our troops have recrossed the Rhine; then, as the soldiers put it, we shall be pell-mell, on top of one another, but with a good river in between us and the enemy . . .

My poor Madelonne [3] is settled in her château. What a fate! Destiny! Destiny! Farewell, dear Count, and fare thee well, my beloved niece.

To Madame de Grignan

Paris, Wednesday 7 August [*1675*].

Can I have forgotten to tell you about Saint Marceau when I wrote about Sainte Geneviève? What an oversight! Saint Marceau came to escort Sainte Geneviève home, else she would not have budged: goldsmiths were carrying her shrine, encrusted with gems worth two million, a dazzling sight. Sainte Geneviève followed after borne by children with the utmost devotion: leaving Notre-Dame the good Saint Marceau proceeded to escort her to a certain spot where the custom obtains they should bid each other farewell. But would you believe it?—it required such a display of strength to prise them apart that an additional ten men had to be called in lest they should join up again! These succeeded, however, and the saints, giving each other a gentle nod of farewell, proceeded on their way. What could I be thinking of to withhold such marvels from you? . . .

[1] A great general under Louis XIII; defeated the Spaniards in 1637.

[2] Praslin defeated Turenne at Rethel in 1650, although at the head of a greatly inferior army.

[3] Monmerqué thinks Mme de S. thus nicknamed her daughter after the exquisite novel *Pierre de Provence*, of which *La Belle Maguelonne* is the heroine.

To The Same

Paris, Friday 6 September [*1675*].

I am leaving, my love, in the depths of misery at having once more to go further and further away from you, and to see our correspondence interrupted for a few days. To still more enhance the amenities of my travels Hélène [1] is in her ninth month, and as you know Marie [2] has broken out in a rash; but do not let these things worry you, I shall soon adapt myself to being waited on with less elaboration and to look after myself. I shall exercise self discipline, and follow your courageous example . . . It would be shameful indeed if I could not emulate Mme de Coulanges, who is learning, admirably, to be bored at Lyons and to do without the companions she likes best: I promise to heed your adjurations; and to pay my debts and eat up my food: How often I shall think of you dearest. I shall study, walk, write, receive letters from you: alas! life goes all too quickly and the candle burns at both ends. I am taking a hundred remedies with me, good, bad and indifferent and I am enamoured of all of them, for each one has its advocate and has cured some one of my neighbours. But, being in excellent health, I hope never to make use of my travelling dispensary.

I went all by myself to Livry yesterday, and wandered in enchantment by the light of the moon; there was no chill in the air and I loitered from six o'clock till near midnight. I was like a real phantom. It did me all the good in the world; I owed it to chaste Diana to pay her my respects, as also to the dear and friendly abbey . . . I have recently been to see Mignard's [3] speaking portrait of Louvigny, but the former was not visible, being engrossed in painting one of Madame de Fontevrault,[4] whom I peeped at through the keyhole. The Abbé Têtu and she were

[1] Hélène Delan, married to her *maître d'hôtel*, Michel Lasnier, known as Beaulieu.

[2] Daughter of Paul, the gardener at Livry.

[3] Pierre M. (1608–68), Court painter.

[4] Marie-Madeleine de Rochechouart (1645–1704), Abbess of F.; sister of Mmes de Montespan and de Thianges and the Duc de Vivonne.

engaged in a lively interchange of wit. The Villars' and I made fun of them from the other side of the wainscot . . .

To The Same

Orleans, [*Wednesday*] *11 September* [*1675*].

I am about to embark on our Loire. Do you remember, dearest, our charming expedition on that noble river? Although I find your Rhône *terribilis*, I wish it were to her safe bosom I was about to commit myself! It is useless to pretend I can ever be happy for a moment without you. I will write whenever possible, and tomorrow I hope for a letter from you which is to be forwarded here. You say that hope is a lovely virtue; it must indeed be all and more than you say since half the world lives on it: I am one of its most ardent devotees . . .

Kéroual has every reason to be satisfied with the treatment she has received in England; she has achieved her purpose which was to be the King's mistress. He spends all his nights with her with the full knowledge of everyone at Court; her son [1] has been acknowledged and has received two dukedoms and withal has amassed great wealth and has succeeded in being feared and respected, at any rate by some persons. But she had not counted on the advent of a young actress [2] whose charms bewitched the King, and from whom she finds herself unable to detach him. In pride and resolution the actress is her match. If looks could kill Kéroual would no longer be alive, the actress makes faces at her, often manages to inveigle the King, and boasts of his favours. She is young, untamed, bold, agreeable and dissolute, and she plies her trade with a will. She has a son by the King whom she insists should be recognised, and to justify herself she reasons thus: "This Duchess wishes to pass as a great lady, claims to be related to all the French quality, and when anyone of them dies goes into deep mourning. Very well, then! If she is so

[1] Charles Lennox, Duke of Richmond, 1674. Her name was distorted to Carwel in English. Of distinguished ancestry and great beauty.

[2] Nell Gwyn, sometimes spelt *Nelgouine* in French [*Monmerqué*].

high and mighty, why has she turned whore? She should die of shame: as for me I ply my trade and pretend to no other. The King keeps me for the time being, and has given me a son whom he should and will acknowledge, as he cares for me any day as much as for his Portsmouth."—The trull has the last word, and proves a great embarrassment to the Duchess. You will agree as to the story being highly original? and from Orleans I could find nothing better to regale you with than this slice of real life.

I am very well, my dear, and am thankful for the fact that I love to think and to read books, for really the dear Abbé does not contribute much to the gaiety of nations. He spends his time gazing at his money-bags but, fortunately, whilst he is thus engaged, Cardinal Commendon [1] keeps me company. The weather and the roads are in perfect order, the days are clear and sparkling, neither too hot nor too cold and we could easily travel by land. In fact it is only to distract ourselves we are taking to the water . . . Farewell, my dearest dear, my love for you is my best, my dearest occupation . . .

To The Same

[*Tuesday, 17 September, 1675*].

Scarcely a red letter day, but an amazing experience!

Dans un petit bateau,
Dans le courant d'eau,
Fort loin de mon château;

And I may as well finish it,

Ah, what folly! [2]

[1] *La Vie du Cardinal Commendon*, Paris, 1671 (translation by Fléchier from the Latin of Gratiani). [*Perrin*].

[2] Quotation from a ditty by the Chansonnier Coulanges, *Pour Mme de Grignan, qui pensa se noyer sur le Rhône, en allant en Provence.*

For the river is so low that we run aground every few yards, and well may I regret my carriages and horses, which travel fast and without delays. It is tedious to travel alone by boat, and the need of a little Comte des Chapelles and a little Mlle de Sévigné to distract me is greatly felt. In short to embark at Orleans, or at Paris, for that matter, is really an act of madness. I can only suppose one does it to be obliging, and as at Chartres we feel [constrained] to purchase rosaries, so at Orleans we hire boatmen.

Nantes is thirty leagues distant from Saumur, we were resolved to accomplish the distance in two days, arriving at Nantes today. With this purpose in mind we travelled for two hours in the dark, ran aground irrevocably, found ourselves a hundred yards from our Inn and with no possibility of landing . . . When finally we did so it was midnight and we took shelter in a miserable hovel where three old hags sat spinning. There was a little clean straw on the ground on which we threw ourselves fully dressed; I should have laughed at our plight, had it not been for my discomfiture at exposing the Abbé to such fatigue. We re-embarked at dawn and were still so firmly grounded that it took us a full hour to resume the thread of our discourse, but so determined were we to reach Nantes, against wind and tide, that every man jack of us took to the oars. I hope to find your letters awaiting me there, and shall leave this missive where a mailcoach is expected to call. I am well, but thirst for good conversation. Farewell, dearest and most cherished one, you are my very dear child. A peck for the " curmudgeon ".

To The Same

Nantes, Friday 20 September [*1675*].

I have just received your letter in which you picture me as a wanderer on the ocean's brink, which conclusions are more than justified. I wrote from the boat whenever possible. At nine o'clock of the evening I arrived at the foot of this great castle which you know so well and from which our Cardinal [1] made his escape. The sound of oars was heard it seems, and a faint " Who goes there ? " reached us over the water. I was about to give an answering call, when the figure of M. de Lavardin appeared at the small gate preceded by six torch-bearers and accompanied by several noblemen desirous of greeting me, which they did with the utmost courtesy. The scene from the river was, I am told, picturesque in the extreme, and greatly enhanced me in the eyes of my boatmen. I supped well, not having eaten or slept for twenty-four hours. I lay at M. d'Harouys' [2] and took part in the festivities both there and at the château . . .

I should arrive at Les Rochers on Tuesday. I have been none too easy about your brother, but I am informed that M. de Luxembourg intends holding Flanders. You must have been shocked to see that Trèves had capitulated. The Marshal is lucky indeed to have been handed over to the enemy tied and bound, but comparatively unharmed ! [3]

To The Same

Les Rochers, [*Sunday*] *29 September* [*1675*].

. . . I left Silleraye on Wednesday, the day after I wrote to you . . . M. de Lavardin handed me into my carriage, and M. d'Harouys filled me up with provisions for the journey. We arrived on Thursday, and the first person I set eyes on was Mlle du Plessis, more hideous, more demented, more impertinent than ever : her craze for me certainly does me no credit. I swear, *here and now on my honour*, not to pander to it by any approbation, kindness, or friendly gesture. I am abominably rude to her but

[1] Cardinal de Retz made his escape from the château at Nantes on 8 August 1654, a prisoner there since 30 March. Mlle de S. had been educated for a period with the Sisters of Sainte-Marie de Nantes.

[2] Silleraye, some 12 miles north-east of Nantes.

[3] Marshal de Créquy, having defended Trèves in a most gallant manner for a whole month, was betrayed into the hands of the enemy by a cavalry officer called Boisjourdan, who was later caught and beheaded in front of the ranks at Metz.

unfortunately, she turns everything into a joke . . . She never leaves me alone for a moment, but I suppose I should not complain as she takes a good deal off my shoulders . . . at the moment she is busy fashioning table napkins.

I must tell you that I find my woods of inexpressible beauty and melancholy; the trees you saw planted have grown to perfection, tall and straight. They have spread out and thus afford delightful shade, and are already forty or fifty feet high: pray observe my maternal pride in giving you these details, and remember I planted them with my own hands and, as M. de Montbazon used to say of his children: "I first saw them when they were only so high." This lovely spot is made for dreams, and you, I know, would indulge in them as I do. If for me their pattern is not uniformly black, (it is certainly tinged with grey). Here I think of you constantly, I think of your health, of your concerns, of your long protracted absence, and you can well imagine how all this piles up at dusk and when the light begins to fall. Do you remember these lines?

Under what unlucky star was born,
The object of such tender love? [1]

In order not to despair entirely of a future such as I envisage, it is necessary to fix my eyes unflinchingly on God and on God's Will, but of this I shall say no more lest I weary you.

Do not worry about Hélène—Marie can do all I require and I am a model of patience. My health is as good as it was six years ago, and I cannot think whence comes this renewal of youth; I can only suppose my temperament is perfectly adaptable. I read, I amuse myself, I pursue my avocations as if the Abbé were not in the room, and sustained by the hope of better things I am spared, as you put it, the expense of a rope to hang myself with . . . No letter from you by the last ordinary . . . I am quite cast down in consequence . . .

[1] Adaptation of Racine's *Iphigénie* V. III.

To The Same

Les Rochers, Sunday 27 October [*1675*].

I have been altogether without letters, dearest, which is a matter of deep concern to me. It never crosses my mind to blame you, for I know how scrupulous you are, and I can well believe your removal to Grignan to have caused the delay . . .

Mme de Chaulnes has sent me the politest messages . . . and I dined there the next day: she expressed much pleasure at seeing me and gave me a lengthy account of all she had been through and of the dreadful dangers to which she was exposed . . . In a word our province has been greatly to blame, but has, I think, been punished beyond its deserts, so much so indeed that it may never recover from the effects. Five thousand men are stationed at Rennes, of whom more than half will remain all winter . . . MM. de Forbin and de Vins do not greatly relish the duties they are called upon to perform, the latter is at my feet; and will, I expect, proceed here shortly. They will be leaving in a fortnight's time, but the whole contingent of infantry remains. Twenty-five or thirty men have been picked out haphazard and are to be hanged. The parliament has been transferred which is the final blow,[1] for without it Rennes is no better than Vitré . . . All these calamities will end in ruin for everyone . . . I am glad to be home, and am making a new alley which fills my leisure hours, my workmen are being paid in bushels of wheat, and I find nothing better to do than enjoy myself, cast off dull care and forget the thought of all the miseries we are heir to.

You say you are concerned as to how my evenings are spent. Dear one, believe me I am never bored, never at a loss. I have much writing to do, or maybe I read, and midnight strikes all too soon. The Abbé retires at ten, and I can endure two hours of solitude as well as anyone. And after all, my dear, life goes so quickly, and so soon must we reach our appointed end, that it is often a matter of surprise to me that we can suffer such profound dejection from purely mundane considerations. I have plenty of time for reflection, and if my woods fail to inspire me

[1] From Rennes to Vannes, as a disciplinary measure.

I have only myself to blame. I am well, and my people obey your injunctions to the letter, and exaggerate the care with which they surround me. At night they foregather, armed to the teeth and are ready to draw the sword at the sight of a squirrel . . .

To The Same

Les Rochers, Wednesday 13 November [1675].

Here are both your letters at once, my very dear one, which I should have received at the usual time had not Rippert caused a delay by going to Versailles. Whatever liking you may have for my letters is not to be compared with the happiness I derive from yours, and, as it appears to be God's will that, for the moment, I should receive no other consolation, this is most fortunate.

But in truth it is painful to be deprived of your beloved presence ; and to have to accept letters as a substitute over so long a stretch of time is a harsh decree which casts its baleful shadow over all my thoughts and dreams. It requires more courage than I possess to bow to this tragic destiny. I grudge every day and hour spent without you, and though I regret the passing of my days, I shall not greatly mind saying goodbye when the appointed hour strikes, since the world has little enough to offer me. Oftimes when I weep I dare not tell you lest I draw down on my head your well deserved reproaches—I seem to fall, quite involuntarily, into these states of despondency, and have not the good sense to know how to extricate myself. Today I am almost in despair having given way so hopelessly ; usually I am a little more self-controlled. Dearest, let us call a truce to such dark thoughts and forebodings. I sometimes entertain myself, sadly enough, by contrasting this year with the last : what delightful evenings were those spent in your company ! What joy it was to see you, to meet you, to converse with you day in day out ! What pleasant home-comings ! I treasure every single moment of all those days even when the moments and the days themselves have fled and are no more . . .

You have omitted to tell me of *Monseigneur* [1] and what were the results of your assembly, and whether the customary donation satisfied His Majesty? Ours is to be increased.[2] I could have beaten Boucherat [3] when I heard of it, and I do not believe the half will be raised. The opening of our *Etats* takes place to-morrow at Dinan; at Vannes the legislative assembly is moribund. Rennes is a deserted city, the taxes and fines have been merciless; it would take an all-night sitting to recount to you all the tragic tales which have come my way.

Does it surprise you to hear I have acquired a tiny dog? This is how it came about. To keep myself in countenance, I had called to a bitch on heat that belongs to a woman who lives at the park gates, when Madame de Tarente said to me: "What! Do you know how to speak to a dog? Then I shall certainly make you a present of one of the prettiest in the world." I thanked her and told her of my resolve never again to become entangled in that sort of attachment. The episode over, I thought no more about it. Two days later, what do I see but a lacquey, bearing in his arms a small dog-basket, stuffed with ribbons, out of which steps an exquisite lap-dog, perfumed, frizzed, ears, coat, sweet breath, small as Sylphide, fair as fair. I have never been more disconcerted, begged in vain he should be taken back . . . He has endeared himself to Marie; he sleeps in his basket in Beaulieu's room, and lives on a diet of bread. I do not take to him, but he makes love to me; I hope to resist. Pray do not repeat any of this to Marphise in Paris lest she reproach me. He is spotlessly clean. He is called Fidèle—a name that would scarcely fit any of the Princess's lovers, though they have been handsome enough. I'll tell you her story one day.

St. Luke's summer is long drawn out this year, and I take endless walks: as I have never made a habit of using a *chaise* [4] I rest

[1] Allusion to the disputed question whether Marshals of France should be addressed as Monseigneur (*see* f.n. p. 132).

[2] The King had demanded 3 million from devastated Brittany: 500,000 from Provence.

[3] Louis B. (1619–99), the King's treasurer to the *Etats* of Brittany, later Chancellor of the Exchequer.

[4] Littré quotes Mme de S.'s early use of the word *chaise*, meaning *chaise roulante*. Here she may be referring to her library chair. The Italian reference is again to *Il Pastor Fido*, "*the burden of my flesh*".

my *corporea salma* along my alleys. I spend whole days all by myself with only a lacquey in attendance and I do not go back to the house until nightfall, when fire and tapers welcome me to my room. I am afraid of spending the twilight hour alone and in silence, and feel more surrounded in the woods than in the solitude of my chamber. Possibly this can be called " stepping from the frying pan into the fire ", but I prefer the sombre melancholy to the tedium of a " chaise ". Do not fear that I shall come to any harm from the evening chill, for these wooded walks are like a cathedral close and afford a perfect shelter. A downpour of rain is more to be dreaded on my account, for then am I driven indoors, where everything I do tries my eyesight, to spare which I oftimes remain out after dark; but have no fear—my health is excellent.

Farewell, my dear one. Are you really convinced I am the most loving mother in all the world? Nothing is truer; you are my heart's dearest concern and nothing and no one will ever supersede you, not even were I to discover the fountain of eternal youth. As for you, dear Countess, your partiality for chocolate makes me tremble, for how can I aspire to be as agreeable, as much to your taste, as perfect and goodness knows what all? For one thing you say it makes your heart flutter: would that I could boast of such good fortune; you should really keep such inconstancies to yourself. Dearest Countess, write and assure me that you sleep well, eat well, that your complexion is in good order, that your lovely teeth give you no pain. Ah, me! Ah, me! How I long to see and hold you to my heart!

To The Same

Les Rochers, Sunday 24 November [1675].

. . . At one fell stroke the other day the Queen lost twenty thousand crowns and missed hearing Mass, and all this before noon! The King observed " Madame, let us calculate what your losses would amount to in a year ": and M. de Montausier said to her the next day: " I wonder, Madame, if you will again forego hearing Mass for the sake of a game of *hoca*?" Upon which the Queen let fly. People who have been at Versailles regale me with these spicy morsels . . .

You treat our suffering lightly; it is true we are not broken on the wheel so frequently, possibly not more than once a week just to keep up appearances; and a hanging seems quite an agreeable novelty. Since I lived in these parts my ideas of justice have changed. I now think of your galley slaves as a company of honest fellows living in comfortable retirement. We have provided them by the hundred for your use; no doubt they are better off than those who are left behind. I thought the *États* would be suppressed altogether as a suitable punishment, but as you will observe they are being held. We are to make a gift of three millions, a mere trifle, ignoring, as quite beneath our notice, the fact that we are totally unable to find the cash wherewith to pay. You ask if this will spell ruin in the countryside. The answer is no—not for those who remain here as they can live on nothing since there are no goods to buy. But when it comes to ready money I can assure you the poor country is sucked dry.

To The Same

Les Rochers, Wednesday 4 December [*1675*].

. . . Guess whom I saw coming towards me, from the end of the Long Walk? Your brother who, at sight of me, fell on his knees; He pleaded guilty to having played truant for three weeks, and to going to bed at unearthly hours; he was afraid of looking me in the face. I meant to rebuke him severely, but was so delighted to see him that my wrath evaporated. You know how he cajoles one; he embraced me warmly and started to make the most impossible excuses seem valid. We walk, we talk, we read, and in this way we shall quickly bring the year to a close, or such as is left . . .

We are greatly disturbed at the number of troops that are arriving from every point of the compass under the command of M. de Pommereuil.[1] It is a great blow for the commanding officers, and they and the Governor are mortified to find such a poor response to their munificent gift of three million. M. de Saint-Malo [2] is back from Saint-Germain and is accused of having mismanaged the whole affair. After putting Brittany's misfortunes before the authorities, he should have remained where he was and tried to make the best bargain possible. M. de Rohan is so enraged that he has not returned, and may, I feel, never do so . . .

NOTE INSERTED BY CHARLES DE SÉVIGNÉ INTO HIS MOTHER'S LETTER.

From what my mother tells you you will realise the precarious state of her health. Although she is not in danger and the excessive sweating she has been subjected to has eased her pains, they are still severe, and to watch her is most distressing for those who love her; you will, I am sure, allow that I am to be counted amongst them, and do all that lies in my power to soothe and assist her. Would that I could be of some real use, but the fact is I am of no use to anybody, and my one and only asset is that I own Larmechin, my good valet—Larmechin, who does prodigies day and night for the invalid. Your letters are beyond price, would that they came oftener than once a week . . .

Farewell, dear sister, we try all we can think of to distract my mother, which is what she is most in need of; for the rest the illness has to run its course, and we expect another three weeks will work wonders . . . Be careful to say nothing when you write which could remotely upset her, it would be most ill-timed, and if she thought you were grieving it might well retard her recovery. My compliments to M. de Grignan and to his beard, since the one adorns the other.

[1] Auguste-Robert, Chevalier de P., President of the Grand Council.
[2] Sébastien de Guémadeuc, Bp. of St. Malo: "*la linotte mitrée*".

1676

To Madame de Grignan

Les Rochers, Sunday 19 January [*1676*].

I am better, dearest ;[1] my stiff neck turned out to be nothing but rheumatics, a most painful complaint which gives bad nights and little rest, but is in no way dangerous. It has lasted eight days, a little good-will and profuse sweating should put me on my feet again ; they have bled me once from the foot, and patience, added to strict abstinence, will do the rest. Larmechin[2] is most devoted and is by my side day and night. Anyway, my dear, I read your letters yesterday with the greatest joy ; how I dote on this way of conversing ! Now do not expect me to believe you when you profess indifference to your notable success in Provence. What can be more pleasing and more promising for the future, and more satisfactory to yourself than a personal triumph ? I received the good news before you did, and when at the same time it was confirmed that the nobles were to be convened it seemed good measure and running over . . .

I would, and I could, write you pages and pages, but I am quite incapacitated and my son must take up the tale. I embrace you, dearest, and today I can do so with my right arm.

[1] Mme de S. had a severe attack of rheumatic fever which left her ill and suffering for a long time, so that her return to Paris was delayed till 24 March.

[2] *Homme de confiance* to the Marquis de S.

M. DE SÉVIGNÉ TO MADAME DE GRIGNAN

Les Rochers, Tuesday 21 January [1676].

To start with, my little sister, you must trust us entirely, and believe what I and Bienbon [1] tell you, and not take fright because, now and again, you fail to see my mother's well known hieroglyphics. Her hands are even now so swollen that we dare not let her expose them outside the bedclothes, and for another thing she has sweated so much since yesterday, the ninth day, in her affected joints that we must guard against a chill if we hope to effect a cure of hands, feet and knees. These are still painful and hugely swollen, but she no longer is in a fever. This then is precisely the state in which our darling little mother finds herself—never imagine for a moment she is neglected, abandoned. Vitré provides an excellent apothecary who has drawn blood from her foot, and she herself is ready to believe she would receive no better treatment in Paris ; in fact we could almost allow ourselves to be lighthearted if only we could devise some contraption by which she could, occasionally, lie on someone else's buttocks instead of always on her own to her grave discomfort. For an initial sickness this has not been a mild one, but these rheumatics are thought preferable to the prevalent chest cold, especially as in this part of the world there are no facilities for drawing blood from a patient's arm. We try to console ourselves for so much wretchedness by pretending to enjoy the sight of our mother, her arms swathed in wet cloths and unable to stand, as much as in old days we enjoyed seeing her run about singing from morning till night . . . I must tell you an incident which happened anon. My mother was dozing quietly, the " little girl ",[2] Bienbon and I were sitting motionless by the fire when in comes la Plessis. We make a sign she should make no noise when suddenly my mother coughs and calls out for a handkerchief. We hasten to get one when la Plessis, who will always be first on the ground, rushes to the bedside and, instead of holding the handkerchief to the patient's mouth, proceeds to blow her nose violently causing her to yell

[1] Pet name for the Abbé de Coulanges.

[2] A little favourite of the Marquise.

out. We had to laugh . . . It is delightfully comforting to think that from now onwards, in all probability, my mother can but improve . . .

M. DE SÉVIGNÉ TO THE SAME, DICTATED BY HIS MOTHER

Les Rochers, Monday 27 January [1676].

Yes—it is quite true—since that first heavy sweat and the succeeding ones I am left without pain or fever, only an immense lassitude. You can picture me flat on my back for sixteen long days, without being able to turn. I have been tucked away in my small alcove where I keep warm, and have been cossetted to my heart's content. I could wish my son were not my amanuensis on this occasion and I were free to sing his praises. My complaint is prevalent in this part of the world, and those who avoid congestion of the lungs fall victims to rheumatics, but to tell you the truth I have always thought of myself as immune from such human weaknesses and have never been so mortified at having to act against all my natural inclinations. I should not be so great a loser had I turned my sufferings to better account: possibly some might envy my state, but I have yet to learn how to get on without the use of hands and feet, legs and knees. You must forgive this invalid's letter, full of selfish preoccupations; next time I hope to write in a different strain . . . Farewell, my dearest. After all, my distemper has only been a painful, not a mortal one, and the intense fever was beneficial, since it helped to consume the humours in my blood. Now we must patiently await the full return of my strength, and watch the swelling subside . . .

I embrace M. de Grignan. The Princess has been a marvel of kindness.

M. DE SÉVIGNÉ TO THE SAME, DICTATED BY HIS MOTHER

Les Rochers, Monday 3 February [*1676*].

My child, give a guess at the following riddle: what in the world is quickest to come and slowest to go? What brings you to the verge of convalescence, and anon snatches you back? gives you the pleasantest sensations and prevents you from enjoying them? fills you with hope which is presently dashed? Cannot you guess? Do you give it up? Rheumatics! I have had them for twenty-three days, for two weeks I have been without pain or fever, and in this blessed state believed I could walk again, which is all I longed to do; when lo and behold I swelled all over, feet, legs, hands and arms, and this swelling, I am told, is a proof I am cured! Instead of exercising my patience in a profitable manner, I am driven to distraction. All the same I think the trick is done and I shall be walking the day after to-morrow; Larmechin encourages me to hope. *O che Spero*! . . . I took M. de Lorme's [1] purge on one occasion, and shall have another dose. It is a sovereign remedy for all such ills and insures eternal health. God willing, my first step will be to go to Paris: so I beg of you, dearest, to calm your fears; you see we have kept you well posted . . . Farewell, dear and lovely one; I adjure you and all concerned to go in fear and trembling of what is called rheumatics, and this with the utmost urgency. Here comes your brother, who for days has been cursing and swearing at you for opposing M. de Lorme's remedy when you were in Paris.

M. DE SÉVIGNÉ TO HIS SISTER

Had my mother but followed the good man's prescription from the first and taken his powders every month she would have avoided a serious illness, caused by an alarming surfeit of morbid infection; but to advise her as you have done to take only one dose is really asking for trouble. Believe me, " this terrible drug,

[1] A doctor, originally from Moulins (1584–1678).

the chief ingredient of which is an emetic called antimony," has no more effect than a glass of water, and gives neither stomach-ache nor gripes. Its only effect is to clear the head and to make you capable, should you try hard enough, of writing poems. "But no," say you, "she must not take it; are you mad, dear brother, to want my mother to swallow antimony? All she requires is a strict diet and a monthly brew of senna tea": So this is your advice?! Goodbye, little sister; I am simply enraged to think, had we applied the right remedy from the very first, that she could have been spared this illness. I hear my mother calling out: "Foolish children, as if anyone can alter the course of a disease! Providence steps in, and we must bow the head." No doubt the saying of a good Christian, but meanwhile let us, on no account, forget M. de Lorme's excellent powders!

To The Same

Les Rochers, Wednesday 26 February [1676].

I am impatiently awaiting your Friday letters: I long to be reassured about your precious health. I embrace you fondly, and my little secretary takes up the tale. My health is of no further interest, with the exception of my swollen hands; if I could write with my feet you would be receiving my usual stream of epistles. In truth I am now too preoccupied with your health to trouble about mine. If you can keep well I shall indeed render thanks to God. Fine weather here will accelerate my departure for Paris.

They tell me that M. le Prince has thrown up his command of the present campaign; I commend him for making this decision. At last M. de Lorges [1] is a Marshal of France; how much better had this honour been conferred on him six months ago . . . Now that you are safely over your lying-in everyone urges me to take to the road; the good news has already provided the incentive and I await further letters with the utmost impatience. My son

[1] Guy-Aldonce de Durfort, Comte, later Duc de L., Turenne's nephew and Saint-Simon's future father-in-law.

is in Paris trying to bring off what would be a miraculous sale of his post of colour-bearer, all through the good offices of M. de la Garde . . .

Note to The Comte de Grignan

Wednesday 4 March [1676].

I am addressing myself to you, dear Count, for you are reported to have said that my daughter's confinements were the models of what confinements should be, and that the oftener she does it the better. Dear God! She never does anything else. I must, however, warn you that unless you call a halt to this business out of common humanity, and if this poor machine is never allowed a pause, you will destroy it utterly, which would be regrettable. I am putting this to you for your serious consideration—the subject can scarcely be called hilarious.

To Madame de Grignan

Laval, Tuesday 24 March [1676].

And wherefore, since I am able, should I fail to write to you today? I left Les Rochers in open spring weather, warm and delightful. The "little girl" was removed early to avoid a scene: she cried without restraint like a child. I dare say she is already dancing after two days of ceaseless tears; I have failed to teach her self-control . . .

All went well with me on the road. My knees ached from the cramped position, but a few steps on foot put that right. My hands are far from well, but maybe the heat will cure them. That will be a great relief, for I long to take up life again and my many activities! I marvel at the way we adapt ourselves to pain and inconvenience! Had I known what I was to be called upon to endure I tremble to think what my state of mind would have been. But each day's troubles are sufficient unto themselves, which gives us strength to meet the next as and when they come. Pray, dearest, keep count of the full moons throughout your pregnancy; so that all possible is done to keep the little one alive . . .[1]

To The Same

Paris, Friday 10 April [1676].

The more I think of it the greater is my conviction that a fortnight's visit from you would be worse than none at all. Should you come to Vichy or Bourbon it must be with the idea of returning to Paris with me, and of remaining with me through the summer and autumn. You can rule over and console me, and M. de Grignan can join you in the winter and do what he pleases with you. By indulging her in this manner you can shew your love for your mother; you can visit her, comfort her for being sick, and, above all, because she has lost the charming illusion that she was immortal.[2] She has become sceptical, full of doubts, and so lowered in her own estimation, she conceives it possible that one fine day she may find herself crossing the Styx in the same boat as the rest of humanity; for Charon shows no favours. So instead of going to Brittany as you intended to do, I am proposing that you should come here.

I shall miss my son very much when he leaves me. Here in Paris there are little else but departures,[3] and even more lamentations than usual over the scarcity of money . . . Do you notice that my handwriting is almost normal again? indeed my writing demonstrates the success of my cure, presently I shall not have to bother about it any more. At the moment I can carry nothing; to lift a spoon is like lifting the world, and I am still subjected to every kind of humiliation; but after all what have I to complain of since I can write to you? . . . I am confined to my room

[1] Several of Mme de G.'s children were still-born.

[2] It was Mme de S.'s first illness. [*Perrin.*]

[3] Since July 1675 a Congress was assembled at Nimuegen for the signing of peace, but no progress had been made.

and have put off my Easter duties for ten days . . . Madame de Coulanges brings her little troubles to my fireside, and I carry my bad knee and my slippers to hers . . . My hand is telling me it wishes to stop and begs to be excused. I owe the poor thing that much consideration for so greatly obliging me.

To The Same

Paris, Friday 17 April [1676].

God be praised, I think my handwriting is not too bad, at any rate the first lines are quite legible, but I must tell you that my hands, especially the right one, resist all blandishments save that of writing to you; which obstinacy I highly commend. When offered a spoon the hand shakes and spills everything on the ground, and every other suggestion is met with stern refusal. To crown all I am expected to be full of gratitude. True it is that I have ceased to make any demands, and can show exemplary patience, for I fully expect Vichy to work the miracle and restore my freedom. Since learning that the douches, baths and drinking waters are as beneficial as those of Bourbon, with lovely country and pure air into the bargain, I have decided to start as soon as possible. I think I have already told you I have no use for your company for a bare fortnight, and I cannot go to Grignan, the rest you must settle yourself. You know the dictates of my heart and how often I am constrained not to listen to my natural inclinations, and you know, as well as I, what can and what cannot be done; you must act accordingly.

To The Same

Paris, Wednesday 29 April [1676].

I can scarcely wait to tell you that Condé [1] was taken by storm in the night of Saturday to Sunday. This news makes one's heart

[1] Condé-en-Brie, repeatedly bombarded during "*la grande guerre*".

beat, much as if it had been a costly victory; not so very dear, our losses were almost nil, not a man of note has fallen. This can almost be called an excess of good things . . .

Madame de Brinvilliers [1] is not in a position to rejoice as much as I do; she is in prison and setting up quite a good defence for herself. Yesterday, it seems, she complained of boredom and asked to play piquet. Her confession has been brought to light. In it she alleges she was seduced at the age of seven, and continued on the same path ever since; that she poisoned her father, her brothers, one of her children, and finally herself: Medea cannot hold a candle to her. She is foolhardy enough to admit her confession to be in her own handwriting, but adds she was delirious at the time and in a high fever, and that what she wrote cannot be taken as evidence.

On no less than two separate occasions the Queen accompanied Quanto [2] to the Carmelites, where the latter conceived the idea of holding a lottery and forthwith ordered all manner of things to be purchased, deemed suitable for nuns. This caused much jesting and laughter in the community. Quanto conversed at length with Sister Louise de la Miséricorde.[3] She asked her if she found herself as comfortable as people said. She answered "No—I am not comfortable; I am happy." Quanto spoke much of Monsieur's brother and asked if she, Sister Louise, would plead with him on her behalf. She answered shortly and sharply: "As you wish, Madame, as you wish." Quanto then said she was hungry and distributed a few coins to be spent on ingredients for a sauce which she proceeded to prepare with her own hands and afterwards consumed with gusto. I am recounting what happened without circumlocution or adornment whatsoever . . .

[1] Madeleine d'Aubray, Marquise de B. (1630–76), daughter of the Governor of Châtelet, notorious poisoner who, with her lover Sainte-Croix, murdered her father, 2 brothers, and finally her lover. She fled to England, thence to the Netherlands, and later sought refuge in a convent at Liège, where she was arrested in March 1676.

[2] Quantova, a nickname for Mme de Montespan, sometimes *Quanto va*.

[3] Louise de la Vallière (*see* f.n. p. 120).

To The Same

Paris, Wednesday 6 May [1676].

My heart is very heavy when I think of my little darling girl,[1] she will be in despair at leaving you and at being cast into prison, as you so aptly put it. I wonder I had enough courage to send you there, but the thought that I should constantly visit and take you out reconciled me to this barbaric custom, which at that time, be it said, was thought essential to a good education. Well, I suppose we must allow ourselves to be guided by an all-wise Providence who knows what is good for us. Mme du Gué,[2] the nun, is entering the Abbey of Chelles to which she brings an important dowry in order, no doubt, to be able to gratify her many requirements. I cannot imagine her remaining there, or anywhere, for long, unless a youth called Amonio whom I saw at Livry, and who is doctor to the Abbey community, should prove an irresistible attraction. My dear, think of it! A young man of twenty-eight with the most beautiful and charming countenance you have ever seen: his eyes like those of Mme de Mazarin, perfect teeth, and otherwise just as one imagines Rinaldo; a head adorned with long black curls completes the picture. He is Italian, as you would guess if you were to hear him speak. He lived in Rome till the age of twenty-two, and after roaming about the world M. de Brissac brought him to France, and as he was in need of a rest, set him down in the Abbey of Chelles of which Mme de Brissac is abbess. The young man has the use of the physic gardens, which are in the abbey grounds, but to me he is Lamporechio to the life.[3] I fancy some of the good sisters burn to consult him about their ailments, but I dare swear he will not cure one of them save in strict conformity with the rules laid down by Hippocrates. You cannot think how much amusement we have derived from this little incident.

I want to talk about the little Marquis (de Grignan); pray do

[1] Marie-Blanche had just been sent to the Convent of Sainte-Marie at Aix, where she was to remain for the rest of her life.

[2] A relation of Mme de S.

[3] *Conte de Mazet de Lamporechio* by La Fontaine.

not let his diffidence disturb you. Remember the charming Marquis [1] who trembled with fear until he reached the age of twelve; and La Troche was such a poltroon as a child that his mother would have nothing to do with him: you should be reassured by knowing that both of these have won distinction for personal courage . . . His stature is another question altogether. You are advised to put him into hose, whereby you can better watch his legs and whether, being undersized, they are getting sufficient nourishment. He requires exercise in order to develop him, and might benefit from a little strait jacket to support his frame. A Grignan who had not a fine figure would indeed be an anomaly; can you remember how pretty he looked in his little jersey suit? The change in him makes me as anxious, need I say, as it does you.—

We are starting on Monday: but I shall avoid Fontainebleau on account of what I went through when I bade you farewell, and I hope never to set eyes on it again, unless it be to meet you there once more. How I pity you, my dear one, for having to swallow such a nasty black draught! My antimony powder is the prettiest little thing imaginable, and is, as old de Lorme tells us, the very bread of life. He wants me to go to Bourbon,[2] but I am disobeying him as everyone says the air is better at Vichy, and it is less crowded . . . I must tell you I cannot close my hands, my knees and shoulders ache, and I have oedema in all my joints. To drain these swamps requires vigorous purging, which can only be done effectively by drinking water from the hot springs. I shall also have douches on the affected parts, after which I should be entirely whole again.

[1] M. de la Chastre.

[2] For a cure. Bourbon-d'Archambault, of Roman origin, had been made fashionable by Richelieu.

To The Same

Paris, Sunday evening 10 May [*1676*].

I start tomorrow at crack of dawn, and this evening am entertaining Mme de Coulanges, her husband, M. de la Trousse [1] and Corbinelli [2] at supper, who are coming to bid me farewell and to partake of pigeon pie . . .

You will be inheriting five or six hundred gold pistoles from your uncle de Sévigné,[3] which I hope you will put by for this coming winter's expenses. I should indeed be sorry if M. de Grignan were forced to spend the summer at Aix, partly because it will cost him so much if only at the gaming table, which is I fear a considerable item in your budget . . . I am glad to see you have turned against coffee, so has Mlle de Méri [4] who has banished it from her house; such are the reversals of fortune. I am certain that dietetics which heat the blood are more apt to lose favour than those which cool and purify. I always return to this thesis for your benefit, and you must know that my dropsy is caused by congestion of the bowels, and when Vichy has put that right I shall be cooled down by a fruit and water diet and a course of internal irrigation. Pray adopt a similar dietary instead of corroding your inside, and keep in good health for the sake of fulfilling your intention of coming to see me. I beg you to grant me this favour as you value your life, and in order that nothing you do should be to the detriment of mine.

My little gathering of friends has just dispersed, my dearest one,

[1] Philippe-Auguste le Hardi, Marquis de la T., first cousin of Mme de S., son of Henriette, *née* de Coulanges; Capt.-Lt. in the Gendarmes-Dauphin, in which regiment Charles de S. was serving.

[2] Jean C. (1615–1716) son of a secretary to Marie de Medici, of Florentine lineage. A scholar in taste as in temperament, writing treatises on Rhetoric, Poetry, History, and a warm disciple of Descartes, which failed to endear him to Mme de G. who doted on this philosopher. Intimate of Bussy's, he became friend and adviser of Mme de S., often being given her pen to add a note of his own to her letters, and accompanying her during the last 20 years of her life. His benefactors were De Vardes, de Retz and the Marquis de Montespan.

[3] Renaud de S., Jansenist, retired to Port-Royal.

[4] Daughter of the Marquise de la Trousse, an eccentric who enjoyed ill-health.

and I am off to bed . . . I kiss you with all my heart. A pity this phrase has been so misused, else it might better serve to express how greatly I love you.

To The Same

Nevers, Friday 15 May [*1676*].

I am embarked on such a charming road that, whatever the impediments, I should be tempted to write to you; where none exist you can judge of my enthusiasm for the task. The weather is delightful; although we have not had any thunderstorms the heat is no longer unbearable. I am better in myself and find the scenery enchanting, and my beautiful Loire as fine as at Orleans, and I have had the pleasure of seeing various old friends in the course of my peregrinations. I am using my largest coach so that we move at our leisure, which gives us time to enjoy the countryside and we find it engrossing. My one source of regret is that in the winter, when you will be travelling, it will be so vastly less agreeable and more fatiguing. We follow in Mme de Montespan's [1] steps and eagerly enquire from everyone we meet what she says, what she does, how she sleeps. She rides in a coach-and-six, we are told, with the little de Thianges; [2] followed by another coach in which are her six serving women, two baggage waggons, six mules, and ten or twelve outriders, apart from officers of rank, in all an escort of some forty-five persons. Wherever she elects to lie she finds a bedroom prepared for her reception, and she retires to bed then and there after partaking of an excellent meal. She stayed here, where M. de Nevers [3] had issued his orders in person, but did not remain himself to receive her. Wherever she goes she is expected to scatter her largesse

[1] Françoise-Athénaïs de Rochechouart de Mortemart, Marquise de (1641–1707), often referred to as "Quantova", the King's mistress; aunt of Diane-Gabrielle de Thianges, who became Dsse de Nevers.

[2] Louise-Adélaïde de Damas de T., younger of two daughters of Mme de Montespan's sister. She married the Duc de Sforza in 1677.

[3] Philippe-Julien Mazarini Mancini, Duc de N., son of Hortense, Mazarin's niece.

far and wide which she does with exemplary grace, for she is open handed in the extreme. Every day a messenger brings her the latest news from the battle-field, and by now she should have reached Bourbon. The Princesse de Tarente arrives in two days and will herself take up the tale . . .

To The Same

Convent of the Visitation, Moulins, where my grandmother[1] *died Sunday 17 May, 1676, after Vespers.*

It has taken me six days to get here, my dearest child; Mme Fouquet,[2] her brother-in-law and her son, met me, and have asked me to lie here tonight. I have dined, and leave tomorrow for Vichy . . . The pupils here are pretty and agreeable, and they recall how you uttered deep sighs when in church, of which I think I was the cause. At the time I was uttering many myself! and still deeper than yours! Is it true that Mme de Guénégaud[3] used to say: "Sigh dear lady, sigh as much as you will, Moulins knows all about Parisian sighs"? I am so grateful to you for your concern over your brother's marriage . . . and it would be just like you to bring the matter off to his advantage. On my side I will endeavour to do my best. You say you were not as alarmed as you should have been by my illness. Good heavens, what could you have done about it? Your anxiety was greater than my sickness warranted. As my twenty days fever were solely due to the pain I was in, no one was unduly disturbed. The fact that I lived exclusively on four cups of broth a day made me

[1] La bienheureuse Jeanne-Françoise Frémyot, Dame de Chantal (1572–1641), celebrated for her piety; she founded the Order of the Visitation, and was canonised in 1667, and beatified by Pope Benedict XIV by a bull dated 13 Nov., 1751.

[2] Marie-Madeleine de Castille Ville-Mareuil, second wife of Nicolas F., who had retired to Pomé, near Moulins, after her husband had been condemned to life-long imprisonment in 1664.

[3] Elisabeth de Choiseul, Marquise du Plessis-G., Dame de Fresnes, whose husband, ruined by Colbert, had recently died. Friend of Mme de S., *par réverbération*, through the Fouquets. [Scudéry's "Amalthée" in *Clélie*].

delirious, besides which ague often induces strange dreams. Your brother made great fun of all these extravagances, and his account will make you die of laughing. Calm yourself, dear love, and believe me you have been unduly concerned.

Mme de Montespan is at Bourbon, where M. de La Vallière had ordered she should be acclaimed from far and wide, but she would have none of it. She has endowed twelve beds at the hospital; has distributed her bounties, enriched the Capuchin monastery, and is quite civil to visitors. M. Fouquet and his niece,[1] who were doing the cure at Bourbon, went to see her; she discoursed with him for two hours on the most delicate matters. Mme Fouquet went the next day and was graciously received by Mme de Montespan, who listened sympathetically to her sad tale. God must have inspired Mme Fouquet to say all the right things about joining her husband (in prison) and hoping Providence would cause Mme de Montespan to remember and take pity on her sufferings . . .[2]

Farewell, my amiable and lovely one. I send you a thousand kisses, and love and thirst for you as we should for our salvation.

To The Same

Vichy, Tuesday 19 May [*1676*].

I am writing today for I long to converse with you, and my letter must go when it will. I arrived last night and was met by Mme de Brissac and the "chanoîne"[3] on the banks of the Allier, such an enchanting river: if we tried very hard I believe

[1] Basile, known as l'Abbé F., brother of Nicolas, the Minister of Finance, and the latter's second daughter, Marie-Madeleine, later Marquise de Montsalez.

[2] It is likely this touching recital had the desired effect, for shortly afterwards Fouquet (*Mémoires de Saint-Simon, Vol. X, p. 101*) was granted permission to see his wife at Pignerol, where he died, still a prisoner, in March 1680, leave to take the waters at Bourbon arriving too late. (*See* p. 243.)

[3] "Le chanoîne", nickname given to the Chanoînesse de Remiremont, Françoise, Mme de Longueval. In 1680 she lost heavily by a suit which her sister the Maréchale d'Estrées lost to Mme de Bussy, and died in 1688.

we should find this spot was haunted even now by the shepherds of Astrée . . .

Mme de Brissac invited me to dine with her, and I assure you it took me no time to see that the " chanoîne " is fed up with the duchess ! Today I rested, tomorrow start drinking the waters . . . This evening we strolled through ravishing country, and at seven your poor milksop of a mother came in, partook of a fowl, after which she sat down to talk with her beloved child. I know not why the sight of others tends to increase my love for her . . . I am glad my beloved " Bienbon " refrained from coming here, he would not have fitted in, and for those who are not doing the cure it is a dull spot, the place is a hotchpotch he would not in the least have appreciated.

Wednesday 20 May.

This morning I started to drink the waters, my very dear child, and how unpalatable they are ! . . . At six o'clock of the morning everyone congregates at the spring : one sips, makes horrible faces (for, would you believe it, the spring is boiling hot and tastes of saltpetre), turns round, paces up and down, walks a little, hears Mass, vomits the water one has taken, which diversion forms an important item of conversation, and does not cease until midday and dinner-time. After dinner friendly visits are exchanged : today I was hostess. Mme de Brissac played *ombre* with Saint-Hérem and Plancy,[1] the while I and the " chanoîne " read Ariosto ; she is conversant with Italian, and thinks mine very passable. Presently some young peasant girls arrived with a flute, and danced a " *bourrée* " to perfection. In this way the gipsy women display their charms, striking such shameless and lewd attitudes the curés can scarcely approve. When five o'clock strikes we scatter for lovely walks ; a light supper at seven, bed at ten. And now, my dear one, you know as much as I do. The waters appear to suit me, and I drank as many as twelve glasses which slightly affected my inside, but that is the desideratum. I shall start the douches very shortly and will write to you every evening . . .

[1] Henri du Plessis Guénégaud, Marquis de, third son of Mme du P. G.

Thursday 21 May.

. . . Today Mme de Brissac is suffering from colic; she is in bed looking lovely and her hair so well dressed as to put everyone else's in the shade; I wish you could see the use she makes of her eyes, her hands, her voice, to indicate the extremity of her sufferings; her arms, her hands twisting and dragging at the coverlet; the attitude she strikes and the pity she evokes are so enthralling that I was riveted with tenderness and admiration, which pleased her I think. Pray note the whole spectacle was got up for the benefit of the Abbé Bayard,[1] Saint-Hérem and Plancy . . . I kiss you tenderly and long for news of you. And goodnight to you, dear Count; shall you not bring her to see me this winter? Do you really wish me to die of inanition?

To The Same

Vichy, Thursday 28 May [1676].

. . . Today I started the douches which serve as a good rehearsal for purgatory. Stark naked you stand in a hole underground, into which water from the spring is carried by a hosepipe, boiling hot. An attendant plays it on you where you will, and it is humiliating to be exposed in a state of nature without so much as a fig-leaf: I had wanted to bring my two serving maids to keep me company. Screened by a curtain someone sits whose rôle it is to keep up your courage. In my case it is a doctor from Ganat [2] whom Mme de Noailles [3] takes around to all her cures; she likes him and deems him an honest fellow, not a charlatan she says, and she sent him here purposely to oblige me. I am keeping him, should it cost me my last penny, for the doctors here I cannot tolerate, while this one diverts me. He in no way resembles the genus

[1] Friend and adviser of Mme de La Fayette.

[2] A nearby village.

[3] Louise Boyer, wife of first Duc de N., Lt.-Gen. in Auvergne. Pious, devoted to her son, later Abp. of Paris and Cardinal, to whom she made her confession every evening [*Saint-Simon.*]

apothecary, nor that young doctor at Chelles; he has both wit and honesty, and is a man of the world; anyhow, he pleases me. So there he sits entertaining me throughout my martyrdom. Picture to yourself, I beg, a jet of boiling water played on to your most vulnerable parts, at first it is generalised in order to stir up the dormant senses, and before the affected joints come under direct attack. When finally it reaches the neck it is like fire which catches you unawares with such an element of surprise that I can give you no idea of. This, no doubt, is the heart of the matter. All I know is that one endures, nay is forced to do so, and comes out unscathed, sinks into a warm bed there to sweat copiously which will, or should effect, a cure. I feel as if I were taking on a fresh lease of life, and if I can see you once again and embrace you from an overflowing heart maybe you will be able to call me, as of old, your *bellissima madre* and I may, after all, not have to renounce the title M. de Coulanges once gave me of *mère-beauté*. It lies in your hands to bring about this transformation. Of course I am not pretending that your absence has been the cause of all my ills, indeed I am told I did not weep enough since so much moisture is left behind, but the truth remains that to live without you is a source of so much bitterness and repining that I am incapable of adapting myself to such a condition . . .

To The Same

Vichy, Monday evening 1 June [*1 76*].

A shame on you, dear Countess, for pleading with me not to write when you well know it is my greatest joy in life, and in this place my most cherished distraction. A pretty way of life you map out for me! Since I cannot serve you in other ways pray allow me the satisfaction of letters and on no account curtail your own. Progress is slow, but since you deign to take so great an interest in my state I shall have the less inclination to change it . . .

The death of Maréchal de Rochefort affords a good subject for meditation. It seems deplorable to die at the age of forty, having achieved all one's ambitions. As he died he begged the Comtesse de Guiche to look after his wife and to fetch her from Nancy. With him she loses everything and it will be a difficult task to console her . . .

A letter I have from Mme de La Fayette will amuse you. She tells me that Mme de Brissac, having come to Aix to be treated for a colic, left without deriving any benefit, but not without dancing and scintillating to such purpose that she reduced everyone, fish, flesh and fowl, to a mere fricassee . . .

To return to those entrancing douches I have already described: I am at my fourth and have four more to complete the number. I sweat so profusely that I soak the mattress; it must, I think, rid me of all the water I have drunk since I was born into the world. When I sink into bed I am in a state of exhaustion, head and body throbbing, wits wandering, pulse racing. For an hour I lie without uttering a word. Then the sweating begins and continues for at least two hours, and for fear I should get restless, I ask my nice doctor to read to me; he would appeal to you as he does to me, I am certain . . . Soon now I shall be quite alone which I shall revel in. As long as I can enjoy the charming scene, the winding river, the woods, the streams, the sweet pastures, the sheep, the goats, the peasants dancing in the fields, I can do without all the rest; this country alone would make me whole . . .

When you call these waters black you are maligning them, assuredly they are hot, but not black. Try putting a plant or a flower into the hot spring, it will come out whole and fresh as the day you picked it, and far from burning or coarsening the skin the water makes it beautiful and soft. Farewell, beloved one: if to effect a cure entails ceasing to love one's daughter, then I adjure all hopes of improvement! Dear Count—are you not a most fortunate man to possess this treasure of a wife? and what do you not owe me for making you so rare, so precious a gift?

To The Same

Vichy, Thursday 4 June [1676].

At length I have finished douching and exuding; in one week I have lost over thirty pints of water, and believe myself to be immune from the rheumatics for the rest of my life. There is little doubt the cure is a painful one, but a wonderful moment dawns at last when, empty and renewed, one sits relishing a cup of fresh chicken broth which joy is not to be despised, indeed I rank it very high: this is an adorable place . . .

Tomorrow I take a mild dose, drink the waters for another week, and the trick is done. My knees are as good as cured, I still cannot close my hands; but using me as a bundle of soiled linen has proved a highly successful operation. We have here an old Madame Barois, who stutters as a result of apoplexy. I am sorry for her, but seeing she is most ill-favoured, no longer young though she decks herself out in absurd little double-crowned hats, falls in love after twenty-two years of widowhood with a M. de Barois on whom she showers her wealth and who, if you please, openly loves another and stoutly refuses to sleep with her for more than a quarter of an hour, and that only to consolidate his gains . . . (a long-winded sentence)—one finds it difficult to keep one's hands off her and not spit in her face.

We are advised Madame de Pecquigny [1] has also arrived or is expected. She is the Cumæan Sibyl, and wishes to be cured of her sixty-six years which she resents; this place is becoming a mad-house . . .

Your letter of the 21st has just arrived, my very dearest one, there are passages in it which make me die of laughing, the one in which you describe being unable to find an appropriate word to fit Madame de La Fayette is superb . . . As to our Pichon [2] I am in the seventh heaven to think that, after all our fears, he may one day attain a Grignan-like stature. He sounds to be a pretty amiable little child, and you need not have worried about his diffidence . . . you will turn him into a good and honest

[1] Claire-Charlotte d'Ailly, mother of the Duc de Chaulnes.

[2] Provençal word for child. The eldest son was now five years old.

fellow. You see how wise it was to put him into hose; boys dressed as girls indubitably remain girls . . .

You say you do not understand about my hands, dear one; I find I can use them up to a point, but they still do not close properly tho' I can just hold a pen. Inside they are as swollen as ever. What say you to these agreeable legacies of a rheumatic attack? M. le Cardinal de Retz tells me his doctors speak of his headaches as membranous rheumatism; deuce of a name! At the word rheumatics I nearly burst into tears . . .

To The Same

Vichy, Monday 8 June [1676].

. . . My one regret is that you should not see the country dances as they are performed here; it is the most fascinating thing in the world to watch these peasants and their women-folk who have as true an ear for music as yours, a lightness, a grace, a natural disposition for the dance—I am mad about them. Every evening I supply a drum and a violin at very small cost, and it is a joy in these enchanted groves to see the *bourrée* danced by the last of the shepherds and shepherdesses of the Lignon.[1] Despite your sedateness I find myself longing that you should join in the revels . . .

You ask me if I am devout—would that I were! I imagine that, after a fashion, I am learning to wean myself from what is called the world. Old age and a touch of poor health give ample time for reflection, but what I withhold from others is, I fear, all given to you: and I make but little progress in the road of true detachment; for you know well enough the rule of the game, which is to rid oneself of what lies nearest the heart.

Mme de Montespan left on Thursday for Moulins in a boat all paint and gilt and upholstered in red damask, which the bailiff had prepared for her reception with a thousand banners and devices of France and Navarre: never was anything done with

[1] Small river made famous by the pastoral novel *Astrée*, by Honoré d'Urfé (1568–1626). [*See* letter 19 May, 1676.]

more zest and gallantry, and the cost will amount to over a thousand gold crowns. But as the lady told him she had written to the King praising his munificence, doubtless he will be refunded in no time. She would not shew herself to the womenfolk but was seen by the men sheltering under the wing of the bailiff (M. Moran). She embarked on the Allier which flows into the Loire at Nevers, and from thence will be carried to Tours, and finally Fontevrault, where she will await the return of the King, who keeps deferring his departure from the battle-front, the truth being that he is engrossed in the art of warfare, a preference which is not altogether to the liking of his people . . .

To The Same

Written from M. l'Abbé Bayard's
Langlar, Monday 15 June [1676].

As I told you I arrived here Saturday. Yesterday I purged myself in deference to the customary rites of Vichy, just as you return the compliments of the season to your visitors who drop cards on you. The warm weather will complete the cure of my hands, but in reality I somewhat enjoy the curb they put on my activities : I stroll before going to bed, which I do at my usual hour, and sleep on in the morning. I am no longer frightened of getting my feet wet, but I feel my way very carefully, and if I were to take a precipitous step, the word " rheumatics " would quickly bring me to my senses. Would, dear daughter, that by the wave of a wand, of good or bad fairy, you could appear before me ! You would, I am sure, appreciate my host's solid virtues . . . A wood nearby, which conjures up the fragrance of your Provence, is haunted by fauns and satyrs, tripping the *bourrées* to the sound of pipe and oboe. Here we talk of you, drink to your health. I was greatly in need of this peaceful interlude.

Wednesday I shall be at Moulins, and hope to find a letter from you . . . The Abbé Bayard is, I think, a happy man and this because he chooses to be so. But I, dear Countess, am unable to make myself happy in your absence. Nay, when I see the flight of time, and the endless days spent far from you I am torn between hope and fear, and am relentlessly pursued by the thought of when and how I shall recapture you. To turn to a less tragic theme, I can recall what a Breton man once told me about a priest's avarice. "You know the sort of man who eats salt cod all his life the more to enjoy choice fish after his death." I was entertained, and ever since have tried to apply it to my own conduct. Caution would have us eat salt cod all our life in the hopes of choice fish hereafter . . .

I am greatly honoured that M. de Grignan should approve my letters, they never wholly satisfy me, but if they meet with his and your approval I can ask for nothing better . . .

To The Same

Paris, Wednesday 1 July [1676].

I arrived here on Sunday, my beautiful one; slept at Vaux [1] with the idea of bathing in the ornamental waters and partaking of two fresh eggs. But the Comte de Vaux,[2] hearing of my arrival, gave a sumptuous repast in my honour and the fountains were silent as they were being repaired . . . At length we reached Paris; I found Mesdames de Villars, de Saint-Géran [3] and d'Heudicourt [4] on my doorstep. The next moment M. de La Rochefoucauld made his appearance, followed by the Coulanges and d'Hacqueville. Here we all sat, sweating away; thermometers had never played such pranks. The river is crowded; Mme de Coulanges says you have to apply for bathing tickets. I perspire so profusely that I am constrained to change from head to foot three times a day . . . I have a constant stream of visitors . . .

[1] Vaux-le-Vicomte, near Melun, Château built by Fouquet, the cost of which was the cause of his ruin and downfall.

[2] Louis-Nicolas, eldest son of Fouquet.

[3] Françoise de Warigniés, Ctsse de S-G., Lady-in-waiting to the Queen.

[4] Bonne de Pons, Marquise d'H. A great beauty, sometime mistress of the King, known as *la grande dame*.

You make me very happy when you speak with no uncertain voice of your visit to Paris; it will put the finishing touch to my cure. I am placing some considerations before you and M. de Grignan relating to your journey. You should avoid Lambesc and not recross the Durance so late in the year. I therefore propose you should start when M. de Grignan is due to go to the assembly. You should make use of litters, you should embark at Roannes, and be assured you will find my coach awaiting you at Briare. It would be a perfectly suitable moment for us to be together. You could joyfully await M. de Grignan who would join you with your equipage; in this way we should have a short spell alone in each other's company which would afford me untold joy; you would be spared useless fatigue, and I unnecessary anxiety . . .

Philisbourg is in a state of siege. The *Gazette de Hollande* reports that they have lost at sea as many as we on land, and that de Ruyter has become their Turenne . . . I am delighted at their discomfiture: the Mediterranean will be as calm as a lake, and you will bless the consequences. My son writes he is being sent to Germany . . . I regret it as I disapprove of this dual campaign. Farewell, my love.

To The Same

Paris, Friday 17 July [*1676*].

All is over at last, and poor little Brinvilliers has gone up in smoke: after the execution her body was thrown into a red hot furnace, and her ashes were scattered to the four winds. No doubt she is in the air we breathe, and when through the agency of wicked little sprites we are overcome by poisonous fumes, we shall be greatly taken aback. Yesterday judgement was finally passed, and this morning the sentence was read out to her, which was that she should make public confession at Notre-Dame, that she should have her head cut off, her body burnt at the stake, and her ashes dispersed. She was interrogated under duress,[1] but she

[1] The practice in Paris was to force the prisoner to drink about four litres of water for *la question ordinaire*, eight litres for *la question extraordinaire*.

assured her inquisitors it was unnecessary as she would confess everything, and so she did, taking several hours to tell the story of her life, which was even more abominable than one had supposed. Her father she poisoned no less than ten times, but was unable to finish him off, her brothers and several besides; all this interlarded with talk of love and mutual confidence. She gave no one away. Even after these confessions, they once again applied torture, but could get no more out of her. She demanded to speak privately with the Public Prosecutor . . . At six o'clock, naked save for a shift, and with a rope round her neck, she was led first to Notre-Dame for public confession, after which she climbed into the tumbril, was thrown on to her back in the straw in her little shift with her mob-cap drawn down over her head, the executioner and a doctor on either side. I assure you the sight made me shudder. Those who witnessed the execution say she mounted the scaffold with great courage. I stood on the bridge with the good d'Escars [1]; never had such a crowd been seen, Paris had never been so moved; if you were to ask me what the spectators managed to see, I should answer—nothing but a mob-cap. The entire day was given over to the staging of this painful tragedy . . .

I must tell you of a ridiculous episode, but you must not repeat it to M. de Grignan. The "Petit-Bon" [2] who is not clever enough to invent anything, naively related that when in bed the other day with *la Souricière*,[3] after some hours of agreeable conversation, she said to him: "*Petit Bon*, I have a bone to pick with you."—"Tell me what, Madame".—"You have not enough devotion to the Blessed Virgin," she said, "no, not nearly enough devotion; it distresses me greatly." I hope you are sufficiently ribald to enjoy this quip as much as I do? . . .

[1] Françoise Charlotte Bruneau de la Rabatelière, wife of Charles d'E., a good friend, who wrote verse and prose.

[2] Comte de Fiesque.

[3] Mme de Lyonne, whose private life was scandalous.

To The Same

Paris, Wednesday 22 July [1676].

. . . One more word about Brinvilliers before closing the chapter. She died as she lived, with great fortitude: when she entered the torture chamber, seeing three buckets of water, she remarked: "I suppose they mean to drown me, for someone of my size could never swallow so much." When the sentence was read out to her she did not flinch nor falter, and asked to have the last part of it read out to her again, as, after the word tumbril, she said, her mind had wandered. On the way she asked her confessor that the executioner should be placed in front of her, "in order to screen me from that brute Desgrais who arrested me". When her confessor rebuked her she said: "I am sorry; very well then, I will put up with the unpleasant sight." She mounted the scaffold, barefoot and alone, and during a full quarter of an hour, and with all eyes bracketed on her, she was shaved, and then alternately flung down and pulled up by the executioners. There was much murmuring at this shocking exhibition of cruelty. The next day people were seen searching for her bones, believing she was a saint . . .

They think M. de Luxembourg will attempt to raise the siege of Philisbourg—a perilous undertaking. At Versailles there are endless gaieties, music, acting, al fresco suppers, meanwhile the siege of Maestricht continues . . . *Reversi* is played daily in the King's apartments, the King and Mme de Montespan at one table, at another the Queen and Mme de Soubise [1] who plays when the Queen is at her prayers; the stake is of two pistoles a hundred. Monsieur and M. de Créquy, Dangeau with his croupiers, Langlée [2] with his: two or three thousand louis are thus won and lost daily.

Wonderful accounts come from Germany: what do you think of these Germans who let themselves be drowned in a brook

[1] Anne, Psse de S., Lady of the royal household, daughter of the Duc de Rohan Chabot; sometime mistress of the King.

[2] Celebrated for his play at cards, son of the Queen Mother's Lady of the Bedchamber.

because they have not the wits to stem the current? I am certain they will be defeated by M. de Luxembourg; and will not capture Philisbourg; it is not our fault if they prove themselves unworthy to be our adversaries . . .

To The Same

Paris, Wednesday 29 July [1676].

Here's a change of scene, my dear, which will appeal to you as much as to the rest of the world. I went with the Villars's to Versailles on Saturday. You know the usual court procedure, the Queen's robing, Mass followed by dinner, but it is no longer imperative to stifle whilst Their Majesties are at table, for at three o'clock the magnificent royal suite is thrown open and the King and Queen, MONSIEUR, MADAME and MADEMOISELLE, the princes and princesses, Madame de Montespan and her suite, the courtiers and their ladies, indeed the entire French Court assemble there. The apartments are sumptuously furnished and as there is no crowd to speak of one does not feel the heat unduly, and the guests move from room to room without being crushed to death. A game of *reversi* sets the tone for the evening. The King stands behind Mme de Montespan who holds the cards; MONSIEUR, the Queen and Mme de Soubise also take part; Dangeau and Co.; Langlée and Co.; a thousand louis are flung on the table, no other counters being used. I watched Dangeau [1] play and realised what innocents we all were compared with him. He is absorbed in the game to the exclusion of all else; he neglects nothing which can be turned to his own advantage, in a word his good judgement overrides the vagaries of fortune, and two hundred thousand francs in ten days, a hundred thousand *écus* in a month all go on the credit side of his ledger. He drew me into partnership with

[1] Famous courtier who asked the King to assign him an apartment in the Château of Saint-Germain. The King agreed, but on condition that his request should be couched in a hundred lines of poetry, these to be composed in the course of a game of cards. This Dangeau did, apparently without effort or distraction from the game at which he won a fortune. [*Fontenelle*].

him, so I was admirably placed. As you instructed me to do, I bowed to the King who bowed back as if I were young and lovely. The Queen talked at length of my illness and cure as if I had lately been through the pangs of childbirth. She also spoke to me of you. M. le Duc lavished his usual meaningless caresses on me . . . Mme de Montespan spoke to me of Bourbon and asked me to tell her about Vichy, and the benefit I had derived from it, saying that far from curing her knee Bourbon had given her a pain in both. She holds herself as straight as a ramrod, in the words of Maréchale de la Meilleraye,[1] but quite seriously, I find her beauty dazzling; she has lost weight, but this has in no way impaired her complexion, eyes, or lips. Her dress was of French point lace, her head adorned with hundreds of little curls, the two longest hanging down on each side of her face, and a black ribbon threaded through the hair. She wore pearls, the property of Mme la Maréchale de l'Hôpital,[2] enriched with curls and festoons of priceless diamonds, as well as three or four bodkins and no coif; in a word beauty triumphant. She was the cynosure of all eyes, sought out by ambassadors, the admiration of the whole assembly. She has met with criticism on the grounds that she deprived the French people of their King and sovereign; now she has graciously handed him back, and you can scarcely believe what rejoicings there are, nor what beauty and sparkle this has lent to the court. This agreeable confusion, this order in disorder among these great and distinguished persons prevails from three to six of the clock. When a courier is announced the King retires to read his letters, returns anon and is always ready to listen to any music being played, which makes a favourable impression. He discourses with the ladies who are specially chosen as recipients for this honour. At six o'clock the players rise from the gaming table, and nothing is easier than to settle accounts, neither markers nor counters being used. The lowest stakes (*poules*) range from five, six, or seven hundred louis, rising to ten or twelve hundred. Each player lays down twenty-five to start with as an ante, making a hundred for the table, and the dealer an additional ten. The holder of the knave of hearts (*quinola*) receives four louis from

[1] Marie de Cossé, Dsse de la M. Her husband was Richelieu's cousin; their son the Duc de Mazarin.

[2] Renowned for her magnificent jewellery. [*Montespan*, III. p. 202].

the other players who pass, and should the pool remain unclaimed sixteen are added to induce careful play. Everyone talks without drawing breath, and no one stops to consider what they are talking about. "How many hearts did you say? two? three? one? no four: he has only three. And Dangeau is delighted to take advantage of the idle chatter in order to decide on his tactics; it is engrossing to watch the skill he displays . . . At six the company move off and are shown to their carriages, the King takes his seat with Mme de Montespan at his side, MONSIEUR, Madame de Thianges [1] and the good d'Heudicourt on the back seat. You know how these *calèches* are made; they do not sit facing each other, but all look the same way. The Queen rides in another with the Princesses, followed by a crowd manœuvring for places as best they can. Later on the guests are rowed in gondolas on the canal to the strains of music, returning about ten, when a play is staged, and at the stroke of midnight *media-noche* is served; thus Saturday draws to its close . . .

Pray tell the Archbishop [2] what the President [3] says on the subject of my health. I showed my hands and knees to Langeron [4] in order that he should report to you. I am using a kind of ointment which I am told will cure me, this will absolve me from the horrid necessity of bathing in bullock's blood, at any rate until after the dog days. It is you, and you alone, my daughter, who can cure me of all my ills . . .

TO THE SAME

Livry, 26 August [*1676*].

. . . Your letter has come just at the right moment for me to affix my signature to this one. What a charming prospect you

[1] Sister of Mme de Montespan (*see* f.n. p. 157) who, with the Abbesse of Fontevrault and the Duc de Vivonne, was the subject of Voltaire's, "*Ces quatre personnes plaisaient universellement par un tour singulier de conversation, mêlé de plaisanterie, de naïveté et de finesse, qu'on appelait 'l'esprit de Montemart'.*"

[2] Abp. of Arles, M. de G.'s uncle.

[3] Guillaume de Lamoignon, First P. of the Parlement of Paris.

[4] Lt.-General of the Fleet, under orders to leave for Toulon.

hold out to me in order to mitigate the horrors of separation, nothing could better contribute to my well-being. Your very first step must be to arrive, when you will find the picture you conjure up quite erroneous, and doubtless these hands and knees which fill you with pity will by then be whole again. I am as strong as a horse, and my present fragile appearance would, in anyone else, pass as rude health.

As for Vichy I expect to return there this summer. Vesou [1] wishes I were going there to-morrow; de Lorme [2] says not at this season of the year; Bourdelot [3] thinks it would kill me since I am a living furnace, and says my illness was brought on by excessive heat! I love nothing better than consulting these men in order to deride them; what more absurd than these contradictions! The Jesuits are right when they say the purpose of certain serious writers is to back all the "probable opinions" which are going round; wherefore am I not at liberty to follow my own judgement? At the moment I am under the orders of my handsome doctor from Chelles. I assure you he knows as much as any of them or more . . . Anyway, he has been successful, no need to be bled, and I strictly observe what he prescribes, after which I shall revert to that other good fellow's powder . . .

Now, dear daughter, are you reassured about me? After raising my hopes so high, pray apply yourself as soon as possible to the task of converting them into realities . . .

To The Same

Livry, Wednesday 2 September [*1676*].

M. d'Hacqueville and Mme de Vins have just spent the night here; they came, most obligingly, to see us. Mme de Coulanges is also here; she is always excellent company, and you know how well we agree . . .

[1] Famous doctor who tended the Marquise de la Trousse and the Dsse de Sully.

[2] Doctor who recommended Mme de S. to visit Bourbon.

[3] Pierre Michou, known as l'Abbé B. (1610–85), doctor to Condé and Queen Cristina of Sweden, whose verses Mme de S. did not care for.

We have all enjoyed the undisguised satisfaction of the King who, despite the strictest admonitions to Schomberg [1] at all costs to relieve Maestrich, has just learnt that the siege was raised as soon as the French made an appearance. The enemy refused to fight: the Prince of Orange [2] would have held out, but Villa-Hermosa [3] would not expose his troops; the consequence being that the siege was raised and a great quantity of booty fell into our hands. It is a great advantage to treat with confederates when wanting to obtain concessions, but best of all is to be in aggreement with the King—thus only can one be sure of meeting with approval . . .

M. de Louvois hastened to carry the good tidings to His Majesty who, transported with joy, embraced him and endowed him then and there with an abbey worth twelve thousand pounds a year, and a pension of twenty thousand for his brother, also the governorship of Aire [4] with a thousand compliments and congratulations which are worth all the rest put together . . .

I am still taking the good fellow's powders, which alarms everyone but myself; indeed they act like a charm. My pretty apothecary (Amonio) stayed by me during the operation which was a great consolation; he spoke in Italian, and entertained me greatly with his stories. His advice first is to plunge my hands into the juice of the vine, then down a bullock's throat, and should neither prove successful to apply the marrow of a deer or wash in the Queen of Hungary's water. I am resolved in any case not to wait for the winter to set in, but to be cured whilst the weather is still favourable. My health, I consider, belongs to you in a special manner, and if only for this reason I give it every attention which lies in my power.

[1] Armand-Fréderic, German in origin and a Protestant (1615–90), he offered his sword in the service of Louis XIV. Marshal of France in 1675. Accompanied Wm. of Orange to England and was killed at the Battle of the Boyne.

[2] William III (1650–1702). Stadhouder of Holland 1672. King of England 1689. The siege had been raised on 27 August.

[3] Governor of the Spanish Netherlands, in command of the forces.

[4] Aire-sur-la-Lys, 20 miles from St. Omer, fortified town taken 31 July.

To The Same

Livry, Friday 11 September [1676].

. . . Here everyone believes that Quanto's lucky star is on the wane. Tears are shed, natural regrets are expressed, there are sulks, there is laughter, and so, my dear, all good things come to an end. People watch, observe, are on the look out for all sorts of possible and impossible things, and the faces of those whom a month ago they considered beneath their notice are now to be seen wreathed in smiles of self-satisfaction. Card playing continues at a merry pace, while the Beauty herself does not leave her room. Some shake in their shoes, others welcome a change of scene at all costs. There is an upheaval in the affairs of men which, say the soothsayers, is seriously disquieting.

The little Rochefort [1] is being married to her cousin de Nangis. She is twelve years old, and if she should shortly bear a female child Madame la Chancelière de Séguier will be able to say: "My daughter, tell your daughter that her daughter's daughter is crying." Madame de Rochefort [2] has hidden herself away in a convent during the wedding ceremonies, and appears inconsolable.

To The Same

Livry, Wednesday 16 September [1676].

How foolish you are to trouble your head about the good man's powders; they have done wonders for me, and four hours after taking them I forget I have done so. This horrific drug, which spreads alarm in others, when I take it is quite innocuous; indeed in Brittany we became such fast friends that we were always

[1] Great granddaughter of Chancelière Séguier, and daughter of the late Marshal (*see* p. 128). The Marquis de N. was her cousin.

[2] Madeleine de Laval Bois-Dauphin, Marquise de R., Lady of the Bedchamber to the Queen, who had eaten no meat since her husband's death.

offering each other fresh marks of esteem . . . gratitude being the basis of this agreeable intercourse. Do not fret yourself over my sojourn at Livry, I live in the lap of comfort and according to my own whims and fancies ; I walk, I read, I have few duties, and although I am no idler I am very sensible of the *far niente* of the Italians . . . I guard against the evening chill and leave Mme de Coulanges to her own devices ; and Corbinelli, who is far more delicate than I, gladly entertains me. Seigneur Amonio prescribes one pill, held in high esteem, to be taken each morning. Swallowed down with a cup of betony soup it clears the brain in a most salutary manner, and is just what I am in need of. After a week of this treatment I am to resort once again to the vineyard. From all this you will conclude that my health is my one preoccupation which, in my case, can be called gilding the lily. So pray do not worry about me, but apply yourself exclusively to the one real and essential remedy which lies in your hands, the bestowal of your beloved presence.

Everyone at Les Rochers and Vitré is dying either of dysentery or the purples at the present moment. Two of my workmen have succumbed lately, and I tremble for Pilois ; millers, farmers, even the " divine " Plessis, have been seized by these cruel disorders. As you stand so high you will I hope escape the unwholesome miasmas rising from your swamps. But you err in thinking this an unhealthy place . . .

How I detest all doctors, and what vain boast is theirs ! I have not yet seen *Le Malade Imaginaire*, in which a sick man becomes a slave to his physicians ; everything he takes has to be carefully weighed and measured, he counts sixteen drops in thirteen drachms of water, all would have been lost had it been fourteen. He swallows a pill and has been ordered to pace up and down : suddenly he stops confounded—what to do ? he cannot remember if it is up and down, or round and round. I was much entertained, for do not like follies obtain with everyone of us ? . . .

To The Same

Livry, Monday 21 September [1676].

I assure you, my dearest daughter, I am not asking you to come in October in order to spare you the fatigue of a journey in December, but only because I want you two months earlier. As you know I did not avail myself of the permission you gave me to insist on your early arrival last summer, and I consider you owe me something for exercising so much self-restraint, and you will start, I hope, at the time agreed upon, that is when M. de Grignan leaves for his Assembly. I expect this concession from you in return for my utter devotion . . .

Why do you say you do not wish me to write you such long letters when of all occupations, so long as we are apart, it is the one I most prize? And now you threaten to return them unread! I should hate to be under the necessity of franking them, and they are so full of frivolities that I sometimes have scruples lest you should have to do so. But, if you want to spare me these repinings, come, oh, come and visit me! Come and take the pen out of my hand; come and tyrannize over me and rebuke me for all my misdeeds; the only way to stem these outpourings and restore me to perfect health.

At length Philisbourg is taken [1]—I never thought our enemies had it in them to effect the capture of a town! But when I asked who had taken it I was straightway told the enemy!!! Forgive my untidy writing—I have got the devil of a pen, which my guests make use of to scribble their notes.

To The Same

Paris, Friday 25 September [1676].
From Madame de Coulanges' house.

This is the eleventh day of our poor little friend's illness which seized her on her return from Versailles to Chaville. Mme Le

[1] Duke Charles of Lorraine took the town after ninety days of trench warfare, after its previous capture by the Germans.

Tellier [1] succumbed likewise, and was driven by coach to Paris, where she received the Last Sacraments. Madame de Coulanges' abigail, Beaujeu, is yet another victim: she has ever followed her mistress devotedly, and the same pattern prevails on this occasion; remedies applied in the bed-chamber are applied in the closet, enema in one, enema in the other; blood-letting in one, blood-letting in the other; Heaven help us! Heaven help us!; exclamations, paroxysms, deliriums, all on the basis of share and share alike. One fervently hopes the partnership may shortly be dissolved. Extreme Unction has just been administered to Beaujeu, who is not expected to live through the night. We fear a paroxysm for Mme de Coulanges since that it was which carried off the young woman. What a dreadful illness, to be sure! But, having observed the doctors at their blood-drawing task, and knowing myself to have a defective circulation . . . I will not submit to these gentlemen working their will on my body. Beaujeu they despatched in an off-hand manner, with a thrust of the lancet . . .

To The Same

Paris, Wednesday 30 September [*1676*].

In truth it is Wednesday, not Tuesday as I alleged. I invariably start my letters which are destined as answers to yours well ahead of time, and I also want to tell you about Mme de Coulanges. To-day is the fourteenth day of her illness: the doctors cannot give us absolute reassurance, as she still has fever and is lying in a state of stupor, so that a return of delirium is feared, but as the paroxysms diminish in intensity, it is reasonable to hope all may yet turn in her favour . . .

Poor Amonio is no longer at Chelles—they had to give way to the inspector's decree. "Madame" [2] is outraged at receiving such an affront, and by way of revenge has forbidden all access to the convent, with the result that my sister de Biron, my nieces

[1] Elizabeth Turpin, the Chancellor's wife, aunt of Mme de Coulanges.
[2] The abbess, Marguerite de Cossé Brissac.

de Biron, my sister de Meilleraye, all friends, relations, and neighbours are sent packing. The parlours are locked, abstinence is observed, Matins are said without the *Miserere*, and discipline is tightened up. There are many groans and lamentations. " Alas ! " says the Abbess, " rules have to be observed." " But, Reverend Mother, you were never so strict ! " " I was wrong, I repent : " Amonio can make the boast he has reformed Chelles . . .

Short of some unforeseen set-back, our invalid can be said to be out of the wood . . .

To The Same

Paris, Friday 2 October [*1676*].

. . . Mme de Maintenon visited Mme de Coulanges yesterday, and showed the warmest interest in the poor sufferer, and joy at her recovery. " L'Ami and l'Amie " [1] had spent the whole day in each other's company : and " la femme " having returned to Paris, they dined together. There was no play in public. In short, all is serene, and jealousy a thing of the past. How everything can change in the twinkling of an eye ! " The Grand Lady " [2] returned by river, she is now as much in " la belle's " good books as previously she was in her bad ones. Tempers are softened, and what is true to-day, to-morrow is falsified, and there is no love lost in this part of the world for the virtue of constancy. Pray, dear one, do not model yourself on this instability in as far as your departure is concerned, and remember 2 October is already upon us . . .

[1] The King and Mme de Maintenon.
[2] Mlle d'Heudicourt. [*See* f.n. p. 167].

To The Same

Livry, Wednesday 7 October [1676].

I am anticipating my letter, as they say in Provence, to tell you that I am returning here on Sunday to profit from the last fine days, and to rest and relax. I like it here, and I like solitude, that is if not unduly protracted. I am going to experiment with one or two little treatments for my hands, for love of you, be it said, as I have not much faith in remedies; and it is for that reason alone that I bother to look after myself, being persuaded that nothing I do will lengthen or shorten my days. But I do believe in taking ordinary precautions, and that by so doing I am submitting my will to the dictates of Providence . . .

On Saturday M. and Mme de Pomponne, Madame de Vins, d'Hacqueville and the Abbé de Feucquières [1] came to collect me for an excursion to Conflans.[2] The weather was fine, and we thought the house a hundred times grander than in Richelieu's day. There are six fountains of great beauty which are supplied from the river by an elaborate system of pipes which cannot fail unless the river should run dry. It is charming to think of this natural source to drink from and to bathe in. M. de Pomponne's mood was gay, and we talked and laughed to our heart's content . . .

As for M. de La Rochefoucauld he was like a child, revisiting Verteuil,[3] and all his old haunts where he used to hunt—I will not say where he used to make love, for of that I think he was never capable . . .

[1] François, uncle of the Marquis de F., who wrote *Mémoires sur la Guerre*.

[2] Château on the bank of the river Seine, now belonging to Abp. of Paris, François de Harlay, who had bought it from the Duc de Richelieu.

[3] Château on the Charente, then in possession of Condé's brother-in-law, François, Cte de La Rochefoucauld.

To The Same

Begun at Livry, finished in Paris, Wednesday 14 October [*1676*].

I thank you, dear daughter for being so dutiful and obliging as to say you will start before M. de Grignan does so for the Assembly. Thank and kiss him from me for consenting to let you go. Well I know how your departure will weigh on him and how it will cause him to grieve, but it is for so short a time that he is right not to envy my good fortune: his is so much the greater. Now I adjure you to procure yourself a reliable guide for your journey; I hate to think how bored you will be . . . take a good provision of literature, and in God's name do not allow those muleteers to attempt any short cuts between Grignan and Montélimar: let them follow the main road: they insisted on taking Madame de Coulanges the short way, and, had it not been for du But seizing her litter just in time, she would have been over the precipice. The thought of it makes my hair stand on end! I have several times been unable to close my eyes for thinking they might hazard the same road with you . . .

I predict that instead of going to the Meuse, whence his unlucky star summons him, my son will come home, for he suffers from rheumatics in his thigh which should earn him some extension of leave . . .

You know how I love to get hold of all the scraps with which to amuse you, but so far I have seen no one. One thing I can never tire of telling you and that is the positive superabundance of my love for you.

To The Same

Paris, Friday 16 October [*1676*].

What tiresome children I have got! since they are responsible for my not returning to Livry as I intended doing . . . Had it not been for you and your brother, I should gladly have protracted my stay: I accomplish more there in one day than I do in a fortnight here. I prayed, read a great deal, discoursed of the next world and of the means of grace. The Father Prior is more intelligent than I gave him credit for, despite which I esteem him an honest man. Anyway, here I am back once more in the hurly-burly of life.

Now for your brother. His ill luck sends him to the Meuse, but his good luck has given him an attack of the rheumatics in hip and thigh which cripple him . . . and he asks me to apply for leave. This entails getting into communication with M. de Louvois, somewhat of a nuisance; am I not justified then in complaining of my children and hurling insults at their head?!

M. de la Vallière [1] is no more: he was operated on more than once, and in the end he died. Sister Louise de la Miséricorde besought the King to retain possession of her brother's province, which could be used as a means of discharging his debts, and to make no mention of her nephews. The King retaliated by handing her back her brother's property, adding that had he thought himself worthy to enter the presence of so holy a nun, he would have brought her news of her bereavement in person. Mme de Soubise has returned from Flanders and we have exchanged visits. I thought her very handsome, save for a gap in her front teeth, which produces a somewhat unfortunate effect; her husband is gay and appears in perfect health. I would like to take a bet their guard relaxed his vigilance these last few nights!

The Grand Lady has had it out, once and for all, with Quanto, and has made her understand she would not put up with any more of her tantrums. Anyway for the present all is for the best with Quanto, though who can say what to-morrow may bring? She is in the seventh heaven, having been given four hundred louis to spend on fine habiliments for Villers-Cotterets, where the feast of Saint Hubert is to be celebrated; it is thought however, that the celebration may not take place, and I am one who has always believed it would lead to nothing save extravagance on the part of the ladies.

[1] Jean-François de la Baume-le-Blanc, Governor and Grand Seneschal of the Bourbonnais, brother of Louise de la Vallière, now a Carmelite nun.

To The Same

Livry, Friday 23 October [*1676*].

Here begins Volume II on the "Frater".[1] I sent a carriage for him all the way to Bourget, and I need scarcely add that I met him here myself in my coach and six. By an unusual stroke of luck we arrived simultaneously at the end of the great avenue. We hastened indoors, we embraced, we talked of twenty things at one and the same time, we questioned one another without waiting for an answer; in a word our meeting was as scatter-brained and joyous as our meetings are wont to be. Monsieur is, however, dead lame, he cries out, he flaunts his rheumatics as soon as I am out of earshot; he knows that I know too much, and in my presence he barely murmurs. When I was ill and delirious I imagined the thigh which pained me most was of a blue colour and I was always thinking and talking of it; so now I tell him I will concede him a blue thigh, if he will allow that he is something of a greenhorn. Lo, there rises before us the portrait of a man, a man with a blue thigh and a feather pate! . . . He is spending a few more days here awaiting confirmation from Charleville, either that he is free to take his leave, or else that he must join his regiment . . . I imagine by now M. de Grignan will have left for the Assembly, and if justice were done you would already be on your way . . . If my writing is all over the place, do not let it worry you, just put it down to the fact that my hands are cold. Farewell, dearest, I will now pass the pen to "*Mr. Hobbler*" . . .

To The Same

Paris, Friday 6 November [*1676*].

Here I am at last! I dined with good Bagnols,[2] and found Mme de Coulanges in that gloriously sunny room where you so

[1] Mme de S. frequently refers to her son by this punning sobriquet.
[2] Cousin of Mme du Gué Bagnols, whom he had married in 1672.

often sat, yourself as glorious as the sun. The poor convalescent received me most agreeably: she wants to pen you a line or two of news from the other world, which I doubt not you will be gratified to receive. She described the new "transparents" to me, have you heard tell of these? Imagine a garment made of the most heavenly gold and azure blue brocade, over which transparent black dresses are worn of the finest English point lace, or maybe of velvet chenil traced on a gossamer tissue, like those winter laces you have seen. Such is a "transparent" . . . and such is the present mode. At a ball in celebration of Saint Hubert, people were dressed in this manner with the result that no one could dance and all was over in half an hour . . . The magnificent embroidered jerkins destined for Villers-Cotterets were donned for evening strolls . . . From Chantilly M. le Prince sent word to the ladies that "transparents" would be ten times more beautiful if worn over their bare skin. I doubt it being an improvement . . .

M. de Langlée gave Mme de Montespan the gift of a gown of gold, lined and hemmed with gold and gold appliqué, and over all rolled gold, richly embroidered, superimposed over yet another kind of gold, the most divine material ever conceived, doubtless the handiwork of fairies unseen by mortal eye. The gift was to have been made in the utmost secrecy. Accordingly Mme de Montespan's tailor brought her the robe she had ordered from him and which he had botched together after a fashion, causing outcries as you can imagine. Whereupon, in a trembling voice the tailor said: "Madame, as you are in a hurry would not this other gown I have brought satisfy your requirements?" The garment was displayed to the cries of: "Oh! the exquisite thing! the stuff is from heaven, there is none like it on earth!" The lining is tried on and fits like a glove. At that very moment in walks the King and the tailor murmurs: "This dress was designed especially for you, Madame." Everyone can see in it the hand of an admirer. But whose? The King says: "Why, it must be Langlée!" "Assuredly Langlée," says Mme de Montespan. "He alone is capable of such munificence." Langlée of course —Langlée, Langlée—everyone echoes Langlée. And I, dear daughter, not to be outdone, take up the cry: "It was Langlée".

To The Same

Livry, Wednesday 25 November [1676].

As I stroll up and down the long walk, whom do I perceive but a messenger coming towards me. Who can it be? Why Pommier! [1] this is indeed a delightful surprise.—And when will my daughter be here?—Madame, assuredly she is already on her way.—Ah! Pommier, come that I may hug you! . . . At last I venture to unseal your letter . . . I must draw a veil over the perfect joy it affords me. To-morrow I leave for Paris with my son, there is nothing more to fear on his behalf and I am writing to tell M. de Pomponne we shall be confiding our mail to him. You, dearest, have left in admirable weather, but I confess I greatly dread the frost; a coach shall meet you wherever you wish . . . Time is short and I must curtail all I am doing. I am in excellent health and send you a thousand kisses to which the "Frater" adds his.

To The Same

Paris, Sunday evening 13 December [1676].

What do I not owe you, dearest child, for the fatigue, the tedium, the cold, frost and hoar-frosts, the late vigils, all you have suffered on my behalf? I seem to be going through it with you, step by step. My thoughts have been with you from the beginning, have followed you everywhere, and ofttimes have I reflected that I am unworthy of the supreme effort you are making for me—that is in one respect only—for where love and tenderness are weighed in the balance I shall not be found wanting. Good God, what a pilgrimage, and at what a time of year! You should arrive precisely on the shortest day, and it should follow that you will bring us the sun. I have seen a motto which I think applicable to my case. Round an old decaying tree the

[1] One of M. de Grignan's gentlemen.

following words are inscribed : *Fin che sol ritorni.* What do you think of it ? Now I will speak no more of your travels, nor probe you with questions ; we will draw a veil over your weeks of extreme exertions, and try to start a new train of thought. I shall not go to Melun for fear of upsetting your good night's sleep by talk and distractions ; but I shall expect you at Villeneuve-Saint-Georges for dinner ; you will find a good hot cup of soup awaiting you, and without prejudice to anyone, you will find the person in all the world who loves you best. The Abbé will be sitting in your room, which will be all lit up, and a good fire crackling in the grate. Beloved one, what joy ! what happiness ! Shall I ever again experience one as great or as satisfying ?

N.B. Madame de Grignan arrived in Paris on the 22nd of December 1676, and only returned to Provence in June 1677.

1677

To Madame de Grignan [1]

Paris, Friday 11 June 1677.

I cannot help thinking that if my chest hurt me, and your head hurt you, we should both laugh heartily; but as things are your chest is of great concern to me, and you, on the other hand, worry unduly about my head. I swear for your sake I will give it far more attention than it deserves—if in return, you wrap up your little chest in cotton wool. I am vexed you should have written me at such length from Melun, where complete rest was what you required. Pray consider yourself only, dear one, and do not conjure up horrid nightmares, but always bear in mind the thought of returning to complete your visit to me which, as you say, Providence elected to cut short in such a ruthless manner. You will be better fitted to carry this out if you are well than if you are ailing, and pray remember it is impossible for my head and my heart to be at rest if your health should not improve. What a sad day! What bitter reflections, how mournful a parting! You wept, my dearest dear, which in my case means little enough, (it is temperamental), but with you it is no light matter. The fact that you are in bad health adds immeasurably to my

[1] Mme de G.'s health had gravely deteriorated and her condition preyed on a mind always of an anxious and apprehensive turn. No doubt it was this which caused friction in her relations with her mother, indeed she greatly resented the latter's solicitude. To this must be attributed the serious rift between them during the year 1677 and the two succeeding years.

grief: it seems to me that I could endure your absence, but when I think of your emaciation, your toneless voice, when I see your sunken cheeks, your full and beautiful figure wasting away and well nigh unrecognizable, I know not how to endure my anguish. If you want to help me to the best of your ability you will endeavour to overcome this disorder.

Dearest—you cannot begin to imagine the triumph at Versailles,[1] the bursting pride, the solid establishment! just such another as the Duchesse de Valentinois' [2] . . . I spent an hour in her room; secure in her new position, she was in bed all got up in her finery and furbelows, resting in expectation of *medianoche*. I gave her your kind messages to which she responded with sugary phrases and vapid compliments. Upstairs her sister revels in her reflected glory, and dotes on looking poor little Io [3] up and down, scoffing at the very idea she should dare to complain . . . Farewell my dear one; without you I feel naked and alone. We must think Providence willed it so, otherwise we should be hopelessly bewildered. Maybe God has chosen this way of restoring you to health. Dear Count, I hope so, I pray so; I pray you to do all you can to promote this happy event.

To The Same

Paris, Wednesday 30 June [*1677*].

You tell me you have arrived at Grignan. The way you keep me posted is a token of your affection . . . You are right in thinking I am in need of reassurance, I could scarcely be more so. It is true, and I cannot deny it, that your presence would have been of still greater support, had you not been in such an extraordinary state of mind that I felt constrained to fall in with

[1] Mme de Maintenon's.

[2] Mme de S. thus nicknames Mme de Montespan because Diane de Poitiers so long preserved her powers of seduction.

[3] Marie-Isabelle, Ctsse de L., "La belle de Ludres," Chanoînesse de Poussay: Lady-in-Waiting successively to MADAME (Minette), Queen Marie-Thérèse, and the 2nd Dsse d'Orléans; the King was enamoured of her at one time, later forsaking her for Mme de Montespan.

your determination to leave me at all costs, and to stifle my own wishes as best I could. My anxiety for your health was accounted to me for a crime. When I saw you declining before my eyes I was forbidden to shed a tear lest by so doing I should become your destroyer, your murderer, the instrument of your undoing —I had to remain passive. A more cruel martyrdom was never imposed on anyone, nor one more inexplicable. If you had only consented to acknowledge your weakness instead of imposing this unnatural constraint on yourself; if your affection for me had made you a little more yielding, a little less obstinate in refusing to take the doctors advice to follow a prescribed diet, a little more ready, now and again, to admit that the good air and quiet of Livry might help you; ah, that would indeed have solaced me! Instead of which you trampled on my most tender feelings, and at the last, my child, we had come to a dead end, and no other course was open to us but to part. Maybe God was imposing His will on us, but instead of driving me to despair as you did, may He not have wished us to see the folly of our ways and to allow our hearts to expand in a little natural freedom, without which there can surely be no peace? Now I have had my say once and for all. Let us, however, reflect deeply in order, should it please God to reunite us, that we may not once again fall into such grave errors. That you should have welcomed the fatigue of such a journey is proof, if proof were needed, how greatly you desired to cast off all restraint. Remarkable persons no doubt require remarkable remedies; no doctor would have conceived such a one as that! . . . May it and the air of Grignan long continue to be beneficial. I had to pour all this out to you just this once, and in addition to say that never again must we expose ourselves to hearing such an abominable suggestion and made with unctuous satisfaction, that you and I would be better apart! To entertain so cruel a thought, even for a moment, requires a fortitude I can but admire.

To The Same

Livry, Wednesday evening 21 July [*1677*].

"Love, love Pauline".[1] I entreat you to love her, yes to love Pauline; cannot you allow yourself this innocent joy? Do not impose upon yourself the cruel martyrdom of separation. Later on, when you judge the time has come, she can always spend a few years at the convent. Cannot you sample that wonderful thing, maternal love? Surely it will taste good, be well seasoned, when the choice is from the heart and when it concerns such an amiable little creature? I am thinking of her and can see her from here and her resemblance to you despite the plebeian streak; the square nose is hard to explain, but no doubt it will fine down and I can answer for it Pauline will be a beauty . . . My son's heel pains him so greatly he thinks of going to Bourbon when I go to Vichy. Do not trouble your head over this journey, and since it is God's will I should be deprived of your goodwill towards me, I must submit; it is indeed a bitter pill, but we must bow to the inevitable. Possibly I should be happy enough, if your friendship were as in the past; it is most precious to me, even when stripped of your bodily presence, and of all the charm and pleasure of your society . . .

To The Same

Livry, Friday 23 July [*1677*].

The Baron is here,[2] and so engrossed is he in our studies that I am scarcely allowed to put foot to the ground. Needless to say conversation holds the first place. We are reading *Don*

[1] Her daughter, Françoise-Pauline, born in 1674, and married in 1695 to Louis, Marquis de Simiane. She was the first copyist and editor of her grandmothers letters and was responsible for destroying those of her mother.

[2] Charles de S. who had recently bought M. de la Fare's sub-lieutenancy in the Gendarmes-Dauphin, in which regiment he was an Ensign.

Quixote, Lucian,[1] *Les petites Lettres.*[2] How I wish you could see how well he acquits himself of the task; read out by him, the letters take on a really divine quality both in the serious parts and the satiric. To me they are eternally new, and I am sure you would share our enjoyment, and opinion of the indestructibility of their matter. The while he reads I embroider, and, as the garden is at our door, we are in and out ten times a day . . . On 16 August I leave for Burgundy and Vichy. Do not be troubled about the cure; since God forbids I should enjoy your presence there I must try and console myself with the thought that you are sleeping and eating and relaxing, that you are no longer hag-ridden by imaginary fears, that your pretty face is resuming its charming contour, and that your chest is not any more that of a consumptive. I look for compensation for your absence in the knowledge of these improvements, and if a little hope creeps in I shall welcome it with open arms. M. de Grignan is with you, I fancy, give him my compliments . . . and tell him I recommend Pauline to his good offices, that he may protect her from your philosophy. Do not deprive yourselves of this exquisite plaything. Alas! It is not often we can boast of a choice of amusements. Surely we must not be so cruel as to deprive ourselves of an innocent one within our reach. So once more I sing the refrain: *Aimez, aimez Pauline, aimez sa grâce extrême* [3] . . .

To The Same

Paris, Wednesday morning, 11 August [*1677*].

. . . Dearest, I have received your letter of the 4th—quite a long one. Please allow us to love and admire your letters; your style resembles the stately flow of a great river, and it causes us to condemn all other styles. You are no judge for you do not read them, whereas we read and reread again and again, and we

[1] Mme de S. was re-reading Lucian and had written to her daughter, "Who that has read him can read any other author?"

[2] The *Lettres Provinciales* of Pascal.

[3] Parody from the opera *Thésée* II, 1, by Lully, 1675.

Statue of Madame de Sévigné "as Sainte-Vierge" at Saulieu

In August, 1677, after spending a happy week at Epoisses, talking, laughing, and entertaining friends, Mme de Sévigné was accompanied by her hospitable cousin, the Cte de Guitaud, as far as Saulieu on her journey, via Chaseu, to Vichy. There she was reported, by her host in a letter to Mme de Grignan, to have drunk so much wine that her projected cure was a work of supererogation. She seems to have repented of her frivolity and, in order to make reparation, sat for a statue of the Blessed Virgin, which she presented to the XIIth Basilica of St Andoche, where it can still be seen.

(*Photo : Combier, Mâcon*)

pride ourselves on being good judges; by "we" I mean Corbinelli, the Baron and myself. To go back to the end of your letter, I find it insufferable: "Since my departure you can do nothing wrong", say you, "I brought disruption into your life, your health, your household: I only did you harm." What words! How could you have conceived them, and how could I have borne to read them? They serve to underline all the cruel things people said when you left. At the time it seemed to me those people were in league to get rid of me; when I thought you were on my side I could afford to laugh at them, but now you adopt the same tone and identify yourself with them! How can I answer you? I can only repeat your words to me the other day: "When life and the events of life appear irrevocably set in one direction we fain must hope it may not be too protracted." The sooner it ends the better, say I; that is what you have brought me to with your blessed Provence. I shall answer your letter more fully on Friday.

To The Same

Villeneuve-le-Roi, Wednesday evening, 18 August [*1677*].

Well dear one, I hope you are satisfied at last, for I am well on the way.[1] I left Monday when the air was full of rumours, and I was longing to know if we had given battle . . . Accordingly I besought M. de Coulanges to let me have word at Melun, where I intended lying, what he gathered from Madame de Louvois:[2] and sure enough a messenger arrived, bearing the news that the siege of Charleroi was raised, that he had seen Louvois' message, and I could proceed calmly on my journey; such a rest to be able to dismiss the war from one's mind! What think you of the Prince of Orange so graciously facilitating the success of my cure? . . . To return to my journey: I am following closely on

[1] To Vichy for a cure.

[2] Anna de Souvré, Marquise de Courtenvaux, Marquise de L., wife of the War Minister. She gave sumptuous repasts at the Château de Meudon.

your footsteps. My heart was rather full at Villeneuve-Saint-Georges, for it was there we wept in each other's arms . . . I have travelled continuously in good weather, through lovely country and on the finest roads. When you passed through here it was winter, now it is high summer and the most charmingly temperate summer you can imagine . . . The good Abbé surrounds me with attentions, he sets out to spoil me with loving care, for which I consider you owe him much gratitude since he says it is done entirely to please you. I said I would tell you . . .

Speaking of La B.[1] she has been guilty of the greatest cruelty, nay barbarity to her mother when she died. In her own interest she should at least have made a display of grief. Her behaviour was inhuman, a public scandal, and she stood talking and cleaning her teeth at the very moment her mother gave up the ghost . . . I am sending you these reflections from Villeneuve-le-Roi which I should never have time for, were I not most peacefully reclining in my own carriage . . .

To The Same

Epoisse, Saturday 21 August [*1677*].

We arrived here yesterday at two of the morning. A thousand times we thought to be hurled into a ravine, which we could easily have avoided had we had even a small candle to light us on our way, but neither earth nor sky was visible. We summoned assistance, however, and arrived at the château just as its master (M. de Guitaud) was getting into bed . . . I had been awake since three, and was grateful to lie in this lovely house where we regretted the absence of our hostess. You know our host, and his charm and welcome to those he likes ; he assures me I can account myself one of them, I believe him because of his good-will towards you ; and he is so grateful to me for bringing you into the world that he cannot spoil me enough. We converse

[1] Elizabeth-Angélique du Plessis-Guénégaud, Ctsse de Boufflers, sister-in-law of the Marshal, and daughter of Mme du Plessis.

endlessly; he loves talking, and once started I think I can hold my own; we get on swimmingly. If your ears burn do not imagine you are on fire; we shall be talking of you, going at it, hammer and tongs . . . I have already been complaining of my bill of eight thousand francs for repairs, and because my wheat was disposed of three days before being fully ripe; this indecent haste will have cost me more than two thousand francs.[1] But who cares! It is just another triumph carried off by Providence over a poor creature; when I am not to blame I can easily console myself . . .

To The Same

Vichy, Monday 6 September [*1677*].

Dear Daughter—do not be vexed with me, it is six o'clock of the evening and I am writing to you far from the waters and the steam, just to give myself the satisfaction of a word with you, having broken off all other modes of intercourse. Do not you agree that we are both too near and too far from one another, which is scarcely a very satisfactory distance? I spend my days with MM. de Termes [2] and Flamarens,[3] they both enjoy poor health and I am their one source of happiness. They have brought with them an artist from the Opera who plays the violin better than Baptiste, it affords us much distraction. And there is an impertinent little hunchback who sings day and night and thinks herself divine: she makes us laugh . . . How are you my love? how is that painful leg-ache? and can it really be a favourable sign? You must have had an infection and not merely overheated blood. If you love, if you truly love me, try and put on a little flesh. How thin you must be, if even M. de Grignan is apprehensive.

[1] Mme de S. had property in the neighbourhood which would devolve on her daughter.

[2] Roger de Pardaillan de Gondrin, Marquis de T., a redoubtable, handsome figure (*see Saint-Simon*); compromised by the "poisonings" scandal.

[3] Jean, Chevalier de F., brother of François-Agésilan, Comte de Grossoles.

Tuesday evening.

I do wish you were here to see the effect produced by the presence of de Termes and Flamarens on the hairdressing modes of the local beauties. From six o'clock of the morning everyone and everything is up in the air, headdresses erect, powdered and frizzed, bonnets wagging, rouge and patches applied, wigs half-way down the back, fans waving, long tight petticoats adjusted: you would die of laughing, and yet the poor dears are forced to drink the waters which they shortly regurgitate from the mouth as well as from elsewhere.

To The Same

From Langlar, M. l'Abbé Bayard's house, Friday 24 September [*1677*].

. . . The end of your letter is charming—come then, come quickly my loved one, and with no scruple to weigh you down or black dog on your chest, since the Bishop [1] has pronounced, *ex cathedra*, that your journey is necessary in the interests of your family.

I am awaiting news from d'Hacqueville about the Hôtel de Carnavalet [2] but to obtain residence is hedged round with such difficulties that should we succeed we shall owe it to Madame de

[1] Archbishop.

[2] In the " *Rue Culture Sainte-Catherine, à l'angle de la Rue des Francs-Bourgeois au Marais* ", in the Quartier Place Royale she always kept close to, now the Rue de Sévigné. It was built in the 16th century by Pierre Lescot, later enlarged by Mansard and others, and acquired by the Ville de Paris in 1866 and thereafter a public Museum. It derived its name from the family of Kernevenoy. It had just been vacated by Mme de Lillebonne, and secured for Mme de S. after much haggling on the part of d'H. and adroitness on that of Mme de Coulanges. It contained ample room for herself and her guests, divided off into several floors with a *petite aile très jolie* for the Bienbon, ample stabling and a good garden. The de Grignans contributed a share of the furniture and provided their own maintenance. Mme de S., staying with the Coulanges in the Place Royale, daily superintended the *déménagement* and received her visitors seated on the pole of her carriage in the courtyard.

Coulanges' cleverness in overcoming them. You ask permission to bring your son. Heavens, dear child, of all things it is what I should most welcome! I know he will be happy with us, and who do you think rejoices most at the project? The Bienbon! He had sworn he would not die satisfied unless he saw the little fellow once again. Since I must return to the subject, we left Vichy to-day. The good Abbé loves and revels in the beauty of this terrace, and I judged M. de Termes worthy to be one of our party because of his enthusiasm at the extraordinary magnificence of the scene. The waters did wonders for me, but this time I could not face the douches, and was afraid they would bring on a feverish attack. It is a remedy which must be treated with great respect. Farewell, most amiable and lovely one.

To The Same

Gien, Friday 1 October [*1677*].

. . . To-day we all crossed the Loire at Châtillon; the weather was admirable, and we rejoiced at seeing the ferry boat recross the river to fetch our second coach. Whilst on board we discussed the merits of the Autry [1] road: we were warned we should come on two highly dangerous escarpments with rocks, woods, precipices, and we who have had many hairbreadth escapes since leaving Moulins, did not fancy the account of what might be ahead of us. So we agreed to re-embark, which we did, laughing heartily at our discomfiture, and we returned in high good humour to Gien, and to-morrow have agreed to separate, each going on his way.

Yesterday evening we arrived at Cosne,[2] a regular inferno, where we discovered the forges of Vulcan. Eight or ten Cyclopes were forging, not arms for Aeneas, but ships' anchors: you have

[1] Property belonging to the Comte de Sanzei, Mme de S.'s cousin, who had been killed at the Siege of Trèves in 1675. His son followed the same profession.

[2] Of Roman origin, in Nivernais, near Le Creusot, on the right bank of the Loire; famous for its iron-works since the Middle Ages.

never seen such accurate hammer-blows, nor heard so rhythmic a cadence. We found ourselves in the midst of four great blast furnaces, and from time to time the fiends who were working there surrounded us, dripping with sweat, wild eyed and with pallid faces covered with long black hair; they would have struck terror in stouter hearts than ours. For myself I could not possibly have resisted any demands these gentlemen might make on us. At length we were enabled to effect our escape by showering four-sou pieces on them which happily distracted their attention . . .

The previous day at Nevers we witnessed the most hazardous race imaginable: four beauties riding in their carriage saw us passing them in our coach, and were so set on renewing our acquaintance that they were determined to overtake us on a road built to hold one vehicle only. My dear, their coachman was rash enough to pass us, missing us by a hair's breadth, and only just avoided toppling them into the river; we cried out for mercy, they continued passing and repassing amid gales of laughter, and in so terrifying a manner that we are still shaken by the experience . . .

To The Same

Paris, Thursday 7 October [*1677*].

. . . You do work on my feelings over that little darling thing, Pauline de Grignan![1] I am sure she is as lovely as an angel and I should be mad about her. I am afraid, as you say yourself, she will lose all her pretty manners and ways before I see her: such a pity! your good Daughters of Sainte-Marie will ruin her; from the day she enters you can bid farewell to all her charms. Could not you bring her with you? Alas! we have only one life to live in this world, why deprive ourselves of these simple joys? I know too well what your answer will be and must not spoil my letter by dwelling on the subject; anyhow there would be plenty of room for the sweet child as we have secured the Hôtel

[1] Mme de G. wished to place her in a convent, to which her grandmother was opposed.

de Carnavalet which is most satisfactory. It will hold us all, we shall be in good air ; as one cannot have everything we must do without parquet floors or modern chimney pieces, but we shall have a spacious courtyard, a fine garden, we shall be in a good quarter of the city, we shall be together : and, best of all, dear child, you love me. Would I could dispel all her anxiety regarding my health from the mind of my best loved treasure ! Question my entourage—they will tell you I am still beautiful ; no more douches are required, nature is the best guide, last year she was in favour of them, this year she is not, and I am careful to obey her to the letter. As for the drinking waters and since I owe the journey to your insistence, I am more than grateful, for they have suited me down to the ground. You spoil me by expressing all sorts of tender wishes that we should travel, read, and talk together : would to God that one day, just by some lucky chance, you were able to prove the depth and sincerity of your words ! Someone was observing the other day that you seemed unable to put the very real affection you have for me to good account, and that, even where my relations with you are concerned, you sadly underrate me. What foolish words ! I only aspire to satisfy your taste as I know I do your heart, if it is possible thus to discriminate. Seriously, my very dearest, to finish this harangue once and for all, let me say that your affection is of greater moment to me than that of the rest of the world put together. This, I know, you will readily believe.

To The Same

Paris, Friday 15 October [*1677*].

. . . I returned here to see the good Abbé, who has been bled and is suffering from a heavy cold ; I feel I should not leave him for a moment . . . We are at sixes and sevens trying to get into the house ; I have been camping in my room, but now I am in the Bienbon's, with nothing but a table to write to you on ; this, however, suffices me : I think we shall be very happy in our Carnavalette . . .

I shall await you here in the expectation that I shall be able to do you all sorts of good turns, be it on a small scale, which I shall much enjoy since you said the other day we could best show our love by the rendering of small services . . .—

So you go for walks by moonlight? That is a sure proof you are well, or it would be forbidden . . . I embrace MM. de Grignan and de La Garde, and I beg they will allow you to come before the roads become impassable. It seems to me there is already an autumnal chill in the air as the calendar puts it . . . Farewell dearest, farewell all my very dear Grignans, I love and honour you all, love me just a little in return. They are removing my desk, my paper, my table, my chair. Go ahead then, do your worst, I can always stand upright!

The young *Mademoiselle* [1] is suffering from intermittent fever which annoys her as it upsets all her winter gaieties: she went the other day to the Rue Bouloi to ask the Carmelites for a remedy, having no one else to advise her. She was given a draught which caused her to vomit excessively: this made a considerable stir; the princess would not reveal who had dispensed the draught but it soon came to light. It was the Carmelites. The King turned to *Monsieur* with the utmost gravity: "So it was the Carmelites", he said, "I always knew they were intriguers, rogues, darners, embroiderers, flower girls; but I did not know they were poisoners." The earth shook at this pronouncement; the pious took up arms, but the Queen was quite unmoved. People tried to tone it down, but what is said is said, what is thought is thought, what is believed is believed. This is a fundamental truth.

The Bienbon embraces you . . . My writing is horrible, but then my pen is demented, it squeaks and makes blots: there—I have flung it in the wastepaper-basket.

[1] Marie-Louise d'Orléans, daughter of *Monsieur* and Minette, who in 1679 became Queen of Spain by marrying Charles II. She died ten years later without issue. (*See* p. 319.)

To The Same

Paris, Wednesday 20 October [1677].

The Chevalier does not know what he is talking about! I ate no fruit at Vichy for the simple reason that there was none to eat; I dined and supped frugally, and when silly folk tried to make me sup on the top of my dinner I laughed at them and waited till eight, when I partook of a wing of partridge or maybe a quail, nothing more. It is true I walked, but if I may not enjoy the fresh air when it is fine, it were better for me if fine weather were taboo altogether. I am always indoors by nightfall, it is a calumny to say I am not . . . What then are these tales M. le Chevalier serves up to you? Pray, Sir, does your arm still make you lame? You will hate to have to use a stick all the winter. And you, dear Countess, I have in truth nothing to reproach you with? Vardes tells me you are sadly undernourished, and to make up for deficiencies you eat wholly unsuitable things. This is what he tells me adding that La Garde is vexed, but no one dares say a word . . .

Let us now discourse for a brief moment on the subject of the Hôtel de Carnavalet. I shall be there before long, but we find ourselves so well off with M. and Mme de Coulanges and they manifest their pleasure so unreservedly at having us that we arrange our new quarters at our leisure, furnish your apartments as we please, and in this way save ourselves all the fatigue and upheaval of moving in. One fine day we shall find ourselves sleeping there quite peacefully, as if we had lived in the house for three months or more. Do not bring any hangings, for you will find everything you require; it is a great source of entertainment to me to contrive that you should be spared, anyhow on arrival, the smallest vexation or annoyance. The Abbé's cold has shaken me badly. I apprehended fever and congestion of the lungs; thank heaven he is better! . . .

Goodnight, lovely one, lovely and greatly loved.

To The Same

Paris, Wednesday 27 October [*1677*].

I am resolved, dear one, to ask you no more questions. In one word you tell me the horses require fattening, that your tooth is hanging by a thread, and the professor is scrofulous! What spectres lurk in these three answers, especially in the second! It would, I take it, be superfluous to ask you if your watch keeps good time, for you would be certain to tell me it was out of order. Pauline's answers are much more to the point, nothing is more diverting than to hear the little reprobate affirm that one day she will be as great a rascal as anyone could wish.

Ah! How I miss that sweet child! But methinks you will soon be consoling me, that is if you follow my injunctions to the letter. If you start next week you will receive no more letters at Grignan. M. de Coulanges left for Lyons to-day in the stage-coach, you should find him there! He will tell you how agreeably we are accommodated in our new house. There can be no question as to the best arrangement, which is that you and I should be on the top floor, M. de Grignan and his daughters downstairs: all is thus perfectly planned.

I entreat all your Grignans, who are so concerned about your health, not to allow you to be flung into the Rhône as a result of your foolhardiness in positively courting danger. I beg of them to give way to their fears and to accompany you: you say you will not allow it! God keep you, I shall have no peace till I hear you have reached Lyons. Dear, how happy it will make me to set my dish of boiled fowl before you, your place at my table is kept warm. The diet your Grignans prescribe is literally made for my ordinaries, and it is understood with Guisoni [1] that no stews or hashes will be served. Come, come my dearest dear, no one can forbid me to receive you with open arms and with infinite tenderness. If only from that angle the banquets I shall prepare for you will be sumptuous indeed . . .[2]

[1] Her doctor.

[2] This letter of 27 October is the last one Mme de S. was to write her daughter in 1677 before the latter's arrival in Paris. She remained a year and ten months, returning to Provence in September 1679.

To The Comte de Bussy

Livry, 3 November [*1677*].

I came here to enjoy the last of the fine weather and to bid a tender farewell to the leaves; they are still on the trees, but are beginning to turn. Fading from green to the rose of early dawn, they have taken on the colours of all the dawns, assuming a magnificent mantle of gold brocade which we admire even more, if only by way of a change. I am settled in to the Hôtel de Carnavalet. It is a fine great house, and I hope to live there many a long year, for moving house has worn me out. I await the beautiful Countess who appreciates your loyalty to her. You speak of Racine and Despréaux.[1] A few days since the King addressed them thus: "I regret you were absent from our last campaign. You would have seen how battles are fought, and you had not far to go." Racine answered: "Sire—we are mere civilians, and have only civilian dress, we ordered our uniforms, but the battle was over before these were ready." This answer appeared to satisfy the King. If I were His Majesty, I would have chosen someone with the proper qualifications, and not given these civilians my history to write! . . .

The good Abbé and I often speak of you, of the excellent table you keep and of the lovely situation of Chaseu,[2] and think it is much to be deplored that we should find ourselves for ever and a day, and to all intents and purposes, debarred from these.

[1] Nicolas Boileau (1636–1711) author of *Le Lutrin* and *Art Poétique*: conjointly with Racine, he had just been appointed historiographer royal, and accompanied Louis XIV on several campaigns.

[2] Bussy's estate in Burgundy, to which he was exiled from Court. Mme de S. had spent a day there in August.

To The Same

Paris, 8 December [*1677*].

La belle Madelonne is here, but as all happiness pure and unalloyed is forbidden us on this earth, mine is greatly marred by the sadness I feel on her account. Picture to yourself, dear cousin, this exquisite little creature you have always so greatly admired, worn to a thread and so frail and delicate looking you would scarcely know her, indeed the deterioration in her health causes me the gravest concern. In restoring my dear daughter to me, God must have willed that I should suffer this heavy trial. This gives much food for reflection . . . You will scarcely credit me when I say that, for once, I have no news. To the great honour and glory of Maréchal de Créquy, Fribourg has fallen,[1] and the *Gazette de Hollande* is constrained to acknowledge that the King's strategy has been beyond praise: in addition to the capture of three large towns, a battle has been won, and what say you to that of Fribourg as a valediction to the departing Germans! Admiration cannot be withheld at such an unusually happy train of circumstances. Farewell, dear cousin, if we continue to love one another, we can scarcely improve on a state of affairs so agreeable to both sides . . .

[1] Fribourg-en-Brisgau was taken by assault after five days of fighting.

1678

To The Comte de Bussy

Paris, 18 March [*1678*].

What say you to the capture of Gand ? [1] It is a long time, dear cousin, since a King of France has made an appearance there. Our King is truly admirable, and deserves better of his country than to have his history written by a couple of poetasters ; you know as well as I do to whom I refer [2] . . . He does not require fiction or verse to acclaim him, but a pure and lucid prose in the hands of a man of quality, a soldier of distinction such as I have in mind . . . Meanwhile these historian-poets follow the court as best they may, on foot, on horseback, up to their eyes in mud and sleeping by the light of the moon, Endymion's beautiful mistress . . . Dumbfounded by all they see they pay their court by manifesting surprise at the strength and number of the legions and at their endurance in the face of fatigue . . . I fancy our two gentlemen have had quite enough of it : I do not know what has led me to discourse on such trifling matters, which, no doubt, should be beneath our notice. My pen runs away with me, I fear.

Let us speak of Mme de Seignelai,[3] who died yesterday morning, pregnant of a boy. It is daring of fate to have ventured to

[1] Ghent itself was captured on 9 March, and the Château six days later. Mme de S. makes a pun on the name, referring to it as the Spanish " glove ".

[2] *See* previous letter of 3.11.77.

[3] Marie-Marguerite d'Alègre, first wife of Jean-Baptiste Colbert, Marquis de S., Minister of State for the Navy.

upset M. de Colbert. He and his family are quite inconsolable. What a good subject for meditation! Here is a great heiress, coveted by all and wooed with much pomp and circumstance, who dies, prematurely, at the early age of eighteen. The *Princesse de Clèves* [1] scarcely lived any longer, but will not be so easily forgotten. This little book, a present from Barbin, is one of the most charming things I have read in a long while . . .

To The Comte de Grignan

Friday 27 May [*1678*].

I want to inform you of a two hour conference recently held by us with the celebrated physician, M. Fagon.[2] M. de La Garde sponsored and brought him here—we had never set eyes on him. He is a mine of learning and out of the common run of doctors whose one delight, I always think, is to fill us with drugs; he believes exclusively in a nourishing diet. He is much struck with my daughter's weakness and emaciation, and would like her to drink milk as the most valuable nutriment, but she is so averse from this that he dares not so much as suggest it; she takes light refreshing infusions and sponge baths, and he is careful not to cross her in any way, but when she says she is not thin and that people tend to alternate between the two extremes, he rebukes her and tells her that in her case loss of weight is due to the condition of her lungs which are dried up and show signs of beginning to wither, and if this should continue she is not long for this life. It is imperative she should put on flesh or die, there is no middle course; her languors, lassitude, loss of voice, prove that it is, in truth, her lungs which are affected. He orders rest, absence of worry, a gentle routine, and above all no writing. He hopes she may improve, otherwise there will be a gradual but steady decline. M. de La Garde was present, you can send him

[1] Mme de La Fayette's anonymous masterpiece had just been published in 4 vols.: *Zayde* had appeared in 1670, under the name of J. R. de Segrais, her collaborator.

[2] Became physician to the King in 1693. Superintendent of the *Jardin des Plantes*, where he died in 1718.

my letter if you wish. I asked M. Fagon if a sultry climate might not affect her unfavourably; he affirmed it. I told him I had wanted to keep her here through the hot weather, and only let her start for Aix in the autumn to spend the winter there, that you wanted nothing but what was best for her, but that she was hard to move . . . I do not want you to be able to accuse me of keeping things from you or minimising the parlous state she is in, all the worse for having lasted so long, (already a full year), and which makes any attempt at treatment so much less hopeful . . . Monsieur, you alone are the arbiter of her fate, take what measures you think fit, and settle all the details of her journey, unless so be you will grant her permission to remain here for another three months, with ample liberty to enjoy and profit by her sojourn, and with the calm and serenity of mind necessary to her recovery. I kiss you from my heart.

P.S. I cannot express surprise at your ignorance regarding her state; it seems to please her to say she is perfectly well. Would to God it were true and she were in your keeping. M. l'Abbé and M. de La Garde will bear out the truth of my words . . .

To The Comte de Bussy

Paris, 18 December [*1678*].

Thrice happy mortals! You are as gods indeed who live remote from the fret and fever engendered by the game of basset,[1] you who possess your souls, who live your life according to God's decrees, who spend your exile as if it were part of God's destiny for you: thrice happy are you who do not regret the past, and who turn your backs on the sins of thirty years ago; and if, in addition, you are free from ambition and avarice you are as Gods walking the earth.

But to return to the game of basset—the whole affair is inconceivable. One hundred thousand pistoles are easily lost at a sitting, and I consider that once you overstep the limits imposed by playing for ready cash the game becomes a gamble, and the

[1] A favourite card game at that period, of Venetian origin.

players like children who stake their all in the endeavour to win back what they have lost.[1] The King disapproves of these excesses, *Monsieur* has put his jewellery in pawn. You will have heard that the peace of Spain is ratified, and that of Germany will shortly follow suit.

My lovely Countess is so penetrated with the cold that she begs you to accept her regretful excuses . . . her chest, her pen, her ink, her thoughts, all are frozen ; she hopes you will believe her heart is not . . .

[1] Mme de Montespan lost four million at a sitting, but she insisted on the holders of the bank remaining at the table till she had won it back.

1679

To Madame de Grignan

[Livry], Saturday evening 27 May [1679].

My dearest—you who know how easily impressed I am by phantoms and spectres should have spared me the painful novelty of the last sentences you addressed to me. You speak of my indifference, of my not caring to see you, of my preferring Livry to your society—if this were so I must indeed live in a state of complete self-deception. Although I have found it impossible not to resent their injustice, I have made every effort to forget your reproaches. If you consent to stay in Paris, how gladly shall I hasten to join you there, sooner than remain at Livry. Thinking of all the things you are doing in my absence has helped me and you will have little time in which to miss me. With me it is altogether a different matter, and whereas time, you say, hangs heavy on your hands, I like to see and always to feel I am near you. Time would drag for me also, were I to continue in my present mood. I wish your lungs could inhale the sweet air I have enjoyed to-night! A thunderstorm broke out here last Thursday when we were dying of heat in Paris, which refreshed the air, leaving it divinely cool. Good night, dearest, I await news of you and wish your health were as good as mine. I wish your health belonged to me that I might have the task of restoring it! My horses are at your service whenever and wherever you wish.

To The Same [1]

Paris, Monday 18 September [*1679*].

I have been anxiously awaiting your letter, and longing for news of you: but I can never read without tears what you tell me of the conclusions you have come to, and still more of the remorse you feel on my behalf. Ah! my dear one, what are these words you make use of? Repentance? Forgiveness? I can think of nothing about you which is otherwise than kind and charming; my heart is, in a manner of speaking, created for you, and I am sensitive in the extreme to everything which emanates from you, a soft word, a kind gesture, a regret expressed, a caress, a tender look, disarm me entirely, and then and there am I made whole as by a miracle. My heart is filled anew with tender love which, though it may manifest itself in many different ways according to my mood, can never grow less. I have said all this before a hundred times, and now repeat it again and again, for it is the truth, of which you, I know, would not seek to take advantage. Certain it is, however, that you alone are the cause of the agitating emotions to which my heart is subjected: judge then how deeply moved I am at what you say. Would to God, dearest, I could see you once again at the Carnavalet, not for a short week, not to do penance, but to kiss, to embrace, to persuade you that, without you, no happiness is possible for me, and I would sooner bear all the pain love can inflict than submit to the monotony, however peaceful, of enforced separation. If you were more open to conviction you could not be so unjust: was it not a crime to believe as you did that anyone could wish to tear you out of my heart, and thereupon to hit out and say harsh things to me? How could I guess what was in your mind? You say you had certain facts to go on; no dearest, believe me, it was all a fiction of your brain . . . Do not allow yourself to fall back into such unworthy suspicions . . . How foolish of me to be tempted into a discourse which probably is useless, or worse than useless . . .

Farewell, dearest and kindest. I assure you I am totally unable

[1] Mme de G. had just started out for Grignan, having remained in Paris from early November, 1678, until mid-September, 1679.

to grasp the full implication of your prolonged absence; you have been unfair to me in many ways and will continue to be so until you learn fully to appreciate what you mean to me. Of this you must allow yourself to be convinced and it will follow that I too shall once more be persuaded of your love and goodwill towards me . . .

To The Same

Livry, 11 October [*1679*].

It was with the greatest impatience I was awaiting your letter of the 1st; rains caused the delay. One of the sorrows of absence lies in the darkness with which all things are invested. I had, of course, thought of the worst disasters, and to speak frankly, I am not easy about your health: I do not believe what you tell me, M. de Grignan does not so much as allude to it; poor Montgobert, in whom I place reliance, is ill; your daughters clearly write to your dictation, and I am left to feed on my imaginary fears. The thought of your cold, inert, lifeless legs, of which you make fun, at any rate before me, distresses me greatly; it is scarcely a matter to brush lightly aside, and in your place I should follow Guisoni's advice when he insists on your undertaking this journey. You can take your time, but you should look on the treatment he prescribes as of pressing importance, and not neglect your limbs, deprived, as they appear to be, of any quickening impulse. In your place I should desire to bring them to life, to put warmth into them, and to set them free from the horrible suffering they nightly endure. To be as hampered, as incommoded as you are is really an intolerable burden, dear child, and if I were M. de Grignan I should use my considerable influence and insist on your departure . . . Why will you speak of my health?—health is the right word for me since I am perfectly well, I have told you this twenty times already; you fret about the good state of my health; I, with how much justification, about the bad state of yours. Guizoni would like to bleed me, to suit himself I suppose. The English apothecary [1] considers it deleterious in cases of rheumatics, and if I lose blood through which the surplus fluid is absorbed, I shall lose all the ground I have gained these past four years. Who to believe ? ! I will take the middle course and purge myself at the new moon, and I shall take linseed infusions, nothing further will be required. How much more would it help me to see you well ! This is a long discourse on a subject which is irksome to you ; but the fact remains that your welfare is my sole preoccupation.

To The Same

Paris, Friday 13 October [*1679*].

. . . A kiss for M. de Grignan : I truly marvel at you both for setting such store on my letters ; I am always freshly surprised when you praise them. They pass through my hands so quickly that I scarcely know if they are worth anything or nothing ; such as they are you will be getting more than enough, and so, no doubt shall I of yours, but sad as yours are compared to some earlier ones they are still a very great consolation, and I live for a return to happier times. I seem to have strayed a long way from my subject. A kiss then for M. de Grignan . . . had he loved Madame de Saint-Simon [2] as much as I love you (my excuses to his prowess in the art of love), he would scarcely have been easy at seeing her in the state you find yourself in ; let him think this over, and since I have appointed myself his teacher in these matters I insist he should apply himself to his task. Meanwhile he shall have my first kiss ; and who shall qualify for my second ? Your step-daughters for whom I have a very soft corner ? The little boy who is so near my heart ? "Paulinote," with her many seductions ?—And you, my beautiful one—what shall I say you have not already said yourself many times, namely that my heart, whose wisdom and understanding you are the first to appreciate, is filled with your image, filled to utmost capacity, and to the exclusion of all else.

[1] The Chevalier Talbot was reputed to have introduced quinine into France and was enjoying a considerable vogue. He later attended the Dauphin.

[2] Diane-Henriette de Budos, Dsse de S–S. *See* f.n. p. 44.

To The Same

Paris, Friday 20 October [1679].

What is this I hear? You intend writing me long letters without making mention of your health!? I am afraid, dearest, you are making fun of me, and in order to revenge myself I must tell you that I put the worst interpretation on your silence, and conclude your legs are in a bad state, for had they improved you would have hastened to tell me . . . In future you must be open with me. I have told you all I know about those precious legs of yours, if you do not keep them warm they will never be cured. To think of you sitting, bare-legged, writing for two or three hours each morning! Good God, how disastrous! I shall soon see how much you care for me. For love of you I shall purge myself on Monday; it is quite true I took only one pill last month—I admire your intuition—but I do not require purging, and only do it to satisfy you. How I dread the swamps and fevers which surround you! . . .

Madame de La Fayette and I were talking about you the other day, and we agreed that alone Madame de Rohan and Madame de Soubise could bear comparison with you and me. Where indeed, if one looked all the world over, could a daughter be found living on more amicable terms with her mother?

Madame de La Fayette is nourishing herself on viper soup, and her strength is returning by leaps and bounds, she advocates it for you. The viper's head and tail are severed, after which the viper is cut open and skinned. One hour, nay two hours after this operation, the victim is still wriggling.

I am returning to Livry and shall remain there until All Saints' Day which I shall spend quietly by myself. I shall take no one with me, I long for solitude; I shall read, and try to reflect on the workings of my conscience; the winter stretches out interminably.

Your pigeon [1] is living like a hermit at Les Rochers, wandering in the woods: he acquitted himself outstandingly at the *Etats*.

[1] A pet name between brother and sister; from the Fable by La Fontaine, *Les Deux Pigeons*.

He played with the notion of falling in love with a Mlle. de La Coste,[1] being desirous to bring off a good match; but it fell through. The affair clearly was suffering from a broken rib [2] . . .

Farewell, dearest and best, I must refrain from telling you of my love lest it weary you . . . Mesdemoiselles how are you, and what of the fever? My sweet Marquis, it seems you care less for me than you did, what have you to say to that? Pauline, my Pauline, where are you my pet?

To The Same

Livry, All Saints' Day [1679].

You should have had my letter written from Pomponne, which went by the same packet as one from Madame de Vins, but your storms disorganized everything. What extremes you suffer from in Provence! Everything there is excessive—the heat, the dew, the mist, the north wind, the unseasonable rains, the autumnal thunderstorms; nothing is ordered or temperate; rivers overflow their banks, the harvest is ruined by floods; as often as not the Durance is possessed by the devil . . . When I think what you in your delicate state of health have to contend with, I tremble. Does this unequal struggle against the forces of nature not alarm M. de Grignan? I find it far from reassuring . . .

The other day I saw little Madame de Nesmond [3] who suffers from extreme delicacy of the chest; she has been instantaneously restored by ass's milk taken night and morning, having been well-nigh speechless. Since it repels you I will not ask you to try this, but I feel it a tragedy you should be deprived of such an efficacious remedy.

My son sits sadly at Les Rochers; he says that when they handed him the keys of my writing desk on the first night, he was seized with such melancholy thoughts that he began to weep as the good

[1] *See* f.n. p. 215.
[2] An expression used by Mme de S. for an unsuccessful undertaking.
[3] Marguerite de Beauharnais de Miramion, wife of a famous lawyer.

Abbé is wont to do when he kneels to receive the Blessed Sacrament. He assures me he will never marry the little creature [1] I wrote to you about, but everyone tells me there are no end of silly goings-on between them; and he wants to go to Tonquedec, only two miles from his lodestar. Tongues are wagging in Brittany, and he is much criticised. In vain does he try to persuade me he will do nothing foolish, adding that each day he is a different man from the last, in fact that he is three different men at one and the same time! I tell him that by going to the girl's home he is tempting Providence, that it only requires a second of time for an irrevocable step to be taken, and that one of his many selves will be the dupe, while another will curse and swear. By then, of course, it will be too late . . . Please make all my excuses to M. de Grignan for having belittled his country; since you have been living there I see nothing but spectres raising their heads . . . As ever I commend his dear spouse to his special care.

To The Same

Livry, Thursday 2 November [1679].

. . . Pray carry out your programme, dearest, and take plenty of milk and good gravy soups, . . . be sure that to cure a delicate chest like yours requires, not only care and a suitable diet, but persistence in the good work, and it is plain as the nose on your face that to drink milk for a fortnight, then give it up and say: "it doesn't suit me" is a mockery for all concerned. Surely you realise that, deprived of good health, one is useless, helpless, and all effort but pain and grief: in a word such a life is not worth living . . . I sometimes wish I could write a treatise on human affection, so much depends on it, and so much could be done to spare our loved ones from feeling frustrated. If we could see more deeply into their hearts and minds how far more indulgent should we be! I would demonstrate in my treatise the hundred

[1] "*L'objet s'appelle Mlle de La Coste; elle a plus de trente ans, elle n'a aucun bien, nulle beauté; son père dit lui-même qu'il en est bien fâché et que ce n'est point un parti pour M. de S.*", Mme S. had written elsewhere.

ways in which we could manifest our love without a word being spoken . . . This is not intended to be personal; but what is written is written.

My son utters such foolish sentiments! He says he adores me with one side of him, and would like to strangle me with the other, and that the two sides fought desperately the other day in the Rochers woods! I tell him I wish the one had killed the other, for there is nothing I desire less than to own three children . . . I am so full of regrets at leaving here, the countryside just now is a thing of beauty: the glades, which were decimated by caterpillars, are as green again as in the finest spring, and the hedges, big and small, are adorned with autumnal beauty such as painters rejoice in. The great elms are well nigh bare of leaves, . . . but as they flutter down one does not regret them, for the landscape all around is smiling and gay; I am happy alone with my books, and only sad as I always must be when you are far from me. I scarcely know what I shall do in Paris, nothing draws me, I have no stake there, no inducements, I go there with regret. The good Abbé speaks of business to be transacted. Very good then, I suppose we must resign ourselves to the inevitable, and be off!

To The Same

Paris, Wednesday 22 November [1679].

You will I know be surprised, nay outraged, dearest one, when I tell you M. de Pomponne [1] has been summarily dismissed; he was told on his return from Pomponne on Saturday he would be relieved of his duties. The King has decreed he should receive a sum of seven hundred thousand francs, and the pension of twenty thousand francs he earned as Minister will not be stopped. In doing this His Majesty wishes to demonstrate his appreciation of Pomponne's loyalty. It was M. de Colbert [2] who was deputed to pass on the compliment with many messages of regret at having to do so! M. de Pomponne immediately demanded an audience

[1] *See* pp. 81–2. Minister and Secretary of State.

[2] Comptroller General.

of the King in order to learn what had brought about his cataclysm. When he was informed it would not be granted, and being ignorant of the pretext for his dismissal, he decided to write to the King of his anguish, adding a plea for his family of eight children. He thereupon ordered his coach to be harnessed and arrived in Paris at midnight. M. de Pomponne is not one of those ministers who require to be humbled in order to learn a much needed lesson in charity; in his case success only served to increase his virtues and thought for others, and he was loved as much as he was revered. As I wrote to you, M. de Chaulnes, Lavardin [1] and I had been at Pomponne on the Friday, and had been received by the ladies with great good cheer. We discoursed and played chess all the evening. Meanwhile what a checkmate was being prepared for our host at Saint-Germain, whence he repaired the next morning! . . . I learnt the bad news from the Abbé de Grignan, and you will readily believe it was a dagger through my heart. I rang their bell that same evening, and found them all three together! M. de Pomponne embraced me without being able to utter a word: the ladies were weeping, and I could not hold back my tears, neither would you at such a sorrowful spectacle . . . Poor Madame de Vins,[2] whom I had last seen so expansive, so buoyant, was unrecognisable; a fortnight's fever could not have wrought more havoc. M. de Pomponne was not in good odour at court, but he much appreciated the privileges of his position . . . and to have his niche there gave him a very sensible satisfaction: alas, what an ominous change! What drastic economies to be practised in his household! Think of it! Eight children to bring up and no breathing space allowed him to try and obtain some palliation of his sentence. They are owing, for rent alone, thirty thousand livres; what will be left? They will have to retrench in all directions. It is said he was unreliable and unpunctual in his secretarial duties, and this, no doubt, contributed to his downfall.[3]

[1] In both Perrin editions this name is given as Caumartin.

[2] Sister of Madame de Pomponne, lost everything as a result of Pomponne's downfall.

[3] M. de Pomponne's disgrace, if partly due to his negligence and Jansenist views, was brought about largely by the machinations of Louvois and Colbert; the former wanting to oblige a friend, the latter to obtain Pomponne's ministerial post for his brother, Colbert de Croissy.

Dearest, your little note rejoiced my heart. It assured me of the boy's improvement, also of yours in a marked degree . . . What a charming picture I conjure up of you applying yourself to getting well, resting, gaining strength. You are spoiling me for the first time . . .

To The Same

Paris, Friday 24 November [1679].

What a delightful letter from you! And how much I enjoy hearing you dissert on the many chapters it contains; the one on medicine is enchanting. With your genius for acquiring knowledge you will soon, I hazard, know more than any physician. Your experience may be limited, but you will not, "with impunity",[1] kill off so many patients; and I shall place much more faith in you than in them, when it comes to diagnosis. It is a foregone conclusion that health is what matters most in the world: "And how are you? How goes it?" we say and reiterate airily, without possessing the most rudimentary knowledge of a science which is vital to us. Study, my child, study, follow your course of lectures, you will need no further qualifications than a red gown such as is worn on the stage . . . But why are you bent on sending us your handsome apothecary? I assure you physicians, with the exception of the two or three who sponsor the Englishman's prescriptions, are not in good odour here. He, by the way, has just saved Marshal de Bellefonds' life . . . No—keep your young man in the country.

Mme de Coulanges was at court a whole fortnight: Madame de Maintenon, who was suffering from a heavy cold, would not allow her to leave. She and Mme de Gramont [2] fell out in the following manner: the latter is ruining her complexion with a surfeit of chocolate. Mme de Coulanges tried to stop her, but was snapped at for her pains. Mme de Coulanges thereupon called her ungrateful, upon which the Countess who, any other day,

[1] Quotation from *Le Malade Imaginaire.*

[2] Lady-in-waiting to Marie-Thérèse of Austria. (*See* f.n., p. 115.)

would have laughed at the adjective, took it into her head to stare insolently at her and in such a determined manner that now they cut each other dead. The Abbé Têtu truculently observed: "But Madame, if she had answered—the pot is calling the kettle black—what would you have said?"—"Sir," she replied, "I am not a pot, but she is a poker." More quarrels, more dressing-down, more cutting dead. Quanto and the bescolded Madame de Maintenon are on very bad terms; this last manages always to be in the centre of things (the King,) hence Quanto's rage. I could go on for ever in this vein if only you were here! . . .

Farewell my beautiful one . . . The Bienbon has a cold . . . I shall be bled in Lent for you have convinced me of the necessity. I am sure the little boy will not lose his cough unless he has ass's milk; measles is apt to weaken the lungs, that is why it terrifies me on your account . . . My dearest, I embrace you, body and soul; than which I desire no greater happiness on earth.

To The Same

Paris, Friday 1 December [1679].

Yes, dear daughter, it is true that I am making you a present of that pretty writing-desk, and I was awaiting your approval before despatching it. The Abbé swears that he was aware of my intention and if, when he sent you his account, he put it down as an item on the schedule of your expenses you must, without delay, draw a big line through the entry in question. It shall be named "The desk of my mother",[1] and well-named I consider—on condition, need I say, that you do not turn it into a weapon of self destruction.[2]

I am sorry you regret having told me of your son's indisposition, but how, I ask you, could it be concealed? I should hate to be so secretive and to force myself, when anxious to speak on indifferent matters. I verily believe the pen would drop from my fingers. I can only approve of complete confidence between

[1] An allusion to one of the walks at Les Rochers: *L'Allée de ma mère.*

[2] Mme de G. was ordered to restrict her correspondence for reasons of health.

those who love one another. Such are my tenets, and such "The ways of my mother"; pray let them also be "The ways of my daughter", and do not regret letting me share your sorrows since you allow me to participate in your joys. Is not that the true intercourse between lovers and friends? Surely! I can conceive of no other . . .

When I allow my thoughts to dwell upon life, my life in particular, which is spent in enforced detachment, I pity those as tender-hearted as I . . . Madame de La Fayette is persuaded that she would have fulfilled all the obligations of our old friendship, had she contrived to attach M. de Grignan to the court, whereby you would have been restored to me. She is, however, encouraged —being so near the fountain-head—to hope for an opportunity in the future which, knowing the inconstancy of human action, must surely arise sooner or later . . .

I am off to dine with the Marquise d'Uxelles,[1] who tells me that M. de Pile [2] expresses himself anxious I should come. M. de La Rochefoucauld and Tréville [3] will be there: they go by the nickname of "the little society". Poor Madame de Lavardin is half dead of a cold, she is confined to her bed with Madame de Mouci at her bedside, the Marquise and I in the wings . . . Farewell dearest, and for my sake pray cherish the person whom I love above all others in the world; I have no news to tell you, doubtless the Chevalier will fill the gap with a dozen items, some true, some false.

To The Same

Paris, 6 December [1679].

. . . To him that hath it shall be given; everything has contributed to assist Mlle Vauvineux [4] to become Princesse de

[1] Marie de Bailleul, Marquise d'U., whose son was Governor of Chalon, lately visited by Mme de S., and later Marshal of France.

[2] L'Abbé, her friend.

[3] Henri-Joseph de Peyre, Cte de T.

[4] Charlotte-Elizabeth de Cochefilet married Charles de Rohan, Prince de Guéméné and Duc de Montbazon in 1699 (1655–1727). Her mother, "La Vauvinette", was a neighbour of Mme de S. in Paris.

Guéméné ; *primo amor del cor mio* [1] is alleged by the bridegroom to be the prime mover in the affair. The whole business was conducted with such discretion that nothing came to light until Sunday morning. They were married at Saint-Paul at midnight. The King was the first person to be taken into their confidence and he signed the contract and gave his blessing to the union. There were twenty-nine persons in the secret who kept their mouths shut. Next day nothing was seen of bride or bridegroom . . . no question of fine clothes or display on the nuptial bed, merely a worthy Princesse de Guéméné, who will live happily for ever after with a husband to whom she rightly feels under a great obligation. He is a strange individual, and one who has never learnt, as you did when young, to master the Trappist's most formidable enemy ; having partaken of salt all his life he cannot do without it ; three months of widowhood to him have seemed like three centuries, and no speculation as to the future can diminish in his eyes the solid advantages of matrimony. The Luynes [2] family are furious : " Only three months after our daughter's death—it is abominable ! He was in tears day and night " ; (easy to see why !) " and did not tell us a word. Shameful ! " . . . I applaud the whole thing, and understand Mme de Vauvineux's jubilations ; not only is the marriage grand beyond all hopes, but she has been spared endless discussions, unpleasantness and expense which might well have amounted to a hundred thousand francs . . . Is it not true, dear daughter, that to him that hath it shall be given—so says the Bible which we know cannot lie.

One hears much gossip about the Queen of Spain, she has given herself heart and soul to that country, and has only kept four French hand-maidens in her service. The King came upon her dressing her hair ; when he entered the room she instinctively fell on her knees to kiss his hand, he did likewise and kissed hers, both remaining on their knees. They were married without any ceremony, after which they retired to converse : the Queen is versed in the Spanish language and both wore Spanish costume. They arrived at Burgos and retired to bed at eight, from whence

[1] *Il Pastor Fido*, III. 6.

[2] The Prince's first wife, Marie-Anne d'Albert de Luynes, had died at the age of seventeen.

they did not rise until ten o'clock the next morning. The Queen has written to *Monsieur* of her happiness and contentment, and adds that she is agreeably surprised to find the King more amiable than she had been led to believe. The King is deeply in love, the Queen has had excellent advice, and her deportment throughout has been unexceptionable. Whose good counsels were followed, do you think? Mme de Grancey's, who, in recognition of her services has received substantial gifts. The King of Spain has endowed her with a pension of six thousand crowns, and a present of a further ten thousand . . .

I fear you will be overdone at Aix by many tiresome duties. I beg you take refuge in the privacy of your sanctum—it is good sometimes to be alone: Mlles de Grignan can do the civilities. Pauline wrote me such a charming letter, we greatly appreciate her style; her letter was instrumental in making Mme de La Fayette forget an attack of the vapours which was threatening to choke her . . .

To The Same

Paris, Wednesday 27 December, 1679.

. . . The court is in the seventh heaven at the marriage of M. de Conti [1] to Mademoiselle de Blois.[2] They are as much in love as characters in a romance; the King has made great play of their lovelorn condition: he spoke tenderly to his daughter and told her he loved her too well to think lightly of parting from her, upon which *la petite* [3] wept for joy. He then said it was evident she disliked the husband he had chosen for her, which so transported her with happiness, that her tears flowed afresh. The King delighted everyone by his account of this little scene. As for M. de Conti he was so elated that he knew not if he was standing on his head or his heels, and brushed aside every obstacle

[1] Louis-Armand de Bourbon, Prince de C., nephew of the Great Condé and of Mazarin, through his mother, Anne-Marie Martinozzi.

[2] Marie-Anne de Bourbon (1666-1739). Daughter of the King and Louise de La Vallière.

[3] She was fourteen.

to get to Mademoiselle de Blois. Madame Colbert [1] forbade he should see her till evening, but he forced his way in, knelt at her feet, and kissed her hand; quite simply and unaffectedly she fell at his feet and once more started to weep. This dear little princess is so meltingly pretty that one would like to gobble her up. The Comte de Gramont, congratulating Conti, said: "Monsieur, your marriage affords me great satisfaction, believe me it is essential you should consider your father-in-law in all ways, be careful never to cross him . . . live circumspectly in this family and I answer for it all will be well." The King is delighted to marry off his daughter and has, without the slightest formality, congratulated the Prince, M. le Duc and Madame la Duchesse, begging the latter to be kindly disposed towards the young bride, who would appreciate her company and good example. He dotes on upsetting Conti by saying the marriage contract offers difficulties and obstacles, and the wedding had better be postponed: hearing which the youthful lover falls in a dead faint, and has to be resuscitated by the young Princess . . . It is all rather quixotic but very charming and romantic. You can well imagine what pleasure is given in certain quarters [2] by the King's attitude. I hope all these details will entertain Mlle de Grignan . . .

To The Same

Paris, Friday 29 December [*1679*].

True it is, my dear one, I am prostrate on my knees before you, pleading with you for the sake of the love we bear each other never again to put pen to paper as you did on the last occasion. I beg this favour of you with such heartfelt, such passionate yearning that you must, I think, feel the repercussion in your own breast. Alas! dearest, it is evident you are exhausted, overdone, at the end of your strength, suffering from your lungs which are in a parched condition; and I, I who love you so dearly, am the

[1] Mme Colbert had brought up Mlle de Blois.

[2] This was ironic, for Mme de Montespan bitterly resented the King's interest in Mme de La Vallière's daughter.

unwitting cause of the pitiful state you find yourself in—yes—I, who would gladly lay down my life for you, have contributed to your overthrow! So little, in fact, do I cherish your well-being that I enjoy reading your letters and getting answers to the missives I send you, even though the effort you make should imperil your very existence! Such a thought is well-nigh unbearable, and I swear to you by all I hold sacred that, if you inscribe more than one sheet, and if you do not employ Montgobert or Gauthier to furnish me with such news as may crop up, I shall cease writing to you for ever and a day . . .

Mademoiselle de Blois' marriage is pleasing to everybody. The King desired her to tell her mother the favours he was conferring on her. People flocked to congratulate the holy Carmelite. I think I and Mme de Coulanges will repair to the convent to-morrow. M. le Prince and his father, M. le Duc, hastened to her side; they say she has admirably succeeded in adjusting her style to the black veil she wears, and in seasoning her passion for Christ with the love she bears her daughter. The King is marrying his child as if, in truth, she were the Queen's, and being led to the altar by the King of Spain; her dowry will be of five hundred thousand écus which is usually reserved for crowned heads, but whereas hers is to be paid forthwith, the latter more often than not, is honoured in the breach rather than in the observance . . .

Now, dearest, I beg of you to relax, to look after yourself and to shut your desk, which is a veritable temple of Janus, remembering that you could scarcely afford a greater joy to those who love you than to preserve yourself for their sake, whereas by writing to them you will, indubitably, succeed in shortening your days.

1680

To Madame de Grignan

Paris, Friday 5 January [1680].

. . . I proceeded yesterday to the great Carmelite convent with *Mademoiselle*, who was well inspired to have arranged with Mme de Lesdiguières [1] to take us under her wing. As we stepped on holy ground we were met by Mère Agnès [2] whose wit delighted me; she spoke of you as knowing her sister.[3] I saw beautiful placid Madame Stuart,[4] and afterwards Mlle d'Epernon,[5] who said she did not find me changed though she had not set eyes on me for thirty years. I, however, found her sadly altered. Little du Janet [6] would not let me out of her sight. Three days ago she took the white veil of the novitiate—she is a model of piety and fervour; I must hasten to write to her mother. An angel [7] then

[1] Paule-Marguerite-Françoise de Gondy, Dsse de L., niece of Cardinal de Retz, first referred to as Mlle de Retz, later as Dsse de Sault.

[2] Judith de Béllefonds, daughter of the Governor of Caen, a success at the Court of Marie de Medici, and *Prieure* at the Carmelites 1684–90.

[3] Marquise de Villars, Mme de S.'s friend, and her daughter's.

[4] "La belle Anglaise"; brought up at the Court of Whitehall, she went to France at the age of 17, and was converted to Catholicism. She wrote her story to Marguerite Périer, Pascal's sister [*Monmerqué*].

[5] Anne-Louise-Christine de la Foix de la Valette d'E., sister of the Duc de Candaule, daughter of Duke Bernard d'E. and Gabrielle de Bourbon, and granddaughter of Dsse de Verneuil and Henri IV.

[6] Daughter of the Gentleman of Provence, mentioned on p. 116.

[7] Louise de la Vallière.

appeared, M. le Prince de Conti having detained her in the parlour. Here was all the fascination and charm we used to admire so well, she is neither puffy nor sallow, not as thin as of old and far more placid; the same eyes gaze at one with their same expression, unchanged by deprivations, austerities and want of sleep; the strange habit she wears has deprived her of none of her natural grace and queenly bearing. She is as modest now as the day she gave birth to a Princesse de Conti, a modesty wholly befitting her state. All she said was full of charm and good sense, and so warmly did she speak of you, and in so fitting a manner, it would be hard to find its equal. M. de Conti loves and reveres her, she has become his spiritual director; like his father he is most devout. In truth her habit and way of life clothe her with a dignity beyond all praise . . .

To The Same

Paris, Wednesday 17 January [1680].

Time was, my poor child, when my greatest solace was to receive a long letter from you, but circumstances have altered, alas! and to-day it has become a real anguish. Knowing the trouble it gives and the harm it does you, I must insist on your curtailing your correspondence as much as possible, and if it incommodes you in the slightest to stop writing altogether . . .

It seems you are appalled by the expenses you incur at Aix . . . you long to be at Grignan which, as you say, is the one place in which you can practise economies: I can see the wisdom of this decision, but nothing must count in the balance where your health is concerned; and surely no one can wish you to remain in a climate which threatens to be injurious to you. You find the north east wind at Aix and Salon most trying—how much more so at Grignan.[1] So, dear daughter, you must resign yourself to

[1] The Château of Grignan stood very high, and was exposed to all the winds that blow. The "*bise*" is a north-east wind considered deleterious to any weakness of the chest.

following the dictates of prudence, and not try to be everywhere at once; agitation does no one any good. With the adverse change in your health and temperament you must adopt a new mode of life, and tell M. de Grignan you cannot travel until you have fully recovered . . . You must in fact reform your ways which have proved so destructive to your well-being. We shall return to this subject anon, but I cannot refrain from telling you what I hope may give food for reflection.

Mademoiselle de Blois has become Mme la Princesse de Conti; she was affianced on Monday with great ceremony, and married yesterday; later there was another banquet and play-acting ensued, after which the nuptial couch was prepared to which the happy pair retired clad in night shifts, gifts of the King and Queen . . .

I must tell you of a most extraordinary incident which took place. M. le Prince—you will scarcely credit it—called in the barber to shave him! This is no invention, no figment of the imagination, but plain sober fact to which the whole court can bear witness. Madame de Langeron,[1] taking advantage of his helpless plight under the barber's hands, had a jerkin adjusted on him adorned with buttonholes sewn with precious stones: the while a valet, also taking advantage of his good-nature, frizzed and powdered him, turning him out the most elegant of courtiers, with a wig which put all other wigs into the shade: this, in fact, was the high light of the whole ceremony.

The Prince was incomparably attired; panels, heavily embroidered in diamonds of great splendour, formed the trimming on a coat of black plush with straw-coloured lining. The straw-colour was a failure, which so upset Madame de Langeron, Keeper of the Wardrobe to the House of Condé, that she fell ill of vexation. From such a blow recovery is not possible. M. le Duc, the Duchesse and Mademoiselle de Bourbon were dressed for the occasion in garments embroidered in precious stones, of a different hue for each day of the ceremonial. Best of all the Prince's sword was studded in diamonds:

La famosa spada
All' cui valore ogni vittoria è certà,

and the lining of his cloak was of black satin, sewn in diamonds.

[1] Wife of the *Lt.-Général des Armées Navales* (*see* p. 173).

The Princess looked romantically lovely, sumptuously dressed, and serenely content.

Happy indeed is she who, in the
adored lover, finds the beloved spouse.

I can tell you no more . . . the sun shone on the wedding ceremony, the moon witnessed its consummation. In her bed the King tenderly embraced the Princess, and begged her to refuse nothing to the Prince de Conti, and to shew herself gentle and obedient. We think she has followed this advice.

To The Same

Paris, Wednesday 24 January [*1680*].

I fear you are going through a bad patch. No one, perhaps, is altogether free of an occasional spasm of pain in the stomach, but yours is unusually sharp and penetrating, and is at the seat of the most intimate sensations. I greatly admire your patience and courage under an ordeal few could sustain with as much fortitude. It is plain enough for anyone to see that you have ample opportunity to rest if you so desire, no one can deny you are well cared for; but alas! the trouble comes from the state of your lungs, of your blood. I am relieved to hear you have followed Fagon's advice to eat more, and have found it has helped you. A nourishing diet for invalids is much in vogue at the present time. The decision as to whether you should drink milk lies entirely with you . . .

Madame la Princesse de Conti is charming as ever: she suffered such a bad internal colic and derangement on her wedding night that the spectators threw off all thought of discretion, but did not get so much as a peep for their pains. She is well, and all are loud in praise of the Prince for his noble and generous instincts; he spends money lavishly, is as benevolent as Henry IV, as chivalrous as Chevalier Bayard,[1] as equitable in his judgements as Sylla: the tales one hears tell are most edifying . . . He has

[1] The celebrated *Preux Chevalier, sans peur et sans reproche* (1473–1524).

given a pension of two thousand écus to Mme de Bury [1] which makes her eligible to a seat in the Queen's carriage, a place much sought after in these circumstances ; there will be further presents from the house of Conti, but she will be dependent on the King's favour. Mme de Langeron must look to it if she wishes to recover her carriage rights, which she lost through Condé's bad offices. It is hard to assess people's conduct at a distance ; Mme de Bury, though fifty leagues away, was sent for to fill a much coveted post ; Mme de Saint-Géran, having despoiled her grand-children of their expectations, gets nothing ; M. de Saint-Brieux [2] is removed from his diocese to Poitiers as he had hoped ; others who make a habit of attending the King's Mass daily, strung out like a row of onions, go empty away. What conclusions can be drawn save that God acts as the spirit moves Him !

Pray listen to this tragic tale. Poor Bertillac,[3] for her sins, falls head over ears in love with insensitive Caderousse [4] ; he watches her catch fire, and does not attempt to offer any resistance to her blandishments. Seeing how the land lies he incites her to pawn her pearls with the object of backing his game of basset. People see him arriving at Mme de Quintin's [5] making great display of the thousand louis he carries on him ; gratitude forbids him to conceal from whence they came. La Bertillac was so stunned at this procedure that she forthwith turned into one of Benoît's [6] wax images, her circulation stopped, gangrene set in, and she is *in extremis*. Coulanges and I looked in yesterday ; her death is imminent and there is no one to mourn for her, husband and father are impatiently awaiting the moment when she can be put under the sod. Opinion is unanimous as to the touching cause of her death . . .

[1] Anne-Marie d'Eurre d'Aiguebonne, Ctsse de, favourably mentioned in Saint-Simon's *Mémoires*. Sister-in-law of Mme de Lavardin.

[2] Hardouin Fortin de la Hoguette, Bp. of St-B.

[3] Anne-Louise Habert, married in 1666 to Lt.-General Nicolas de Bertillac, Governor of Rocroy.

[4] Juste-Joseph-François de Cadar d'Ancezune, Duc de C.

[5] Suzanne de Montgomery, Ctsse de.

[6] Celebrated artist in wax figures.

To The Same

Paris, Friday 26 January [1680.]

. . . Mme de Soubise [1] is forgotten—no one so much as gives her a thought and many other events have helped to put her tragedy into the shade . . . For the last two days everyone is on tenter-hooks, asking each other for the latest news, going in and out of each other's houses, and up to date this is what has transpired.[2] M. de Luxembourg,[3] who was received in his customary manner by the King at Saint-Germain, was warned of an impending order for his arrest: he thereupon notified his wish to see the King, and you can imagine the feelings this aroused. His Majesty told him that if he were innocent all he need do was to give himself up, and that such wise judges had been appointed to examine into his case he could confidently place himself in their hands. M. de Luxembourg begged not to be taken to prison and was accordingly driven straight to the Père de la Chaise [4] . . . After an hour spent with the Jesuits, he was

[1] Enraged at not being appointed Lady-in-Waiting to the Queen, she had left the Court. She was not exiled, but had the measles (*Monmerqué*).

[2] La Voisin, la Vigoureux, and a priest named le Sage, well known in Paris, had added to their fame as soothsayers that of purveyors of deadly poisons. The account of their trials can be seen in the archives of the Arsenal Library where many celebrated names appear, those of the Ctsse de Soissons, Dsse de Bouillon, Duc de Luxembourg and a tribe of others. Amongst other horrible indictments le Sage accused the Marshal of having sold himself to the devil in order to get Louvois' daughter to marry his son. In addition to so many horrors, whose perpetrators were more suitable for lunatic asylums than the guillotine, the King handed the Dsse de Foix a note alleged to have been written by her to la Voisin couched in the following terms: "The more I rub the less they grow." Asking what was meant H.M. was told it related to a recipe for expanding the bosom. La Vigoureux, wife of a tailor, was condemned and executed. *See* p. 237 for La Voisin's end. Her name was Catherine Deshayes, wife of Antoine Montvoisin.

[3] The King had instituted a Court of Justice, "*La Chambre Ardente*", at the Arsenal after the mysterious revelations in the Brinvilliers case. The Marshal went of his own accord to the Bastille and was later rehabilitated; after the death of Turenne, he led the French army against the Dutch, whom he was to defeat at the battle of Fleurus. *See* p. 365.

[4] Father Francis, Jesuit, confessor to Louis XIV, who gave his name to the famous Paris cemetery.

removed to the Bastille, himself handing over to Bezemaux [1] the order for his arrest. He was first shown into an agreeable room where Mme de Meckelbourg [2] visited him in tears; an hour later the order came through he was to be transferred to a heavily barred cell in one of the towers, from whence the sky is not visible and visitors are excluded. Here, my child, is a lesson which should be taken to heart. Consider this man's brilliant career, the great honour conferred on him, that of leading the King's armies into battle, and try and picture to yourself what he must have endured on hearing the door of his cell heavily barred and bolted, and if he slept the sleep of exhaustion what then must have been his awakening! No one believes that poison was a genuine factor in his case, but trumped up by his enemies.[3] Such a misfortune, believe me, puts all others into the shade.

Mme de Tingry's [4] case is adjourned. As for Mme de Soissons,[5] she could not face her sentence, and has been allowed to make her escape. On Wednesday she was enjoying a game of basset, when M. de Bouillon [6] entered the room and asked her to follow him into his study, where he conveyed to her that she must either leave France or submit to imprisonment. She did not hesitate for a moment; she threw in her hand and left with Mme d'Alluye: they were not seen again. When supper was served the guests were told that Mme la Comtesse was supping in town, they immediately departed, realising something grave had occurred. Great activity was displayed over packing up; money, jewels were collected, grey jerkins provided for the lackeys and coachmen, and eight horses for the coach. Mme la Marquise d'Alluye,[7] it is thought reluctantly, took her place on the front

[1] Governor of the Bastille.

[2] His sister, formerly Mme de Châtillon. *See* p. 376 for her end.

[3] His downfall was the work of Louvois, who never forgave the Marshal for passing him over in favour of Colbert.

[4] Marie-Louise-Antoinette d'Albert, Psse de T., sister-in-law of the Marshal's, Lady-in-Waiting to the Queen, accused of having poisoned her children.

[5] Olympe, Mazarin's niece, accused of having poisoned her husband.

[6] Her brother-in-law.

[7] Bénigne de Meaux du Fouilloux, accused of having poisoned her father-in-law.

seat beside Mme la Comtesse, the two waiting women on the back seats . . . Mme de Tingry told her household they must not be concerned for her as she was innocent, and that " the vile women " had betrayed her . . . She left Paris at three of the morning, in tears. It is thought she is going to Namur and that she will not be allowed to make her escape. Her trial will be held, if only to clear her in the eyes of the world; Voisin's calumnies are black indeed. The Duc de Villeroy, who has been overwhelmed at these untoward events, is shut away in his room and sees no one . . .

I am greatly touched, and so is M. l'Abbé, that you should have written with your own hand: did you not know, dear one, that we should be unable to read your missive without tears? What, I wonder, will you say next? You tell me you are good for nothing, useless, worthless—this to me, whose world you are and more beside. I pray you to cease decrying your own wares. Yours are a heart and mind too perfect and flawless to be obscured by any fleeting shadow . . .

Dear one, I count my life as worthless until such happy time as we are reunited.

To The Same

Paris, Wednesday 7 February [*1680*].

Is it really so that you can enjoy a game of chess? I am besotted about the game, and only wish I were as proficient as you or your brother; it is the best, the most reasonable of games, and one in which luck plays little or no part: whether things go well or badly, the player remains quite unperturbed and master of the situation. Corbinelli tries to persuade me to take a hand, he thinks I have an inkling, but in truth it takes three or four moves before I see what is coming to me . . . I assure you I shall be horribly vexed if I do not succeed in achieving some degree of mediocrity. Everyone was at it when I went to Pomponne on that last ill-fated occasion, and at the very hour our host was busy defeating M. de Chaulnes, he himself was being checkmated at Saint-Germain . . .

No one alludes to M. de Luxembourg: the tragedy which befell him is a nine days' wonder—it would seem as if a great flood had swept all away. We are however assured there will be some astounding revelations . . .

To The Same

Paris, Friday 9 February [*1680*].

So your carnival is in full swing, my beautiful one: those intimate little suppers for eighteen or twenty ladies, how well I know them! and the expense entailed by the kind of life you lead at Aix; but it seems you are at least able to rest between whiles. Some people say they must get their money's worth of fun, but you declare you must get your money's worth of rest; rest I pray you, for nothing is more worth while. I confess to feeling somewhat astonished that the minuet should not have tempted you: not so much as a tremor in the legs? or a swaying of the shoulders? This is scarcely credible! I have never seen you passive on these occasions, and am forced to conclude that you are less well than you pretend.

Last night at the Hôtel de Condé an enchanting fête took place. Madame la Princesse de Conti stood godparent with the Prince de la Roche-sur-Yon [1] to a little daughter of M. le Duc.[2] The christening was followed by a collation, and such a collation! Next came a play—and what a play!—interlarded with five stanzas of music and the best dancers from the Opera house. A theatre designed by fairies, with a background, recesses, orange trees festooned with fruit and flowers, perspectives, pilasters; in a word a charming little entertainment costing more than two thousand louis, and all for a pretty Princess . . .

The opera is superior to all others. The Chevalier tells me

[1] François-Louis de Bourbon, who became Prince de Conti on the death of his brother.

[2] Marie-Anne de Montmorency, born 24.2.78, later known as Mlle d'Enghien, daughter of Henri-Jules de Bourbon, son of le Grand Condé.

he has sent you several of the airs, and that he saw a gentleman who said he had sent you the words; I dare say you will like it . . .

Friar Ange [1] has restored Maréchal de Bellefonds, and cured his chest, which was in a most parlous condition. Mme de Coulanges and I visited the Grand-Master, who has been at death's door for the last fortnight, the gout having invaded his system, and the oppression was such, he appeared to be at his last gasp; cold sweats followed by stupor proclaimed a state of the utmost gravity. The doctors were baffled, Friar Ange was summoned, who brought him back to life with the most palatable and agreeable remedies; the oppression lifted, the gout centred once more in feet and knees, the danger was averted.

Adieu, my dearest. I am following my customary routine which you know well, I am either at the faubourg,[2] or else with the good widows; [3] sometimes here, at others partaking of a fowl with Mme de Coulanges, only too thankful to feel time is passing and bearing me along, ever bringing me nearer to you.

To The Same

Paris, Wednesday 14 February [*1680*].

. . . The little Prince de Léon [4] was christened at Saint-Gervaix yesterday by a Breton bishop. M. de Rennes,[5] representing the states of Brittany, stood godfather, Madame la Duchesse [6] godmother. The governor of Brittany, the lieutenants-general of Brittany, the treasurer of Brittany, the bishops of Brittany, the

[1] A Capuchin doctor. The Capuchins had been expelled from the Louvre, and taken refuge at Rennes, under the protection of M. de Chaulnes, where they made themselves famous as physicians (*see* pp. 281–2).

[2] Saint-Germain, with Mme de La Fayette.

[3] *Les Veuves:* Mesdames Lavardin, de Moncé and d'Uxelles.

[4] Louis-Bretagne, Scion of the House of Rohan Chabot, son of Louis, Duc de Rohan and Marie-Elisabeth du Bec.

[5] Jean-Baptiste de Beaumanoir de Lavardin, Bp. of R., who later lodged in Mme de G.'s apartments in the Hôtel de Carnavalet.

[6] Anne de Bavière, Dsse d'Enghien.

deputies of Brittany, the nobles of Brittany, the presidents of Brittany, son and father—you can never have seen so much Brittany gathered together. If they had danced it would have been to the Breton steps, had it not been a fast day they would have partaken of Breton butter. I can assure you my son appreciates the strength of the ties which bind the Breton to his homeland—he returned full of enthusiasm. For the first time Tonquedec [1] was accorded his meed of praise and thought worthy of imitation. One might as well aspire to deflect the course of the Rhône as to stem this torrent which carries with it his firm resolve to sell his commission [2] . . . All M. de La Garde and I can obtain is that he should leave well alone. We rejoice at his absence, as he would be sure to decry his own goods. I told him how unfortunate it was to put a price on his commission merely as it accords with his individual taste : the rank of standard bearer stands sky high because he adored it, that of sub-lieutenant correspondingly low because he found it tedious. Is it wise or sensible to proceed thus when buying or selling one's possessions, unless of course one wishes to cut one's own throat ? Farewell, dear one, do not allow what I have said to disturb you, it behooves us to cling to Providence ; in matters which are not vital it is easy enough. My liberty is not curtailed, far from it, neither am I cut off from you—this I can say most emphatically.

M. de Luxembourg has twice been to confront his judges at Vincennes [3]—but his affairs remain obscure.

To The Same

Paris, Friday 16 February [*1680*].

If I am preoccupied about your health it is not without good reason. I wrote Montgobert the result of a consultation I had the other day with Friar Ange . . . I shall await Montgobert's

[1] René de Quengo, Marquis de T., a Breton Gentleman, much admired by Charles de S.

[2] The Sub-Lieutenancy in the Gendarmes-Dauphin bought by Charles de S.

[3] Persons charged with administering poisons were detained at Vincennes.

answer, that is to say yours; all hinges, it seems, on whether you can digest milk. It is possible you do not derive sufficient nourishment from it, or maybe your blood is in such a state of ferment that your system is unable to assimilate it, otherwise fresh milk should have cured you. Friar Ange made the matter clear by using the simile of cold water poured upon a hot shovel. Fagon holds the same view, and now it is for you to judge whether the fever in your blood is still at a high pitch in which case the remedies of Friar Ange, which are gentle, strengthening and cooling, might happily pave the way to a fresh milk diet and thus possibly to a cure as in the case of Maréchal de Bellefonds, the Queen of Poland and a thousand others.

Duchesnes [1] still abominates coffee, but the Friar is not prejudiced against it . . . It seems that drinking coffee makes some people fat and others thin; what enormities it is capable of committing! I do not see what more can be said of such an unpredictable beverage . . . Consult your good doctor, I should like to ask him why, if your chest is not affected, you should suffer from this intolerable sense of fulness and burning in your side; why you feel the cold in such a marked degree, and why you are so emaciated, especially about the chest? Hence my fears that you are suffering from something worse than fever in the blood . . . You ask after my health; I have not failed each time the moon has waned, to take two pills swallowed down with water . . . I have got into the habit of drinking one or two glasses of linseed tea which is sovereign against neuralgia; if M. de Colbert is alive today France owes it to the effects of this magical draught . . .

To The Same

Paris, Friday 23 February [*1680*].

What a successful week this has been for the Grignan family! [2] If Providence were disposed to favour the eldest member in proportion to the rest, we should have the pleasure of seeing

[1] Court doctor.

[2] The Abbé de G. had been nominated to the bishopric of Evreux.

him admirably settled in life; meanwhile it is most agreeable to have one's brothers singled out for distinction. No sooner had the Chevalier rendered suitable thanks for his pension of a thousand crowns than he was picked out of a dozen men of high standing as the most suitable to form part of M. le Dauphin's retinue,[1] a post which carries with it a pension of two thousand crowns, making a total of nine thousand francs a year . . . I congratulate you all . . .

I must confine myself to telling you about la Voisin: she was burned at the stake yesterday, not Wednesday as I had told you. She already knew her fate on Monday. That evening she is reported to have said to her gaoler: "How is this? no *medianoche* for us?" She partook lightheartedly of their supper as it was not a fast day, drank much wine, and sang bawdy songs. On Tuesday she was put to the torture, ordinary and extraordinary, was confronted with Mesdames de Dreux,[2] Le Féron and others, on the rack: silence is kept on what she said, but strange revelations are expected.[3] She supped that evening and, broken as she was, she scandalised everyone by her ribaldry. They rebuked her and adjured her to turn her mind to higher things and to sing an *Ave Maris Stella* or a *Salve* sooner than lewd ditties. She thereupon intoned both in a farcical manner, after which she slept. Wednesday was spent in more confrontations, debaucheries and songs: she refused absolutely to see a priest in confession. When at length Thursday dawned she was offered some broth, but she complained saying it would not give her sufficient strength to testify before her judges. Driven by coach from Vincennes to Paris she started choking and gasping for breath, but when told to confess she refused. At five they bound her, and she could be seen in the tumbril, torch in hand, dressed all in white, the accredited dress for these occasions. Scarlet in the face, she violently threw off the priest who was holding up the crucifix. From the Hôtel de Sully Mesdames de Chaulnes, de Sully, "the Countess," and many others saw her pass. At Notre-Dame she

[1] The Dauphin was engaged to Marie-Anne-Victoire of Bavaria, granddaughter of Henri IV through her mother, the Dsse de Bavière.

[2] Catherine-Françoise Saintot, wife of the Sieur de la Judicière, accused of poisoning her husband, who came to meet her at the prison gates (*see* p. 245).

[3] She had gone so far as to accuse Racine of poisoning the actress du Parc.

refused to recant, and when they came to the Grève [1] she would not leave the tumbril, had to be removed by force and thrown on to the pyre in a sitting posture, bound with ropes, and covered with straw which was heaped on her, but which she managed to throw off time and again. At length the flames obscured her from our view, and by now her ashes have been scattered to the four winds . . . When my son commented to a judge the other day as to the custom of roasting people at a slow fire being somewhat strange, the judge answered: "Undoubtedly there are small palliations for the weaker sex." "Sir," said my son, "can it be they strangle them first?" "Dear no!" said the judge, "logs of wood are thrown at their heads, which afterwards the stokers wrench off with pincers." So you see dearest—it is not so terrible after all. What think you of the tale? I confess it set my teeth on edge . . . These charming anecdotes form the staple of our conversation the while you play and dance. I long to hear news of your festivities; you will do little else during the feast days, but you must hurry up for Lent is hot on our heels.

To The Same

Paris, Wednesday 28 February [*1680*].

. . . Let us entertain ourselves by conversing of the King's journey: the Abbé de Lannion, who has recently returned from Bavaria, says Madame la Dauphine is amiable and possesses a ready wit and much virtuosity; she is conversant in three languages, and is much better looking than her portrait by de Troy [2] led us to expect. His Majesty set out on Monday to meet the young Princess and escort her home. That morning in the courtyard of Saint-Germain a new and splendid coach was drawn up to which eight horses were harnessed, gaily caparisoned; yet more chariots, baggage waggons, fourteen mules escorted by

[1] The square where executions took place.

[2] One of the family of 16th-century artists, of whom Jean-François de Troy (1679–1752) was the most famous.

attendants in grey liveries: and into the coach stepped the most beautiful young woman at court.[1]

Mme de Villars passes on plenty of agreeable gossip to Mme de Coulanges, who does likewise to us . . . It appears the Queen of Spain is plump and comely, the King lover-like and jealous, he knows not of what nor of whom. The bull-fights are brutal in the extreme, two grandees barely escaping death the other day, their horses killed under them, the arena is often bespattered with blood; thus does a Christian country seek to entertain itself: our ideas are opposed to anything of the kind and are, we hope, none the worse for that and certainly less destructive. . . .

Our minds being wholly taken up by this royal pageantry M. de Luxembourg was forgotten before four days were out; a whirlwind carries all before it, and there is no time to dwell on any one thing for any length of time; too many preoccupations succeed one another. The King has been informed by his ladies that the Dauphine exceeds all expectations,—her mother and grandmother were renowned for their endearing qualities. . . . When the young Princess went through Strasbourg she asked to be addressed in the French tongue and said she would not hear a word of German spoken . . . *Monseigneur* must now put the finishing touch to the good work, and make her forget the country she is leaving with so little regret. Mme de Maintenon tells the King her figure is as perfect as are her neck and shoulders, hands and feet, and she shows a marked desire to please; withal she is imbued with dignity and good sense.

To The Same

Paris, Wednesday 13 March [*1680*].

. . . I have some Court news for you. Madame la Dauphine is much admired: the King could scarcely wait to see for himself

[1] Marie-Angélique de Scorraille, Dsse de Fontanges with a huge pension by Louis XIV; known as *La Singulière*; she had lavished Christmas presents on her friends, especially on Mme de Montespan her rival, but given nothing to Mme de Coulanges, who had helped her choose them.

if her figure was up to expectations. He sent Sanguin [1] to reconnoitre, a man incapable of flattery. "Sire," said he, "if you can get over your first impression you will be well satisfied." This is apt, for there is something about the nose and high forehead which is out of proportion with the rest, and which spoils the general effect . . . *Monseigneur's* attitude was impeccable, and if he forgot to embrace her at the start he did not forget certain other things in which M. de Condom was scarcely qualified to prompt him . . . I conclude this Princess is very devout . . . Desiring to confess before making her final marriage vows, no Jesuit priest could be found speaking German . . . the situation was awkward, it was imperative a remedy should be found,[2] for this lady can go one better than the Queen in the matter of frequent communions . . .

You seem to outdo us in tragedies. I like your story of the son who fell dead on seeing his father hanged, all honour to him. In the matter of devotion fathers have long ago proved themselves. The jealous lover who ran amok at Arles easily outstrips any lovers in these parts; we scarcely have time here for such unbridled passions, or else we are too easily distracted by everyday events, too scatterbrained . . . and then your climate is better than ours . . .

To The Same

Paris, Sunday 17 March [1680].

Although this letter cannot leave until Wednesday I feel compelled to write today to announce to you the sad news that M. de La Rochefoucauld died yesternight. I am overwhelmed with grief for myself, and on account of our poor friend.[3] Yesterday

[1] Claude S., Seigneur de Livry. He had purchased the position of *maître d'hôtel* to the royal household, after meeting the King through Mme de Maintenon.

[2] The services of a Canon from Liège were enlisted, who was much embarrassed, asserting his only penitents were the wounded in the trenches. He and the Princess together made the best of a bad job.

[3] Mme de La Fayette.

it was thought the Englishman's remedies had worked wonders . . . Victory was proclaimed, head and lungs had cleared, the fever had abated, nature had reasserted herself, when at 6 o'clock there was a change for the worse, fever redoubled, oppression, delirium, in a word the gout laid its stranglehold over the whole system, and although his strength bore up in spite of five blood-lettings, he died at the end of a few hours, at exactly midnight, in the arms of M. de Condom. M. de Marsillac [1] did not leave him for a moment; he will derive some consolation from the King and the Court; and so will the rest of the family, from the place he enjoys. Where will Mme de La Fayette find such a unique, such a faithful friend, such good company, so much urbanity and solicitude for her and her son? She is ill, almost bedridden, and M. de La Rochefoucauld's sedentary habits accorded perfectly with her way of life, and nothing could equal the intimacy and charm of their intercourse. If you think of it, dear child, you will see that no loss could be more devastating or more irreplaceable. I have not left her side since it happened, she is keeping aloof from his family, and is in need of succour . . . All this sadness has awakened my own fears and dread of separation, and my heart is like lead . . .

To The Same

Paris, Friday 29 March [1680].

How right you were to say that, sooner or later, I should learn what sort of life you were leading in the absence of M. de Grignan and his daughters; [2] a strange enough life in truth! So you have "entered" a convent? One scarcely can be said to "enter" Sainte-Marie as one enters the Carmelites; you have slept in a cell and were, I suppose, given a little meat in the refectory: your doctor would scarcely allow you to commit the last follies.

[1] His eldest son, who had been accorded the Governorship of Berri in the place of Lauzun and was later made *Grand Maître de la Garde-robe* and *Grand Veneur de France*. He did not wish to assume his father's name.

[2] The two daughters of M. de G.'s first marriage.

You contrived, you say, to avoid the recreations. You do not mention little Adhémar; was she not allowed even a glimpse of you from some hidden corner? Poor child, she was so looking forward to your retreat.

Mme de Chaulnes took me with her to court the day before yesterday. I saw Madame la Dauphine, whose plain looks did not shock or displease me. If her face does not favour her her manners do so in a marked degree, which can be seen in everything she says and does. Her eyes sparkle with intelligence and she has a quick understanding, she is natural and at ease, and might have been born and brought up at the Louvre. Her gratitude to the King is extreme, but not that of a sycophant . . . she has a noble mien, much dignity, likes poetry, music, and conversation, and is perfectly happy spending four or five hours alone in her room, and cannot understand this feverish pursuit of amusement. The other day La Ferté [1] wanted, as a joke, to tell her a secret about poor Princesse Marianne, [2] whose troubles deserve to be respected; the Dauphine gravely retorted: "Madame, I have no curiosity." . . . Mme de Maintenon unexpectedly paid me a flying visit . . . and left in a whirl, which heralded the entrance of none other than Mme de Soubise, back at Court after an absence of three months to a day . . . She was well received by the Queen and all present . . .

M. le Duc spoke feelingly to me of M. de La Rochefoucauld, and with tears in his eyes. There was a poignant scene between him and Mme de La Fayette the night the poor man was *in extremis*; I have never witnessed such a flood of tears, nor so genuine, so touching an exhibition of grief . . .

Farewell, dear one, I know not how you are, and fear the effects of your journey—Salon, Grignan—in a word I fear whatever ill may betide you, and if only on this account I beg you may write less frequently.

[1] Formerly Mlle de Touci, third daughter of Marshal de la Mothe-Houdancourt, Dsse de la F.

[2] One can guess the secret, remembering what was said by the Prince de la Roche-sur-Yon when he saw his sister-in-law (Princesse de Conti) dancing: "There goes a trull who knows perfectly how to dance."

To The Same

Paris, Wednesday, 3 April [*1680*].

I am profoundly moved, dear child, at the news of the death of M. Fouquet:[1] I do not remember the loss of so many good friends one on top of the other, and to feel oneself surrounded by ghosts is a mournful experience. But what really pierces my heart is the thought, nay the conviction, that all your troubles have returned, and though you try to keep it from me, I feel it in my bones. Yes—your consuming fever, your heaviness and languor, the stitch in your side are as if they were mine, and as you yourself so aptly put it, a smouldering fire is apt to burst into flame . . . Is not M. de Grignan alarmed at your condition? . . . it would be worthy of his good sense and care for you, were he to concentrate on your return here in October. There is no other suitable place in which you can winter; but I will say no more for the present—too much foresight ends by defeating itself . . .

There is no longer any question of undertaking a long journey; Fontainebleau is mentioned . . . As for me I shall wend my way to Brittany with death in my heart. I go there in order to get there, to remain there a short while, and finally to have been there and have done with it. Next to bad health, which I account the worst calamity, nothing is more tiresome than miscalculation and disorganisation of one's every day existence, and I must resign myself to this cruel necessity. You can judge of the extent of my anxiety, knowing how impatient I am at any delay in the mail; what will it be like when I have so much time on my hands in which to give way to my fears? I must drain the cup of sorrow to the dregs and turn my thoughts to the happy moment when I shall see you and embrace you once again, which is the main purpose of my existence, but of which, whatever small merits I may otherwise possess, I find myself unworthy. I must work out my destiny however, and offer to God the grief, which is a necessary and integral part of my tender love for you, in

[1] At Pignerol (*see* p. 73).

reparation for the devotion I give you, and which rightly should belong to Him alone . . .

Poor Mme de La Fayette is at a loss to know what to do, M. de La Rochefoucauld's death leaves her so desolate that she is more than ever conscious of the inestimable price of their friendship. When all have forgotten she will remember him whose death leaves her without resource or occupation of any kind . . .

Farewell, dearest, most amiable one—I am yours, yours wholly and entirely and more so than I am capable of putting into words.

To The Same

Paris, Friday 12 April [1680].

You ask about Madame la Dauphine ; the Chevalier can tell you much more than I. It looks as if she had cleverly avoided being tied to the Queen's apron strings. They went together to Versailles, but they mostly take their walks alone. The King will often spend the afternoon with the Dauphine where he never finds himself encumbered by a crowd. She holds her court between eight and nine thirty of the evening ; for the rest she leads a life of strict privacy, and remains in her apartments with her ladies : the Princesse de Conti is constantly in her company, and being still a child she will profit greatly from such an example. Madame la Dauphine sparkles with wit and intelligence, and her notable good sense is the result of a wise education ; she speaks of her mother with the utmost tenderness, and says she owes all her happiness to her upbringing . . . She is learning to sing, to dance, to read, in fact she is a person to reckon with. I confess I was anxious to see her, so I went to her apartments in the company of Mesdames de Chaulnes and Kerman :[1] she was at her toilet conversing with M. de Nevers. We were presented, she gave us a frank, straightforward look, and one could see that, with the slightest encouragement, she would burst into animated conversation . . . The Court, dear child, is no longer a country I wish to explore, neither do I any longer aspire to be

[1] " La Murinette " (*see* f.n. p. 68), wife of Henri de Maillé, Marquis de K.

esteemed there. Were I young, I should enjoy being singled out by this charming Princess, but as things are I have no wish whatsoever to qualify for this distinction . . .

To The Same

Paris, Wednesday 1 May [1680].

I know not what your weather is like in Provence, here it is so deplorable that all travel, including mine, has had to be postponed [1] . . . Maybe the new moon will bring finer days, and allow me to start. I cannot tell you what my feelings are at increasing the distance between us by yet another hundred leagues. How I abhor business : it devours us, sends us pirouetting, flying hither thither obeying its behest. I shall be so sad when I step into my carriage, and those who see me off will, no doubt, think it is for them I am shedding tears. Well—if there were no departures, neither would there be any returns to gladden the heart. . .

Mme de Dreux left prison yesterday ; she was admonished, a light enough sentence, and a fine of five hundred pounds was imposed. The poor wretch was confined for a year in a cell without light or air save for a small hole in the ceiling, and was deprived of all news or other consolation. Her mother, who was still young and well-looking, and who adored her daughter, died two months since of sorrow at her plight. Mme de Dreux, who had not been told of her mother's death, was received with open arms by her husband and family, who went to escort her from the Arsenal. The first question she asked was : " And where is my mother ? Why is she not here ? " M. de Dreux said she was waiting at home, but the poor thing kept on asking if illness had prevented her mother coming to meet her. When she finally reached the house, she rapidly ascended the stairs calling out her mother's name. All were weeping, none dared tell her the truth. At length Father Célestin, her confessor, told her she would not see her mother until she went to Heaven—it

[1] Mme de S. was leaving Paris for Les Rochers.

was God's will. The poor woman fell into a swoon and came to uttering most heartbreaking cries alleging she was responsible for her mother's death, wishing she had died in prison, for she could no longer enjoy her liberty without her beloved mother . . . Is it not ironical, dear daughter, that all this happiness, this joy, this family reunion, should turn into dust and ashes? . . . It is thought M. de Luxembourg will meet with as much leniency as Mme de Dreux. In fact his judges decided that he should not even be admonished . . .

I am off then with the good Abbé and with my books, and with the ever present thought of you in my mind, who are the author of all my joys and all my pain. You may rest assured the thought of you will prevent my exposing myself to the evening chill, for I know how you dread it; it will not be the first time you have driven me indoors. I promise ever to consult you and follow your precepts; do likewise by me and have no fear, you can rely for my safety on my extreme cowardice. I cannot be said to have as much ground for confidence in your behaviour and find I have many things to reproach you with, and without going as far as Monaco have I not the Rhône to dread where you insist your family should follow you against their better judgement? and pray remember I nearly died of fright in traversing the "Vaux d'Olioules": [1] may the thought of me have a restraining influence on you, as the thought of you ofttimes has on me . . . I am starting by the Loire and Nantes, which are in no way formidable. I think my son will accompany me as far as Orleans. I am convinced of M. de Grignan's admirable intentions; he has really noble attributes added to courtesy and kindness of heart, but there is another side, the reactions of which are more difficult to assess, together with a social charm which is inimitable—it is all a question of facets. One loves him and wants to scold him, one esteems him and wants to rebuke him, to kiss and to smack him. Farewell, dearest—I must tear myself away . . .

[1] A narrow pass between two precipitous mountains in Provence, through which flows a small river. [*Perrin*].

To The Same

Paris, Monday 6 May [1680].

When you say, lightheartedly, that if we use a little common-sense, we are sure of finding compensations in human events, I can only hope I shall be as commonsensical as you, and that time and change of air will contribute to make me less unhappy than I am at present. I seem to have spoken to you of this mania we both possess for putting ever greater distances between us: it would appear that, even now, we are not satisfied, and after due deliberation, we feel called upon to add yet another hundred leagues . . . I can only hope the sea will set a limit to this furious tug-of-war, and when we have stretched the line to its utmost capacity we shall retrace our steps instead of striding in opposite directions. For two persons who long for each other's society no stranger destiny can well be imagined. Were my eyes not steadily fixed on Providence I should be completely at a loss. If it lay in our hands to settle or unsettle, to arrange or disarrange, to have in fact any choice in the matter I should never again have a moment's peace, but when I turn to the Creator I can submit to His decrees, albeit not without pain or grief, as being in the natural order of things. Thus it is ordained there should be a Mme de Sévigné whose love for her daughter passes the love of mothers, from whom she has constantly to be parted and who, quite unwittingly, is the cause of all her earthly suffering. I still, however, venture to entertain the hope that Providence may relent, and on second thoughts allow us to meet once again . . .

I have just had a visit from your bailiff, his keyhole was very rusty,[1] but I gathered he greatly admired you: he spoke of you as truly magnificent, says you are still beautiful, but often sad and cast down, and he could see what self-restraint you imposed on yourself . . . The Abbé Arnauld came yesterday to bid me goodbye. As for Madame de Coulanges, she has simply taken possession of me, body and soul, she feeds me, follows me about, and will not let me out of her sight till she has " seen me hanged ".[2]

[1] Expression used by Mme de S., meaning a confused way of talking.
[2] Quotation from Molière's *Le Médecin malgré lui*.

The Dauphine is at Paris for the first time: Mass at Notre-Dame, dinner at Val-de-Grâce, visit to La Vallière . . . every day fresh entertainments for the lady . . .

To The Same

Orleans, Wednesday 8 May [1680].

We have arrived without undue misadventures: the weather is as fine as one could wish, the roads are admirable, our turn-out is all it should be, and my son has escorted us so far with his own horses. He has cheered me on my sad journey and we have discoursed, argued and read out loud to each other; our mistakes, being identical, have helped in maintaining a perfect harmony between us. Our axle broke in a heavenly spot, and we obtained assistance from a man, the very spit of "M. de Sottenville"; [1] here is a man who could himself have written Virgil's *Georgics*, had they not already been composed, so learned is he in country lore. He introduced his wife to us who belongs "to the House of Prudoterie where a prominent belly is esteemed an adornment." [2] We spent two hours in this agreeable company without tedium, owing to a language and an approach which were wholly fresh to us. Later we reflected on the happy state of this gentle knight, of whom it can be said:

> "*Happy he who drinketh the milk of his own lambs,*
> *And whose garments are spun of their wool.*" [3]

Daylight is by now so prolonged that we shall scarcely need to rely on the light of the most beautiful moon ever seen, when we embark tomorrow, and by the time you receive this the Loire will have carried us to Nantes: today I made the discovery, by drawing a line on the map, that Nantes is no further from you than Paris. But these are small alleviations when I consider I have not even the relief of hearing from you . . .

[1] *Ref.* Molière, the father-in-law of *George Dandin.*

[2] *George Dandin*, I. 4.

[3] From *Les Bergeries* by Racan.

Farewell, my child—what can I find to say to you which you will not already have heard from others? It seems I no longer serve any purpose save that of loving you, and I can make little enough use of this amiable virtue which, for one of my eager temperament, is sad indeed. The Bienbon sends you expressions of his homage, I am anxiously watching over him, for at his age journeys are no light matter.

To The Same

Blois, Thursday 9 May [*1680*].

I want to be able to write to you every evening dearest, it is the only occupation I find completely satisfying. I pace up and down, I " turn round " and take up my book, I try " turning " things round and round in my head ;—I am still hopelessly bored and long to sit down at my desk. I want, nay I find I must converse with you, and whether my letter goes today, tomorrow, or the next day, each evening I am constrained to furnish you with every detail of my news . . .

We embarked at six o'clock of a beautiful evening, and my great coach is decked in such a manner that the rays of the sun cannot reach us : we lower the windows, and have a fine view from an aperture in the front of the carriage, and we also have peeps from the side-doors and interstices. I and the Abbé are alone in this charming seclusion, reclining in comfort on soft cushions, in good air and at our ease, while the rest of the passengers are stowed away like pigs in a sty. We have partaken of hot soup and pap, there is a small stove, and we are served on a ship's plank inside the coach like any King or Queen ; you can see how conditions on the Loire have improved, and how refined we have grown since the days when " we wore our hearts on the left side " : [1] one thing certain is that mine, whether to right or to left, beats only for you. If you question me as to my activities in this charming equipage, where I feel myself to be in perfect safety, I will answer that I think of my dear daughter and commune with myself on the tender love we bear one another,

[1] *Le Médecin malgré lui*, II, 6.

on the infinite stretches of country which lie between us, on how deeply concerned I am for her welfare and how greatly I long to see and embrace her . . . All this provides a little of "the mood of my daughter", despite the fact that "the mood of my mother"[1] prevails all around. I gaze out of the window and admire the view, so greatly esteemed by our painters. I am touched by the dear Abbé's kindness who, at the age of seventy-three, traverses land and water at my behest. Then I take a book M. de La Rochefoucauld made me buy, *Histoire de la Réunion du Portugal*, in a two-volume 8vo translation from the Italian; both story and style are equally estimable. In it one sees the brave young prince Sebastian of Portugal, hurrying headlong to his predestined fate; he perished in Africa in a war against the son of Abdalla, uncle of Zaïde:[2] it is certainly a most diverting story. Then I come back to Providence, and remember you saying that our conduct is determined by eternal decrees. . . . Finally we arrive early in the morning, the company disperses, we stretch ourselves, everyone shaves himself the while I sit romantically in this Inn where you have been (called La Galère) by the side of the river, writing away . . .

As I listen to the songs of a thousand nightingales I am thinking of those you are hearing, this moment maybe, from your balcony. I scarcely dare tell you into what depths of melancholy the thought of your delicate state of health has thrown me . . . If you love me try, try to get better . . . this place will be the touchstone, I feel. Goodnight, my loved one, goodnight till tomorrow at Tours.

Tours, Friday 10 May.

Everything prospers, and this mode of travel is the most agreeable you can imagine. Have you taken in the fact that our coach is

[1] Certain alleys at Livry and Les Rochers were thus named (*see* p. 219).

[2] Sebastian I of Portugal, who perished 4 August 1578, in a battle against the Moors. At the death of his uncle, Cardinal Henry, who succeeded him, Philip II of Spain reunited the two kingdoms. Zaïde is an allusion to Mme de La Fayette's novel *Zayde*. Don Sebastian is mentioned by Chapman (*The Conspiracie of Charles Duke of Byron*, II, i.) and is the subject of Jonathan Griffin's recent verse trilogy *The Hidden King*. An English translation of Conestaggio's Italian was published in 1600.

berthed sideways on in the barge, which means that we are sheltered from the rays of the sun; it rises on our right, and sets on our left and the barge protects us. As the stream carries us down, an ever-changing panorama unrolls itself before our eyes, an endless variation of scenes and landscapes which would enchant M. de Grignan. I would like to make him a present of one of my own choosing!

Farewell, kindest, most amiable love. Farewell, M. de Grignan.

To The Same

Saumur, Saturday 11 May [1680].

We have arrived here, my beautiful one, having left Tours this morning where I posted a letter to you. I should find myself gravely embarrassed were I to be deprived of the power of thought, but more especially on this journey. I spend twelve solid hours in this coach, comfortably and thoroughly well ensconced, some are employed in eating and drinking, others in reading, others in looking about and admiring, and many more still in dreaming and thinking of you. I am certain, dear child, you know this to be the bare truth and no flattery on my part. I dissect you, thumb you over, wind and unwind you time and time again; I come upon bad patches, regrettable ones, others tender and kind. I think of your radiant youth, of your health and how greatly it has been mismanaged, in defiance of all good sense, and how when danger first reared its ugly head, we were not alarmed until it was too late. What thoughts do not pass through my mind who have ample leisure and solitude in which to indulge them? . . . Meanwhile: I think, *ergo* I am,[1] I think of you tenderly, *ergo* I love you; I think exclusively of you, *ergo* I love you exclusively . . . Here comes the Abbé to send you his compliments. I am happily perusing my history of Portugal, but I have perused nothing of yours since the 28th of last month which is by far too long. I read and reread your old letters. Farewell, dear heart, my pen is giving out.

[1] Celebrated axiom of Descartes, *Cogito, ergo sum.*

To The Same

Nantes, Monday evening 27 May [*1680*].

I am writing to you tonight as I shall be leaving tomorrow at crack of dawn, praise be . . . Like Harlequin I answer a letter before I receive it.

I went to Buron [1] yesterday, returning the same evening; I nearly wept at seeing the havoc my son has wrought there: on his last visit he gave orders the most beautiful woods in the world should be razed to the last tree—all came under the axe, and he went so far as to sell the only remaining little coppice, which is of great beauty—pitiable indeed. He made a hundred gold pieces out of the transaction, of which not a sou was left him by the end of the month. Impossible to understand what he is driving at, and although he dismissed his lackeys and coachman in Paris, only retaining the services of Larmechin, his valet, God knows what he managed to get rid of. He seems to have made the following discoveries: how to spend with nothing to show for it; how to lose without betting; how to discharge debts he has not incurred. In war, as in peace, he has an insatiable thirst for ready cash, he is like a bottomless pit: having no expensive tastes all he does is without rhyme or reason. Dear daughter, pray bear with me; would not any heart be wrung by the sights and sounds I witnessed yesterday? [2]—dryads bereft of shelter, ancient genii of the forest, homeless and bewildered, ravens croaking out their doom who, for centuries have nested in these sombre woods, and when darkness fell the hooting of the owls seemed to proclaim all the sorrows of the world . . . The place is a regular *luogo d'incanto*,[3] and I came away sick at heart . . . How I rejoice to be returning to my own home woods at Les Rochers which I venture to hope will not all have been laid bare in my absence.

[1] Mme de S.'s estate near Nantes.
[2] In the woods her son had levelled.
[3] The enchanted spot in Tasso's *Jerusalem Delivered* Canto XIII. [*Perrin*].

To The Same

Les Rochers, Wednesday 5 June [*1680*].

Considering the vast distance which lies between us, I console myself whilst awaiting your letters with the knowledge that I receive them only nine days after they are despatched. I cannot but admire the goodwill of these knight-errants, (they are treated most scurvily in the *Essais de Morale*) who do our behests in so honest and obliging a manner, however mean or subservient, they fly to carry our letters two hundred leagues distant, they climb upon the roofs of our houses to save us from being flooded out, and even worse things besides. It is, no doubt, a wise dispensation of Providence who in this manner turns the deadly sin of cupidity to good account. I have brought with me a fine assortment of books which I disposed this morning on my shelves. I cannot lay my hand on a single one I do not long to read from beginning to end; one whole shelf is set aside for books of devotion—I can scarcely imagine a more ideal setting for its practice! Another to historical works of merit, another to morals, yet another to poetry, short tales and memoirs. Romance and fiction meet with little consideration and are relegated to a closet. When I go into my study I find it difficult to reconcile myself to the thought of ever leaving it again; it is, I think, worthy of you as are our lovely walks, but not so our visitors for whose benefit my pot is kept on the boil all day on Sundays.[1] The only consolation lies in the fact that everyone scatters at six o'clock on account of supper, which, as you know is my favourite hour for a walk and this helps me to recover my equanimity.

Mme de Coulanges recounts much gossip which I would pass on to you were it not folly to do so. Her friend, Mme de Maintenon, continues to be in high favour; the Queen accuses her of being responsible for the breach between her and Mme la Dauphine: the King endeavours to console her, and their interviews last so long that it sets everyone dreaming . . .

[1] On Sundays Mme de S. felt herself under an obligation to do the honours of Les Rochers—which she called keeping the pot boiling. [*Perrin*, 1754].

To The Same

Les Rochers, Whitsunday 9 June [*1680*].

. . . As for me, the days seem endless, and I scarcely know when they draw to a close; seven, eight, nine o'clock of the evening to me are one and the same. When formal visitors make an appearance I take up my needle, for I find them quite unworthy of my beautiful woods, and when the time comes I gladly escort them to the gate where the knight springs into the saddle, the lady riding pillion, and off they go to supper and I to my walk. I try to think of God and find myself thinking of you; I want to say my rosary and lo my thoughts wander; I come across Pilois and we talk over the project of fresh alleys and drives, after which I hasten indoors for fear of evening chill and of incurring your displeasure.

Hoping for a possible incursion into my solitude of the Third Person of the Holy Trinity, I have been studying books of devotion; but the wind bloweth where it listeth and He chooseth the heart in which He wishes to dwell; He it is who prays for us with groans which cannot be uttered. St. Augustine is my informant—I find him and St. Paul out-and-out Jansenists: the Jesuits like to conjure up a spectre they name " Jansenius ", upon whom they heap insults, without appearing to notice from whence he derives . . .

I wish my dear Sisters of Sainte-Marie (of Nantes) were at Vitré! I have no liking for your chatterboxes from Aix. If I were you I should place my little girl with her aunt; [1] she would become an Abbess; it is the home of doubtful vocations where pleasures and success are not ruled out . . . I cannot help feeling the child would be better off there than at Aix, which will, I imagine, see you no more. The child will be lost to you for ever, since M. de Vendôme is likely to succeed you as Governor,[2] and she will fall into despair. There are privileges in an abbey which are not to be met elsewhere. Once in a while one may be

[1] M. de G.'s sister, who was Abbess at Aubenas.

[2] Mme de S. was always hoping the Duc de Vendôme would succeed M. de G. in Provence, and the latter obtain an appointment at Court.

permitted to accompany Reverend Mother, to enjoy her company, to visit one's ancestral home, to take the waters . . . One is the Abbess' niece, and for this reason all becomes less harsh . . .

To The Same

Les Rochers, Wednesday 12 June [1680].

. . . The other day someone addressed me thus : " Madame, it is warm in the mall, not a breath stirring and the moonlight superb." I could not resist the temptation, summoned my body-guard, donned all my available bonnets, coifs and cloaks, none of which was necessary, and sauntered to the mall which was like a hothouse. It was filled with wraith-like figures, figures of black and white monks, grey and white nuns rising, vanishing, black men, hobgoblins peering from trees, terrified priests . . . Laughing heartily at those strange apparitions we decided they were spooks, mere figments of our imagination, and we returned straightway to the house without the slightest sense of dampness or chill . . . I am sorry, dear child, but I felt compelled to emulate our forefathers . . . and pay my respects to the moon. I can assure you I feel the better for it.

What say you to this ? The most lovely rosary dropped from the skies the other day to my great astonishment, it must have been a recompense because I excel at this particular devotion. This rosary, made of a kind of wood of aloes, has a diamond cross and death's-head in coral . . . Can you throw any light on its origin, and why and how it has traversed many continents to end up here in my lap ? Meanwhile when I recite the decades I fear I shall have even greater distractions than is my wont. Pray write and tell me all you know on the matter of this rosary . . .

To The Same

Les Rochers, Saturday 15 June [1680].

. . . The other day I made Mme de Vins guess which virtue I most willingly put into practice. I told her—that of generosity. There is little doubt I have dispensed large sums since my arrival: one morning eight hundred francs, on another occasion it was a thousand, on another five, and again three hundred pieces; it sounds like a joke, but is true nevertheless. My farmers and carpenters owe me all that and more, and as they have not a farthing piece between them with which to pay their debts I have no choice but to advance them the wherewithal . . . The other day I saw coming towards me a pretty young farmer's wife, with shining eyes, and a fine upstanding figure, in a gown made of Dutch cloth over rich moiré silk, with elaborately-fashioned sleeves . . . Good heavens! this time I shall be ruined once and for all, thought I, for she is owing me eight thousand francs! M. de Grignan would have doted on her, she is on the same model as his Paris beauty. This morning a peasant walked in slung all over with sacks, he carried sacks under his arms, his pockets were stuffed with sacks, as also were his hose—in this country the custom prevails of wearing them unstrapped, whereas that of buttoning the jerkin from the bottom upwards does not yet obtain here, the result being an economy in stuff, and the ungainly appearance of the inhabitants. The good Abbé, who always jumps to conclusions, thought our fortune was made and cried out: "Ah! my good man—I see you are weighted down, how much have you brought with you?" The fellow murmured under his breath that he thought he had as much as thirty francs, and all in two-farthing pieces. I think all the farthings in France must have taken refuge in our poor province . . .

To The Same

Les Rochers, Friday 21 June [1680].

Bad weather still prevails, dearest one, and a lull between the storms only serves to wet us through. Under the auspices of St. Swithin I venture out between two cloudbursts to return drenched to the skin, and, in order to insure that we shall have better protection than bonnets and cloaks can afford, I have erected a small tent at the end of the mall and another at the extreme end of "The Infinite",[1] in which we shall be able to take shelter, to converse, to play games and to read: these objects will serve the twofold purpose of a parasol and an umbrella, and will be a great convenience at a negligible cost. Such is the resounding piece of news from our woodland retreat worthy I venture to think to be chronicled in the *Mercure Galant* . . .

I am told His Majesty's conversations with Mme de Maintenon grow in beauty and in stature, and last from six till ten when the daughter-in-law pays them an impromptu visit to find them still seated in two great armchairs; no sooner has she left than the conversation is resumed. My friend [2] advises me that the lady is treated with universal respect and homage [3] . . .

Mme de la Sablière [4] is one of those Incurables who has been cured of an incurable disease, much to everybody's satisfaction. She is in that blessed state enjoyed by the truly devout; she makes good use of the gift of free will—but then is she not inspired in her actions by Almighty God? Is it not God who snatched her from the burning? Who changed her heart? Set her on the right path? Caused her to love and desire Him alone, thus putting a seal on His munificent gifts? If this goes by the

[1] One of the principal alleys at Les Rochers.

[2] Mme de Coulanges.

[3] Louvois and Marsillac had wanted to re-establish Mme de Montespan at Court, but failed to do so.

[4] Wife of Antoine Rambouillet, Marquis de la S., secretary to the King, she had formed a passionate attachment to the Marquis de La Fare. She was celebrated for her wit and learning, as well as for her beauty. Author of *Pensées chrétiennes* and friend of La Fontaine. She died in the home for incurables in 1693.

name of free will, pray ask me another! Let us now for a moment leave our good Saint Augustine and return to Mme de Coulanges.

She has taken Mme de La Fayette to see this pious soul, in the hopes, maybe, that she will perceive that her own sorrow is not past repair. Up to the present, however, she remains singularly obdurate to all distractions even to that of seeing her own son; but how can we tell what may befall any of us? I am tempted to say this when I think of mine, and wonder how on earth to set about finding a wife for him. At the moment he is devoted to his fat cousin de V . . . and speaks of her in a ribald manner, scarcely a good approach to success and fortune. Look at that wretched little minion, de Chiverni,[1] with his scrubby looks and cold heart, who has succeeded in attracting Mme de Colbert and marrying her niece. Mark my words we shall hear before long that the mortgage on his fine estates is paid off, his debts discharged, and that he has been rescued from the almshouse whither he was indubitably heading. But who can change himself? We are in the hands of Destiny: I scarcely dare to envisage what will be that of your brother. I can see no grandchildren at my knee from his side, only from yours, all so pretty, so well-grown, so charming: and for the improvement in your health I am devoutly grateful. But do not take advantage of it, my dearest, for fear of an early relapse.

To The Same

Les Rochers, Sunday 14 July [1680].

At length, dear one, I have received both your letters—which arrived by the same ordinary. I shall never get used to the tricks the post delights in playing on us, neither shall I ever succeed in curbing my imagination. The very thought of that moment when I am assured your letters have or have not arrived sends me into a turmoil over which I have no control, although I can

[1] Louis de Clermont, Marquis de Montglas, Cte de C., attached to the Dauphin, and one of the "grands seigneurs" of France. Wrote *Mémoires*.

laugh at myself when it is all over . . . the same weakness causes me to start at my shadow every time I think your affection is in doubt; and when the post is late I am frantic; and only recover when I am proved wrong. Would I could follow M. de Grignan's example and be as placid as you wish one to be, then he and I could be of one mind like twins . . . Anyway, dearest, we have to put up with our ego and, comparing our earthly lot with life eternal, echo the words of the song which assures us that one day our suffering will surely come to an end . . .

I am told there has been a rumpus between the King and *Monsieur* in which the Dauphin and Mme de Maintenon are involved: but as yet no one knows what took place. I am amused, in the fastness of my woods, to have had this news from the fountain-head . . . Mme de Coulanges will tell you all she knows which may not be much. M. le Prince de Conti is to be one of the escorts on the King's journey, and the young Princess will remain at Chantilly, she is as sharp-fanged as a viper with her husband . . .

You ask me what caused the breach between La Fare and Mme de La Sablière: believe it or not, it was basset: he prostituted himself for *la bassette*, and for *la bassette* abandoned his revered, his adored one: no doubt the moment had come for a change of objective for his emotions, and basset procured a means of escape, shall we say of salvation, a strange one to choose out of five hundred thousand available ones . . . Mme de la Sablière divined what lay beneath his desertion, his trumped-up excuses, his pretexts, self-justifications, ill-concealed impatience to leave her side, his expeditions to Saint-Germain (where he went in order to gamble), his boredom and silence; and observing the total eclipse of his affection and the mere simulacrum of what had once been an overwhelming passion, she decided to act . . . Disdaining to have recourse to recriminations, without fuss or useless explanations, she herself disappeared, vanished into space without so much as putting her shutters up . . . or announcing her intention of abandoning a mundane existence with all its pomps and vanities. She now devotes the greater part of her life to the "Incurables", only too grateful that her sufferings are not as theirs. The superiors of the hospital are delighted by her charm and ready wit, indeed she subjugates everyone, and her friends crowd to visit her. La Fare goes on playing basset, and the curtain goes down on a nine days wonder which shook the universe. This pretty creature had not waited with folded arms for grace to fall into her lap—God had mapped out the road she should pursue . . . Heavens above! the grace of God is aware of all the turnings, the divagations, the ways and byways, the lure of basset; is acquainted with sorrow and with glory, with the proud and with the lowly; in short all things whatsoever serve the purpose of this great Executant to whose decrees, in the end, we all must submit . . .

To The Same

Rennes, Tuesday 6 August [1680].

. . . I must tell you of a reception given here yesterday in honour of Mme la Princesse de Tarente. The Duc de Chaulnes sent a detachment ahead of forty guards led by their captain as a mark of respect . . . Next came Mme de Marbeuf,[1] two Presidents, friends of the Princess, and finally M. de Chaulnes himself, M. de Rennes, MM. de Coëtlogon, de Tonquedec, de Beaucé, Kercado, de *Crapodo*, de *Kiriquimini*, a *drapello eletto*. Everyone stops dead, embraces, sweats profusely, no one can hear himself speak: on they go to the sound of drum and trumpet, ready themselves to burst into loud acclamations. As we passed by Madame de Chaulnes' house I suggested a pause. There we found her surrounded by a bodyguard of at least forty women and maidens of high degree, the female counterparts of the advance guard. I forgot to mention the presence of six coaches harnessed with six horses each, and ten others with four horses. To go back to the ladies I found myself face to face with three or four of my "daughters-in-law",[2] scarlet in the face with discomfiture. I could see nothing there to discourage me from wishing them to find husbands other than your brother. Everyone kissed and embraced, men and women indiscriminately—a

[1] Louise-Gabrielle de Louet, a good friend, with whom Mme de S. stayed.
[2] Charles's lights-of-love.

somewhat strange manœuvre, the Princess leading the way, and I following in perfect step. In the end I found myself glued to my next door neighbour, so bathed in sweat that by the time I had clambered into the coach and arrived at Mme de Marbeuf's I was totally unrecognisable . . . we then proceeded to lock ourselves in our rooms, for what purpose I leave you to imagine. Personally I changed down to my shift, and forgive me if I appear boastful when I say that I made myself so beautiful I put my said daughters-in-law completely in the shade . . . After Mme de Chaulnes had paid us her state visit we returned with her to find a similar display, grand illuminations, two long tables spread to accommodate sixteen persons . . . at which the guests seated themselves, each evening being a replica of the last. After supper there were games and general conversation : one thing which did not altogether please me was to see a very pretty young woman, who could not boast that she was any cleverer than I, check and checkmate M. de Chaulnes no less than two times, with an air of perfect self-assurance which filled me with envy . . .

Wednesday morning 7 August.

Yesterday was taken up with dinner and a ceremonial supper at M. and Mme de Chaulnes, with hundreds of formal visits to private persons and convents, with comings and goings, fatigue, exhaustion . . . I long with a great longing to be out and away from here where I am too much in request, and I pine for silence, prayer and fasting. I am not very well endowed, but such gifts as I possess are, I consider, wasted in this place, dissipated ; like pence they are scattered to right and to left, and I am left emptied out, bankrupt . . .

Farewell, dear child, I must get ready to dine with M. de Rennes. Oh ! those unending festivities ! Would that I could die of inanition and never open my mouth again.

To The Same

Les Rochers, Wednesday 21 August [1680].

I preface my letter by offering my best congratulations to the Grignan family on the death of the good old Bishop of Evreux.[1] It must be admitted that this event, although wholly unsolicited, is timely to say the least of it. The Chevalier is the richer to the tune of a thousand crowns, and the young prelate [2] finds himself in possession of one of the finest ecclesiastical endowments in France. It all points to Condé's [3] being vested in your family estates. M. de La Garde is acquainted with the amenities of this property, its size and dignity, and the advantages which will accrue to the owner. One can reside there with next to no outlay.

How well I understand your reluctance to look into your budget, it is one of those infernal machines which, if you touch it, is apt to explode. The magnificence of your house and your table, the footing on which you live and entertain and the wastage which ensues are unbelievable; and when you assert they are negligible you take my breath away: to me it savours of black magic or the mendicity of courtiers who, though penniless, travel extensively, follow the drum as they ape the fashion, are to be seen wherever a candle is lit, have tickets in every lottery, and this despite the fact they are head over ears in debt; . . . I forgot to mention the gambling tables; their estates may fall into bankruptcy, on they go, nothing stops them . . . My child—I must admit this line of conduct leaves me completely baffled, but as I am devoted to my dear daughter and to her interests it affects me more than does my own. This truth is plain to see, but let us refrain in our letters from dwelling on so painful a subject, which is only too apt to haunt me in the solitude of my woods and to deprive me of sleep.

The Princesse de Tarente is delighted with your messages; she was amused at the use you made of Hungary water by injecting some into M. de Grignan, and of the word gout to indicate what

[1] Henri de Maupas du Tour, author of *Vie de Sainte Chantal.*
[2] L'Abbé de G. [3] Rest house of the Bishops of Evreux.

the doctors politely term arthritis: your letter is really divine. She was telling me of a German Prince living in Denmark who ran a sharp pin into his side when in a somewhat embarrassing situation. He naturally kept silent, and gangrene set in two months later necessitating the use of incisions; I wished she had killed him outright. Think how Pauline would have derided your jealous proclivities, had M. de Grignan wounded himself on a similar occasion! My son is at Rennes paying court to Sylvia (Tonquedec's daughter is so called); never have I seen such an unlucky fellow when it comes to embroilments, the last one, as he told you, was a long way from being of snow and ice! Mesdames de Coulanges and La Fayette assure me we shall find a way this winter of extricating him from his present abode which, no doubt, he would soon be disgusted with were M. de La Trousse to disclose his heartless designs in favour of M. de Bouligneux.[1] I am half ashamed to own that I am in agreement with you in thinking he would not be averse to spiking his guns by inflicting this deadly blow on our poor little subaltern . . .

Mesdemoiselles de Grignan . . . Adieu, my pretty ones, the truth is I long to embrace you; if you succeed in caring for me the least little bit be assured you will not be the losers. As for the Count I embrace him warmly, and sympathise greatly with him in the matter of that dastardly pin: our poor bodies are indeed subject to humiliating vicissitudes.

To The Same

Les Rochers, Wednesday 28 August [*1680*].

Of course I am delighted to hear that you have retired to bed instead of writing to me, and dearly as I love your letters your well-being is nearest my heart. My son arrived soon after my letters were posted.

My child—believe me, there are women in this world who should be stamped out, erased from the face of the earth; mark

[1] Louis de la Pallu, Cte de B., whose mother was a de La Trousse, Bussy's aunt. The Marquis de la Trousse wished him to marry his daughter.

my words, they should be summarily dealt with, for perfidy, treachery, insolence and effrontery are their stock in trade, and crass dishonesty the least of their shortcomings. They cannot boast of a single kindly impulse, I will not say a loving impulse, for that is unknown to the brood, but even a decent or charitable or humane one, they are fiends in human shape, with soft words and pretty wit, they are utterly brazen. Invulnerable themselves, they delight in turning human frailty to their advantage, and gloating over their triumph. Pray assemble my thumb-nail sketches, frame them together, and there will emerge the portrait of a certain lady who shall be nameless; would to God she were alone of her kind! The health of certain persons we know is so seriously affected that it will be little short of a miracle if recourse to extraordinary measures can be avoided. . .[1]

I am informed the Queen is in great favour at Court,[2] and has been so assiduous in visiting the fortifications in the course of her journey, despite the inconvenience of great heat and fatigue, that she has reaped her reward in the shape of favours and gratuities . . . How is your husband whom we both love? And how is the pin? and is he still unable to use his right hand when he embraces me? I return the embrace with both arms, but very gently in order not to hurt him. Adieu, my dear and lovely one.

Note enclosed from M. de Sévigné

I have seen the letter you wrote my mother which sent me into fits of laughter, despite the panic I have been in these last few days. I hope, however, it will soon be dissipated and that my disease, though it may not boast a resounding Greek name, can at least be spoken of in French without a blush . . . What say you to the picture my mother has drawn of wicked females who deserve to be smothered between mattresses? She is a real child of nature, and herself deserves to be immortalised . . .

[1] Allusion to one of Charles de S.'s mistresses.

[2] Mme de Maintenon had worked for a reconciliation between the King and Queen. Fontanges was dying, and at all costs the King must not fall again under the influence of Mme de Montespan.

To The Same

Les Rochers, Wednesday 11 September [*1680*].

I should never have believed that a letter from you announcing your arrival in Paris could reduce me to tears, yet that was precisely the effect produced, partly by the happiness this assurance gave me, and partly by the noble sentiments expressed by that most pious and saintly girl.[1] We do not only weep when we are sad, the ingredients of which tears are composed are many and diverse . . . Keep me informed of your intentions in order that, if possible, mine may conform with them . . .

I had no idea of the manner in which the Bishop of Evreux met his death. What a terrible catastrophe! You are right in thinking I am appalled. Indeed I am, and more than ever convinced that God's ways are not our ways. He uses this old man's whim as the vehicle whereby he meets with a terrible doom, death by mutilation, to be drawn and quartered by his own horses. See how a ruthless fate takes him in hand, ordains that at the advanced age of eighty he should elect to ride in a coach drawn by a fresh team of horses, and against all advice without a postilion, that he should be killed, torn in half, and that his death should be to the great advantage of the house of Grignan. I could dissert endlessly on this topic. As they say, it never rains but it pours—consider for a moment how well placed will be our dear Chevalier, and what favourable repercussions this will have on his family . . .

I send kisses to the little ones. Montgobert[2] tells me Pauline reads the *Letters of Voiture* with as much understanding as we do.

[1] The eldest of M. de G.'s daughters notified her intention of taking the veil.

[2] Mlle de, governess to the de G. children, sometimes referred to as "la Dague", "Montgo", and as "La Gogo" by Pauline.

To The Same

Les Rochers, Sunday 29 September [*1680*].

Your Château is a little world in itself, a state, a republic, in my day there was never such a crowd collected there as you describe. Montgobert speaks of a " quintille ",[1] a word with which I am not familiar, but although we are hermits in comparison with you we frequently have no less than three card tables set out for backgammon, ombra and reversis. At the moment we have Mme de Marbeuf who is easy and obliging . . . and other folk from Vitré with whom you are no better acquainted than you are with the " Solitary " [2] . . . Far from wishing to add to the number I am well satisfied with things as they are and only regret I have not more time to talk and read. The " Solitary " is just where you think, and you would be agreeably surprised with its straight lines and admirably planted trees . . .

I feel the time has come when I should turn my thoughts in other directions. When I consider that at the end of my journey I shall find you waiting for me I can scarce believe in such happiness and dread some difficulty cropping up . . . But I am persuaded all will be well and that your hosts of visitors will make themselves scarce. They appear to resemble that conjuring trick played with pawns in which a King is guarded on either side by nine men ; when four are removed it still leaves nine, when four are put back nine still remain ! That is your case to a t. When you are by yourselves you are full up to the brim and yet there is always room for three times the number. May God preserve in you this gift of multiplicity, with which you are notably endowed, and which is so valuable where expenses far outrun the constable . . .

Adieu, sweet child ; have no care regarding my health which is perfect. Would to God I could say the same of yours ! I have erected small pavilions in the shape of tents, which serve to shelter us in the woods, they are most handy . . . we read

[1] A new card game, five-handed *ombre*, with the same rules as for *quadrille*.
[2] A new walk at Les Rochers, mentioned in a previous letter.

LES ROCHERS Château de Mme de Sevigne (Ille et Vilaine)
(Chemin de fer de l'Ouest — Ligne de Bretagne)

Château des Rochers—Bretagne
19th-century lithograph by Becquet Frères after J. Jacottet

VUE DU CHATEAU DE GRIGNAN (ÉTAT ANCIEN

Château et Ville de Grignan—Provence
17th-century drawing in the *Bibliothèque Nationale*
(*Photo :* B.N.)

there and converse at our leisure, we let the mists disperse after which we wander home through the mall which is as safe and sound and snug as any corridor or gallery.

To The Same

Les Rochers, Wednesday 9 October [1680].

How greatly I pity you for allowing yourself to become such a hopeless prey to anxiety; in truth you have not the requisite strength to endure it. You are in a fever of apprehension, over-straining your eyes and over-stimulating your brain, ever fearing the worst. By now you will know that your brothers are well again,[1] they, and the other invalids, were cured by the English apothecary's draught. You alone are to be pitied because of your tender heart and your too vivid imagination . . .

I conjure you not to be over-anxious on your little brother's behalf; he is far from well and is bound to suffer a good deal; but as he possesses the courage and determination to be cured, and there is no real danger, I beg of you, my pretty one, to rest content about him and about me—his illness is not catching through the medium of books or conversation. He is so happy here that he will not hear of going to Paris as was suggested, he by litter on account of his severe megrims, and I by coach. I feel he cannot face the separation which life in the capital will impose on him; here it is altogether different, and, moreover, he has a touching belief in his physician, and sacrificed one whole week to his treatment, at the end of which he was as one who has been dipped seven times in the river Jordan. One day you shall have the whole story . . .

When in Paris my son confided his troubles to Mme de La Fayette and a dozen of her friends. What think you of this secret in the hands of some fifteen persons? I confess I have never been more astonished than by the lighthearted way he treats this whole business—I should have thought one would die sooner than give oneself away, but seeing how frank my son is I shall endeavour to follow his example.

[1] The Grignan brothers had fallen ill of a prevalent disease.

To The Same

Malicorne, Wednesday 23 October [*1680*].

We are well on the way, and longing to get to Paris as quickly as possible. Indeed there is no time to be lost in obtaining relief for your poor brother, the pains in his head and their deleterious effect on his emotions, together with the Lauzun-like beard he now affects have made him unrecognisable; we are entirely preoccupied with the task of getting him safely to his destination, everything must give way to this urgent necessity; as he never falls asleep till dawn we cannot start before eight or nine of the clock, and arrive when we may . . . do not trouble yourself unduly—the right treatment, which I believe will prove to be the river Jordan I spoke of the other day—this, I am sure, will make him whole again, meanwhile his state is pitiful to behold. You say you only speak of Providence when you have a pain in your chest; as for me, when I am once embarked on that subject, I find there is so much to be said, to argue about, to look into, that I could go on talking till my chest became unbearably sore . . . Impossible to describe to you all that has happened at Les Rochers in the last two months, the blindness which overtook us, the paralysis, lethargy, procrastination, love of home maybe . . . then, of a sudden, all changed overnight from black to white, we hated what we previously adored, we longed for the Paris we had previously contemned . . . we moved house in two days, and here we are dying to get to our destination and to bathe in the river Jordan which, after all, is our main objective . . .

To The Same

Paris, Wednesday 6 November [*1680*].

I adjure you, my child, to embark on your travels at the first opportunity: if you wait until M. de Grignan has fulfilled his obligations, you must abandon the thought of coming this winter. It would appear to me scarcely to conform with the affection he professes that he should contemplate exposing you to the vicissitudes of treacherous weather and bad roads—it really is not credible . . . It is evident that from birth you were not intended to enjoy a moment of peaceful happiness, since you are unable to let your thoughts rest on your sojourn in Paris, but must, even now, be agitating about your return journey. It is surely unnecessary to make a bugbear of leaving Paris whilst you are still in the throes of departure from Grignan. When you do arrive, you will find your quarters comfortable, your lease renewed for four years, your budget cut and dried, and, if you and M. de Grignan should wish to avoid reckless expenditure, this is the one place where you will find you can draw in your horns. Your outgoings at Aix are outrageous, and I imagine you have somewhat revised your views on the wonderful economies you affect to practise at Grignan, where you think you can live on air; air is apt, it could scarcely be more so! Your three tables spread in the gallery, your unending flow of visitors, the state you keep; the feeding of man and beast which in these times no one but you would attempt; the famous Inn you run for the benefit of all and sundry—in my eyes, and despite your protestations, I can only see a relentless flood which I dare not contemplate, and which carries all in its train. But here I hope you may be able to relax and rest from your labours; and pray do not think of leaving before your financial situation is once more secure . . . the one important thing is to arrive, which is also my dearest wish . . .

Ah, my child—if you knew how adaptable I really am, how easy to get on with! In my case a little kindness, good will, sociability are half the battle—indeed I am the most easy-going of mortals . . . I only wish you had been here when my cousin confided to me her desire to know more of my son's misfortunes, and I felt constrained to satisfy her curiosity—the natural give and take between two creatures living side by side in this world. But when all one says is a grievance, when every carefully chosen word is subject to misconstruction, when barriers are erected on every side, and the most common-place things bear a sinister interpretation . . . when suspicion, bitterness, nay, aversion inform every word and action I get disheartened, disabused to say the least of it . . . One is not, I suppose, used to so rough a passage, such harsh treatment, especially from a child one has brought into the world . . . If I put this before you at the present moment it is because I am sensible of a little change for the better of which I am overjoyed . . . if it cannot be called a reconciliation, it is, at any rate, an easing up . . . surely one is not always beyond the pale! I am pleased—it takes so little to please me . . .

I now wish to recommend to your care the person I love best—your own most precious self, and if for no other reason pray take every precaution, whatever else may induce you to do so . . . The Dauphin and Dauphine are once more suffering from a feverish attack—their minions will be obliged to deputise for them . . .

NOTE.—*Shortly after this letter was written Mme de G. arrived in Paris, and mother and daughter were together until September 1684, when Mme de S. left for les Rochers.*

1681

To The Comte de Bussy

Paris, 3 April [*1681*].

Shall we call quits, my poor cousin? I am, however, constrained to admit I am in the wrong. My niece, I hear, is in poor health; alas, there is no stable happiness to be looked for in this world. The law of compensations ordains that all men shall be equal, or at any rate that the favoured ones, by occasionally suffering a setback, may come to understand the hard lot of their less fortunate brethren, the victims of sorrow and misfortune. I shall believe in your projected journey in April only when I know my niece is well enough to accompany you . . .

You really must not allow such sombre, such useless thoughts to possess you: much better to believe what Corbinelli preaches daily for my benefit, that God rules all things according to His will, that your place in the Universe is pre-ordained and you can occupy no other. Père Bourdaloue preached a sermon the other day against prudence in human affairs which, as he said, are wholly dependent on Providence, adding that the one and only way of salvation is that which God ordains for us. How consoling a thought is this, and how easy in that way to accept at His hands the worst that can befall us! Life is short and passes like a thief in the night and we are scarcely aware of the flood which inexorably bears us along. These are suitable reflexions for Holy Week, and they fit my pessimistic mood when I observe that, with the exception of yourself, all men are proud and boastful, but you must know, despite the pious maxims I preach, I am ever conscious of my own shortcomings and human frailty.

Adieu, dear cousin . . .

1682

To The President de Moulceau [1]

Paris, 7 August [*1682*].

Madame la Dauphine was brought to bed of a Duc de Bourgogne[2] on Thursday at ten o'clock of the evening: your friend will tell you of the joyous clamour which broke out at court when the news became known, and with what frenzied haste people rushed to offer their congratulations to the King, the Dauphin, and the Queen; the shouting and yelling which ensued, the fireworks, the wine which was spilled whilst the Swiss guards, to the number of two hundred, disported themselves among the hogsheads, the cries of "Vive le Roi", clanging of bells, cannon firing, discourses, compliments flying around. Then, in a moment of time, in the twinkling of an eye, all is over.

To The Comte de Bussy

Paris, 23 December [*1682*].

If, my very unfair cousin, you were to receive as scant justice as you have meted out to me, I should strongly urge you to refrain from coming to Paris . . .

Nevertheless you must know that love is playing many a prank

[1] President of the Council Chamber of Montpellier, friend of all at l'Hôtel de Carnavalet: said to be jealous of Corbinelli.

[2] Louis, for whom Fénelon later wrote *Télémaque*. (*ob.* 18.2.1712).

in this capital. The Comte de Soissons [1] has openly avowed his marriage to Mlle de Beauvais.[2] The King received her most graciously, and she appeared both beautiful and modest. It is alleged she has been married two and a half years and for fear her husband should be surfeited before the appointed time she withheld her favours until after her twenty-fifth birthday which was celebrated last Friday; we could, I think, converse endlessly on this subject, and one day, when you come and dine on your return, we will argue the wrongs and the rights of her action: it seems to me that when a man of this quality honours a young lady by asking her in marriage, it is scarcely probable that the said young lady will have nothing better to offer him than an overweening ambition allied to a frigid mistrust. I remember a verse of Ariosto which pleased me: Angelica, having roamed the world in the company of Roland, returns unscathed as when she left her father's house. The author comments: "*Forse era ver, ma non però credibile.*" It must, however, be conceded that the manœuvre has met with resounding success.

The King has endowed the Count with a pension of twenty thousand livres; his mother having long since disinherited him, and his grandmother, Madame de Carignan,[3] in despair, having followed suit. From another quarter news reaches us that the Marquis de Richelieu [4] has absconded with Mlle de Mazarin [5] from the portals of Sainte-Marie de Chaillot, in the rôle of lover, or in my view that of husband, the while her father is consulting Grenoble,[6] Angers [7] and the Trappists as to whether or no he

[1] Louis-Thomas de Savoie, son of Olympe Mancini, brother of Prince Eugène, the famous general and victor at the battle of Malplaquet.

[2] Uranie de la Cropte de B., Lady-in-Waiting to *Madame*, whom *Monsieur* had discovered talking to the Cte de Soissons and thereupon forbade him entry to the Palais-Royal. The marriage was not recognised till three years after it took place.

[3] Marie de Bourbon, with whom her granddaughter-in-law went to stay before leaving France.

[4] Louis-Armand du Plessis, nephew of the Duc de R.

[5] Marie-Charlotte de, daughter of the Duc de Meilleraye and Hortense Mancini. The Duc de Mazarin was so jealous of his daughter's charms that he desired to have all her teeth extracted: two years later he forgave his son-in-law.

[6] Cardinal le Camus, brother of Nicolas, *Procureur Général.*

[7] Henri Arnauld, brother of Arnauld d'Andilly.

should give his daughter in marriage! One really loses patience with such lunacy . . .

My daughter has been seriously indisposed; she is cured however, and so therefore am I, for both you and I know what it is to suffer all our daughter's ills. I embrace yours and I embrace you also, that is if you are ready to atone in full for your many shortcomings.

1683

To The Comte de Bussy

Paris, 15 December [1683].

At last, at length and after many vicissitudes my poor son is about to be married.[1] I crave your power of attorney to enable me to sign the marriage contract . . . This event is a proof one must never despair of a change of fortune. I have long feared my son had forfeited all hope of making a suitable match after his most outrageous conduct and his many shipwrecks, added to the fact that he is without fortune or prospects of any kind ; and just as I had come to this sad conclusion Providence destined us, or maybe long ago had so destined, that we should bring off a marriage more prosperous than I could have dared to hope for, even in his earlier and more innocent years. It seems we go through life feeling our way as do the blind, and in our total ignorance mistaking good for evil, evil for good ? . . .

[1] His marriage to Jeanne-Marguerite de Bréhan de Mauron took place 8 Feb. 1684.

1684

To Mademoiselle de Scudéry

Monday, 11 September [1684].

If I were to let my tongue run away with me there is only one truth I would wish to express, and that is, Mademoiselle, the assurance of my undying love and veneration for you, added to the appreciation I have of your extraordinary merit. I admire it, and am conscious of my great good fortune in possessing a share, however small, of your friendship and esteem. As constancy spells perfection I assure myself that you will not change towards me, and I venture to make the boast that, whatever punishment God may have in store for me, it will not be to deprive me wholly of your presence . . . I am taking your *Conversations* [1] to my son, hoping they will afford him as much delight as their perusal, undoubtedly, will give me.

[1] Mlle de S. had sent the first two volumes of this work to Mme de S. in 1680. The date of this letter is determined by the fact that a further two volumes appeared in 1684.

To Madame de Grignan

Etampes, Wednesday 13 September [1684].

You can well believe, my very dearest, that despite all your good advice, I found myself on leaving you at the mercy of many a sharp pang and thrust from dagger and sword, try as I might to elude them.[1] I dared not so much as think or pronounce a word; to be so vulnerable is painful indeed! . . .

I tried to formulate the reasons which impelled me to make this journey, and found them so convincing that I was able to understand the why and the wherefore of my resolution, but I have to begin all over again in order to endure your absence with any kind of equanimity . . .

I am delighted you went to Versailles, as I think the change of scene will have afforded you some distractions—certainly more than did Châtres [2] or Etampes in my case. I hope your journey may prove propitious—how could one grudge it you? I recommend your good health to your attention: it is a vast consolation to me to dwell on the thought of your plump little cheeks—pray do not allow them to wither in my absence . . . Thank Mademoiselle d'Alerac's [3] beautiful eyes for the tears they have shed on my behalf: but how to thank you for your tenderness and grief? We must however put that quickly from us: and you must believe me when I say that my heart is yours, yours to the exclusion of all else, over which you reign, shall reign and reign supreme for evermore.

To The Same

Les Rochers, Wednesday 27 September [1684].

At last, my dearest, three of your letters have arrived. When no other consolation offers, to receive them is like being born

[1] Mme de S. had reluctantly decided she must return to Les Rochers.

[2] Old name for the town of Arpajon.

[3] Françoise-Julie, M. de G.'s second daughter by his first wife, Angélique d'Angennes. She became Marquise de Vieraye.

anew, they are vivifying, exciting, sustaining; without them one is apt to fall into a state of abandonment when all other correspondence is utterly distasteful and the longing to hear from the one we love becomes imperative . . .

Here we lead a somewhat quiet and melancholy existence, any other would not at present suit my mood. My son has suffered an attack of his boils; my daughter-in-law is seldom cheerful, she suffers from the vapours and changes countenance a hundred times a day without ever hitting on the right one: she is extremely delicate and can scarcely walk a step, she is always shivering with the cold, and by nine o'clock at night she is played out, extenuated, for her the days are all too long. Her habits of extreme sloth leave me free to do what I like, on condition that she can do likewise—that at any rate is gratifying. No one could possibly think Les Rochers possessed more than one mistress, and although I never interfere I find all my wishes forestalled as if by an invisible agent. I take my walks in solitude, but dare not linger till nightfall lest I should cry aloud or burst into tears; no—I cannot face the dark in my present mood, but should I gain sufficient strength to do so I shall not venture for fear of your displeasure: at the moment my health stands in the way, but that, I think, is how you would have it; in fact it is you, and you, and always you . . . Your account of Versailles has vastly entertained me: Mme de Maintenon's status at court is unique, in the annals of history nothing has ever equalled it nor, I venture to think, ever will . . .

To The Same

Les Rochers, Sunday 1 October [1684].

Although my letter is dated Sunday I am writing on a Saturday; it is barely ten o'clock of the evening and everyone has retired for the night: it is an hour in which you belong to me in a very special manner, more so than at other times of day when my room is filled to capacity: not that I allow anyone to coerce me—I know how to shake off the importunate. I take my walks by myself, and despite all you say, am thankful for my freedom. To think of you is as necessary to me as to see you, and if only those swords were blunted I wrote to you about from Etampes, and

I less vulnerable to their thrust, the long hours I devote to you in my thoughts would be as beneficial to my body as they are to my soul . . . I was telling you an unpalatable truth when I said that you left me in so vulnerable a state that my very thoughts were as open wounds. But let us not dwell on it . . . as I sit writing to you I am composed and at peace . . . You say you regret me as you would the loss of good health, but I do not agree with your premises, for I am convinced you rejoiced far more in the five or six visits I was wont to pay you each day, and in the solace of our close communion than in any sense of well being. You are not being fair to your powers of devotion. For my part I have nothing to reproach myself with, there was not a moment of the day or night when I was not acutely conscious of the joy your company afforded me: when I returned from Mass, from a walk or a visit to the Bienbon all was sensible delight: in fact I cannot deny that leaving you dealt me a mortal blow from which I had scarcely recovered by the time your visit came to an end. Are you not amazed at the want of control I display, and the havoc wrought by my unbridled emotions? . . . but remember I am alone, defenceless, and profoundly stirred, which I imagine will not be the case with you when you peruse what I have written. But no matter, dear Countess, you must try and learn to be indulgent . . .

It is Sunday, and time to despatch our packet . . . My son has left for Rennes, where he hopes to be told that his boils are innocuous. His wife surrounds me with attentions, but she is more than ready to observe the pact we made, namely to meet as little as possible in the course of the day. I have spent the morning in my grounds with my dear Abbé Charrier; [1] when she wishes to take a stroll I shall be waiting in my study—I assure you this all fits in perfectly. She has good points, at least I suppose so, but up to the present I am disposed to confine myself to negative praise. She is not this, nor that, nor the other, the day may come when I shall say she is the other. She sends you her kind wishes, and desires our goodwill, but without alacrity. In fact she shows not the slightest alacrity for anything. I can say this in her favour that she does not speak Breton, and has not the accent of a native of Rennes.

[1] Abbé de Quimperlé.

To The Same

Les Rochers, Sunday 5 November [1684].

I can assure you I will not fret unduly about your pains and aches, my best and dearest one; I adjure you to keep nothing from me. It is clear that you are faced with having to survive your remedies. It was cruel to submit you to a third bleeding when already a second one proved a mistake, and it is certain your drugs are badly composed; our good Capuchins strongly deprecate the use of polycrest;[1] I fear you have been very badly advised, my poor love . . . To me you try to minimise the gravity of your sore throat and the dangers of your superfluous blood-lettings, you must however not allow these unduly to disturb you, and must once more have recourse to that wholesome infusion of green and bitter periwinkle, a specific for your troubles, which has already helped you so much; it will no doubt cool your poor inflamed lungs . . . Ask M. du Plessis[2] to write to me . . . but pray scribble a line top and bottom of the letter that I may see your handwriting, and I shall be charmed to know you are resting and talking to me, instead of sitting up writing in a posture which is fatally bad for any delicacy of the chest. For the pain in your side I am tempted to send you the remainder of my soothing balsam by the Abbé Charrier, who is however afraid of breaking the bottle . . . this balsam is sovereign, but for rheumatism it would require oceans; drop eight drops into a very hot plate, apply to the seat of the pain, rubbing gently until well absorbed, then apply a hot cloth on the painful spot; miraculous cures are known to have resulted; some people believe in adding a like number of drops of the essence of urine . . . I entreat you not to neglect your side . . .

As for our well-being, dearest, I must tell you I am in perfect health; when it is fine, I walk, avoiding the mist and fog, but as soon as they rise my son hastens to fetch me indoors . . . My daughter-in-law never stirs her stumps, she is immersed in dosing herself with the remedies of our Capuchin brethren, which

[1] A purgative salt.

[2] Tutor to the Marquis de G.

consist of potions and herb baths—these have exhausted her without doing her any appreciable good . . .

The Abbé is greatly incommoded by distention and wind, although he is familiar with such troubles. The Capuchins insist on his taking daily doses of crayfish powder, and assure him that these will in time prove beneficial. As for me I am rid of the vapours. I believe they come because I dread them, now that I disregard them they will attack the more credulous. This is a truthful recital of our state at the present time . . .

To The Same

Les Rochers, Sunday 26 November [1684].

. . . Let us start by discussing you and your concerns. To me it is scarcely credible that when you were conversing with the King you got so confused, so rattled, that you well nigh took leave of your senses and could only stand and gape at your sovereign. I can scarcely credit that my beloved child, usually so self-possessed and resourceful, should be reduced to such a plight. From what you told me that His Majesty said about wishing to benefit M. de Grignan I did not think this merely implied that his huge expenditure in Provence would be taken into account. By the King's answer I took him to mean : " What you are asking is little enough—my intention is to do something more." . . .

Madame de La Fayette says you looked beautiful as an angel at Versailles, that you were received by the King, and it is thought you pleaded that your husband might be granted a pension. But if questioned, I intend replying quite casually that you were drawing His Majesty's attention to your excessive commitments in Provence.

Our dear Bienbon has contracted one of his heavy colds, and is shut away in his small alcove where he is much better off than in Paris. As for my daughter-in-law she has taken all the Capuchins' most violent remedies . . . which appear to have left her quite unmoved. When it is fine weather, as it has been these last three days, I start at two o'clock and walk *quanto và* ; I pass and repass the woodmen sawing wood with a will and looking to the life like classical effigies of winter, and when I have basked once more in the last rays of the setting sun I go back to my room, and leave tougher, coarser-grained folk to enjoy the dusk since, having become a timid damsel at your dictation, I have adopted these sedentary habits. The Coulanges armchair, the books my son reads aloud to perfection, a modicum of conversation—these will constitute my in-all and by-all through the winter, to your entire satisfaction be it said, since in so doing I am following your prescriptions to the letter . . . We have read many volumes in folio in the course of the last twelve days, Nicole, *The Lives of the Fathers of the Desert*, *The English Reformation* : if one is fortunate enough to fancy this kind of diversion one can never be dull.

1685

To Madame de Grignan

Les Rochers, Wednesday 7 February [*1685*].

You could scarcely do better than air your troubles at Versailles unless you were to do better still and get rid of them altogether. I fear the " powder of sympathy "[1] is useless for old folks' ills. It has only succeeded in healing the very smallest of my sores, and I now make use of that admirable black unguent which has so nearly cured me that, in future, your only concern must be to love me . . . I have no fever, I eat well and discreetly; having no inflammatory symptoms I am encouraged to walk a little when fine, I read, write and sew, and welcome your letters with open arms—this is the truth about myself, naked and unashamed, my dear one, and you need not put spies upon my tracks, for I shall never tell you a lie, I am far too anxious not to be hoodwinked by you to practise any deceit myself. At this very moment the sun is pouring into my room which tempts me to take a turn in the Mall. Now, dear Countess, curb your imagination, draw back the curtains which obscure your view, and exorcise this image of a weeping female with a " pious Aeneas " at her feet; it is a false one I assure you. But I want to preserve

[1] A fashionable remedy. Sir Kenelm Digby had delivered his famous discourse on his invention at Montpellier in 1658. Mme de S. suffered from erysipelas, for which certain herbs were laid on the part afflicted for a certain time, and then buried in the ground: as the herbs rotted there so the inflammation was supposed to subside.

the use of my legs as long as possible, for once they rebel they are difficult to subdue. The other day I wanted to purge myself with those broths of Fr. Ange, they had suited me on a previous occasion, but they only served to stir things up, which fain must simmer down again and I am resolved on no account to have recourse to drugs or potions, and not to try and improve on perfect health. To play about with remedies is a cruel game. Enough—I must stop, leaving you in a whirl of gaiety, or so I imagine, where I know I am not forgotten by you any more than I am in the quiet of your bed-chamber, and of whom is it possible to say as much? But then no one could appreciate more warmly than I the many charms of your devotion!

To The Same

[*Les Rochers*], *Wednesday 13 June* [*1685*].

. . . Speaking of vapours, my kindest dear one, I was on the verge the other day of welcoming their return when I had recourse to eight drops of essence of urine and although I was unable to close my eyes all night long . . . I am glad to have renewed its acquaintance. I should indeed be ungrateful if I complained of the vapours: so long as my leg troubled me, they stayed in the background, which was obliging of them you will admit.

Yes—our dear Capuchins are faithful to their threefold vows: their journey to Egypt, where all the women are naked as Eve, disgusted them for the rest of their days. Their worst enemies can find nothing detrimental to say of their morals—what a testimony is this! . . .

My dear—pray acquaint yourself with the new fashions for men this summer; I shall be asking you to send me a suitable length of material for your brother, who begs you to put him in the way of being dressed in the present mode, without undue expense of course, and to acquaint him of the latest fashion in sleeves, choose him a trimming and send all you think he may require for the reception of our good governors. My son has a local tailor, and M. du Plessis will hand you over some ready money to spend on ribbons . . . pray consult Madame de Chaulnes on the subject of a suitable summer gown for me to wear when I meet her at Rennes . . . I shall return here to pack up and get ready for the red letter day when I shall see and embrace you again and again. I have a silk gown; it is bronze colour and studded with silver tassels, looped up at the sleeves and hem, which I take it is scarcely in the present mode, and one must not risk being made a mock of at Rennes where everything is done on such a sumptuous scale. I shall be well satisfied to be guided by you in the matter of dress, bearing in mind the necessity of economy and a modest demeanour. No "*toupers*" for me; good Madame "Dio" has my measurements. You will know better than I at what date the garments will be required since you will be apprised of M. de Chaulnes' movements . . .

We are told (*fuor di proposito*) that the "Minims"[1] from Provence have dedicated a thesis to the King, in which they compare him to Almighty God, if anything to the disadvantage of the latter. It was shown to the Bishop of Meaux,[2] who passed it on to the King urging His Majesty to spurn such a missive. The King was of the same opinion, the thesis was returned to the Sorbonne for a pronouncement to be made. The Sorbonne forthwith turned it down; there is a limit to everything, and I should never have thought the Minims capable of committing such an enormity. I like to recount the latest gossip to you from Versailles and Paris: ignoramus that you are!!! . . .

To The Same

Les Rochers, Sunday 26 August [*1685*].

Does the twenty-sixth appeal to you, dear child? Surely it is better than the twenty-second and you will see, if God pleases, how well it will all pan out. I say if God pleases for that is the crux of the matter. Let me know the exact date of your arrival at Bâville [3] that I may so contrive as to be there on the following

[1] Monks of the order of Saint François de Paul. [2] Bossuet.

[3] Country house of M. de Lamoignon (*see* p. 173), the great book collector.

day, do not attempt to push on any further but rest the while you await my arrival, and above all do not overdo yourself. Were you for one moment to question my perfect and overwhelming happiness at our reunion I should have to turn the tables upon you and begin to question yours; let us not offend, neither attribute any unjust motive to one another. As for me I refuse even to contemplate the possibility of any unpleasant complication in the future lest it should upset my digestion.

Yesterday we visited the Princesse de Tarente whose son was there; what a fine figure and what an ugly countenance! He is not alone in possessing these contradictory attributes [1] . . . Farewell, my most agreeable daughter, I embrace you on both cheeks and long to hear if you are still plump and beautiful? If God spares me a little longer I hope to be reassured on that head.

NOTE.—*No more letters were to pass between mother and daughter until September 1687—they spent the two intervening years together in Paris.*

[1] An allusion to M. de G.'s physique.

1686

To The President de Moulceau

Paris, Friday 13 December [1686].

Sir—I wrote you a long and confidential letter a month since, full of esteem and affection, but it must I think have gone astray . . . at any rate you have not answered me. In spite of this I feel constrained to write once more to tell you of a tragic event, and another of happy augury, namely the death of M. le Prince [1] which occurred at Fontainebleau on the 11th instant at a quarter past seven of the evening, and the return of Conti [2] to the Court of Versailles at the instance of M. le Prince, whose earnest request to the King received a favourable hearing. When on his deathbed the Prince had the consolation of knowing his prayer had been granted, but seldom have so many tears been shed over an event so joyous. M. de Conti is inconsolable, and his loss is the more overwhelming in that he spent the period of his disgrace at Chantilly under the auspices of his master, whose great attainments and flawless character he endeavoured to emulate, and from whom, in addition, he received untiring devotion. M. le Prince had gone post haste from Chantilly to Fontainebleau upon hear-

[1] Le Grand Condé, aged 65.

[2] François-Louis de Bourbon, Prince de la Roche-sur-Yon, who had recently succeeded to the title of Prince de Conti on the death of his brother Louis-Armand from smallpox. He had been exiled from Court for a dangerous letter, in which he had referred to "*le Roi de théâtre*".

ing that Madame de Bourbon [1] had contracted smallpox, and in order to prevent M. le Duc [2] (who had hitherto been immune) from endangering his life by attending on her; by so doing he forfeited his own . . . he became desperately sick, and died of a mighty oppression. Thinking he was coming to Paris he uttered the ominous words he would shortly be embarking on a longer journey. He summoned his confessor, Father Deschamps, and after lying unconscious for twenty-four hours he rallied, received the Last Sacraments, and died to the extreme sorrow of his family and friends . . .

Before the Prince's departure for Fontainebleau the following curious incident took place. Returning at three of the clock from a day's hunting one of his gentlemen named Vernillon, as he approached the Château saw, framed in the window of the armoury, the phantom of one long since dead and buried. He drew up and dismounted to look more closely at the strange apparition when his valet cried out he too had seen a spectre; they proceeded to enter the Château, and having obtained the keys from the guardian, they advanced into the armoury. Vernillon found it undisturbed as if silence had reigned there for the past six months. When this tale was repeated to M. le Prince he soon dismissed it, but all the world heard it and trembled for his safety. I am telling you the story because it bears the stamp of truth, and may give you to think, as it has us . . .

[1] Louise-Françoise de Bourbon, formerly Mlle de Nantes, daughter of the King and Mme de Montespan.

[2] Her husband, le Duc d'Enghien, grandson of Condé.

1687

To The President de Moulceau

Paris, Written on Feast of the Epiphany, 1687.

I really cannot frame an answer to all your religious and moral reflections, for my answer would be a mere repetition—yes, my letter would be an echo of yours since, in this instance, I am happy to find myself in agreement with you. Therefore I greatly prefer scolding you, and telling you that you must indeed be finical and over-nice if finding yourself a grandfather throws you into a state of decrepitude. I see your daughter has taken the liberty of doing it a second time. What a misfortune! And you dare complain to me, Sir, to me whose granddaughter may, at the age of sixteen, take the veil in the Convent of the Visitation at Aix. What a life you prepare for yourself! Whereas I succeed in disregarding the affront I have not yet suffered, and in displaying heroic courage, knowing myself to be helpless. I try and dwell on what I owe to God for leading me in so gentle a manner to my appointed end, for encouraging me to spend my days in preparing for it, and, not being tempted to drain the cup of life to the dregs. Extreme old age is ugly and humiliating. Corbinelli and I have a painful example before our eyes in that of poor old Abbé de Coulanges, whose crippled state and many infirmities are a warning to us not to follow in his steps . . . These sentiments are inspired by Christian philosophy which we devoutly hope you will put into practice when your granddaughter reaches the age of sixteen . . .

To The Comte de Bussy

Paris, 2 September [*1687*].

I have this moment received your letters from Cressia,[1] my dear cousin, which have afforded me much solace, for I must tell you that I am stricken with grief having, in the course of these last ten days, seen my beloved uncle [2] die before my eyes. You know what he meant to me. Everything he could possibly do he did, making me the recipient of his worldly goods, and restoring the fortunes of my children. He raised me from the abyss into which I had sunk at the time of M. de Sévigné's death, he prosecuted my lawsuit, transformed the estate my son now owns into one of the most lovely and pleasant in the land; promoted the marriages of both my children: in a word it is to him I owe the comfort and security of my days. You can well imagine what it means to me to have lost one to whom I was under every manner of obligation, and bound by the habits of a lifetime . . . My uncle was eighty years of age, and bowed down with years and infirmity, his life had become a burden and one could not wish it prolonged . . . I am filled to overflowing with sorrow and gratitude.

Adieu, dear cousin; if you come, we shall converse endlessly . . . I pray God to preserve you, which is tantamount to saying you may love me for many a long year for I cannot contemplate imposing any limits on our affection other than those prescribed by the number of our days on earth.

To Madame de Grignan

Bourbon,[3] *Monday 22 September* [*1687*].

We arrived here yesternight from Nevers . . . true it is we did it in a day, but what a day! What an endless ten leagues! We

[1] In Franche-Comté, property of the Colignys.

[2] L'abbé Christophe de Coulanges, her guardian. He died 29 Aug., after a week's illness. The Abbaye de Livry was thus left vacant.

[3] Mme de S. had gone there to do a cure.

travelled from early dawn till late at night, pausing only a short two hours for dinner; it was raining cats and dogs, the roads were atrocious, and we proceeded at a snail's pace for fear of upsetting into the yawning ditches—the longest fourteen leagues I ever traversed. And all this after enjoying five days of perfect weather under a glorious sun, and with countryside and roads to match. We might be in a different zone, a country covered in low cloud like Brittany, a dark forest which the rays of the sun never penetrate . . . We have slept well, visited the bubbling springs, heard Mass at the Capuchins . . . We like our doctor Amiot, who knows and esteems Alliot [1] . . . he is against blood-letting, and approves the Capuchin remedies. He assures me all my small ailments are due to the spleen, for which Bourbon is specific. He dotes on Vichy, but for my condition this resort is to be preferred. As for the douches he advocates they should be given very lightly or preferably not at all, and he is sure he can convince M. Alliot . . . that by throwing off the bad humours, and sweating profusely all will be for the best; he has my case well in hand . . . Mme de Chaulnes finds this resort an antidote for her troubles, which are far from negligible, but Madame de Nangis has nearly passed out with the colic. Our lodgings which we share are commodious enough; but of this place it must truly be said that heaven can ill afford it a smile . . .

Providence, in a devious way all her own, has taken me by the hand and led me here. In my heart I find myself ever turning to you for counsel and support and I seem to hear your reassuring answer: courage my dear—you have done the wise thing, no other course was possible . . .

NOTE.—*At the time of Mme de S.'s return from Bourbon, Mme de G. was residing at Fontainebleau. Mother and daughter thereafter remained with one another until the early days of 1688.*

[1] Doctor-in-Ordinary to the King.

1688

To Madame de Grignan

Paris, Wednesday 20 October [1688].

Your letters from Thézé [1] have reached us; what you say of it is wholly delightful. One would scarcely expect to find such polite amenities on the top of a mountain: the mistress of this domain does indeed deserve to be loved and admired [2] . . . But let us speak of you, my lovely one: so you successfully forded that arrogant, turbulent, brute of a Rhône for which I think the Durance, when in spate, would be a suitable mate? What an awe-inspiring couple to be sure! We are impatiently awaiting news of you from La Garde; can youth and health stand up to the spectres you conjure up? to your black moods and cruel nights? The thought of it is my undoing, for I am sensible of the grave danger which is entailed. But indeed you have allowed your imagination to run away with you: were you with us you would be getting constant news as we do, and you would know our dear little crony [3] is already quite settled in, and started off on his new career. He writes lightheartedly and with good cheer has twice been in the trenches . . . and is in good health . . . The Chevalier is pleased with him. He told him: "You are no longer my little lad, nor my nephew—you are my comrade."

[1] Mme de G. had once more set out for Grignan.

[2] Ctsse de Rochebonne, sister of M. de G.

[3] The young Marquis de G., on his first campaign as a volunteer in his uncle's regiment (Champagne).

Thus he feels himself amply rewarded for all he has been through. They think the worst is over, and they do not believe the regiment will again be called upon to go into the trenches. What rejoicings there will be the day I can write and say: "Philisbourg is taken, your son is safe!"

The Prince of Orange, dismasted, is a prisoner in our hands. The ships he was sending, in the hopes of enticing the English fleet, would have been defeated without doubt, and four or five were scattered on their return journey. The King, James II, succeeded in rallying the country by wisely relaxing all stringencies in regard to liberty of conscience; God is on his side.

Farewell, dearest and best. Words fail me adequately to express the strength of my passion for you; they are, I find, wholly inadequate.

To The Same

Paris, Friday 22 October [*1688*].

Indeed I understand all your fears concerning your dear child, and do you not suppose that we share them in full measure? But we, of course, have constant news to hearten us, whereas you languish in ignorance for days on end. And we know, that M. le Dauphin himself goes into the trenches, indeed we are told he got covered with mud the other day from a cannon ball which exploded at his feet . . . I and the Chevalier also draw consolation from the fact we are convinced the siege will shortly be raised, and that Vauban,[1] who is not pressed for time, will do all to preserve his men as is his invariable habit. *Monseigneur* is adored for his generosity and thought for the wounded; he sent three hundred louis to the Marquis de Nesle; [2] assists those deprived of equipment; distributes largess to the soldiers; brings the officers and their needs to the King's notice; all this because he finds himself deeply moved by the dire poverty he sees all round. Indeed, my child, to have followed *Monseigneur* in one's initial

[1] Sébastien le Prestre dev., Marshal of France.

[2] Louis de Mailly, Marquis de Nesle, died of wounds received at Philisbourg.

campaign is, I consider, a matter of no small moment, and I am certain you would not have deprived your son of such a God-sent opportunity in order to keep him with you, whatever your fears and torments may be. . .

Yesterday one of His Majesty's equerries was wounded by a stag, and the horse killed under him; Saint-Hérem's young son, who, with the Comte de Toulouse,[1] was following hell for leather was thrown from his horse and rendered unconscious for a space of three hours . . .

To The Same

Paris, All Saints, 9 o'clock of the evening, 1688.

"Philisbourg is taken," my child, "your son is well." I could turn this phrase round and round and inside out, for I do not wish to talk on any other subject. This note then will give you the following news: Your son is well, and Philisbourg is taken. As yet few details are known save that the town was not stormed . . . You can breathe again, and thank God here and now . . . You can sleep once again as you read these magic words, and if your thirst for fresh torments be unabated you must look elsewhere since God has spared your son: we are overjoyed, and kiss you with a tender gladness of which you cannot doubt.

To The Same

Paris, Wednesday 3 November [*1688*].

How your heart must glow at the thought that you will receive no more letters which can throw any doubt on your son's safety! Pray relax and allow yourself to expand in the exquisite peace engendered by the knowledge you need no longer harbour any fears on his behalf, they are things of the past; think of his delight

[1] Louis-Alexandre de Bourbon, son of the King and Mme de Montespan.

at paying his court on the occasion of *Monseigneur's* inauguration in his role of victor; you will relish, as I do, the delectability of such a triumphal occasion. We must hope M. le Chevalier will be well enough to pay his respects at court . . . His pains and aches scuttle in and out like mice, and are now in one hand, now in another, now in the knee, which is pitiable as it prevented him last night from dining with Dangeau . . . but, when at length he is able to return to Versailles, you can count on his good offices at court with the full co-operation of our little Marquis, a young gentleman of no mean standing, and who need give way to none in the manner he has borne himself throughout the campaign. He is brave, cool in the face of danger, applies himself to the matter in hand; he amused himself the other day, if you please, by training a battery of two guns as nonchalantly as if he were practising at a target at Livry . . .

A propos of Livry . . . Père Gaillard [1] was preaching a sermon on All Saints day when M. de Louvois came to announce the fall of Philisbourg: the King raised his hand, the preacher stopped dead, and after announcing the news to the congregation His Majesty fell on his knees to render thanks to God. Whereupon the Father resumed his discourse, introducing the matter in hand in such eloquent terms, throwing in Philisbourg, *Monseigneur*, His Majesty, God's blessing on all His works, serving up, in fact, such a beautiful hotchpotch that all who listened were reduced to tears . . .

To The Same

Paris, Friday, 5 November [1688].

Yesterday I swallowed a little draught much on the same lines as those prescribed by my Capuchins; it was intended to rid me of humours and succeeded in drastically purging me; this was hailed as a grand success. I was a little sad this morning not to see you come in and take possession of my room, not to hear you question me, examine me, throw epilogues at my head,

[1] Honoré G., a Jesuit preacher.

manage me, destroy me, and smile on me just as I was about to have the vapours. Ah! child of my heart—what a charming and agreeable intercourse it was, and how I miss those filial attentions: and your coffee, your toilet, your friends who come to visit you, and against whom my door is barred. In truth the loss of you is a grievous one, for no one lends as much charm as you to the pleasures of friendship. You know I am always telling you you spoil the running for others whose converse appears flat and insipid when one has tasted of yours. How often M. de La Garde would say so to me, but at the time I thought you cruel, and that you were concealing your treasures from me. Now I know the exquisite qualities of your heart, and it is filled with tender kindness towards me. You want to console my old age by giving me this happiness, which alas! is overshadowed by your absence. But, dear one, is not love illimitable? Whereas absence, sooner or later, will come to an end . . .

Five o'clock of the evening.

The weather is abominable. Your letters have failed to arrive. I, most unworthy of the honour, am in the Chevalier's room looking after him to the best of my ability. He is in bed, but as his pain is now centred in his knee, he thinks he can write to you. We have been conversing about your son, whom we are awaiting. The Chevalier considers it a wholly unnecessary expense for the lad to go to Provence, and that he would be better advised to take advantage of his recent campaign and spend the winter here, and that M. du Plessis, with all his qualities, is a heavy drain on your coffers. To-morrow you will receive the great news: Philisbourg is captured—your son is safe. No one doubts that Mannheim surrendered without much persuasion, or having to be smoked out by our bombs. You can sleep in peace once again . . .

To The Same

Paris, Monday 8 November [1688].

. . . M. le Chevalier is better. Irony has it that the weather which is beneficial to him, may prove the undoing of the King of England, and instrumental in bringing about the loss of his throne. Contrariwise the poor Chevalier was crying out in pain and distress the while the Prince of Orange's fleet was scattered by wind and storm: the Chevalier regrets being unable to contrive that the state of his health should conform with the good of Europe. Universal joy was felt at the defeat of the Prince whose spouse is Tullia to the life.[1] How remorselessly would she trample on her father's dead body! She has assigned to her husband the prerogative of annexing the throne of England to which she pretends to be the rightful heir, and if the Prince should be killed (sensibility is scarcely her strong point), M. de Schomberg [2] has orders to claim it on her behalf. What say you to this hero who so grossly misuses the end of a valuable life? He witnessed the wreck of the flagship in which he was to sail, and as he and the Prince followed in the wake of the flotilla of ships (which, full sail and in superb weather, headed out to sea), a sudden storm blew up which sent them scuttling back to harbour, the Prince greatly incommoded by asthma, M. de Schomberg no less by chagrin. Only twenty-six vessels reached port, the rest were scattered far and wide . . . M. d'Aumont [3] informed the King by courier that ships had been sighted at the mercy of wind and wave, and wreckage identified. A flute [4] with nine hundred men on board foundered in sight of the Prince of Orange. The Hand

[1] Mary Stuart, daughter of James II, married the Prince of Orange, who annexed the English throne and reigned as William III. Tullia, to whom Mme de S. compares her, is alleged to have driven over the dead body of her father, Servius Tullius. She was the wife of Tarquinius Superbus.

[2] When he went over to England in 1688, Louis XIV was heard to remark: "Strange that M. de Schomberg, who was born a German, should wish to have himself naturalised English, French, and Portuguese."

[3] Louis-Marie-Victor, Duc d'A. Gentleman-in-Waiting. Governor of Boulogne.

[4] Long flat transport vessel.

of God is visible in the destruction of those proud ships; many may yet return to join in the fight, but for a long while they will be powerless to inflict much damage . . . it would seem that by a wise decree of Providence a miracle has been performed . . . Would you like to hear of the many wounds inflicted at Philisbourg, (other than at the siege) on M. de Longueville?[1] *Monseigneur* had come to inspect the march past of the troops when the little Chevalier jumped out of the trench; a soldier mistaking him for a snipe on the wing, fired his gun at the young fellow who died the following day. His death was scarcely less remarkable than his birth . . .

Remember me warmly to the dear Count . . . and if you care to kiss Pauline for me you will be affording her the greatest happiness, for I am told she worships the ground you tread on. There is, I think, no other way of loving you.

To The Same

Brevannes,[2] *Thursday 11 November* [*1688*].

I arrived here last night, my dear one, a well-chosen time, you will say, to set out for the country; nevertheless I am glad to take this opportunity for much needed exercise after a whole year's residence in Paris. But, mind you, I do not regret my protracted stay there since Philisbourg remained to be captured, and your son to be salvaged, no insignificant tasks. Now that I have nothing more to do save render thanks to God for his safety and your peace of mind, I have chosen this charming place in which to practise these virtues. I really believe I brought the Chevalier ill luck by my insistence on wishing him well, for the moment my back was turned he gathered strength to dine with Abbé Têtu; I am delighted, as that is the high road to Versailles on which his heart is set . . . Here the order of the day is to do as you please; it pleases me to take long walks, read, be alone, pray,

[1] Charles-Louis d'Orléans, illegitimate son of the Duc de Longueville (*see* f.n. p. 107) and the Maréchale de La Ferté.

[2] Residence of Mme de Coulanges.

once again forgather, and partake of sumptuous repasts; I have not been here twenty-four hours, but have had some fair samples up to date.

I am awaiting a letter from you to-morrow, but not the one I long for more than all others, the one you will write when you know about Philisbourg, and when I shall be able to think of your heart expanding with the peace and comfort you have been a stranger to these last two months . . .

Farewell, my dearest, to be absent from so beloved a daughter is pain and grief indeed. I am acquiring M. le Tourneux's new book *Rules for a Christian Life*; I hope from reading it to obtain the required grace to submit myself with a better heart and will to the harsh decrees of Providence.

To The Same

Paris, Friday 3 December [1688].

The news should reach you to-day that His Majesty the King yesterday appointed seventy-four Knights Chevaliers du Saint-Esprit,[1] of which I enclose the list. As he has done M. de Grignan the honour of including him in the number you must expect to receive endless compliments and congratulations. Persons, better qualified than I am, advise you to exercise the greatest restraint both in speaking and writing, not to wound the sensibilities of others less fortunate, and that you would be well inspired if you were to write to M. de Louvois, telling him you are happy to think the honour which has been done to M. de Grignan meets with his approval. You will turn it better than I should, and it will in no way prejudice what M. de Grignan chooses to write on his own account . . . The Knights were proclaimed at Versailles yesterday; the ceremony will take place on New Year's day: time is short, and some will be dispensed from appearing in person—it is possible you may be of the number.

[1] Order founded in 1579 by Henri III.

To The Same

Paris, Wednesday 8 December [1688].

Would you believe it? That little rascal,[1] after announcing himself for Tuesday evening arrived, without the slightest compunction, the day before yesterday at seven of the clock, and before I was back from town. His uncle received him with open arms, and as for me, when I saw him gay, debonair, charming, we set to embracing one another with a will, our one bone of contention being that he wanted to kiss my hands, and I wished to kiss him on both cheeks. I seized his head in my two hands, and embraced him to my heart's content: I next asked to see his bruises, but as they are, pray do not think me indelicate, in the region of his left thigh, I could scarcely expect him to accommodate me by taking down his breeches. We conversed all evening with our little crony. He admires his dear Mama's portrait and pines for her, but he takes his role of warrior so seriously one dare not put forward any suggestion. I wish you could have heard the nonchalant manner in which he told us how he came by his injury, and how little he made of it, whereas those who were present with him in the trenches were greatly perturbed. The truth is, had he lent an ear to your usual exhortations to hold himself upright, doubtless he would have been killed, but luckily he was sitting sideways, which comes naturally to him, leaning across in earnest conversation with the Duc de Guiche.[2] This demonstrates how providential it may be, on occasion, to be of a stooping disposition.

My pockets are stuffed to overflowing with compliments in your intention. L'abbé de Guénégaud [3] started stammering one out at such length this morning that I was obliged to interrupt . . . It seems the Grignans are on everyone's tongue just now . . . Anyway I no longer have to assure you your child will return, which

[1] The 17-year-old Marquis de G. returned from the wars with a contusion on his left thigh caused by a bomb explosion at the siege of Mannheim on 9 Nov. No doubt his uncle, the Chevalier, and his grandmother were justly proud of his exploits.

[2] Antoine de Gramont, son of the deceased Cte de Louvigny.

[3] Claude-François, nephew of Mme du Plessis-G.

you do not altogether appreciate, but that he is here which you long to be told. Bless my soul! Here he is, he himself, in person, in the flesh.

To The Same

Paris, Monday 13 December [*1688*].

Had anyone told me I should be glad not to see M. de Grignan at the New Year I should have denied it; but the fact remains that I and M. le Chevalier are very well satisfied the King should so graciously permit him to be absent. You must do like those other absent ones, and collect your blue ribbon when you are advised; but you will have, I imagine, some time in the coming year to assist at the final rites, receive the collar in person, take the oath, and complete the process of turning out the Perfect Knight . . .

To return to the little Marquis. Pray do not imagine for one moment we were otherwise than greatly moved to see him return and not find his Mama to whom he had so lately bidden farewell. I purposely omitted to dwell on that side of the picture . . . Had you but seen his buckled sword, and the piece of shell which drove it into his thigh, you would think him happy indeed to have escaped so lightly and that God should have spared him; and you would worship the Hand which guided him so opportunely for his and our good, for do we not all bear this captain a most tender love . . . Do not fret about your child's health, he requires no bleeding, no dosing, in fact he requires no treatment whatever, he enjoys a healthy appetite, a good night's sleep, is not in a state of fever, and shows a great power of resistance, just what a doctor would hasten to deprive him of were he called in.

My goodness gracious, child, how nonsensical your womenfolk must be, whether dead or alive! You horrify me over these be-ribboned top-knots! [1] How profane it is, and smells of pagan

[1] In Provence the custom prevailed to bury the dead with their faces uncovered, and those women who affected hair ornaments retained them in their coffins. [*Perrin*, 1737].

rites ; and the wicked folly of it ! Unless you swear you will not call in the wig-maker when the undertaker is summoned, Heaven preserve me from dying in Provence ! [1] . . . Fie ! let us drop such an unpleasing topic . . .

You should not blush at retrenching, as far as your table is concerned, since the King models himself on his Grand-Master [2] in doing so at Marly.[3] Old Madame de Leuville [4] tells me she now offers supper to no one, and she certainly is not alone in taking this decision.

The King of England, forsaken to all appearances by his most faithful subjects, has returned to London suffering from severe nose bleeding : had he followed his own devices he would have fallen into the hands of the Prince of Orange. It appears he was rushed into promising a free parliament by next month, thereby signing his own death warrant. His son-in-law, the Prince of Denmark, and his younger daughter, another Tullia whom I have dubbed " La Demoiselle de Danemarck " [5] have joined the Prince of Orange who is the scourge of our times. They say the little Prince [6] is not to be found at Portsmouth where he was thought to be in hiding, but from whence he has made his escape ; this has all the makings of a great romance. No one doubts his father will follow him into exile. Short of a miracle, the Prince of Orange remains head of the state and will be crowned King in the near future. This at the moment, as the clock strikes three, is the great news, maybe to-night the Abbé Bigorre [7] will have something to add to it.

[1] This passage reads like a presentiment. All happened as she apprehended, she died in Provence, and when her coffin was opened she was found decked out in her finery.

[2] G.-M. of the Bedchamber and *Grand Veneur de France*, François VII, Prince de Marsillac, Duc de Rochefoucauld, eldest son of the deceased Duc.

[3] The superb Château de Marly-le-Roi built by Louis XIV and destroyed during the Revolution, except for the hydraulic apparatus for supplying Versailles with Seine water.

[4] Marguerite de Laigne, a widow, and friend of Mme de Caylus.

[5] Anne Stuart, wife of Prince George of Denmark, later Queen of England, after the death of her brother-in-law, William III. Allusion to *Amadis*.

[6] James Francis Edward, born 20 June 1688, died 1766.

[7] " Le plus aimable de tous les hôtes ", in close touch with Rome.

To The Same

Paris, Friday 24 December [*1688*].

The Marquis has been alone to Versailles, where he has acquitted himself admirably; he honoured M. du Maine [1] and M. de Montausier with his presence at dinner, supped with Mme d'Armagnac, attended all the court functions with assiduity both night and morning, *Monseigneur* ordaining he should hold the candle; [2] in fact he is launched in the great world where he cuts a fine figure. He has become the vogue, and no début was ever more auspicious, I could run on for ever if I were to repeat to you all I hear in his favour . . .

But how comes it that I am gossiping away, and forgetting to tell you the latest news? Just a trifle, a snippet, scarcely worth mentioning—the Queen of England, the Prince of Wales, his nurse and one attendant should be here at any moment! The King has despatched his carriages on the road to Calais, where the Queen landed last Tuesday 21st, escorted by M. de Lauzun. [3] This is what M. de Courtin [4] related to us yesterday, who himself had been to Versailles. You will have heard of M. de Lauzun's resolve, made some weeks since, to proceed to England: he could scarcely put his leisure to better use. Whereas the King of England's own subjects were forsaking him, M. de Lauzun alone remained loyal. On Sunday last, 19th of the month, the King, having come to a firm decision on his future actions, retired to rest with his Queen, dismissed such of his attendants as remained to him, rose an hour later and ordered a valet to admit a certain gentleman who would be found stationed at the entrance; the gentleman in question was no other than M. de Lauzun. The King addressed him thus: "Sir, I wish to confide the Queen and our son to your

[1] Son of Louis XIV and Mme de Montespan, Louis-Auguste de Bourbon, Duc du M, married Condé's daughter, Mlle de Charolais.

[2] To hold the gold candle-stick at the *Coucher* of King or Dauphin was a much-prized honour (*faire donner le bougeoir*).

[3] Recalled from Pignerol, he had rejoined *Mademoiselle* at Amboise, but separated from her in 1684.

[4] Honoré, Councillor of State and Ambassador, whose son, the Chevalier, had been killed at Philisbourg. He was Governor of Calais.

care; you are to take any risk you deem necessary in the endeavour to bring them safely to France." M. de Lauzun thanked him in suitable terms, but said he wished to press into his service a brave and reliable man, a gentleman from Avignon named Saint-Victor —the latter it was who concealed the little Prince under his cloak, whom people believed to be still at Portsmouth, when in truth he was in hiding in the Palace. M. de Lauzun proceeded to take the Queen's hand in his—I beg you for one moment to cast your eyes on Her Majesty as she bids farewell to the King, her spouse. Followed by her two waiting women she steps into a hired coach which they are presently transferred to a small boat on the river bank where they encounter such heavy weather that they are unable to keep under shelter. At the mouth of the Thames a yacht awaits them, M. de Lauzun remaining at the owner's side lest he should prove a traitor. But the owner, not realising his passengers are other than the usual run of common folk he is accustomed to handle, sails, unknowing and unnoticed, in the close vicinity of fifty ships of the Dutch fleet, who do not so much as take heed of the small craft. By the grace of Heaven and under a lowering sky its precious cargo is safely landed at Calais, where M. de Charost [1] receives the Queen with all the courtesy you would expect . . . Orders had been given that the King's equipages should meet Her Majesty and escort her to Vincennes, which is being furnished with due regard to her requirements, and where the King will attend her. This is only the first chapter of a royal romance, and the ensuing ones shall be related to you in due course. We are assured that to crown his actions M. de Lauzun, having placed the Queen and young Prince in M. de Charost's safe keeping notified his intention to return to England with Saint-Victor to share the fortunes of her ill-fated Monarch. I marvel at M. de Lauzun's lucky star, which continues to shine on his good name which we had long thought buried in obscurity. His was a noble action, dearest one, crowned by his return to a country [2] where it would seem he has no choice but to perish

[1] Armand de Béthune, Marquis, later Duc de C., followed his father as Captain of the King's Guards; brother-in-law of Fouquet.

[2] He did not after all return to England, for in recognition of his services he received from Louis XIV a gracious invitation to return to the French Court.

with the King at the hand of a revengeful enemy. I leave you to ponder over the tale I have unfolded, and I embrace you, dear child, with a love of which it can truly be said it is out of the common run of human affections.

To The Same

Paris, Monday 27 December [1688].

Would you believe it—our young captain has embarked on the road to Châlons with the purpose of inspecting this fine body of troopers you have recruited for him. He started out on Christmas day, intending to lie at Claie, and to salute Livry in passing; he returns on Sunday. The Chevalier has mapped out his days, and M. du Plessis, highly gratified with the confidence you have placed in him, accompanies the lad everywhere—you can count on him absolutely . . . I hear you think our Marquis has put on flesh; on the contrary he is slimmer in the waist, and has shot up, but you cannot expect anyone to grow so many inches in two months . . .

The Queen of England is on everybody's lips: she begged to be allowed to remain incognito at Boulogne until news came of her royal spouse who has escaped from England but whose whereabouts is unknown. Our King despatched three coaches of ten horses apiece, and in addition litters, pages, valets, guards, a Lieutenant and other officers to wait on her . . . M. de Lauzun must congratulate himself on the part he played; he showed ability, coolness, judgement, dignity and courage, these attributes have put him on the highroad to Versailles, *via* London, a highly characteristic procedure. The Princess is outraged at the King's attitude and that Lauzun should be taken back into favour.[1]

The ceremony [of Knighting] will take place in the chapel at Versailles with as little formality as possible.[2] The inauguration

[1] *Mademoiselle* de Montpensier, who in the first place was instrumental in getting Lauzun liberated from prison, had much cause for complaint at his ingratitude and brutality.

[2] Knights of the Saint-Esprit were, at that time, dubbed with scant ceremonial in order to fall in with the King's wish to avoid any kind of extra expense on their behalf.

will take place on Friday, and more will follow at Matins and again at Vespers on New Year's day. The King has ordained that partaking of Holy Communion shall not be obligatory; and His Majesty will not be wearing his great cloak, but only his collar; cloaks will be lent, so many will be dispensed from wearing them . . .

Farewell, my charming and beloved one—I have much else to tell you, but am fearful of overwhelming you entirely.

To The Same

Paris, Friday 31 December [1688].

Per tornar dunque al nostro proposito: the uncertainty which prevailed as to the whereabouts of the English King, reported by M. de Lamoignon to be in Calais, is now removed, for it is learnt he was arrested in his own country or perished by the way since he was due to embark but a few hours after the Queen. In this belief we ring the Old Year out and the New Year in, for which events of great moment were long since foreshadowed. Certain it is, however, that nothing will happen save as Providence ordains, and the same obtains for all our actions and activities, our comings and our goings. One must submit and put a brave face on events—that is the long and the short of it—the issues are buried in the womb of time . . .

Mme de Barillon is greatly perturbed about her husband,[1] but although no letters have come through she is assured of his safe arrival, despite the rumoured destruction of the King's private chapel and of that of the French ambassador . . . My dear child, your "Madame", who swore not to touch a card until the King of England was successful in battle, will not, I fear, play cards for some time to come, poor soul! The Prince of Orange is already in London, they say; this phrase is repeated wherever one goes, and I find myself going back and back to it—each holds his own view as to the enactment of the final scene in this great drama.

[1] French Ambassador to the Court of Whitehall. [*See Macaulay*].

The Queen is still in a convent at Boulogne, weeping her eyes out for a husband she adores . . .

A new play is said to be in rehearsal, to be represented at Saint Cyr ; it is called *Esther*[1]. The carnival does not promise to be very gay . . .

[1] *See* f.n. p. 314.

1689

To Madame de Grignan

Paris, Monday 3 January [*1689*].

Your dear boy returned this morning, and we were overjoyed to see him and M. du Plessis: we were at table and they dined, miraculously well, on our remains. You should have heard all the Marquis told us on the excellence of his Squadron. On arrival he at once enquired as to the bearing of his men, and was told they could not be smarter, that the Company *had been formed long ago*, and none of *more recent* years could hold a candle to it. You can well imagine the delight of such a compliment, coming from one who was ignorant of the fact that he was destined to command it. The child was transported with joy on seeing, the following day, the splendid troopers whom you helped to select with so much judgement and acumen, horses and men seeming to be turned out in the same mould. M. de Châlons[1] and his mother shared in his delighted appreciation, and he was welcomed as a son of M. de Grignan: but why am I taking his tale out of the mouth of our young Marquis? . . .

The ceremony of your Brothers the Knights was duly performed at Versailles on New Year's day, Coulanges tells us . . . it all started on the Friday, the professed wearing their fine apparel and chains of office; two Marshals of France remaining over the Saturday. The Maréchal de Bellefonds was a figure of fun, having

[1] Louis-Antoine de Noailles, Bp. of Châlons, later Abp. of Paris.

forgotten, partly out of modesty, partly out of indifference, to wear ribbons below his knee-breeches, thus appearing quite undressed. The assembly was magnificent, M. de La Trousse outstanding; his wig, however, with its side-pieces, would insist on working itself to the back of his head, leaving his cheeks bare, and he trying, unsuccessfully, to readjust it, which caused slight embarrassment. Walking in a line with him were M. de Montchevreuil [1] and M. de Villars, [2] who got inextricably entangled, swords, ribbons, laces, jangles, hopelessly interlocked, and the jagged particles so viciously hooked together that hand of man could not have disengaged them; like the links in Roger's armour [3] the more they tried the worse it got. When at length, after the ceremony, the marching, the bowing—in fact the whole bag of tricks—had been brought to a standstill, the gentlemen were forcibly torn apart, the strongest carrying off the prize. But what finally upset the gravity of the occasion was d'Hocquincourt's [4] get-up. So used is he to the garb of a Provençal or a Breton he found himself seriously incommoded by his page's breeches, and his shirt would ride up despite all his coaxings; in fact he never ceased trying to restore order until at last the Dauphine could no longer suppress a loud guffaw. It was regrettable, and His Majesty was greatly put out, for in all the records of such happenings there is no precedent for so absurd an interlude. That evening the King was heard to say: "My rôle seems always to have to uphold poor d'Hocquincourt—of course his tailor was in fault." . . .

The King of England was captured, [5] they say, trying to make his escape. He is at Vittal [*sic*]—I don't know how to spell the word. He is surrounded by his own Captain of the Guards, his Guards, and Milords who attend his levée: nevertheless he is under strict surveillance. The Prince of Orange is at Saint-Jean [*sic*], at the further end of the Gardens. Parliament will be in session; may God protect this frail craft! The Queen of

[1] Henri de Mornay, Marquis de M.

[2] Pierre, Marquis de V. Ambassador to Spain. Father of the Marshal who had so distinguished himself in the recent wars in Germany. Often referred to as *Orondate*, on account of his prowess and distinguished mien.

[3] Allusion to *Orlando Furioso, Canto* X.

[4] Governor of Péronne, now living in retirement.

[5] He escaped 28 Dec. and reached Ambleteuse, near Boulogne, 3 Jan.

England is expected on Wednesday; she is moving to Saint-Germain to be nearer the King and his beneficent attentions. Farewell, my dearest, dear and most amiable one . . .

To The Comte de Bussy

Paris, Sunday of the Epiphany [*1689*].

I must preface this letter, dear cousin, by wishing you a happy New Year; which is tantamount to wishing you may persevere in your Christian philosophy, through which alone true happiness can be found. Unless we can accept God's will, which in any case is imposed on us, we cannot know a moment of happiness in this world. Thus sustained, however, we can pass through the crucible of suffering with courage and fortitude . . . I do not desire to go back on the past, and all that you should have been and have failed to be, and which since I love you, has caused me to suffer so greatly on your behalf; this chapter must be closed . . . The Court is all blue ribbons; one cannot pay a visit without finding the place adorned with four or five. Nothing could be more appropriate than this decoration to do honour to the arrival at Saint-Germain of the King and Queen of England . . . As it happens to-day is the true Feast of Kings,[1] a happier one for the privileged who can dispense favours than for the beggar at the gate . . . It seems certain that the Prince of Orange facilitated the King's escape in order himself to become master of the situation without having recourse to criminal action; and on his part the King showed wisdom in abandoning the struggle and putting no faith in a parliament which had condoned his father's murder, despite the religious beliefs which he shared with his people. Here grave issues are at stake for which no foreseeable solution can be found . . . That same Providence who ordains all things, will doubtless elucidate all things in her good time. We spectators are as blind as we are ignorant. The second volume of M. de Lauzun's epic tale is worthy of the first. He had the

[1] On the Epiphany, "Le Jour des Rois", Louis XIV was receiving and giving succour to the English monarch.

honour of being closeted for an hour with the King. *Mademoiselle* is furious, and says she will not meet him, but I doubt if her tantrums merit serious attention.

To Madame de Grignan

Paris, Monday 10 January [*1689*].

Our minds seem to work on the same lines, for my last letter from Les Rochers mentions time in the very same terms as does yours which crossed it. The burden of each day is no longer so dear to me, so precious, as to make me wish to spin it out. At the Hôtel de Carnavalet, when you were with me, it was otherwise. I never returned there—and this I have often told you—without a sense of joyous excitement; I hoarded every moment as a miser does his gold. But in the absence of the loved one all is changed, days pass as a shadow, unnoticed; our only wish is to speed them along, and our only hope lies in some future when we shall lay down our laborious task. Meanwhile I am prodigal of time, and my days and hours can be had for the asking . . .

The Abbé Têtu suffers from insomnia to a degree which induces grave anxiety. The doctors fear for his reason, he is aware of his state which causes him much suffering, he lives on opium, and seeks distraction in the pursuit of pleasure and entertainment. We want him to go to Saint-Germain to see the King and Queen of England and the little Prince of Wales installed in state, for no spectacle could be grander or more diverting . . . The King was allowed to proceed to Exeter with the secret connivance of the Prince of Orange, the main door of his residence being heavily guarded, whereas the back door remained wide open. The Prince does not seem to have harboured criminal intentions towards his father-in-law, but has elected to remain in London and assume his rank, if not his title, and confine himself to the task of re-establishing the religion he believes in, and restoring order without shedding blood. We judged him too harshly. Meanwhile our beloved King showers his bounties on the English Sovereigns in a truly divine manner, for is it not an attribute of the All High to succour the poor wanderer, the outcast, the betrayed? The rôle of saviour is admirably adapted to one of such noble and generous instincts, and greatly to the liking of our Monarch. He met the Queen at the head of his entire retinue consisting of a hundred carriages, each drawn by a team of six horses. When the coach came into sight in which the little Prince of Wales reclined, the King dismounted and embraced him tenderly before hastening to the Queen's side, whom he likewise greeted, and after conversing awhile he placed her at his right hand in his own royal coach where *Monsieur* and *Monseigneur* were presented to Her Majesty. In this manner they proceeded to Saint-Germain where the Queen received all the attentions due to a reigning sovereign and where presents of fine trappings and wearing apparel were showered upon her, and a casket of great price containing six thousand gold louis. The English Monarch was expected at Saint-Germain on the following day, and the King went from Versailles to receive him, crossing the whole length of the guard-room to greet him. As he entered the King of England prostrated himself before ours, as if to embrace his knees, but His Majesty would none of it, raised him up and kissed him fervently on both cheeks,[1] after which they conversed in private for near a quarter of an hour . . . Before taking his departure the King addressed the English Monarch thus: "You must look upon this house as yours, and must do me the honours when I visit you, and when you visit me at Versailles I shall do likewise." . . . A further gift of ten thousand louis was despatched to the King of England who looks weary and sadly aged; the Queen is thin, and her beautiful black eyes are dim with weeping, she is pale, has a large mouth with fine teeth, a distinguished mien and much ready wit; in fact all the making of a charming and agreeable person. These events should serve to furnish the populace with a subject of conversation for a long time to come . . .

Yesterday Mme de Coulanges offered a supper to the victims of gout: there were present the Abbé de Marsillac,[2] the Chevalier

[1] Mme de La Fayette records that the two sovereigns embraced tenderly but with this difference, that the King of England's deportment was humble as befitted his misfortunes.

[2] Henri-Achille, Rochefoucauld's son.

de Grignan, M. de Lamoignon (whose nephritis stands him in lieu of gout), his wife and *Les Divines*,[1] as always much congested; I on the merits of the rheumatics I had twelve years since, and Coulanges who, if he has not gout, richly deserves to have it . . . Meanwhile your child was enjoying himself vastly with the Mlles de Castelnau; [2] it is clear he admires a younger sister who is pretty and charming, and he would like to palm off the squinting one upon Sanzei; he brought an oboe, and dancing continued till past midnight . . .

Adieu, my dearest—study your health, in other words your beauty, which is so very near my heart.

To The Same

Paris, Friday 14 January [1689].

Here am I, dearest child, closeted in the Chevalier's room: we have partaken of dinner; he is sitting in his chair suffering acutely from lancinating pains in every limb; he slept well but is confined to the house, which makes him peevish and gives him the vapours . . . The cold is intense, our thermometer registers below zero and the river is frozen over; snow is falling and it thaws and freezes at one and the same time. You cannot stand up out of doors, so I stay in and keep delightfully snug in the Chevalier's room . . .

Mme de Maintenon is occupied with a performance she is organizing for her young ladies at Saint-Cyr—they say it will be enchanting.[3] She visited the English Queen, who expressed her regrets at having kept her waiting, and received her most royally. All speak highly of this Queen, who is most intelligent . . . her husband is brave and gallant, but his mind is set in a commoner

[1] Mme de Frontenac and her friend Mlle d'Outrelaise.

[2] Daughters of the Marquis de C., whose mother was a friend of Mme de S.

[3] The Superior, Mme de Brinon, first introduced play-acting among her pupils, but when they performed Racine's tragedy of *Andromaque* the love passages were rendered in so realistic a fashion, that she entreated Racine to provide a play of impeccable morals, if not of historic interest. Thus it was that he came to write *Esther*. Mme de S. attended the first performance.

mould, and he speaks of events in England with such lack of feeling that he inspires little enough for himself; he is however a good-natured fellow, and enjoys the amenities of Versailles. Madame la Dauphine refuses to visit the Queen, unless she should be allowed a seat on the Queen's right hand; which would be against all precedent; so she will remain in bed, and takes for granted she herself will be visited . . . *Madame* will be satisfied with a seat on her left, and the Royal Princesses who will accompany her must fain put up with tabourets [1] . . .

M. de Lauzun's star has waned, he is no longer in residence, and has been shorn of many of his privileges; his adventure has lost much of its zest, has, in fact, fallen flat, a sign alas! of the times in which we live.

To The Same

Paris, Monday 17 January [1689].

. . . The English Court, by now, is firmly established at Saint-Germain, and is run on a footing of fifty thousand francs a month, the offer of a more considerable sum having been refused. The English Queen is a universal favourite; our King finds her conversation agreeable, and her judgements well-disposed and shrewd. He desired the Dauphine to make the first advances, but the latter had so insisted on her poor health that the Queen called on her three days ago clad to perfection in a black velvet robe with a sweeping skirt and fine headdress, and with the figure and majestic bearing of Mme de Conti. The King welcomed her as her carriage drove up and escorted her to his apartments where she was shown a seat immediately above His Majesty. After conversing they proceeded to Madame la Dauphine's room who, to everyone's surprise, had risen to receive her guest. The Queen said: "Madame, I thought to find you in bed?" The Dauphine answered: "Madame, I rose, being sensible of the honour Your Majesty was conferring on me." The King left them very shortly,

[1] *Tabourets* were stools which duchesses were privileged to use in the King's presence.

as Madame la Dauphine is not entitled to be seated in his presence; the Queen took her appointed place with the Dauphine on her right, *Madame* on her left, and seats were allotted to the three young princes: [1] they conversed agreeably for half an hour of the clock, the court was crowded, many duchesses being present . . . I did not learn how far the Dauphine escorted Her Majesty when she took her departure, but the King was apprised of it, and having seen her into her carriage was heard to sing her praises in the following terms: "She is a model for any queen, both in her person and for the qualities of her mind; she well knows how to inspire respect in her subjects." He paid tribute to her courage in adversity, and to her loyalty and devotion to her royal spouse . . . Some court ladies, who aped the Princesses, avoided making their obeisance and certain duchesses followed their example, which His Majesty considers in deplorable taste; so now they fall over themselves to kiss her feet.

A greeting to you, dear Count, I hear you two are in absolute agreement over your situation and reckless extravagance. Would to Heaven you had been so in the past! A greeting to my charming Pauline; and what do I hear, Miss? That after cogitating for six weeks on a suitable name for me, something between "Grandmother" and "Madame" you have finally plumped for "Madame"?

To The Same

Paris, Monday 24 January [*1689*].

At length your Durance has relented, and allowed our letters to cross her in safety; how clever of the ice to have dammed up such a raging torrent! Here we have suffered a most cruel spell of cold and frost, but I have been happily immune from chills. I have several times been confined to M. le Chevalier's room, and as Mme de Coulanges puts it, he alone was to be pitied for the

[1] The Dauphin's three sons, the Duc de Bourgogne who became Dauphin and the Ducs de Berri and Anjou. The latter (2nd son) became King of Spain under the name of Philip V.

inclemency of the season; but between you and me, I think he quite enjoyed my being there . . .

Last night your son attended M. de Chartres' [1] ball looking, I must say, very handsome. But you must not count on his devoting himself to study; yesterday he told us, quite simply, he was incapable of it at the present time; the call of youth is so insistent he is deaf to all else. Would that time alone were at fault, but alas, the right impulse is lacking! He is so sincere that we have not the heart to rebuke him, but we din it into his ears, and Corbinelli gets quite heated . . . We feel it is not possible that with so much good sense and natural bent for the art of warfare he should not aspire to learn more of the heroic deeds of the past, with Caesar's exploits at the head of the list. You must be patient and bear with him—he would indeed be a paragon of all the virtues if he cared for reading.

You astonish me about Pauline. Ah! Dear daughter, I pray you to keep her under your care; do not for one moment imagine that a convent is capable of making good the defects of a faulty education in religious matters, about which nuns are wholly ignorant; as indeed they are on every other subject. How much better at Grignan if you had time to devote to her! She could read the right books . . . converse with you . . . be more profitably employed, I am persuaded, than at any conventual establishment the world over.

To The Same

Paris, Friday 4 February [1689].

I was awaiting M. le Chevalier yesterday, who had advised me he was returning in the evening with your child, adding that he had forwarded the warrant whereby you are entitled to claim your blue riband. It and the cross which are gifts of the King will reach you shortly. You must cherish this friendly Order *ad multos annos* and let it adorn your beautiful person, and pray do not forget it during the three hours you daily devote to

[1] A masked ball at the Palais-Royal. He was to marry Mlle de Blois.

love-making, for it is an ornament which can only heighten the enjoyment of your connubial bliss. You see, dear Count, that I find myself addressing you almost without meaning to, and I will finish my discourse with a kiss.

To turn once more to you, dearest daughter . . . We supped Wednesday, Mme de Chaulnes and I, in Coulanges' study, on Mme de Coulanges' famous capon. Coulanges is suffering from gout, due, I fear, to his excesses: he calls out, has to be carried pick-a-back, cannot sleep, but he makes a joke of everything, even of his anguish.

I dined yesterday at Mme de La Fayette's with Tréville and Corbinelli; we partook of partridges from Auvergne and capons from Caen. Her son who, as you know, keeps an eye on the little Marquis, reports very favourably of him, says he keeps good company, sits down with the finest in the land who esteem him and sometimes address him as "The little curmudgeon",[1] others more politely call him "pussy cat". All this I consider highly gratifying . . .

To The Comte de Grignan

Paris, Monday 7 February [1689].

I salute you, Monsieur of the blue ribbon! Are not you magnificent! And how well it becomes you! My best compliments and congratulations on the new turn-out.

To Madame de Grignan

Paris, Ash Wednesday 23 February [1689].

Dear child—I rejoice to hear of your life in charming Marseilles, I feel I love this city which resembles none other in the world. And how well I understand Pauline's naive enthusiasms, her

[1] *Le Minet* was at one time Mme de S.'s nickname for her son-in-law.

fervours, her surprises; the pretty creature has an intelligence I much appreciate. And do I not love her better than you do? You expect perfection to which, on leaving the convent, she never pledged herself . . . you look for a prodigy, yes, a prodigy of prodigious proportion such as does not exist. I feel I should make an excellent partisan, were I present to curb your imagination and make you appreciate a loving little creature who is out to please and satisfy you, who adores and trembles before you . . . What more can you want?

This morning, Ash Wednesday, went to Mass and wrote peacefully to my daughter, such is your poor mama's ritual, the while our pussy-cat and the Chevalier disport themselves at Versailles, where all the gaiety changed overnight giving way to the lamentations of *Monsieur* and *Madame*. This poor Spanish Queen [1] was only a year older than her own mother when she died in an equally mysterious manner; she vomited for two whole days without drawing breath . . . Her courage, her endurance and her truly Christian fortitude sustained her throughout and she affirmed, when speaking to the King, that she died without regret and from natural causes, and not, as she first alleged, in the same way as her mother. The word poison is not mentioned, it is strictly forbidden throughout the country . . . Unexpected news has reached us from England; after great opposition the Prince of Orange is proclaimed King: a week ago we heard otherwise, but then what can you expect of the English! . . .

To The President de Moulceau

Wednesday, 2 March [1689].

What memorable events are taking place, Monsieur! And is not the reception of the English King by our Monarch an epoch-making one in the annals of France! Consider, too, the gifts His

[1] The Queen of Spain, Marie-Louise d'Orléans, daughter of *Monsieur* and Henriette d'Angleterre (*see* f.n. p. 200) had just died in Madrid. Mme de La Fayette says she was poisoned by a cup of chocolate, Dangeau by eel-pie, while Saint-Simon says Mme de Soissons administered the poison, suborned by the Earl of Mansfield.

Majesty showered on his guest when the latter took his departure to Ireland, and from thence to Brest where ships awaited him, ships, frigates, troops, officers, not to speak of an Ambassador Extraordinary in the person of the Comte d'Avaux,[1] who will act as financial adviser and superintendent of the armed forces. The sum of two million was given as a send off, and there will be more to follow for the asking. And to crown all and bring him luck our Sovereign handed over, for his own personal use, his armour, his helmet and his shield; and further equipment for ten or twelve thousand men. And as if this were not good measure and running over there are fine post-chaises, barouches, carriages and riding horses, canteens of gold and silver, raiment, linen, camp beds, jewelled swords and service swords, pistols and every imaginable adjunct. When the Kings bade each other adieu ours of France spoke thus: "You cannot think I am unmoved at seeing you depart, but I am constrained to admit I never hope to witness your return. If, however, you should, unfortunately, be obliged to do so, you will find me (of this you must rest assured) precisely as you leave me." Well and nobly said, and such a display of kingly magnanimity is edifying to all beholders . . .

TO MADAME DE GRIGNAN

Paris, Friday 11 March [*1689*].

The Duc de Chaulnes has acquitted himself as befits his station in order to do honour to the English Monarch. Halts for supper were prepared at appointed intervals on His Majesty's route, one at ten, another at midnight. The King, however, pushed on to the second, which was beyond Nantes; M. de Chaulnes he embraced warmly, having known him in the past. The latter informed him a room was got ready for his convenience, the King replied he only desired to eat. Accordingly he was ushered into a great hall where, by the touch of a fairy's wand, a hot supper was served. There were sea fishes and river fishes, all was of the

[1] Jean-Antoine de Mesme, Cte d'A, nephew of the negotiator of the Peace of Westphalia, late Ambassador to Holland.

greatest excellence, both as to the viands and as to the company, many nobles were present and a fair number of ladies in attendance. When M. de Chaulnes handed the King a napkin and proceeded to wait on him in person His Majesty insisted on his supping at his table, together with other notables. His Majesty ate as unconcernedly as if, in truth, the Prince of Orange were a myth. He left the following day, and embarked for Brest on the sixth of the month. This Prince I consider a scourge who can set all Europe by the ears, but, alas, his lucky star persists . . .

To The Same

Paris, Friday 25 March [1689].
Feast of The Annunciation.

So far we are without letters from you, but I persevere with mine, as is my wont. It seems you have set a great example on this notable feast-day which is, after all, at the very root of Christianity and of all church feasts—that of Easter and of the Incarnation: today Our Lady reigns supreme as she has on many other occasions . . .

Pray, listen to the following tale. Do you remember hearing of M. de Béthune,[1] the so-called shepherd of Fontainebleau, otherwise known to many as *Cassepot*? And do you recall his appearance? Tall, haggard, pallid, crazy looking—in point of fact a regular wolf in sheep's clothing and, such as he is, he lodges at the Hôtel de Lyonne with the Duc and Duchesse d'Estrées [2] and Mme and Mlle de Vaubrun. Two months since the latter was known to have retired to the Convent of Sainte-Marie du faubourg Saint-Germain, it was thought her sister's happiness had turned her thoughts heavenwards . . . What do you think kept *Cassepot* busy at the Hôtel de Lyonne? Making love, dear daughter, love with Mlle de Vaubrun. Such as I have described him the poor

[1] Henri de B., Cte de Selles.

[2] François-Annibal III, Marquis de Cœuvres, whose first wife, Madeleine de Lyonne, had died. Mlle de Vaubrun was the sister of his second wife, Mlle de Bautru de Vaubrun. She was 17, *Cassepot*, 60.

girl loved him. As Benserade [1] said of Mme de Ventadour who loved her husband [2]: "Good—if she can like him she will like another." This child of seventeen has, I tell you, capitulated to Don Quixote, and yesterday, armed with logs and followed by six or seven of M. de Gesvres' [3] guards he demolished the Convent gates with repeated blows, and entering with one of his men found the young lady awaiting him. He seized her bodily, carried her to his coach and drove her to M. de Gesvres where they went through a form of marriage and slept together that night; the next day they vanished, and have not been heard of since. It would be apt at this point to quote Molière: "Agnès and the corpse have eloped together".[4] Béthune says it is a betrayal of hospitality, and Mme de Vaubrun would like to see his head chopped off. M. de Gesvres denies that he knew who the young lady was, and the Béthunes do not wish proceedings to be taken against anyone of their flesh and blood . . . There, my child, you have the gospel of the day and no one talks of ought else. What think you of that little god of love? He sickens me when he picks out such unpleasant victims for his darts.

To The Same

Paris, evening of Wednesday 13 April [*1689*].

After all, dear daughter, we are only leaving twelve days hence, as M. de Chaulnes finds himself obliged to go to Nantes. Mme de Chaulnes wishes me to spend ten days with her at Chaulnes.[5] That is settled, Madame de Kerman agrees—we start tomorrow . . . So far so good for us, but you are at Grignan, my lovely one, worn down with strain and anxiety. You feared there would be no war, and wondered to what corner of Europe you would be constrained to dispatch your son. Fate has belied your fears

[1] Isaac de B., member of *l'Académie Française.*

[2] Louis-Charles de Lévis, Duc de, married Mlle Houdancourt.

[3] Léon Potier, Duc de, Governor of Paris.

[4] From *L'Ecole des Femmes.*

[5] In Picardy, near Péronne.

and the whole of Europe is alight, you had not reckoned with the Attila of his day—the Prince of Orange. The great piece of news which is on everyone's lips is that Poland, on divers pretexts, has declared war on the Emperor with whom the Turks are still fighting. This would make a great diversion and the Rhineland can scarcely be regarded as a danger point. Well, dearest, all is in God's Hands! Our little lad is so capable, already so experienced in his profession, having been present before the tender age of seventeen at no less than three sieges: had you known this was to be his destiny you would not have believed it, but no doubt it was foretold from all eternity . . . Farewell, dearest, you are a woman of iron will who, were wars to cease, would be utterly at a loss, and you must believe that God watches over your son and will preserve him . . . think of the many perils from which the Chevalier has been rescued, doubtless your child will follow in his uncle's footsteps.

To The Same

Chaulnes, Tuesday 19 April [1689].

I am awaiting your letters: the mailcoach calls here three times a week, which makes me wish to remain. I am seated at my desk, with the intention of setting before you everything which crosses my mind, for other news I have none: such missives cannot be called entertaining, and you will doubtless find nothing that you do not know already such as that I love you, and how I love you: perchance you would do well to leave my letters unread, since what your mother tells you is ancient history, but, as I cannot believe you will have the heart to act in this manner, let me say that I yearn, O how deeply I yearn after my daughter; her health, her poor aching brow fill my thoughts. The climate at Grignan alarms me: "this terrible wind which uproots trees whose topmost branches reach the sky and whose roots are planted in the Kingdom of the dead"[1] makes me tremble for you. Will it carry my daughter away? Beat her down? Shrivel her up?

[1] From La Fontaine's fable, *Le Chêne et le Roseau.*

Deprive her of sleep and despoil her beauty? These terrors, which haunt me, rob me of all peace of mind. As I pace my woods alone I am pursued, weighed down by melancholy reflections, but even in this extremity it is best to be alone . . .

To The Same

Chaulnes, Sunday 24 April [*1689*].

We intended leaving today, my dear child, but have put off until tomorrow. Mme de Chaulnes was seized with a violent sore throat yesternight, which made it impossible for her to swallow; this, together with a huge swelling under her ear, left Mme de Kerman and me hard put to it to know what to do for the best. Had she been in Paris she would doubtless have been bled, but here the only remedy to hand was to rub her gently with a well corked and soothing balsam, and apply blotting-paper to the affected parts; she slept in a warm bed, slightly feverish I think, and the results are nothing short of miraculous. The precious balm cured her in a night, the swelling is gone down, throat and tonsils no longer sore, so much so that the very next day the invalid was off to play chuck-farthing! . . . I call this remedy divine, pray hoard what you have of it with care, and fly to it when occasion offers. But, beloved, I am troubled by your aching brow, and what in heaven's name are you thinking of when you liken your case to that of M. Pascal? Do you want to finish me off altogether? No doubt it is desirable to have his pen, and his writings are, we know, divine; but to have a sensitive brain like his, to be constantly on the verge of exhaustion as he is, must be a torment, which indeed has resulted in spoiling his life and in cutting short his career—that surely is to be deprecated! A lesser mental strain than that imposed by the problems of Euclid may have as ominous results. What I dread for you are the vagaries of your climate, and lest already it should have reduced you to a shadow. Would to Heaven that you could have the benefit of ours, which I do not hesitate to classify as perfectly salubrious! . . .

To The Same

Pecquigny, Wednesday 27 April [1689].

We left Chaulnes on Monday, lay that night at Amiens where Mme de Chaulnes is an object of veneration as you are in Provence —I have never seen the like. The steward (M. Chauvelin) offered us a fine, nay grand, abstinence supper for the eve of Saint Mark, and yesterday a splendid repast for the feast day . . . After dinner we pushed on to the Château where, to satisfy the inordinate pride of the heiress to Pecquigny,[1] her possessions are displayed in all their glory. It is a feudal castle built, like Grignan, on a height overlooking the city and, like Grignan, having a remarkably fine Chapter, a Dean and twelve Canons; I do not know if the endowment be as grand, but here there are terraces overlooking the river Somme which winds endlessly in and out of vast meadow-land; these natural advantages you do not enjoy at Grignan: one of Caesar's encampments is to be seen half a mile away, the trenches of which exist to this day, and which is comparable to the Pont du Gard.[2] I can hear you saying: " My dear mother, what are you doing? And why are you not in Brittany? " I answer: " My dear daughter—we shall be leaving shortly . . . but have had to put off our departure ", no harm will come of it, and I am laying my plans to go to Nantes in June or July: meanwhile I expect no joy or happiness, and look for none, since you are absent. I live for the day, in a state of suspense, with my eyes now and again turned on some distant future, which belongs to God and depends on His goodwill, as do all things in this world. I sit thinking of your poor health, of your headaches, of the scorching winds which burn you up . . .

[1] Claire Charlotte d'Ailly, heiress of Philibert, Seigneur de Pecquigny, who married Honoré d'Albert, Marshal of France, father of the Duc de Chaulnes.

[2] The triple-arched Roman bridge over the Gardon in Bas-Languedoc, of great architectural beauty.

To The Same

Caen, Thursday 5 May [1689].

. . . A word about our journey. It took us three days to proceed from here to Rouen, uneventful days and charming spring weather. We ate well, went early to bed, and suffered not the slightest inconvenience . . . M. de Chaulnes awaits us at Rennes with all the impatience of a lover. We lay at Dive which is situated on the sea: the country is delightful, and Caen the most attractive, inviting, and gayest of towns with its fine position, wide streets, noble buildings and churches . . . and to crown all it is renowned as a Seat of Learning . . . Farewell, dearest. I picture you smothered in the dust raised by your building activities.

To The Same

Rennes, Wednesday 18 May [1689].

Thank God! At long last they have bled you; I can scarcely wait to know the result, and if your head is clearer. Mme de Chaulnes sends her love to the dear Countess, and wishes her to be told that her legs suffer from much the same kind of agitation as yours, which is most unfortunate considering the state into which it has pleased God to call both of you; she is anxious to know if the blood-letting has proved beneficial? So pray let us know; I should greatly object to my own blood being spilt in vain.

We laughed immoderately at the injunctions contained in your letter that I should purge myself, for at the very moment your letter arrived I was mixing myself a dose of my Capuchins' manna, despite the fact that I was not in need of it, and only taking it as a precautionary measure in view of the approaching austerities of Lent . . . You have been bled, I have been purged with, I trust, excellent results. In the evening we entertained a goodly company. M. and Mme de Chaulnes, Messieurs de Rennes,[1] de Saint Malo,[2] de Revel,[3] Tonquedec, and other Breton notabilities . . . The Duke is constantly in demand, troops are to be billeted, parades to be held, pipe and drum, soldiers, officers eighteen served at one table, ten at another, all in magnificent style; as the Chevalier remarked: "It works like a ferry, with the cable out of control." . . . We are off on Monday to Les Rochers to rest and relax, my son longs for it, his wife has need of it, and I live for the hour when I shall see my woods again. We pretend we shall return at any moment: God, no doubt, will inspire us when the time comes . . .

To The Same

Rennes, Wednesday 25 May [1689].

I am accompanying my son and his wife to Les Rochers . . . We remained here purely to oblige; as for me I am surfeited with visits and social engagements, and quite worn out: I require nothing so much as complete rest and silence, and to be alone once more in my charming woods; we arrive tonight, but to please you I promise to commit no imprudence. Yesternight we supped with M. de Rennes; it is an unending succession of entertainments, and this is the land of good cheer and good roast meat, well larded, and of the famous Prévalaie butter. M. and Mme de Chaulnes send you a hundred thousand good wishes, they would write if they were not up to their eyes in work. She bade me goodbye in tears.

The latest news from Brest is that M. de Château-Regnault[4] has disembarked his troops in Ireland, as also his armour and his coffers. M. de Gabaret, whose flotilla is ranging the high seas, has been attacked by Lord Herbert. M. de Château-Regnault,

[1] Bp. Lavardin.

[2] Bp. Guémadeuc.

[3] Charles de Broglie, Cte de R., brother of the Marshal de B., Lt.-General in Brittany, under orders of M. de Chaulnes.

[4] François-Louis Rousselet, Marquis de C.-R.

having left his convoy strictly guarded, sailed to the relief of M. de Gabaret; went into action and fought for seven hours, when the English disengaged and, badly mauled, made for their home port. The French pursued, and encountering seven Dutch ships on their return, brought these into Brest, a prize estimated at a million crowns.

To The Same

Les Rochers, Wednesday 15 June [*1689*].

What a contrast our lives present, dear Countess, yours at Avignon on such generous lines, brilliant, dissipated, extravagant, whereas here plain living is our motto, with loneliness thrown in, all no doubt in order and according to God's intentions; but I cannot believe that even from the anchorite's cell in which you hide away you are not gratified by the sincere homage laid at your feet by those who are both estimable and exalted—I should not believe it if you were to say so . . . What vexes you arises from purely domestic considerations and from cruel wastage; after all, if the place can be kept warm for our handsome young Captain he will not be doing too badly for himself. Meanwhile I have to watch you involving yourself in such reckless expenditure that, were it to continue, I should have to tell you as I did Mme de Chaulnes that " you are seated in a ferry of which the cable is out of control." But all this is over, you are back in your Château, and although you have not a moment of leisure neither are you in a perpetual whirl: no one could keep it up all the time, and to relax and lay down your arms becomes a necessity . . .

I embrace you, my dearest, you have been hard pressed—I beseech you to rest. As for me I am in such good fettle, and so perfectly well, that I am wondering what God wants of me! I am reading " Treatise on Submission to His Will ",[1] which to me is ever new and admirable. How lucky are those who can read! I have written to our Marquis; from what I hear of our

[1] The second Treatise, Vol. I, Nicole's *Moral Essays*.

little crony nothing is too good for him . . . My love to you and to all around. M. le Chevalier—Is that you I hear? And pray how have you borne the fatigues of the journey?

TO THE SAME

Les Rochers, Wednesday 22 June [1689].

What a grand procession [1] you describe! Both reverent and magnificent; and how fitting are such demonstrations in their deep devotion, compared with the horrid profanities exhibited at Aix with its display of worn-out effigies—"Gods of Love and hobby horses".[2] I can see the respectful salutations addressed by the crowd to you and M. de Grignan, who evidently did justice to the occasion by looking at his best: I am greatly touched by all you tell me. Your blue ribbon decorations were admirably suited to the occasion, all the more so when worn by someone of M. de Grignan's noble birth and exalted station . . . I must admit I am somewhat surprised that the Sacrament should be administered on such a noisy occasion; after all the feast of Pentecost has only recently been celebrated—but no doubt the position you occupy requires such observances—otherwise I cannot credit you with being more devout than Saint-Louis who, we are told, did not partake of it more than five times in a year. The author of the noted life of Saint-Louis was closely interrogated at La Chaise as to his authority for this statement, and he produced a manuscript . . . which is to be found in the King's library. However that may be, dearest, no doubt you know best about your religious duties and observances . . . the serious study of these questions requires a scientific approach . . .

Mlle Descartes [3] professes the profoundest admiration for your

[1] Procession of the Blessed Sacrament held on the Feast of Corpus Christi at Avignon, where Mme de G. was staying.

[2] Hobby-horses figured in a religious procession at Aix which had given rise to much comment, including the satire *Querela ad Gassendum.*

[3] Catherine, niece of René Descartes, a quick versifier. Mme de Chaulnes gave her a pension.

beauty and for the qualities of your mind. She scouts the very idea that anyone in Brittany is worthy so much as to cast an eye on your letter save one highly estimable person, whom she refers to as her mentor, and whose admiration equals or even excels hers. True enough—your letter was divine and free from any trace of philosophical balderdash.

To The Same

Les Rochers, Sunday 26 June [*1689*].

Dear daughter—I see you have, at last, torn yourself away from that most engaging city of Avignon [1] . . . Your descriptions diverted us extremely, not least your brother who, like you, fell in love with its delightful situation, and the delicious freshness afforded by the junction of those two noble rivers.[2] But you will have observed with closer attention than he did the antiquity of the churches, dignified as you say by the presence of Popes who, from time immemorial made their residence in the city. The beautiful Chapter House which, from its magnificent display of canonicals,[3] might, even now, accommodate a body of Cardinals : there is nothing like it in the whole of France . . .

You speak triumphantly well on the Jewish question, one needs must pity the Jews and emulate the Church which ceases not to pray that they may be brought to believe in the risen Christ; but as the Queen and Mme de Béthune could not persuade them, neither will you, I imagine, succeed in doing so . . . the antipathy felt for the Jewish race is unaccountable. In Racine's *Esther*

[1] Seat of the Papacy from 1309 to 1377, the city was ceded to Pope Clement VI from the House of Provence in 1348 for the sum of 80,000 florins, and restored to France only in 1791. In 1663 Louis XIV, on account of an affront to the Duc de Créquy, his Ambassador in Rome, seized Avignon, which became an integral part of Provence and of great benefit to the Governors. When it was handed back to Rome in 1689, Mme de S. uttered many complaints on behalf of the Grignans.

[2] The Durance flows into the Rhône a league below the city of Avignon.

[3] The robes worn by the Canons of the Chapter were scarlet like those of Cardinals.

such an alluring picture is drawn of young Jewesses I feel they could not have antagonised the most ardent Christian . . .

But will the time never come when you might return to Avignon without living in such a hideous turmoil? When you could enjoy the company of reasonable people and insure yourself an adequate amount of sleep? And not be exclusively preoccupied with that ruinous basset? How charming it might be if everything were different! Even M. le Chevalier should reap some advantage since Grignan is less salubrious than Avignon. I hear you have won every heart in the place, which I have little difficulty in believing.

Farewell, dear child, dear and most worthy to be loved . . . I enclose a line from Mme de La Fayette in which you will see what Boufflers [1] says of our lad: I am assured Barbantane [2] will never be tempted to throw a dice-box at his head when playing backgammon with him, as he did at P. d'E—— [3] who retaliated with a chandelier. Swords were drawn, great confusion ensued, and in attempting to separate them the Chevalier de Vassé was killed.

TO THE SAME

Les Rochers, Sunday 17 July [1689].

. . . I like to picture your life, dearest Countess, and confide its secrets to my woods. You enjoy such good company and so much good sunshine that, for you, it is easy enough to sing: " The north wind doth blow and we shall have snow; and who cares? " Our ceaseless rains might try you less; now that there is a let-up I have once more started on my solitary perambulations. What are you trying to tell me, dear child? That, having been to Mass, partaken of dinner, spent five hours in my daughter-in-law's company she and I may not separate for a short space

[1] Louis-François, Marquis, later Marshal, and Duc de B., Governor of Lorraine.

[2] Son of a friend of Mme de S. Captain in the King's Regiment.

[3] Maximilien de Béthune, Prince d'Enrichement, was the Duc de Sully's eldest son.

and enjoy our well earned liberty? She would scarcely thank you for this! She is a comely and agreeable female, and we agree very well, but we both treasure our privacy, and meet again the more agreeably because of it. When I am with you, dear daughter, it is altogether a different story, and *you* I should never leave of my own free will, but this, you will allow is perfectly natural, since no two persons exist who feel for each other as I do for you. So pray do not grudge us our mede of sanctifying freedom; with the help of books time passes somehow and as quickly maybe as in your brilliant surroundings. What a disadvantage to have no zest for reading! I fear your child is of that number—he should, however, know how to express himself in a letter. I am desirous he should visit you in November. He will be eighteen, high time to begin thinking of his marriage, fatherhood and the rest. But on no account must you toy with the notion of Mlle d'Or——; [1] her father is a ne'er-do-weel, whose behaviour is in the worst taste—the very thought of him puts me in a rage . . .

The life and air of Grignan should do much to restore the Chevalier's health: he is in good company, is no longer at the mercy of indiscreet visitors nor of hordes of sycophants who, says he, give him the gout. He is not tried by severe cold, at most a touch of north wind which, in order not to alarm him, is referred to as "A breath of native air." In face of all these advantages I cannot understand the blackness of his mood, the obstinacy of his vapours . . .

Good to hear that sometimes I am wanted by the Grignan family . . .

To The Same

Rennes, Sunday 24 July [*1689*].

I need not tell you I was welcomed with open arms by our kind Governors, who were deeply grateful to me for leaving my

[1] Mlle d'Oraison, daughter of André, Marquis d'O.

beloved Rochers in order to visit them. M. de Chaulnes I found reviewing the "Noblesse"—the regiment is a fine one and well disciplined. My son was highly gratified by the compliments he received, but I could not help reflecting I had brought him up with a very different end in view. Providence, however, would have her say as usual, thus sparing us the trouble of harking back on the past, and trying to unravel the tangled skeins, an endless task. God grant I may preserve this hardly acquired philosophy till the end of my days!

The other night we saw a young man dance, he is a son of that old lunatic, the Procurator of Rennes. The son is as pretty as a picture; he is twenty, married to the daughter of a President of the Law Courts of this locality who, no sooner had she looked upon the young fellow than she became pregnant, was married in haste, and six weeks later gave birth to a child. She is under the impression that a sight of her husband would exonerate her in all eyes; true enough that if you could see him dance you would be of the same opinion. Picture a young Adonis, perfectly fashioned, a hero of romance who dances with the stately grace of a Pécour, a Favier, a Saint-André.[1] His masters assure him they have nothing to teach him. He treads a measure to the tune of the Spanish fandango, and with his wife proceeds to execute steps of the most exquisite grace, no set pieces, but ever maintaining an impeccable rhythm. At one moment he improvises figures, the next jogs merrily along in the wake of the other dancers, anon can be seen facing his wife in a stately minuet: motionless for a second of time and before you know where you are he is off again flying through the air with feet barely touching the ground. Madame de Chaulnes, who was a noted dancer in her day, declared she was quite carried away . . .

In three or four days we shall all have scattered which, for me, is a good thing, for I find the life I lead here killing; I am in constant request and know not where to hide away—it puts me in a fever. I beg you will never again suggest I should be lured out of my retreat, for I dare swear I should not survive. The peace and quiet of Les Rochers encourages the hope that your mother will live to see you once again—life here is impossible . . . Farewell, my dearest—you know how greatly I love you.

[1] Three famous contemporary opera dancers.

Heavens! How dull and drab the sound of these words when they serve to express something so infinitely rare and precious.

To The Same

Auray, Saturday 30 July [1689].

Guess where I am, my dearest! At the seaside on the south coast of Brittany. Gone the time when you and I were sitting side by side in that small study in Paris—do you recall it? May we, happily, one day, meet there once again! Meanwhile fate has taken me by the scruff of the neck and flung me down in this spot. From Rennes I wrote you my impressions of the journey. Nothing could have exceeded Mme de Chaulnes' care of me; she herself looks into every detail, and I am not allowed to suffer the slightest inconvenience. And M. de Chaulnes, when he is my neighbour at supper, murmurs in a low voice: "I assure you this will do *her* no harm—see how well *she* is looking. Here is a lovely melon, (do not imagine Brittany cannot boast of melons!) *she* must eat a slice." When I ask him what he is muttering he says he is talking to *you* on the subject of *my* health. Of this banter he never appears to tire which makes us laugh heartily. It took us three days from Rennes to Vannes, a matter of six or seven leagues a day, affording a delightful and commodious way of travelling. Wherever we halted we were met by deputations . . . bearing complimentary addresses, and all the hubbub and din which forms a necessary part of travelling with Their Excellencies. There were detachments of soldiers with their officers, whole regiments manœuvring in the most warlike manner. The Kerman Regiment is composed of Lower Bretons, of splendid physique, they speak no French, but carry out their drill as if performing step-dances in a ballroom. I have heard tell that when leading the Bretons into battle the great Bertrand du Guesclin believed himself to be invincible. We arrived at Vannes on Thursday, and lodged at the Bishop's Palace . . . a fine house, and most sumptuously furnished. A magnificent supper was served such as leaves one dying of hunger . . . I was offered a partridge, when I pined for a cut of veal; and a pigeon when above all I coveted a wing of one of those fatted pullets from Rennes . . .

M. de Faluère [1] did the honours of the table to the best of his ability; he stared at me as if rendered speechless, finally exclaiming: "Madame de Sévigné! Can it be she!!" Yesterday, Friday, he regaled us with fishes, thus we have sampled the finest specimens land and water can produce . . .

Mme de Chaulnes never stops insisting on the satisfaction she has afforded you by removing me from the dangers and bad air of Les Rochers. Once said, there is no gainsaying it and you, dear daughter, have been instrumental in routing me out and sending me a-roving. It is true I am easy-going, and can accommodate myself to most things, and I love M. and Mme de Chaulnes; but I assure you that when God ordains I should return to Les Rochers, which you so wrongly decry, I shall do so with no little alacrity . . .

To The Same

Auray, Saturday 6 August [*1689*].

A festive spirit reigns abroad on account of the sudden arrival at Brest of Chevalier de Tourville.[2] So little was he expected that it was thought the enemy was at the gates until he revealed himself in person to the joyous surprise of all and sundry. He displayed great skill and daring in the performance of his duties, estimating that the enemy would be driven out of the shelter of the Isle d'Ouessant by the very wind which brought his fleet into Brest. This became apparent when the ships which set sail from Ushant took to the open sea . . . the Chevalier, not knowing their whereabouts, and with all sails set, made for Brest harbour where he was applauded for having judged so accurately of the situation and taken advantage of wind and weather . . .

[1] First President of the Breton Parliament.

[2] Anne-Hilarion, later Cte de T., created Marshal of France in 1693, after defeating the English and Dutch fleet.

The regiments here are being demobilised, and the "Noblesse" disbanded, sign of more peaceful days to come . . .

Adieu, dearest Countess—I embrace you most tenderly; you seem to absorb both coffee and chocolate in a singularly unsuitable climate, and in the dogdays to boot; have a care both for our sakes, and in order to allay any unnecessary apprehension which, at this distance, rears its horrid head only too easily.

To The Same

Auray, Friday 12 August [1689].

We are due at Rennes on Tuesday, two or three days in advance of our time-table, as M. de Chaulnes is recalled to Paris on affairs of state, or so it is surmised. In any case he is off, I will let you know my movements and when I return to the haven of my Rochers. We made a delightful excursion to Port-Louis three days since, an enchanting place whose whereabouts you are cognisant of, with its vast expanse of sea to rejoice the eye. Should one perchance turn one's back on the sea, one might be confronted with the hideous mask of Mazarin.[1] Despite his extensive domains he has chosen this one, which is not his by right, but belongs to his son and is in M. de Chaulnes' province. Nothing can equal the fellow's eccentricities; he is a lunatic, dressed in rags and hag-ridden by a kind of misguided piety. We wished to persuade him to fetch his wife back from England, where she runs the dual risk of being driven out or perverted, and where she sides with the King's enemies. He always ends by saying her duty is with him—with him! Good heavens! When we look at Mazarin, we must allow she is dispensed from all obligations.

The following day we inspected the locality in which Lorient[2] is situated, a league distant from the sea, and to which merchants from the Far East have access and may deposit their merchandise

[1] Armand-Charles de la Porte, Duc de Meilleraye, husband of Hortense Mancini. Governor of Alsace at the time.

[2] At that time Lorient was a port of call for merchant vessels, blossoming into a city in 1720.

for safe keeping. A M. le Bret, recently returned from Siam, is in charge of these commercial undertakings, and his wife from Paris, arrayed in all her glory as if for some state function at Versailles, invited us to dine with them. The husband entertained us vastly with an account of his travels, and we were urged to inspect a display of merchandise, porcelains and furnishings we thought of moderate appeal. Were you not queen of the Mediterranean I should have hoped to find you a suitable length of material or gingham for a houserobe, but it would have been an insult to your high standards in such matters. We returned on the tide that same evening, lying at Hennebon [1] in delightful weather—you will find these name-places on your map . . . Farewell, dearest, I shall write from Rennes . . .

TO THE SAME

Rennes, Wednesday 17 August [1689].

Dearest child—I have so much to tell you and so many questions to answer! To return to the courier who came to Hennebon to find M. de Chaulnes, bearer of a letter from the King. Well, the letter he brought was one which sends you flying to the ends of the earth to accomplish the impossible, and in it we recognised M. de Louvois' [2] unequivocal and forceful style in which he deigns not to ask if one is able to go to Rome here and now, but assumes that all is in order, and indeed brooks no excuse or delay. The King decrees " that he be sent forthwith to Rome,[3] judging him to be alone capable of bringing to a successful conclusion an event greatly to the advantage of all concerned by procuring as head of the Church one both capable of governing the Church and at the same time satisfying the laity throughout the world, and France most of all; that he (the King) has learned that the Pope is not long for this world,[4] and that the manner in which

[1] On the Blavet, some 10 leagues from Lorient.

[2] Minister for War.

[3] M. de Chaulnes had been sent to Rome as Ambassador Extraordinary on two previous occasions.

[4] Innocent XI had died 12 Aug., but the news had not yet reached France.

M. de Chaulnes acquitted himself at the two previous enthronements has convinced His Majesty that this one will be carried out with equal felicity, for it is of great import. Therefore M. de Chaulnes must hold himself in readiness to receive his orders from the French Cardinals who will be awaiting him . . . No doubt he will obey with alacrity since his absence will be a short one and its object redound to his credit; but meanwhile "the strictest silence must be observed." You can well imagine the effect in our small circle: M. de Revel and I have our lips sealed . . . We dined with the Bishop, who gave us the largest and best meal you can conceive . . . We induced M. de Chaulnes to tell us tales of his past embassies to Rome, and we found him in such a good mind, and so admirably equipped to negotiate in a country where his memory is still revered, that we could but applaud His Majesty's choice. M. de Chaulnes assured me, had the object of his mission been to make peace with the Pope, he would have declined the honour for your sake, but he wants you to rest assured he will never work against your interests; that is to say, until death has claimed His Holiness he will take no step whatever . . . Our intentions were to spend the winter in this part of the country . . . as it is M. and Mme de Coulanges are off in four days . . . and I to Les Rochers with your brother and his wife. Having parted with our much beloved Governors I shall spend a far happier winter at Les Rochers than elsewhere . . . and I shall be sustained by the hope of seeing you in Paris, if so be it is the Will of God, for on man-made projects I have long ceased to place any reliance whatever. I am persuaded M. de Chaulnes will recommend my son for a commission when speaking with the King on matters relating to Brittany, and I think he will not meet with a refusal . . . I esteem myself fortunate to love Les Rochers as I do, and those who rule over it, and that our existence there should be so greatly to my taste. I rejoice at a return to my natural habitat, from whence I shall not emerge unless, happily, you summon me . . .

To The Same

Les Rochers, Wednesday 24 August [*1689*].

. . . To possess a portrait of Pauline would transport me to the seventh heaven! Bring it with you, I am sure to like it. I can picture her with a something of the Comte des Chappelles,[1] to which ingredient I should add a small pinch of the best kind of Grignan, and out of this hotchpotch there emerges a handsome pretty young woman with noble mien and a ready wit which becomes her well, and I embrace her with all my heart. Take good care of yourself, dear Countess, for the sake of your house, of your son, and of your mother. I shall not forbid you to touch melons since you have such good wine in which to cook them: M. de Chaulnes forbade them to me on your behalf, and as they were not delectable I took it in good part; but I insisted on being allowed to sweat freely. I would return to Auray, after a short walk, in a bath of perspiration as if I had taken part in a game of tennis; after being rubbed down and changed, I turned up perfectly fresh for supper, and took the wind out of everybody's sails by laughing at myself; judged by its results the régime could not have been improved upon . . . I have always been prone to sweat profusely, and at an advanced age it may be better to leave well alone sooner than adopt new habits . . .

I ardently hope M. de Grignan's troubles are modified; it is a miracle that your health can stand up to the onslaught of such heavy anxieties . . .

To The Same

Les Rochers, Wednesday 31 August [*1689*].

I am suitably impressed by the state you keep at Grignan, and the fact that your two dining tables are laid and served, simultaneously and to the stroke, certainly does great honour to Flame,[2]

[1] De Rosmadec, a friend of the family who stayed at Les Rochers.

[2] Butler to the Grignans.

who appears to run Honoré [1] very close in excellence. He must be of vast assistance to the lady of the house, but how ruinous is this display. The upkeep of a great estate like yours can scarcely be said to cost nothing, and I have recently seen an example of it at the Chaulnes', where by a wave of his wand Honoré can conjure up all he wants out of thin air—such powers are both serviceable and admirable on occasions, but the results are plain for all to see . . . I was wont to say that M. de Rennes [2] marked the pages of his breviary with slices of ham: it would seem your Valence [3] would not despise the possession of a similar bookmarker: I remember well this luminary of the Church, when midday struck, putting himself to the affair in hand with a will and a positively beaming countenance . . .

M. de Chaulnes leaves for Rome on Saturday 27th—he travels by river; when he reaches your beautiful Rhône you would get a view of him if you held up a telescope. A body of Cardinals will join him at Lyons, and at Toulon, they will find twenty galleys awaiting to convey them to Leghorn: Coulanges is of the party . . . You are a good fairy to have written to M. de Chaulnes about your brother's commission; he thanks and embraces you tenderly . . .

I scarcely know what to say about our fleet: since you despatched those powerful reinforcements and the whole flotilla set sail for the open sea, we have heard nothing further. A witty person was heard to remark that no decisive naval victory has taken place since the battle of Actium, cannon are fired, ships are scattered and sunk; and they all turn up again in a month's time, scatheless!

Farewell, dear and amiable one—I am persuaded you will lavish attentions on our dear Duke on his way back from Rome . . . I mourn the Pope and the loss to you of the Comtat d'Avignon [4] —God hath given, God hath taken away . . .

[1] Butler to the Chaulnes.

[2] Charles-François de Vieuville, Bp of Rennes, died 29 Jan. 1676.

[3] Guillaume Bochard, Bp of Valence, nominated 1687, consecrated in 1693.

[4] The Pope allowed M. de G. the revenue of the Comtat Venaissin. There was danger that he might be deprived of his Governorship after the new election.

To The Same

Les Rochers, Sunday 11 September [*1689*].

. . . I am not fully reassured about our poor Marquis' activities. With so much going on all around it is difficult to believe that Boufflers' flying unit can remain passive. Whilst they were fighting a very creditable action, the Maréchal d'Humières was sustaining a heavy defeat at Walcourt. Think of this mere brat, sword in hand, fighting his way into the castle, and slaying or capturing eleven or twelve hundred men! This child, all in a moment assuming man's stature, nay that of a god of battle with a flaming sword! Dear one, these thoughts would be well-nigh unbearable did we not know he is in God's keeping. You never spoke a truer word than when you say I am not indifferent where you and he are concerned, not only am I not indifferent, and identify myself with every turn of your fortunes, but I can truly say I am in it up to the neck. How badly off should I be if it were not so! These are the preoccupations, the emotions which keep me going, and fan the spark of life in me, all too fiercely perhaps.

I must tell you that for the last year Corbinelli has allowed himself to be absorbed in the supernatural to the exclusion of all else. He possesses a copy of Malaval [1] which he finds enchanting; perusing its pages he has made the discovery that their love of God, to which my grandmother and my "grandfather", Saint François de Sales, bore witness in so unmistakable a manner, was on as spiritual a plane as that of Saint Teresa herself . . . From this work he has extracted five hundred maxims of unexampled beauty; he goes daily to visit a pretty young woman called Mme Le Maigre, in whose house the only subjects of conversation are those relating to God, to Christian morals and to the Gospel of the day. These so-called religious conversations, at which he is an adept, have become his one preoccupation . . . he confides in Mme de Coulanges, who approved all he does, and is encouraged by the Carthusians to continue in the good work.

[1] The works of François Malaval were put on the Index on the grounds of unorthodox teaching.

But this he will not do, for as you know, he burns all his scribbles before they are read . . . Corbinelli has no time to write to me, what would I not give to be assured that, in his case, the inner structure of the man were as secure as the exterior is pleasing, and to know the effect of true devotion on a mind so enlightened, so progressive, as his: if I were worthy to ask God to grant me this favour, I would do so from the depth of my heart.

Our weather is atrocious—it is mid-winter. I am attempting to keep warm and dry by picturing your gorgeous sun at Avignon; Good Heavens, I forgot! At all costs we must avoid talking of Avignon. Should you forfeit that splendid Comtat the Duke will be responsible, you must scold him: I dare not allow my mind to dwell on the enormous benefits you derived from it in the past, and what their loss will mean to you . . .

My daughter-in-law sends you her love, she and I have been alone together and find we get on famously well without your brother's help.

To The Same

Les Rochers, Sunday 18 September [1689].

I have at length received your letter of September 1; it went on the Grand Tour as my letters sometimes do; they find their way into the wrong bag; one knows not whom to blame. But this one has turned up to my great delight, as it is a link in the chain of our correspondence . . . Let us at once proceed to converse of M. de Chaulnes' visit, and of the warm welcome and magnificent reception you gave him; [1] he will have seen the grandeur of your house, tasted of your excellent fare, two tables laid in great style as he is used to in Brittany, enjoyed the fine company you keep and the timely absence of tempestuous winds which would have deafened you and put an end to conversation—the guests, no doubt, were making enough noise without that! It seems Flame did his work to perfection and with a great air. I can see it all, and I can scarcely exaggerate the joy it has given me, for I wanted you to be seen in all your glory—your glory, that is, of the country variety, for at Aix it is still more dazzling,

[1] The Duc de Chaulnes visited Grignan on his return journey from Rome.

and I like to think that with you he enjoyed a more lavish fare than the homely fowl or bacon omelette which is all our humble table can supply. Now the Duke knows of what you are capable, and this will prove a good investment and one which will enable you to do just as you please when you come to Paris: he will have sampled your feast days and your fast days, your mutton pasties and your raised pigeon pies. Coulanges [1] too seems to have been on his best behaviour, and not to have let you down—I am afraid it may not last, as with him enjoyment is half the battle, and he revelled in it all to his heart's content; furthermore he was enamoured with Pauline's divine attributes. I know you have it against him that he only shows his best side in the company of the high and mighty, but he can make himself most agreeable in a family gathering and you yourself told me of an intimate little supper you partook of with him five years since, which was little less than hilarious. M. de Chaulnes has written to me . . . he tells me you often spoke of me, and drank toasts to my good health, and that on one such occasion Coulanges actually climbed up on a chair—how dangerous for such an unsteady, round-about, little ball of a man! . . . You are indeed magnanimous, as you say, to put yourself out for an Ambassador who is doing you such a bad turn: he is greatly upset. It seems the Papal Conclave is hedged around with difficulties . . .

Your beloved child is well: everywhere he follows close on M. de Boufflers' heels, sword in hand. O dear daughter!—that little beloved mannikin—think of it! I must ever harp on the same theme. *May God preserve him!* Mainz has surrendered; [2] this news is great news indeed. One was so confident about it that one mocked M. de Lorraine's [3] fears. We are told M. d'Uxelles comes out of it with enhanced prestige, from friend and foe alike. I tremble lest the Dean's brother [4] be among the killed

[1] Emmanuel de C. had been of his company.

[2] Mainz fell after a siege lasting seven weeks, for want of ammunition. M. d'Uxelles made twenty-two sallies, in the course of which he killed five thousand of the enemy, but his gallant defence was severely judged in Paris. Louis XIV thought this ill-considered, telling him he had "acquitted himself as a stout-hearted man, and capitulated as a man of understanding".

[3] Charles V, Léopold-Nicolas-Sixte, Duc de Lorraine (1643–90) had laid siege with an army of 50,000 men.

[4] One of the brothers of M. Rippert, Dean of the Chapter at Grignan.

or wounded: none of these splendid brothers is long lived. If one can judge by the laconic manner in which he received the news from M. Prat [1] doubtless he is used to bad tidings. I pity Martillac; [2] how does a legless man acquit himself in a besieged city which falls into the hands of the enemy? What hellish noise, what utter confusion, what a shambles! I confess I am not without anxiety . . .

You ask me to describe our life here—I hasten to obey: we rise at eight, hear Mass at nine, walk or not as the weather permits, each on our own: we dine copiously, possibly a neighbour drops in; after dinner we discuss the news and take up our needlework . . . at five we separate, enjoy a little exercise, meet anon in some lovely glade, each carrying a book, we recite our prayers, and I dream of my dear daughter and build castles in Spain, in Provence, sometimes gay, more often sad. My son reads aloud, suitable books, books of devotion or historical works which help to distract us; he is an indefatigable reader, and when wanted can read aloud for five hours at a stretch. A great part of my leisure is occupied with correspondence; we have had visitors and shall have more, we could do without them, but when they are here we make the best of it. My son is employing his workmen in the task of further beautifying his alleys, pleasances and parterres . . . My dearest, it is indeed strange how in a life spent in so insipid and monotonous a manner the days seem to fly by and elude us; and God knows what else eludes us at the same time. "Let us avoid the subject", though ofttimes our thoughts will be our masters. We sup at eight: Sévigné reads aloud, something light and breezy so as not to induce sleep: the young people retire at ten, I not before midnight; this then is approximately the rule of our convent, on the door of which is inscribed "Liberty Hall" or "Do as you please".[3] How greatly I prefer our life here to that at Rennes: it will be high time to seek sustenance there for body and soul when Lent is upon us . . .

[1] Curé at the village of Grignan.

[2] Probably a relation of the Mlle de Martillac who was in the service of Mme de G.

[3] Rabelais writes of the Abbey of Thélème: "The only rule of their Order was do as you please." *Gargantua*, I. Chap. lvii.

To The Same

Les Rochers, Sunday 25 September [*1689*].

I am getting somewhat restive under M. de Grignan's watchful eye: he suspects my every movement, does he think I shall saddle him with a father-in-law? His attitude will end by making me commit some folly, but it will not be for *Monsieur* le Comte de Revel; yes Sir—not simply just *Monsieur*, but *Monsieur le Comte* de Revel.[1] In this province no one is thought to be worth mentioning who does not bear a title, though we sometimes forget ourselves and say plain Revel, but, if we do, it must be under the strict seal of the confessional. I do not, however, want to marry him—he is too dashing. You wish to know who are his "Chimènes". You mention two Breton ladies—here are three more: the wife of a sheriff of Rennes who was recently in this neighbourhood; Mademoiselle de K—— a beauty; and heading the list little Madame de C—— none other than *your niece*, I say your niece since she is a granddaughter of *your father* Descartes: she is no fool, and understands perfectly that he who plays with fire is apt to burn his fingers . . .

To The Same

Les Rochers, Wednesday 28 September [*1689*].

I am surprised you should care to give me so graphic an account of M. de La Trousse's infirmity: I understood he was paralysed from the waist downwards, but the details you underline are catastrophic, and place him out of bounds of normal society which, in his case, means he is bereft of all consolation. I cannot imagine the waters of Bourbon being of any avail. How can waters, whose property is to relax, succeed in binding one who is already relaxed, nay paralysed? His derangement is really quite out of the ordinary and I condole with him, far more I think than he would with me in like circumstances . . .

[1] Charles-Amédée de Broglio.

We have here an Abbé de Francheville, who is witty, agreeable, and perfectly unassuming; learned without conceit. He is a Parisian to the tips of his fingers and says he has met you on two occasions, that you are divine and that your image has remained indelibly printed on his memory: he is a Carthusian and Mlle Descartes' tutor: she showed him your letter, for which he expressed great admiration as he does for your enlightened understanding. In return I appreciate his . . . and it is a long time since I have enjoyed such good company. He speaks of my son as *nate dea*; [1] it follows that I am a divinity . . . but, in my own eyes at any rate, a bucolic one: in order however to reassure M. de Grignan, who probably thinks I wish to marry the young man, I should like him to know that another widow, young, rich, of estimable family has forestalled me; she married him two years since for his ready wit and sterling qualities, having previously rejected offers made to her by no less than two Presidents of the Law Courts; further one can scarcely go. As for him, the pursued who should have been the pursuer, he capitulated at the ripe age of sixty, left his convent and fain must now be satisfied with practising as a Christian philosopher, and the most honest man to be found in this province. He lives in his château, and his comely young wife cares for nothing so much as to be with him. He came to see me and my son, and if we enjoy conversing with him, we think he fully returns the compliment . . .

To The Same

Les Rochers, Sunday 2 October [1689].

Tomorrow, as ever is, a year will have gone by since I saw you, embraced you, heard your voice, bade you farewell at Charenton. It seems but as yesterday, and I dream of a future which shall reunite us, when I shall once again embrace my beloved treasure, never, nevermore to be torn from her embrace. Would that I could end my days on earth with the one person who has filled them to the exclusion of all else! Dearest, I am

[1] From Virgil's *Aeneid.*

opening my heart to you, almost involuntarily, in order to celebrate our mournful parting of yesteryear. After telling you what is in my mind I should like you to know that the vivacity, cheerfulness, *currente calamo* of your letter quite carried me away. I feel that no one who was not lighthearted, and enjoying good health, could express herself in so agreeable a manner. Let us turn for a moment to the Chevalier—he must have vastly improved since I last saw him. Is it possible that, at this very moment, I can hear him stamp with his right foot!—we used to think he was wont to boast of the prowess of the left, although the state of the right kept him from being unduly elated and worried us as much as it did him. It is nothing short of miraculous to see this foot restored, for it was fast going the way of M. de La Rochefoucauld's, which was truly lamentable . . . Tell M. le Chevalier our delighted congratulations on his convalescence; soon I trust we shall be able to say—on his recovery . . .

Well, my beautiful one, we no longer feel aggrieved with our good Governors, such a relief, for I could scarce endure to think they were in the wrong. It now appears, and all are agreed, that the Duke was never given an opportunity of speaking to the King on the subject of our commission, nor on Brittany, nor indeed on any other matter, since Rome occupied the whole of the royal conversation . . . now we must endeavour to put it all behind us and if, by an extraordinary chance, the affair were to come off, we should know it was due to miraculous intervention . . .

To The Same

Les Rochers, Wednesday 12 October [*1689*].

. . . I must tell you that Mme de La Fayette writes to me in the tone of one issuing a decree from on high, with Mesdames de Chaulnes and de Lavardin in the role of collaborators, in which she threatens to cease loving me if I do not consent, here and now, to return to Paris: saying that I shall fall ill, that I shall die, that my mind will suffer deterioration. So persistent are these ladies, so pressing and urgent, and this in so friendly a manner, I cannot help but be gratified, and Madame de La Fayette goes on to tell me what steps I must take to put the plan into instant execution: I am to go to Malicorne in my son's equipage, where I shall find M. de Chaulnes' carriage in which I shall proceed to Paris, where I am to be the Duchess's guest . . . best of all I shall be able to lay my hands on the sum of a thousand crowns which someone is falling over himself to lend me and, if you please, will want no interest nor seek to be refunded: above all I must start *here and now*. It is somewhat of an effort to receive such a long missive when one is barely recovering from an attack of fever, but I answered gratefully, if in a tone of banter, that I scarcely expected to be bored to tears in my son's company and that of his wife, not to speak of my library, nor at the prospect of returning to Paris in the summer, to my own house, in my own carriage, and without having to borrow from any generous soul, thus finding myself under an even greater obligation than if I were dunned by the police. But I ended up by swearing I would not fall ill nor grow into a garrulous dodderer just yet, and that, despite her threat, I counted on her love for ever and aye. Thus did I reply to my three kind friends. One day I must let you see Mme de La Fayette's letter. Just imagine suggesting to me to live in someone else's abode, on someone else's money, to drive there in someone else's carriage! In truth, my child, I am incomparably well off where I am: the horrors of a winter spent in the country, which at a distance seem so formidable, when nearby lose all their sting. Do you not approve my decision? If only you were in Paris, would not that be a trumpet call! But woe is me you are not there. I have, however, taken all my dispositions on the remote possibility that you might take it into your little poll to fly like a bird in this direction . . .

Your dream has intrigued me. You think it must have been imaginary, as in it you could see no tree in front of the house, well this turns out to be nearer the truth than you imagined, for my son had every one, nay every single one, felled two years since; he is so proud of the view, just as in your dream, that he is building a protecting wall for his parterre, turning the tennis court into a bowling-green with yet another moat and wall beyond. If this plan is carried out, it will be an enchantment and the gardens of surprising beauty, closely resembling the designs favoured by M. le Nôtre, and our "Place Coulanges" planted with orange trees. You must have anticipated all this in your dream.

To The Same

Les Rochers, Sunday 16 October [*1689*].

What a joy to know that quinine has produced its customary effect in the case of M. le Chevalier, for with his temperament all new remedies have to be used in fear and trembling; I duly trembled on opening your letter. How good to know that a potion containing such heat-inducing properties should have been efficacious for his inflammatory symptoms! . . . I rejoice at your success, knowing full well that in the realms of conduct, as of health, you would deservedly have the last word. I am, if anything, still more surprised that gout should have cured M. de Grignan's bowels, and fine weather rid him of gout, as I am to know that quinine can reduce fever! Perhaps the gentle diet of rice you prescribe may have effected these miracles . . .

I appreciate all the praise lavished on Pauline by M. de Coulanges which fits her like a glove, and makes me understand her claim to admiration, only very slightly tempered by the fact that someone has, most inadvisably, poked his *nose* into her concerns. Had the Count been satisfied to give her his eyes and splended figure, and left the rest to you, Pauline would have "set the world alight".[1] Such an excess might have been an embarrassment whereas the charming combination has turned out a wholly delightful creature . . . Here am I alone once more—my son and his wife are at Rennes . . . I can assure you I am not in need of pity . . . At Rennes all is festive and gay at the return of parliament in the near future and the opening of the *Etats* on the twenty-second of the month; the new Marshal [2] has agreeable

[1] Expression used by Tréville when speaking of Mme de G. when she made her first appearance at court.

[2] The Maréchal d'Estrées was in command of Brittany during the absence of M. de Chaulnes. [*Perrin*].

manners, the Bretons like him and all appreciate a change. Do not regret my solitary state—I like it . . . I look after myself I walk when it is fine, when there is rain or mist I stay at home I have learnt wisdom. But you, who reign with omnipotence over the health of others, I pray you take care of your own, rest from your labours, and remember that your present intercourse is of more value to them than any benefit you may hitherto have conferred on them . . .

To The Same

Les Rochers, Sunday 23 October [*1689*]

I am alone, which, my dear one, is not an unusual occurrence and anything but bored ; I am in good fettle, I have a fine selection of books, work to do, the right weather to tempt me abroad with a small admixture of good sense you will admit all this should go a very long way. I can see, through my son and his wife's protestations of their longing to be with me, that in reality they are enchanted to be at Rennes, wherefore I wish nothing better than that they should remain there . . . At Rennes one need never be dull, the atmosphere is lighthearted and frivolous, the Bretons have not begun to feel the pinch of the dues which will presently be extorted from them ; they see no further than their noses—namely the return of Parliament to their poor city and to its noble palace, the most beautiful in France, where the *Etats* are wont to be held. No sight is more superb, and a great crowd will be attracted at the thought of seeing so many new faces, the Maréchal d'Estrées, M. de Pommereuil, M. d'Eaubonne[1] . . . in the place of M. de Chaulnes . . . M. d'Harouys ; the world revels in nothing so much as change. M. de La Trémouille[2] came to Vitré a few days since, where he was given a tremendous ovation on account of his new Knighthood, at such times honours are

[1] Gervais le Fèvre, Seigneur d'E., Pommereuil's son-in-law.

[2] Charles-Belgique-Hollande, Seigneur de la T., Duc de Thouars, Prince de Tarente et de Talmont, son of Prince Henri-Charles de T. and Amélie de Hesse-Cassel. Mme de S. had already remarked on his extreme ugliness.

ꞏedoubled in proportion to the holder's territorial rights. Despite ɿis fine upstanding figure and blue ribbon it cannot be contested ꞏhat he has a fearful countenance withal; M. de Grignan's alone ꞏan bear any comparison, and were I not afraid of giving umbrage n a certain quarter I might add, "save in the realm of physical beauty," for in that M. de La Trémouille far surpasses your husband.

I feel I have dished you out good gossip about Brittany, and only trust I have not wearied you, but are we not sometimes compelled to display our own wares? After which I hasten to return to Provence . . .

I end my letter, dearest and most beautiful one, by sending you my love which I esteem beyond compare. I dare not broach my plans so early in the day—but it looks now as if I should be free at the end of the summer when there will be plenty of time for us to put our heads together and arrive at some conclusion; our aim being identical in every respect, this should not present any grave difficulties.

To The Same

Les Rochers, Sunday 30 October [*1689*].

To speak of the many and grievous farewells and partings you have been subjected to I have long feared the effect these might have upon you, and predicted that you would come to regret the loss of such an entertaining galaxy of friends. On the subject of the Chevalier I see you have changed your mind: I suggested to you this summer that he would do well to spend the winter at Avignon or elsewhere in Provence, and that a gracious winter spent in your glorious sun would be a fitting climax to the waters of Balaruc; many persons do this to avoid the rigours of a Paris winter: but you would none of it and sent me about my business, adding that, should he remain, it would be a sign he was not well enough to leave . . . it would indeed be a sad winter for him spent in that little Paris closet, with only your portrait to look at, which remains mum however much one tries to induce it to utter, and if it be God's will he should have to suffer and cry aloud, how bitterly he will regret you for, dear knows, he is no one to be satisfied with small mercies . . . since he is willing, I am all for his trying out the climate of Provence this year . . .

Why do you say you are no longer beautiful? Why should your blood be at fever pitch? Mine, I confess, runs cold at the very thought. You are too sensitive, too easily overthrown, your days of feverish agitation make inroads on your nights: pray endeavour to compose yourself, bring all your courage, philosophy and faith to bear on the subject, and thus you will be enabled to endure the burden Providence has placed on your shoulders . . . Pauline writes me such an enchanting letter . . . You are teaching her Italian, she says, and she is reading *Il Pastor Fido*. The saucy baggage dares to ask me a most insolent question! I vow I shall have no choice but to refer her back to her parents.

To The Same

Les Rochers, Sunday 6 November [1689].

M. de Chaulnes writes in a most tender and engaging manner: he says he thinks he could boast of having carried out a satisfactory mission were it not for the necessity he was under to hand over your lovely Comtat [1] to His Holiness [2] as a gift; this he did with so bad a grace that he thought it would not be accepted: far from it—the alacrity shown by His Holiness further enhanced its value in M. de Chaulnes' eyes. The deed is done, dear child: God hath given, God hath taken away, and the loss must, like so many others, be discounted. I must repeat once again that if you want to do him justice you must never allow yourself to think the Duke played you false. Before our last *Etats* were held he was remarking how times had changed, and that he was no longer, as of yore, incontestable master in his own house, and that to

[1] The Comtat d'Avignon had made part of the Grignan's prerogatives in Provence.

[2] Pietro Ottoboni, a Venetian, had been elected Pope on 6 Oct. as Alexander VIII.

keep in good odour at Court he found it necessary, now and again, to put in an appearance at Versailles . . .

Let us discourse once more of our *Etats*. The Holy Ghost, according to Fra Paolo,[1] arrived at the Council of Trent in a portmanteau, whereas the deputation to M. de Rennes was in a sealed warrant—one method seems as unusual as the other: the Maréchal d'Estrées will not let my son out of his sight for an instant, he speaks to no one else, knows no one else, will not stir a step without him . . . in fact knows so mighty little of Brittany that had he not found open house with the Marquise d'Uxelles, he would have been in a pretty fix. The Marshal keeps a horrifically copious table, outdoes even M. de Chaulnes, having two tables spread for eighteen persons both night and morning furnished with new and splendid porcelain services festooned with fruits and flowers; each vies with the other, and the devil take the hindmost; there are twenty tables of the same calibre of wild extravagance.

My son is at Rennes, his wife takes no end of trouble to keep me amused. M. de Lauzun, like a troubadour, wanders romantically off to Ireland at the head of six thousand men. Take care of yourself, my dearest, and love me with the tender solicitude which I dare venture to think is, in a very special manner, my sole prerogative.

To The Same

Les Rochers, Sunday 20 November [1689].

You make me very happy when you tell me that your Marquis has been promoted to the rank of colonel in his uncle's famous regiment; at eighteen nothing could be more honourable, he could scarcely have aspired to greater dignities. Your anxiety is a thing of the past, and your alternations between hope and despair have come to an auspicious conclusion. I defy even you, with your genius for discovering the worst in everything, to find the smallest fly in this ointment. Now your only trouble will be on

[1] Pietro Sarpi, author of *History of the Council of Trent.*

the financial side, as a colonel's life is, of necessity, more costly than a captain's. Of course the Chevalier must be refunded—pray for what sum?—and I trust you will be allowed to sell that admirable company of troopers for which you were responsible. So, my child, the drawbacks and the advantages of this affair balance each other. Your son's honours will increase your expenses, but despite the difficulties which will accrue, one could not want it otherwise—such is the way of the world. Does not your little colonel intend to pay his mother a visit, surely he could find time to do so? I must write to him and indulge my fancies in addressing the letter.

You say you are often as many as a hundred souls at Grignan, and eighty besides are accommodated in the grounds and out-buildings. It seems that no one has the smallest scruple in taking advantage of your notorious hospitality. I commend you for not exposing your beauty and Pauline's to the dangers of the smallpox, that most formidable menace . . . You have drawn such an alarming picture of the north wind at Grignan during the winter! I feel M. de Grignan will not be able to resist the temptation of seeking shelter at his good town of Aix . . . Keep me ever informed of your plans and intentions . . .

To The Same

Les Rochers, Wednesday 30 November [*1689*].

How grateful I am to you for sending me on that letter from good M. de Saint-Pouanges.[1] It is a joy to have seen with my own eyes the tribute he pays to the high merits and good character of our Marquis, and so apt to the days we live in . . .

I see you were struck with Mme de La Fayette's phrase,[2] written in all love and affection, be it said. Although I do not allow myself to forget the inner truth of her comments I admit I was somewhat taken aback, not having observed in myself any

[1] Gilbert Colbert, Marquis de S.-P., Colbert's cousin who acted as the young Marquis' protector. *Grand Trésorier des Ordres du Roi.*

[2] "*You are getting old, your faculties and shrewd wit will decline.*"

sensible signs of advancing age or decay. But ofttimes I reflect on the sadness of life, and make assessments and computations which lead me to the inevitable conclusion that, without knowing it, I have advanced to the very brink of old age; yes—we have come face to face, and my one concern is not to take another step on the downward path which leads to infirmity, suffering, loss of memory and those horrid blemishes which will inevitably disfigure me. I hear a still small voice saying there is no other choice but to advance or die, however repugnant to human nature . . . When all is said and done is not this the fate of mankind? Acceptance of this universal law should steady us and give us patience: may you too have patience, my dear, and not allow your tender heart to cause you to shed one tear of which your reason does not approve.

I found little difficulty in saying no to my kind friends . . . Their alarming picture of a winter spent at Les Rochers portrays in reality one of the sweetest things on earth; their idea of wintering in the woods makes me laugh! Mme de Coulanges writes: "leave your cold, damp Rochers," and I retort: "the boot is on the other foot, it is your Brévannes which is damp and cold!" . . . We are on a height, like Montmartre—our sun-drenched woods, our beautiful dry terraces are incomparable, so also our Place Madame which is in the very eye of the midday sun; at another point the sunsets are gorgeous, and when it rains there is a good fire crackling; sometimes two card-tables are set as at this very moment: I do not greatly object to visitors, for I do as fancy prompts me, but I dare swear I like it best when no one comes, for then we read and read to our hearts content . . . I wanted you to know this in order to remove from your mind any possible disquietude on my account . . .

To The Same

Les Rochers, Wednesday 7 December [1689].

My dear one—it is as I said—when one is thoroughly settled in for the winter the months of November and December pass as a flash. But I admit your gales alarm me; here we have no record of anything approaching their severity. I do not want you to be alone this winter, and if the Chevalier is destined to spend the coming one in a sick bed it should be in your home, not in his small chamber in Paris; it would I think be a consolation to both. You say you are resolved to spend the winter at Grignan, giving M. d'Aix all the trump cards to hold, with regretful excuses at your enforced absence, and inability to hold your court as you and M. de Grignan were wont to do for three or four months every year! . . . Like you I am beginning to lose hope of your effecting a sale of the company, it has hung fire too long! My son and I were talking with admiration the other day of the manner in which you moulded the Marquis' career, so successfully indeed that he finds himself, as if to the manner born, at the head of his uncle's regiment; all this just as it should be, M. de Grignan inaugurating him in the Philisbourg campaign, which caused you so many tears, thus crowning the good work. Neither his military training, service with the Musketeers or Light-Horse, gained him as much experience as the three sieges under Monseigneur his uncle, not to speak of the famous contusion he bore so lightheartedly, so gallantly. Up to the present nothing could well be more auspicious, may God watch over him to the end . . .

My health is excellent, of yours you speak unconcernedly: how then is your side, your colics, your exhaustion, the whole of your most precious self? Are you still beautiful, for that is the touchstone, the framework of the whole edifice? Adieu, my beloved, my enchanting daughter—can you, I wonder, fully comprehend the all-compelling nature of my devotion to you?

To The Same

Les Rochers, Sunday 11 December [*1689*].

I cannot credit what you tell me of the rate of *six* as a rate of interest, I have not heard the like since the son of Molière's *Miser* raised a loan at that preposterous figure. I think you must

brand and addicted to war, he is doing himself scant justice by neglecting to study the art, and to seek acquaintance with those heroes who have excelled in it. I scold and torment him in the hopes I may succeed in rousing him—it would be the first time he set himself against our wishes. I do not, however, object as much to his knack of day-dreaming (since he can be relied upon to wake up in a twinkling where his honour is concerned), as I do to his habit of gambling at cards. I have given him to understand it will be his undoing. If he should restrict his play his losses will follow suit, but the lightest rain is apt to be the wettest, and if he should play badly he will, for a certainty, be fleeced and someone will have to pay the piper; again, should he have no ready cash he will either have to go by default, or encroach on his allowance. And then there are the innocents who, apart from being dupes, are invariably the losers. It would be a sad day for you, my dear one, who would have to bear the brunt and feel the repercussions. Yes—the Marquis would be a happy man if, like Pauline, he could acquire a taste for books and learning. Most blest and happy state, which puts us out of reach of two formidable enemies—boredom and sloth . . .

To The Same

Les Rochers, [*Sunday*] *18 December* [*1689*].

. . . What say you to the good example set by the King who has had his finest silver melted down? Our Duchesse du Lude is in despair but feels obliged to follow suit; Mme de Chaulnes has given her ornamental tables, Mme de Lavardin her silver service which came from Rome, in the belief her husband will not be recalled there; pray look into your affairs and see if you can contribute in any way . . .

I am hoping to enlist your interest by sending you a letter from M. du Plessis: do not appear to have seen it, or allude to it to him . . . I am full of sympathy for the poor fellow; to be addicted to the state of matrimony is a dangerous disease: far better take to drink in my opinion . . .

1690

To Madame de Grignan

Les Rochers, Sunday 22 January [*1690*].

O my dear one—what a cataclysm has overtaken you! And how greatly do I participate in your tribulations! But regrets and lamentations are useless on such occasions, are indeed a mockery, and it would be idle for me to asseverate that if I could lay my hands on a sum of ready money it should be yours for the asking. In my own small way I find myself overwhelmed by creditors whom I have no means of satisfying, being swamped by the obligation I am under to pay, here and now, no less than five thousand francs in dues on the land I recently purchased from Mme d'Acigné, and in order not to have to pay ten thousand in another two years time. I am only telling you this in order to explain to you why my hands are tied. Your brother feels your situation acutely, and I am certain, were it not so difficult to raise money at the present time, he would be far more generous than your two rich prelates . . . He can see what an ambiguous position our young Colonel is in, and shares our regrets that M. le Chevalier is no longer there to direct and keep him in the right path . . . In the face of such adverse circumstances God alone can help you to resign yourself to His will. My son is also greatly disturbed to see a lad of such tender years in command of a horde of old veterans . . . The whole thing is most regrettable. Can you not think of some wise head who could be relied upon to give him sound advice? His career is of all others one requiring judgement based on experience. I entreat you to allow him to join you forthwith at Grignan; of what avail would a companion be to him in Paris or Versailles where they will want to open his eyes to every kind of intrigue. Possibly I am doing him an injustice, but would he be capable of acquitting himself properly at Court or of performing the duties required of him?—too much I think for such young shoulders to carry. I am handing the pen to my son, and will resume it anon.[1]

I agree with your brother when he points out that this promotion, which pleased and delighted us all, will to you be a source of financial embarrassment. Do not forget, my dearest, that Bourbilly is yours. It is, I know, only a small thing to have in reserve against a rainy day, but you must be thankful for small mercies. Have you tried to ingratiate yourself with President Berbisi?[2] Write to him—he might advance you something if you raised a mortgage on the property: anyway my endorsement will not fail you . . . It is useless to write to me about your health; haunted as you are by bogies, how then can you expect to sleep, or to keep cool when anger and indignation are working havoc within? . . .

Farewell, best and dearest, I grieve for you, how can it be otherwise? Two years without seeing any return on your money which is tied up in this concern, and the considerable upkeep involved; and arrears of rent; and Paris; and God knows what all . . .

To The Same

Les Rochers, Wednesday 1 February [*1690*].

We seem to have struck a bad patch, what with snowstorms, rain, and severe gales; but when we come through it will be to

[1] M. de S. writes sympathising over the young Marquis having to command old veterans—he calls them an array of mustachios and camels.

[2] Jean de B., President of the Burgundian Parliament.

open weather, and longer brighter days: what is heartbreaking is to see that, however fast the days and hours go by, you can never catch up on your losses. Good heavens! What a miscalculation you made over the years 90 and 91,[1] and as far as the eye can reach! At a distance an argument is difficult to sustain, as the necessary rejoinders are missing, but I must be allowed to heave a sigh and to feel, that whatever suffering is entailed, a little knowledge is better than none. I can see very well that, in your case, the only apparent remedy has its drawbacks both in respect of your relations at Court and your good name in the province . . . and if a better way could be found it would certainly not be advisable to hide your head all winter in your château: . . . You are fortunate, I think, in finding that your friends' misfortunes tend to lessen your own; it is a great solace to be able to converse and lament with one another, but I fear that in the state you are in it is out of the question that reading can afford you any pleasure, and when I urge you to do so it is only to quiz you, for what interest can we find in the annals of the Kings of France when we are beset with troubles of our own? I know it all too well and oft find myself reading the same page twenty times over, and I can assure you, although my son is an admirable reader, I suffer endless distractions, and find myself making such frequent excursions into Provence that I can well picture those countries you would explore were you to attempt to fix your mind on a book! My one prayer is that God should sustain you through these heavy trials. My heart is wrung for you, for your misfortunes will be highly prejudicial when it comes to settling your poor son in life. At length he has arrived in Paris, having dawdled unpardonably when it came to leaving his regiment. But now he is engaged in paying his court at Versailles for the very good reason that he hopes to sell his company . . . I always find it difficult to picture him in these royal surroundings, but soon he will tire of sojourning there, and think of nothing but joining you . . . To-day the new Parliament assembled at Rennes in its noble palace amid feasting and jubilations. I respond to my dear little d'Adhémar's [2] message with the most

[1] M. de G. was forced in those years to put some order into his affairs and to forego his revenue in order to do so. [*Perrin*].

[2] Marie-Blanche, who had taken the veil at the Ladies of Sainte-Marie at Aix.

ively sentiments of goodwill; poor dear child! How good it will be if, in lieu of happiness, she finds contentment. This, of course, goes without saying, but you will not fail to observe the nnuendo in my remark.

TO M. DE COULANGES

Les Rochers, 18 March [*1690*].

I am posting this missive hot on the heels of the other three I wrote telling you, dear cousin, all about my imperfections which I should like proclaimed in Rome as they are in Paris. I have perused your charming letter more than once, the last time in the silence of these woods where I could the better appreciate your verse and your prose, both when you are grave and when you are gay. I reflected on life in Rome and its mixture of the profane and the "Santissimo", and on those beautiful gardens where art and nature vie with each other. I thought of that ball [1] to which you climbed with the agility of your twenty years, and with the many advantages men have over women when it comes to climbing, circumscribed as we are at every step; and again I thought of the days and the years I shall be roaming these alleys from end to end before ever I reach those giddy heights. I think Mlle de Scudéry's madrigal very well turned and flattering, and I think you most fortunate to include the Abbé de Polignac [2] (since Cardinal) in your circle; I am gratified at his messages for he is one of the most agreeable of men, as thinker, as conversationalist; his address is informed by knowledge, and is lively and agreeable in the extreme . . . When I returned from my walk I had every intention of writing to you about him, and it went out of my head. What an omission, my dear Coulanges! And how can one venture to rely on one's memory? Ever since I have reproached myself, turned a cold shoulder on myself, refused to walk with myself, and I must beg you to reconcile me with myself

[1] The ball at the summit of the cupola which surmounts the dome of St. Peter's.

[2] Melchior de P., brother of the Marquis.

by telling that kind Abbé that, albeit I forgot him, I remembe him perfectly. I intended to advise you to cultivate him as friend rather than as a rival; and furthermore to continue lovin me as much as I do you, should such a thing be possible.

To Madame de Grignan

Les Rochers, 26 April [*1690*]

At length the poor Dauphine is no more;[1] she died a tragic a sordid death. La Troche has furnished me with details, and will do likewise for you when she writes as she intends doing The King and *Monsieur* were present at the death-bed. Sh craved the King's forgiveness for her shortcomings and wante to kiss his hand, he embraced her; her sobs prevented he addressing the Dauphin, who did not long remain in the sick chamber. She blessed her little ones adding: "I bless you a well, my little Berry, although you are the cause of my death" but this she said in error, as it was known she was not affected ir those parts . . . To Bessola[2] she made a gift of forty thousan livres, and recommended her warmly to the King's good offices; to *Madame* she bequeathed a diamond; to Mme de Rochefort a ring worth fifty thousand louis: mourning will be worn for six months only. I am in my dotage, I think, to give you all the news with which, no doubt, you are already acquainted . . . I know not on whom the task of delivering the funeral oratior will devolve, but the Ducs de Berry, d'Anjou and de Bourgogne will furnish, I think not unworthily, the salient points in the panegyric of our Dauphine.

NOTE.—*Mme de S., having remained at Les Rochers for another seven months, must have written many more letters to her daughter covering this period; of these all have been lost or destroyed save three which are in the private collection of M. le Marquis de Garnier.*

[1] Marie-Anne-Christine-Victoire de Bavière, probably due to bad nursing after child-birth. Fléchier delivered her funeral oration.

[2] Lady-in-waiting, who came with her from Germany.

To The Comte de Bussy

Les Rochers, 12 July [1690].

I must tell you about the great battle [1] fought and won by M. de Luxembourg, dear cousin, which is uppermost in all our minds. Does it not appear that God is ever on the side of His Majesty the King? Nothing could redound more to his credit than this glorious prowess in arms, this resounding victory . . . Little de Grignan, who was serving in de Boufflers' army may, by now, have been seconded in order to join up with M. de Luxembourg. There are still a handful of young fellows in whom I take a personal interest, and I shall not be easy until I know how they have fared: beyond this nothing is left but an all-embracing compassion for those who have fallen in battle . . . I pity the bereaved mothers . . . not so the young widows who, doubtless, will appreciate their liberty, or still more a change of lord and master. I rejoice for the King; the repercussions of this great news will be felt far and wide. To M. de Luxembourg I tender my friendship and humble obedience . . . You can see, dear cousin, from what I am saying how full of preoccupations I have been these last days, but in the country one badly requires to be roused from time to time by some strong emotion lest one should become fossilised. Peaceful surroundings induce a state of torpor. Thank God I have come to life with a bang—the Queen of Hungary's water has never produced a more sensational effect . . .

To The Same

Les Rochers, 13 August [1690].

I duly received the letter you sent me on your departure from Paris, dear cousin, which I took to be in lieu of farewell. Despite your usual courage and the buoyancy of your temperament, which

[1] Fleurus, near Charleroi, where the French defeated the Dutch and captured 7,000 men, of whom 900 were officers. They lost 2,000 men, killed or wounded, and more than 300 officers.

enables you to surmount obstacles and defy depression, I thought I could detect in you a note of chagrin at not having been granted your request at Court. This was enough to drive me, who have so much less strength of character, into the abyss. Had we but met we could have said so many things which must now remain unspoken.

I have been receiving letters from Paris which tell me the Prince of Orange is alive [1] and that only M. de Schomberg was killed at the battle of the Boyne . . . The Flemish armies are in such close proximity that it looks as if they were still intent on fighting, whereas those of Germany, with only the Rhine between them and the enemy, stand as if moonstruck, and gape at one another. We must commend all to the God of Battles who, in his own good time, will assume the mantle of the God of Peace. To Him I turn regarding the future, and endeavour to conform in all ways to His designs. Farewell, dear cousin, and to you, my charming niece.

To The Same

Grignan, 13 November [*1690*].

When you see the date and address at the head of this letter you will think of me as a bird on the wing. With commendable courage I transferred myself from Brittany to Provence. Had my daughter been in Paris I should have joined her there, but knowing she intended spending the winter in this beautiful part of the world I resolved to take advantage of her sun and return with her to Paris in the course of the coming year. Having devoted sixteen months to my son I felt I owed something to my daughter, although the execution of the plans did present certain difficulties. I took three weeks to cover the distance, travelling partly by litter, partly by the Rhône. After taking a few days much needed rest, I was received with great cordiality by my daughter and

[1] For some days it was believed he was dead, and indecent rejoicings were the order of the day. He was wounded in the shoulder on the eve of the battle.

M. de Grignan, nay with such warmth and gratitude that I feel well repaid, and my journey of a hundred and fifty leagues an inadequate tribute to offer these kind good people: I am not unduly fatigued. One day I shall entertain you with an account of the grandeur, beauty and magnificence of this domain. I wanted you to know my change of address in order that you should write to me here and not to Les Rochers—here where I am basking in a sun whose beneficent rays should give me back my youth. At our age, dear cousin, we cannot afford to despise any small mercies which come our way . . . We have been apprised of the recent death of M. de Seignelai.[1] Favoured by fortune he had youth, wealth, great possessions—it seems as if splendour itself had died with him. It is the more surprising to hear Madame de Seignelai[2] intends relinquishing all part in the social life of the community because of her husband's debts, which amount to fifty million. Is this not a proof that no wealth, however great, is adequate when exceeded tenfold by expenditure? Anyhow, dear cousin, before death all men are equal, and at its portals we may confidently await life's favoured few. Their pride and vainglory will be humbled to the ground, thus affording much solace to their less fortunate brethren. A few Christian maxims would, I think, not come amiss at this juncture, but I have no wish to preach a sermon . . . only to ask news of my dear cousin and his amiable daughter . . . and to entreat their continued love for me. To become fickle at our ages is scarcely worth the trouble.

To The Same

Lambesc, 1 December [*1690*].

I am gratified, dear cousin, that you should approve my pilgrimage from Brittany to Provence: it would have been worth

[1] Jean-Baptiste Colbert, Marquis de S., eldest son of Colbert, was made "Ministre Secrétaire de la Marine" at the age of 36. He died of languor 3 Nov, aged 39, when Minister and Secretary of State.

[2] Catherine-Thérèse de Matignon, his second wife, who subsequently married Charles de Lorraine, Comte de Marsan.

while if only to bask in the glorious sun. To spend a winter in this favoured climate is altogether delightful, and to have found my Madelonne here is sweeter to me than any spring.

Together we have read, admired, and approved your offers of service to His Majesty. They are couched in your own incomparable style; you have presented to perfection the attributes which rightly belong to one seeking the post you aspire to fill, and I see so many advantages accrue to the recipient that I am induced to think the rôles should be reversed and he should be imploring you. As you so truly say you are well equipped to further enhance the might and glory which are his by divine right . . .

You will I know, dear cousin, keep me informed of any developments in this affair. I am grateful for your confidence, for no one can be more interested than I. Indeed I believe I have brought you ill-luck by being as sensitive as I am to anything which touches our illustrious name. By punishing you God has humbled me, but you are far too brave and too wise to feel humiliated . . . it is I who am weak and foolish . . . Sometimes I am tempted to think you have inherited the virtue of resignation from our grandmother (Sainte-Chantal) . . .

We are spending the winter peacefully at Grignan. M. de Grignan has been suffering from severe colic and fever for the last ten days; when he has recovered he intends leaving for Paris. He sends you his compliments, and my daughter her kind remembrances . . .

1691

To M. de Coulanges

Grignan, 26 July [1691].

I am so greatly shocked by the sudden death of M. de Louvois [1] that I scarcely know where to begin. This great statesman is no more, this man of unique stature and lofty attainments, and as M. de Nicole put it, whose *self* spread far and wide in many directions, who at his zenith could lay claim to be the hub of the universe: how many projects, secrets, plots had he not unravelled; how many wars had he not averted; intrigues had he not forestalled! In politics he played chess on a grand scale, moving the pawns in a masterly manner. Ah! If you give me pause for a moment how dearly should I like to mate and checkmate both the Duke of Savoy [2] and the Prince of Orange at their game!

In as far as the things of God are concerned, or those more nearly related to God, I can see, dear cousin, that what has occurred in Rome and at the Conclave has deeply disturbed your inner life: you should not let that be. I have heard tell of a man of sound judgement who, from personal observation, drew very different conclusions, which were that to survive so many disorders and blasphemies the Christian religion can be no less than

[1] Son of Chancelier Le Tellier, Louvois was Minister for War under Louis XIV. Born in 1641, he died of apoplexy.

[2] Victor-Amédée II, later King of Sicily, and finally of Sardinia.

divinely inspired. Try to see it from his point of view, and remember this very city of Rome was bathed in the blood of martyrs, and that in the early years of the Church, and indeed for centuries, the main purpose of the Conclaves was the choosing of priests possessing enough zeal and devotion to face martyrdom ; no less than thirty-seven Popes remained firm in the face of the most terrible and painful death. If you read the history of these events you will surely agree that, if true religion can be established and can subsist in so miraculous a manner, it is no figment of man's imagination . . . Duly assemble these facts, and do not jump to rash conclusions. Whatever machinations the conclave may be up to the Holy Ghost can be trusted to look after the Pope . . . I have come across this wise saying : " What evil can overtake a man, who knows that all things come from God, and who loves the work of His Hands ? " On this highly moral note I will leave you, dear cousin.

1692

To the Comte de Bussy

Paris, 27 January [*1692*].

We arrived here, dear Cousin, in time to see M. de Grignan knighted, but not soon enough to embrace you . . . You warned me you would have left for your châteaux, and would be there or at Autun to enjoy in peace the gracious distinction conferred on you by His Majesty. You were badly in need of solace . . .

The Court is full of rejoicings for the marriage of M. de Chartres [1] with Mademoiselle de Blois.[2] There is to be a grand ball which is made an excuse by all those who proclaim they are penniless, to spend two or three hundred pistoles. It makes one sceptical and inclined to disbelieve in their tales of penury, which, possibly are very real. But the French always have ample resources when it comes to doing honour to their Sovereign such as you would scarcely credit did you not see it with your own eyes. Courtiers, young and old, will be adorned with more or less magnificence according to age and rank . . .

M. de Grignan and my daughter send you their respectful

[1] Philippe, later Duc d'Orléans, nephew of the King.

[2] No trouble was too great for Louis XIV when it came to finding suitable matches for his illegitimate children. Not content with placing one in the House of Conti, and another in that of Condé he elected that Mme de Montespan's daughter should espouse the Duc de Chartres, thereby raising her to the very steps of the throne. Bussy, indeed, thought to see her Queen.

compliments. Their little daughter is here; without possessing her mother's famous good looks she has succeeded in so mitigating and toning down the Grignan countenance as to be almost a beauty. One day you must judge for yourself . . .

1694

To M. de Coulanges

Grignan, 5 July [*1694*].

I heave a sigh of relief at your news of the improvement in Mme de Coulanges' health; her last letter had so gravely disturbed me. I am sorry Carette [1] is leaving her—he would do well to appoint the Maréchal de Bellefonds as his locum tenens to guide her in the way she should go. It is most unfortunate to place all one's faith in an apothecary who happens to be firmly persuaded he has sovereign rights in Italy: pray keep me informed of the end of the chapter . . . M. de Grignan has left for Nice at the head of a big detachment, to stave off an attack, if one be attempted by that flotilla which met with so bad a reception at Brest. [2] You know how easily the Lieutenants-General of our provinces tend to become lieutenants-general of our armies? They find it quite irresistible even though it prove their undoing. Here we play *hombre* with passing visitors, we read, keep to our rooms, the days and hours go by. Our small gathering sends you love and salutations.

Note.—*Mme de G., having spent the years 1692 and 1693 with her mother in Paris, forestalled by a few months only Mme de S.'s return to Grignan.*

[1] An Italian doctor who was looking after her.

[2] The English and Dutch fleet under Admiral Russell had sailed into the Mediterranean to rally the Spanish squadrons and protect Barcelona, threatened by the Maréchal de Noailles. [*Montmerqué*].

To The Same

Grignan, 9 September [1694].

I have received several letters from you, dear cousin, fortunately none has gone astray, for each has its own individual merit and rejoices all our hearts. We shall not quarrel with you over your mode of address: "To the Royal Château of Grignan". It is a striking address, and gratifying to know that in a mind as well stocked as yours with the noble and beautiful, this château, unique of its kind, should succeed in retaining its niche . . . by no means its smallest title to fame: since you love it as I do I should like to exchange a few impressions. That unsightly gradient which led to the upper courtyard, much to the shame, be it said, of those Adhémars who designed it, has been replaced by one which is perfectly agreeable, I will not say in the grandiose style—they were cramped for space—but the result is a real *chef d'œuvre*. The vestibule, which can be used for a dining hall, is reached by a flight of steps under a covered way and has the Grignan arms over the door, which you would appreciate. The apartments reserved for dignitaries of the Church are suitably furnished . . . and we make use of them in a highly agreeable manner. But, as we are on the subject of Grignan, I must allude to the merciless habit of almost continuous banquets in which they indulge, more particularly at times like these. It is not that the constituents are so very different from those to be found elsewhere—partridges, for instance, are common fare—but whereas in Paris everyone sniffs at them and cries out: "Fie! this is a dung heap", here our partridges feed on thyme, marjoram and the ingredients which go to make our perfumed sachets; the same can be said of our plump quails, and of them it is expected that the leg can be parted at the first stroke of the knife. The turtle doves are of unsurpassed excellence, and so are our melons, our figs, our muscat grapes, and, believe it or not, should the fancy take us to eat a really bad melon, we should have to send to Paris to get one, here such a thing is unknown; crystallised figs, grapes the colour of amber which melt in the mouth and which, if you indulged in them, would make your head go round as though you were slowly imbibing, sip by sip, our most delicate vintage wine, our wine of Saint-Laurent. What a life we lead, dear cousin! . . . And how far removed from that of the good Trappists! . . .

1695

To Madame de Coulanges

Grignan, 3 February [1695].

I beg you never again to mention Mme de Meckelbourg's [1] name in my presence. In face of the dire poverty which surrounds us how is it possible, holding any Christian belief, or indeed out of common humanity, to enjoy such vast possessions, such accumulations of gold, silver, furnishings, fine trappings, precious stones? How can she wish to cut such a sorry figure in the eyes of the world, a world whose esteem and approbation she covets above all else both now and hereafter? How can she want to show herself for what she is—a miser to the backbone, grudging to the poor and to her dependents whom she has disinherited; so tight-fisted even towards herself that she is brought to the verge of starvation, and when she dies her deadly sin, the sin of avarice, will stand revealed in its true colours. Dear friend, were I to discourse on this subject for a year it would not suffice to express my abhorrence for such abasement of the human understanding, and I resent Mme de Meckelbourg's name being brought to my notice. We were wont to love each other as sisters, but now I renounce her and all her works for ever and amen. This book is closed. . .

Our time is still much taken up with ceremonial visits after our

[1] The beautiful Dsse de Châtillon, sister of the Maréchal de Luxembourg; she died 24 Jan., leaving a colossal fortune.

wedding [1] from the Mesdames de Brancas, de Buous and other ladies of consequence who, though they know we wish to dispense with their presence, break the windows or crawl under the doors to come and pay their compliments at the peril of their lives. Thus do we proclaim our love in this part of the world—not so, I imagine, in Paris? I should be content with rather less of it, I confess, but I dare swear that to see you would transport me with joy.

To M. de Coulanges

Grignan, 3 February [1695].

Mme de Chaulnes wishes to remind me of my good fortune in being where the sun shines; she seems to think our days are spent in drinking and making merry. Alas, dear cousin, she could not well be under a greater misapprehension, the cold here is more severe a hundred times than in Paris; we are exposed to every wind that blows—the south wind, the north wind, the very devil of a wind, they vie with each other for the honour of confining us to our rooms, or hurling the biggest insult at us: even the obstreperous Rhône, hard-bound, is a prisoner; our desks are frozen, our hands are blue with cold and can scarce guide a pen, snow is on our breath. After their brutal rape our snow-capped mountains stand as in a virginal trance, and no day passes but that I find myself wishing for some artist to immortalise the horrific splendour of the scene—this is the pretty pass we have come to. I pray you to acquaint the Duchess with these facts, whose fancy sees us strolling, parasoled and veiled, under the orange trees. The pastoral splendour of our wedding festivities you have drawn to the life; all desire to claim their share in your congratulations; but none of us understand your allusions to the wedding night? How ribald you are to be sure! I was enchanted with the modest demeanour of all concerned, and I told Mme de Coulanges how the bride was escorted to her apartments where her night apparel,

[1] That of her grandson, Marquis de G., with Anne-Marguerite de Saint-Amand, daughter of a *fermier général*, Treasurer of the Languedoc *Etats*.

linen and coifs were laid out, her hair was braided, and after disrobing she stepped into bed; no one was aware of any comings or goings in the bridal chamber, and the next morning all arose, including the happy pair, who had remained undisturbed, left discreetly to themselves; no awkward questions as to their new claims as son and daughter-in-law, no formal breakfast, everyone helping himself according to his needs; no bawdy jokes . . . all this I found most unusual, and none the less commendable and proper. The cold is so penetrating that my pen drops from my hands . . . Respecting the vast fortune bequeathed by Mme de Meckelbourg, I told Mme de Coulanges it was a great source of joy to me to know that, when the time comes, I shall die penniless but owing nothing, which is I think the appropriate way for a Christian to meet her end.

To M. de Sévigné

Grignan, Tuesday 20 September [1695].

And so you are back once more at our poor Rochers, my dear children, and enjoying that peace and immunity from fatiguing duties which, by affording her a breathing space, should be of untold benefit to our dear little Marquise. I am greatly affected by your poignant account of her extreme delicacy, and from the depth of my heart identify myself with your anxieties. May God spare you the ultimate sorrow which I cannot readily accept, believing as I do that if this dear creature be wisely cherished she will live as long as any of her contemporaries . . . I pray you to keep me informed of every development. . .

As for your poor sister's health, her condition, alas! is far from reassuring. The hemorrhage is stanched, but has left its aftermath; she is so sadly changed you would scarcely recognise her for the same person. This is due to grave digestive troubles, of which the cause is a diseased liver, and this of long standing. With her it is constitutional and to me a source of deep apprehension. Such remedies as could be applied for the liver might risk a return of the flux, and these contra-indications make any treatment difficult and her state lamentable. If, as they still hope, time can effect improvement we shall start post haste for Paris . . . I shall keep you informed . . .

NOTE.—*At the back of this letter of eleven pages is inscribed in the Marquis' hand: "From my mother, 20th of September 1695." It may well have been the last letter he was to receive from her before her illness, and subsequent death on 10 April 1696.*

A SELECTIVE INDEX OF PERSONS

(N.B.—M de (without full point) indicates "Marquis de". Figures in italics refer to footnotes: the first usually supplies biographical details.)

Abbé (le bel), *see* Grignan, L-J. de
Abbé (le bon), *see* Coulanges, C. de
Adhémar, *see* Grignan, Chevalier de (Also used of Marie-Blanche, *la petite* A.)
Amonio, Dr, 86, 154, 162, 174-5, 177, 179-80
Anges, Les, 90
Anne of Austria, wife of Louis XIII (1601-66), Regent, *24*
Anne-Marie of Austria, wife of Philip IV of Spain (1634-96), *78*, 84
Anne of Denmark (Queen of England), *303*
Ariosto (1474-1533), *65*, 160, 274, *310*
Arles, Abp. of, *see* Grignan, F. de
Armagnac, Ctsse d', 304
Arnauld, A. (Le Grand (1591-1661), 28
Arnauld d'Andilly, R. (1588-1674), 28, *103*
Arnauld, Abbé de Chaumes, eldest son of above, *ob.* 1698, *123*, 247
Arnauld, H., Bp. Angers, *274*
Arpajon, Dsse d', 49, 110

Bagnols, *Intendant de Flandres*, 184
Balzac, J. G. de, 14
Baptiste, *see* Lully, J-B.
Barbin, C., 86, 206
Barillon, Paul de, 75, 307
Bayard, Abbé, 161, 166, 196
Bellefonds, M de, 91, 93, 218, 234, 237, 309-10, 373
Bellefonds, Judith de (*Mère Agnès*), 225
Béthune, M de (1603-65), 321-2
Béthune, Marquise de, 330
Blois, Mlle de, M-A. de (Psse de Conti), (1666-1739), *222*-4, 227
Blois, Mlle de, F-M. de (Dsse de Chartres), *317*
Boileau Despréaux, N. (1636-1711), 203
Bossuet, J-B., Bp. of Condom, 1669: 23, *120*, 127; Bp. of Meaux, 1681: 241, 286
Boufflers, L-F., Maréchal de, 331, 341, 343, 365
Boufflers, Ctsse de, *194*
Bouillon, Cardinal E. de, 129
Bouillon, G-M., Duc de, *77*, 231
Bouillon, Dsse de, 104, 230, 231
Bourdaloue, L. (1632-1704), 19, *51*, 114, 271
Bourgogne, Duc de, 273, 364
Brancas, Cte de, 110
Brinvilliers, Marquise de, 26, 153, 168-70, *230*
Brissac, Dsse de, *53*, 83, 95, 154, 159-63
Bussy-Rabutin, Celse-Roger, 32-3, *39*
Bussy-Rabutin, Roger de R., Cte de B., 14, 16-17, 22, 30, 32, *38-41*, 102-3, 112, 131, 371-2

Cadaval, Duc de, *49*
Caderousse, Duc de, *229*
Canaples, Cte de, *91*
Capmas, C., 35-6
Capuchins, The, 114, 234, 281-2, 285, 292, 296, 326
Cardinal, The, *see* Retz
Carmelites, The, 120, 153, 200, 225, 241
Castlemaine, Dss of, *87*
Chaise, Père de la, *230*
Champmeslé, Mlle de, 28, *54*, 86
Chantal, C.-B. de Rabutin-, 20
Chantal, La Bienheureuse Jeanne-Françoise Frémyot, Dame de, 20-1, *158*, *262*, 341, 368

Chapelain, Jean, 21, *66*
Charles II of England, 87, 91, 134
Charles II of Spain, *78*, 221–2, 224
Charmes, M. de (Pres. Aix Pt), 71, 72, 91
Charost, M de, *305*
Chartres, Duc de, 317, 371
Chaulnes, Duc de, Gov. Brittany, 18, 19, *68*, 70–2, 91, 125, 217, 232, 260–1, 286, 320–3, 326–7, 336–40, 342–3, 350, 352–3
Chaulnes, Dsse de, *68*, 70, 72, 91, 125, 139, 244, 260–1, 286, 292, 318, 324–5, 327–8, 333–5, 338, 347–8, 359
Coadjutor of Arles, *see* Grignan, J-B. de
Coadjutor of Rheims, *see* Le Tellier, M.
Coëtlogon, M. de (Gov. Rennes), *70*, 260
Colbert, J. B. (1619–83), 97, *206*, *216–17*, 231, 236
Colbert, Mme., *46*, *223*, 250
Condé, le Grand, Louis II de Bourbon, (1621–86), known as *M. le Prince*, *38*, *47*, 58–9, 91, 93, 101–3, 105, 114, 117, 121, 149, 185, 223–4, 288–9, 298
Condé, Psse de (*Mme la Princesse*), 23, 288–9
Condé, Henri-Jules de Bourbon, Duc d'Enghien (*see*), *M. le Duc*, after the death of his father, *M. le Prince*
Condom, M. de, *see* Bossuet
Conti, Armand, brother of le Grand Condé, Prince de (1629–66), *83*
Conti, A-M. de Martinozzi, Psse de, wife of above, 82–4
Conti, L-A., Prince de, son of above, 83, *222*, 227–8, 259
Conti, M-A. Psse de (Mlle de Blois), wife of above, 226–8, 259
Conti, F-L., Prince de la Roche-sur-Yon, *233*, *288*
Corbeau, le Seigneur, *see* Grignan, J-B.
Corbinelli, Jean, 24, 61, *156*, 177, 193, 232, 271, 290, 318, 341–2
Corneille, P., 15, 18, 23, 86
Coste, Mlle de la, *214–15*
Coulanges, Anne-Marie, *see* Sanzei
Coulanges, Christophe de, Abbé de Livry (uncle), "Le Bienbon", *21*, 22–5, 30, *50*, 61–3, 64, 67, 85, 89, 98, 107–8, 135–6, 138–9, 146, 160, 187, 197, 199, 200, 201, 203, 207, 215–16, 219, 232, 246, 249, 250–1, 280, 282–3, 290–1
Coulanges, P-Emmanuel, M de, 20, 24, *45–7*, 85, 113, *135*, 161, 167, 193, 201, 202, 309, 313, 318, 338, 343, 363–4, 369–70, 373–5, 377–8
Coulanges, M–A. du Gué, wife of above, 20, 24, 45, 108, 133, 167, 174, 177, 178–9, 180, 182, 184–5, 196–7, 201, 218, 234, 239, 247, 253, 257–9, 263, 313, 318, 338, 341, 358, *376–7*
Countess, The, *see* Fiesque
Court of England: at Saint-Germain, 311–16, 320
Court of France, 239, 244, *264*, 257, 264, 362, 366.
Créquy, Maréchal F. de, *77*, 93, 204

Dangeau, M de, *94*, 170, 173, 296, *319*, *357*
Dauphin, le Grand, *see* Louis, eldest son of Louis XIV
Dauphine, La, *see* Marie of Bavaria
Delan, Hélène, 44, 133, 138
Descartes, René (1596–1650), *251*, 329, 345–6
Descartes, Catherine, 329–30
Despréaux, *see* Boileau
Devilles, the, 43–4
Digby, Sir K., *284*
Divines, Les, 314
Dreux, Mme de, *237*, 245–6
Dubois, Postal Agent, *46*, *93*
Duc, M. le, *see* Condé, H-J. de
Duchesse, Mme la, *see* Enghien
Duclaux, Mme, 36–7

Enghien, H-J de Bourbon, Duc d', known as *M. le Duc* (1643–1709), son of le Grand Condé, 15, *59*, 90, 105, 117, 121, 171, 223–4, 227, *233*, 242, 289
Enghien, Anne de Bavière, Dsse d', *Mme la Duchesse*, *44*, 90, 223, 227, 234
Enghien (children), Anne d', 1671–5: Henri d', 1672–5: Louis, Duc de Bourbon, *m.* Louise, Mlle de Nantes, *233*, *289*; Marie-Anne de Montmorency, *289*
Englishman, The, *see* Talbot, Chevalier
Estrées, Duc and Dsse d', *321*, *349–50*
Evreux, Bp. of (Henri du Tour), 262, 265

Faluère, M. de la, *335*
Fare, M. de la, 191, *257*, 259–60
Fare, Marquise de la (after 1681 known as Mme Bonneval),
Fénelon, F. de la Mothe- (1651–1715), *273*
Fiennes, Mlle de, *87–8*
Fiesque, Cte de (le Petit Bon), *169*

Fiesque, Ctsse de (The Countess), *169*, 237
FitzGerald, Edward, 25, 26, 36
Flamarens, Chevalier de, *195–6*
Fléchier E., Bp. of Nîmes (1632–1710), *135*, *364*
Fontanges, Dsse de, *239*, *264*
Fontenelle, B. de (1657–1757), *171*
Forbin-Janson, Bp. of Marseilles (The Bishop), *79*
Forbin, Capt., 18, 126, 131, 139
Fouquet, Abbé Basile, 158–9
Fouquet, Nicolas, 22, 24, 71, *82*, 159, *167*, 243
Fouquet, Marie, 2nd wife, *158–9*
Fouquet, Marie, daughter by 1st wife, *158*
Fouquet, Louis-Nicolas, son, *see* Vaux
François de Sales, St, 20, *80*, 341

Gailly, Gérard, *31*, 35–6, *102*
Games, Card, *Bassette*, 207–8, 259; *fredon*, 87; *hoca: ombre*, 166, 178, 266, 373; *piquet: quinitille*, *266*; *reversi* (or *-is*), 171–2, 266
Gesvres, Duc de (Gov. Paris), *322*
Gesvres, Dsse de, *83*
Gourville, J. de, *58–9*
Gramont, Antoine III, Duc de (1604–78), 114
Gramont, Dsse de, wife, 115, 218
Gramont, Armand de, eldest son, *see* Guiche
Gramont, A-C., brother, *see* Louvigny
Gramont, Catherine, daughter, *see* Monaco
Gramont, Philibert, Chevalier de, *128*
Grand Master, *see* Lude
Grignan, F. A. de M, Cte de (son-in-law), *22*, 25–6, 29, 31–2, *40*, *42*–4, 60, 62, 65, 67, 71, 73–5, 81, 87, 94, 97, 108, 110–11, 113, 116, 123, 127–8, 130, 144, 147, *150*, 182–4, 195, 214, 215, 243, 251, *287*, 300, 302, 316, *318*, 329, 339, 345, 346, 356
Grignan, Françoise-Marguerite (daughter), wife of above, 16, 17, 23, 24–31, 40. Thereafter refer to Contents Table
Grignan, Louis-Provence, Marquis de (their son), 23, 26, 30, *53*, *72*–6, 89, 122, 154–5, *164*, 197, 212, 214, 218–19; his first campaign, 293–303; at Versailles, 304; his squadron, 306; at the wars, 309–10, 322–3, 331, 341, 343; Colonelcy, 353–6; social life, 317–19, 328–9; marriage, 357, *377*
Grignan, Marie-Blanche (elder daughter), *43*, 44, 66, 68, 69, 75, 83, 84, 262–3
Grignan, Pauline de (younger daughter), Marquise de Simiane, 27, 30, 32–4, *191*-2, 198–9, 202, 212, 214, 263, 265, 299, 316, 318–19
Grignan, Charles-Philippe de, "The Chevalier" (brother), *80*, 84
Grignan, F–A. de, Abp Arles (uncle), *41*
Grignan, Jacques, Bp Uzès and Cte de (uncle), *41*
Grignan, J-B. de, Coadjutor, later Abp. of Arles, "Seigneur Corbeau" (brother), *43*, 44, 69, 74, 86, 173
Grignan, Joseph *Adhémar* de, succeeded C–P. as Chevalier, "Le Glorieux" (brother), 80, 201, 220, 237, 244, 262, 265, 267, 293–9, 314, 316–19, 324, 329–32, 347, 349, 351, 353–4, 356–9, 360–1
Grignan, Louis-Joseph de, "le bel Abbé", Abp Evreux, 1681, Carcassonne (brother), *113*, 217, *236*, 262, 265, 267
Grignan, L-C. de (eldest daughter), 223
Grignan, F-J. de (Mlle d'Alerac, second daughter), 29, 202, 214, 241, 263, 278
Grignan, Marie-Adhémar de (sister), abbess, 254–5
Grotius, P., *77*
Guarini (*Il Pastor Fido*), *106*, *141*, *221*, *352*
Gué, Marie-A. du, wife of P–E. de Coulanges
Guémadeuc, S. de, Bp. St. Malo, *327*
Guénégaud, Abbé, *301*
Guiche, Antoine de Gramont, Cte, later Duc, de, 301
Guiche, Marie-C. de Noailles (wife), *52*, *115*, 163
Guiche, Armand de G. (eldest son), *92*, 95, *105*, *114*, *129*
Guiche, M. de Béthune, later Dsse du Lude (wife), *115*
Guise, Duc de, 15, *69*, 71
Guise, Marie de (aunt), *49*, *69*–70
Guise, Elizabeth d'Orléans, Dsse de, 50
Guisoni, Dr, *202*, 211
Guitaut, Cte de, *88*, 194–5
Guitaut, Elizabeth, Ctsse de (2nd wife),
Gwynn, Nell, *134*–5

Hacqueville, Abbé d', 27–8, *56*, 59, 65, 79, 85, 113, 115, 123, 167, 174, 196

Hamilton, Count Antoine, *128*
Harcourt, Cte d', *132*
Harcourt, Ctsse d' (aunt of Mme de S.), 69
Harcourt, Prince d', *49*
Harouys, G., Seigneur de Silleraye, *125*, 137, 360
Hauterive, Mme de, *47*
Hébert, *50*
Heudicourt, Marquise d' (La Grande Dame), *167*, 173
Hocquincourt, Cte de, *128*, *310*
Humières, Duc d', 93, 341

Innocent XI, Pope, *337*, 340
Irvine, Lyn, 26–7

James II of England, *45*, *298*, 303–4, 307–8, 310–13, 319–20
Janet, M du, *116*
Janet, Mlle du, 225
Jansénius (Jansenists), 254
Jesuits, The, 174, 254

Kerman, Marquise de, *see* Marinais, *244*, 322, 324
Kerman, Regt, 334
Kéroual, *see* Portsmouth
Kerrich, Mrs., 25, 36

La Bruyère, Jean de (1695–6), *113*
La Chaise, le Père F. de (1624–1709), *230*
Ladvocat, Mlle de, " le petit ministre ", *123*, *see* Vins
La Fayette, Ctsse de (1634–92), 15, 23, 24, 30, *44*, *56*, 57, 81, *86*, 97, 99, 101, 113, 114, 163, 164, 206, 213, 220, *234*, 240–2, 244, 250, 258 (her son), 263, 267, 282, 318, *319*, 331, 347–8, 354
La Fayette, *Psse de Clèves*, 15, *206*; *Psse de Montpensier*, 86; *Zayde*, 206, *250*
La Fontaine, Jean de (1621–95), 15, 17, *44*, 64, *76*, *104*, *113*, *213*, *257*, *323*
Laisné (Vincent Léna), *97*
La Garde, M de, *113*, 116, 150, 200–1, 206–7, 235, 293, 297
Lamoignon, G. de, *173*, *286*, 307, 314
La Mousse, Abbé P. de, 24, *61–2*, 64, 67, 71, 89, 107
" La Murinette ", *see* Murinais
Langlée (Gambler), *170*, 185
Larmechin, *144*–5, 148, 252
La Rochefoucauld, François VI, Duc de, 15, 16, 24, *56*, 57, 90, 94–5, 99, 106, 113, 167, 181, 220, 240–1 (death), 242, 244, 250, 347
La Rochefoucauld, François VII, *see* Marsillac, Prince de
La Roche-sur-Yon, Cte de, son of Conti, *233*
La Trémouille, Seigneur de, *350*–1
La Troche (Trochanaire), Marquise de, *52*, 92, 125, 155, 364
La Trousse, M de, 117, *156*, 263, 310, 345
La Trousse, Marquise de (aunt), *50*, *75*, 85, 88–9, 95, 98, 103, *174*
Lauzun, Duc de, *45*–7, 73, 79, *241*, 304–6, 314, 353
La Vallière, Chevalier de, 159, 183
La Vallière, Louise, Dsse de, 16, *45*, 120, 183, *223*, 225–6, 248
Lavardin, M de, *61*, 137, 217
Lavardin, Marquise de, *125*, 220, 347, 359
Lavardin, J-B., Bp. of Rennes, *234*, 260, 327, 338, 353
Le Brun, C., *96–7*
Lenclos, Ninon de, 18, 23, 28, *53*, 56
Le Nôtre A. (1613–1700), 90, 349
Lennox, Charles, Duke of, *134*
Lesdiguières, Dsse de, *225*
Lesdiguières, Duc de, *94*
Le Tellier, C-M., *179*
Le Tellier, Michel, *see* Louvois
Locmaria, M de, *70*
Longueval, Françoise de, *159*
Longueville, Duc de, *101*–3, 105–7
Longueville, C-L. (son), *107*, 299
Longueville, Dsse de, *101*, *103*–6
Lorges, Cte, later Duc de, *149*
Lorme, Dr, *148*–9, 155, 174
Lorraine, Charles V., Duc de, *178*, *343*
Lorraine, P., Chev. de, *87*–8, 90, *104*
Lorraine, Louis de, Cte d'Armagnac, *88*
Louis XIII of France (1601–43), *46*
Louis XIV of France (1638–1715), 14, 16–17, 47, 49, 58–9, 77–9, 83, 93, 96, 99, *104*, *107*, 114, 122, 128, 141–3, 166, 170–3, 175, 185, 203, 204, 205, 208, 216–17, 219, 221, 223–4, 228, 230, 239–41, 253, 259, 264, 273–4, 282, 286, 296, 298, 300, 302–6, 310–13, 316, 319–21, 337–8, 347, 357, 359, 364–5, 368
Louis, le Grand Dauphin, son of above (1661–1711), *237*, 239–40, 259, 270, 273, 294–6, 304, 357, 364
Louvigny, Cte de, *129*, 133
Louvigny, Ctsse de, *115*
Louvois, M de (M. of War), 91, *93*, 128, 175, 193, *217*, *257*, 296, 300, 337, 369
Lucian, *112*, *192*

Lude, Cte, later Duc du, *Grand Master and Gov. Versailles*, *92*, 128, 130, 234, 259
Lude, Ctsse du, *292*
Ludres, Ctsse de, "Io", *189*
Lully, J.-B. (Baptiste), *97*, 192, 195
Luxembourg, Duc de, *79*, 117, 137, 170–1, 230, 233, 235, 239, 246, 265
Lyonne, Mme de, *169*

MADAME (official title of the wife of the King's brother)
Marguerite, 2nd wife of Gaston d'Orléans, *90*
Henriette d'Angleterre (Minette), 1st wife of Philippe d'O., 57, *106*, *319*
Elizabeth of Bavaria, *73*, 171, 319, 364
Madame la Comtesse, *see* Soissons, Ctsse de
Madame la Duchesse, *see* Enghien, Dsse de
Madame la Grande Duchesse (Marguerite-L. d'Orléans),
Madame la Princesse (official title of the wives of the Prince de Condé)
MADEMOISELLE (daughter of the King's brother)
Anne-Marie de Montpensier, d. of Gaston d'Orléans, *46–7*, 50, 90, 225, 306
Marie-Louise, d. of Philippe d'O. & Henrietta, 200, 319
Maine, Duc du, *304*
Maintenon, Françoise d'Aubigné, Marquise de (1635–1719), 180, 218–19, 242, 253, 257, 259, *264*, 279, 314
Mancini, Hortense (Nevers), *55*, 104, *336*
Mancini, Marie-Anne (Bouillon), *104*
Mancini, Marie (Colonna), *104*
Mancini, Olympe (Soissons), *104*
Marans, Ctsse de (Merlusine), *57*, 99
Marey, Dsse de, *90*
Maria-Thérèse (Queen of France), *47*, 49, 50, 94, 118, 142–3, 153, 170–3, 200, 222, 224, 240, 242, 253, 264, 273
Marie-Anne de Bavière (Dauphine), *237*, 239, 244–9, *248*, 253, 257, 270, 315–16, 364
Marsan, Cte de, *104*
Marsillac, Prince de, *101*, 102, 113, *241*, *257*, *303*
Marsillac, H-A. de, Abbé, *313*
Marsillac, J-B., Chevalier de, *101*
Mascaron, Jules (1634–1703), *57*, 82
Massillon, J-B. (1663–1742), 19
Mazarin, Mlle de, *274*
Mauron, Mlle de (d.-in-law), *276*
Meckelbourg, Mme de, *231*, *276–8*
Meilleraye, Duc de la, *52*, *104*, *336*
Ménage, Abbé Gilles, 21, 23, *66*
Méri, Mlle de, *156*
"Merlusine", *see* Marans
Mignard, P. (1608–88), *133*
Minims, The, 20–1, *193*, 286
Molière (J-B. Poquelin, 1622–73), 54, 63, 66; *L'Avare*, 356; *L'Ecole des Femmes*, 64, 322; *George Dandin*, 248; *Le Malade imaginaire*, 177, 218; *Le Médecin malgré lui*, 247, 249
Monaco, Psse de, *95*, *115*
Monmerqué, *31*, 35–6, *58*, *97*, *101*, *110*, *132*, *134*, *225*, *373*
Monmouth, Duke of, 97
MONSIEUR, (brother of the King)
Gaston d'Orléans, *46*
Philippe d'O., *46*, 93, 173, 208, 222, 259, 319, 357, 364
Monsieur le Duc, *see* Enghien
Monsieur le Grand (Grand Ecuyer), *see* Lorraine (Cte d'Armagnac)
Monsieur le Prince (official title of P. de Condé)
Montaigne, M. E. de, 13, 18
Montausier, Duc de, Dsse de, *79*, 142–3, 304
Montespan, Marquise de (Quantova), (1641–1707), *107*, 153, *157*, 159, 165–6, 170–3, 176, 185, *208*, 219, *223*, *257*, *264*
Montgobert, Demoiselle de, 211, 224, 235, *265–7*
Montpensier, Duc de, *see* Lauzun
Montpensier, Marie de Lorraine, Dsse de, *see* MADEMOISELLE
Moulceau, Président de, 30, 273, 288–90, 319–20
Murinais, Mlle de, *68*, 72

Nantes, Mlle de, *289*
Nevers, Duc de, *157*
Nicole, Pierre (1628–95), 18, 43, 61, 253, 283, *328*, 369
Noailles, Dsse de, 161
Noailles, L-A. de (son), Bp. Cahors, later Abp. Paris, *161*, *309*

Orange, Prince Wm. of, 1650–1702, 117, 175, 193, 294, 298, 303, 310–12, 319, 321, 323, 366, 369
Ottoboni, Pope Alexander VIII, *352*

Palatine, Edward, Count, *44*
Pascal, Blaise (1623–62), 18, 43, 61, *192*, 324

Perrin, le Chevalier, 34, *78*, *122*, *135*, *151*, *217*, *246*, *252*, *253*, *302*, *349*, *362*
" Petit Bon ", *see* Fiesque, Cte de
Pilois, *63*, 65, 177, 253
Plessis, M. du, 281, 285, 306, 309, 359
Plessis, Mlle du, *63*, 65, 67–9, 137–8, 177
Plessis-Guénégaud, Elizabeth (Mme du Plessis, *158*, 160
Plessis-Praslin, Cte du, *91*, 132
Pomenars, M de Pontménard, *68*
Pommereuil, Chevalier de, *144*, 350
Pomponne, M. de, 24, 28, *81–2*, 101, 116, 123, 126, 181, 186, 216–17
Portsmouth, Dss of, *87*, *134–5*

" Quantova ", *see* Montespan, *153*
Queen of England, *see* Mary
Queen of France, *see* Maria-Thérèse
Queen of Spain, *see* Anne-Marie and Marie-Louise

Rabutin-Chantal, Baron Celse-Bénigne de, (father), 20
Racine, Jean, 15, 18, 23, 86, 203, *237*; *Andromaque*, 86, *314*; *Bajazet*, 86; *Iphigénie*, *138*; *Esther*, 308, *314*, 330–1 (1639–99)
Rambouillet, Marquise de, 22–3, 40
Rarai, M. de, *113*
Rennes, Bp. of, *see* Lavardin
Retz, Cardinal de (Mme de S.'s uncle), (1614–79), 15, 22, 24, *56*, 95, 121–3, 125, 130, *137*, 165
Revel, Mlle de, 45, 338, *345*
Rheims, Abp. of, *see* Le Tellier
Richelieu, M de, *274*
Rippert, *76*, 140, 343–4
Robinet, Mme, *43*–4, 74
Rochebonne, Ctsse de, 108, *293*
Rochechouart, Mme de, *133*
Rochefort, M de, *128*–9, 162–3, 173
Rochefort, Marquise de, 163, *176*, 364
Rochefort, Mlle de, 176
Rohan, Duc de, 144
Rohan, Dsse de, Psse de Léon, 213
Roquelaure, Duc de, 102
Ruyter, Adml., 98, 168

Saint-Armand, Anne M. (Marquise de Grignan), *377*
Saint-Brieux, Bp. of, *229*
Saint-Esprit, Chevaliers du, 300–18
Saint-Géran, Ctsse de, 167, 229
Saint-Hérem, M de, *75*, 160–1, *295* (son)
Saint-Hérem, Marquise de, *75*
Saint-Malo, Bp. of, *see* Guémadeuc
Saint-Simon, *Mémoires*, 27, *55*, *75*, *91*, *159*, *161*, *195*
Saint-Simon, Dsse de, *44*, 212
Sainte-Beuve, C-A. de, 13
Saintsbury, George, 13–14
Sanzei, M. de, *197*, 314
Sanzei, Mme de, 122
Sault, Duc de, *94*; Dsse de, *45*
Scarron, Paul (1610–60), *81*, *104*
Scarron, Mme, *29*, *81*, 84, 113, *see* Maintenon
Schomberg, Mme de, *57*
Schomberg, Maréchal A-F., *175*, *298*, 366
Scudéry, Madeleine de, 24, 36, *277*, 363; *Artamène*, *105*; *Clélie*, *101*, *158*; *Conversations*, 277 (1607–1701)
Segrais, J-R. de (1624–1701), *206*
Séguier, Pierre, *82*, *93*, 96, 115
Séguier, Mme, *115*, *176*
Séguier, Charlotte (daughter), *49*, *95*, *97*
Seignelai, *see* Colbert J-B.
Seignelai, Mme de, *205*, *367*
Sévigné, Charles, M. de (son), 17, 24, 28–9, 53–5, 61–2, 65, 67, 71, 92, 98, 99; at the wars, 101–3, 112, 143, 168, 184, 191–3, 214–16, 232, 238, 248, *264*, 267; marriage, *276*; 277, 279, 280–1, 285, 327, 342, 346, 349–50, 353, 360, 366
Sévigné, Marquise de (his wife), 29, *276*, 279–83, 378
Sévigné, Henri, M de (husband), 22–4
Simiane, Pauline de, *see* Grignan
Soissons, Cte de, 274
Soissons, Ctsse de, *230*, 231, *319*, 341
Soissons, L-T. de Savoie (son), 274
Soubise, Dsse de, *170*–1, 213, *230*, 242
Stuart, " la belle anglaise ", *225*
Stuart, J. F. E. " The Old Pretender ", 303–5, 312–13
Sully, Duc de, *49*, *95*
Sully, Dsse de, *52*, *174*, *237*

Talbot, Chevalier, " The Englishman ", *212*, 218, 241, 267
Tarente, Psse de, *63*, 141, 147, 158, 260–4, 287 (son)
Tasso, 66, *252*
Termes, M de, *195–7*
Têtu, Abbé Jacques, *81*, 84, 113, 133, 219, 249, 312
Thianges, D-G. de (Nevers), *157*
Thianges, L-A. de (Sforza), *157*
Tingry, Psse de, 231–2
Tonquedec, M de, *235*, 260, 263, 327

Toulouse, Cte de, *295*
" Trochanaire ", *see* La Troche
Tulle, Bp. of, *see* Mascaron
Turenne, Maréchal, 38, *77*, 93, 98, 114, 117, 123, 127–32

Uzès, Bp. of, *see* Grignan, J-A.
Uxelles, Marquise d', *220*, 353
Uxelles, M d' (son), 220, *343*

Vaillant, *63*
Vardes, M. de, Gov. Aigues Mortes, *69*, *201*
Vatel, 58–9
Vaubrun, Mlle de, 321–3
Vauvineux, Mlle, *220*–1
Vaux, Cte de, *167*
Vendôme, Duc de (Gor Provence), *42*, 254
Verneuil, Dsse de, *49*, 92, 110
Vertus, Mlle de, 103
Vieuville, C-F., Bp. of Rennes, *340*
Villars, M de, 134, 171, *310*
Villars, Marquise de, *49*, 120, 134, 167, 171, 239
Vins, M de, 18, *126*, 139, 256
Vins, Marquise de, *123*, 174, 214, 217
Virgil, 15, 21, *248*, *346*
Vivonne, Duc de, *102*, *173*
Voisin, La, 230–1, 237
Voiture, V (1598–1648), 15, 23, 265
Voltaire (1694–1778), 33, 36, *173*

Wales, P. of, *see* Stuart, J. F. E.

INDEX OF PLACES

Aix-en-Provence, 60, 66, 156, 207, 226, 233, 329–31, 342, 354
Allier, R., 90, 166
Auray, *334–6*, 339
Avignon, 328–*9*, *330–1*, 340, 351, 352

Balaruc, 351
Bâville, 287
Blois, *249*
Boulogne, *298*, 306–8
Bourbilly, *112*, 361
Bourbon-d'Archambault, 151, *155*, 158–9, *291–2*, 345
Boyne, Battle of the, 366
Brest, 320–1, 322, 327–8, 335
Brevannes, *299*, 355
Buron, Le, 167, 252, 355

Caen, 318, *326*
Calais, *304–5*, 307
Carnavalet, Hôtel de, 29, 32, *95*, *196*, 198–9, 201, 203, 210, 234, 312
Chalon, 56
Châlons, 306
Champagne, Regt. of, *295*
Chantilly, *58*, 185, 259, 288–9
Charenton, 346
Charleroi, 98, 117, 193
Charleville, 184
Châtres, 278
Chartres, 136
Chaseu, 203
Châtelet Prison, *127*, *153*
Châtillon, 197
Chaulnes, Château de, 322–5, 340
Chaulnes, Hôtel de, 178
Chelles, Abbaye de, 154, 179–80
Conflans, *181*
Cosne, *197*
" Coulanges, Place ", 349

Dijon, 20
Dinan, 141
Dive, 326
Durance, R., 168, 214, 293, 316, *330*

Epoisse, *194–5*
Etampes, *278–9*

Flanders, 79, 84, 123, 137
Fleurus, Battle of, *230*, 365
Fontainebleau, 121, 127, 155, 243, 288–9, *292*, 297, 321
Fontevrault, 133, 166
Fougères, 165
Fribourg-en-Brisgau, *204*

Ganat, 161
Gand (Ghent), *205*
Gard, Pont du, 325
Germany, 79, 85, 98, 127, 131, 170, 208, 366
Gien, *197–8*
Gramont, Hôtel de, *114*
Grignan, 29–31, 56, 66, 226, 242, 316, 323, 325, 339, 354, 361, *366–7*, 369–70

Hennebon, 337
Holland, 79, 104
Huy, 122

Ireland, 320, 353

Kaiserslautern, 357

Lambesc, 168, *367–8*
Langlar, *166*, *196–7*
Laval, *150–1*
Leghorn, 340
Le Mans, 126
Liancourt, 59
Limbourg, 121–2